ENGAGING YOUNG READERS

Solving Problems in the Teaching of Literacy

Cathy Collins Block, Series Editor

ENGAGING YOUNG READERS:
PROMOTING ACHIEVEMENT AND MOTIVATION
Edited by Linda Baker, Mariam Jean Dreher, and John T. Guthrie

ENGAGING YOUNG READERS

Promoting Achievement and Motivation

Edited by

Linda Baker
Mariam Jean Dreher
John T. Guthrie

THE GUILFORD PRESS
New York   London

© 2000 The Guilford Press
A Division of Guilford Publications, Inc.
72 Spring Street, New York, NY 10012
www.guilford.com

Printed in the United States of America

This book is printed on acid-free paper.

Last digit is print number: 9   8   7   6   5   4   3   2   1

Library of Congress Cataloging-in-Publication Data

Engaging young readers : promoting achievement and motivation /
edited by Linda Baker, Mariam Jean Dreher, John T. Guthrie.
    p. cm. — (Solving problems in the teaching of literacy)
   Includes bibliographical references and index.
   ISBN 1-57230-554-1 (hc.) — ISBN 1-57230-535-5 (pbk.)
   1. Reading (Elementary) — United States.   2. Academic
achievement — United States.   3. Motivation in education —
United States.   I. Baker, Linda.   II. Dreher, Mariam Jean.
III. Guthrie, John T.   IV. Series.
LB1573.E655   2000
428.4—dc21   99-056748

About the Editors

Linda Baker, PhD, is Professor of Psychology at the University of Maryland, Baltimore County. She teaches courses on children's development in school settings and on the processes involved in reading development. She coedited (with Peter Afflerbach and David Reinking) the 1996 book *Developing Engaged Readers in School and Home Communities*, which introduced the National Reading Research Center's engagement perspective on reading. Her research addresses such topics as parental influences on early reading, experiences related to the development of word recognition, metacognitive aspects of reading, and children's motivation for reading.

Mariam Jean Dreher, PhD, is Professor of Curriculum and Instruction at the University of Maryland at College Park, where she teaches reading education courses. She is a former classroom teacher and Title I teacher in schools serving at-risk students. She has published in such journals as *Reading Research Quarterly, The Reading Teacher,* and the *Journal of Literacy Research*. Her research interests include effective early literacy instruction, as well as helping elementary school children become more facile at reading for learning and research-related reading.

John T. Guthrie, PhD, is Professor of Human Development at the University of Maryland at College Park. From 1992 to 1997, he was codirector of the National Reading Research Center, which emphasized classroom research on motivation and contexts for developing reading engagement. Much of that work was summarized in a 1999 book entitled *Engaged Reading: Processes, Practices, and Policy Implications,* coedited with Donna Alvermann. He has collaborated with teachers in developing and studying Concept-Oriented Reading Instruction, which has been shown to increase motivation, reading strategies, and children's knowledge in content areas.

Contributors

Peter Afflerbach, PhD, Department of Curriculum and Instruction, University of Maryland at College Park, College Park, Maryland

Patricia A. Alexander, PhD, Department of Human Development, University of Maryland at College Park, College Park, Maryland

Janice F. Almasi, PhD, Department of Learning and Instruction, State University of New York at Buffalo, Buffalo, New York

Linda Baker, PhD, Department of Psychology, University of Maryland, Baltimore County, Baltimore, Maryland

Michelle Buehl, BA, Department of Human Development, University of Maryland at College Park, College Park, Maryland

James P. Byrnes, PhD, Department of Human Development, University of Maryland at College Park, College Park, Maryland

Marilyn J. Chambliss, PhD, Department of Curriculum and Instruction, University of Maryland at College Park, College Park, Maryland

Kathleen E. Cox, MA, Department of Human Development, University of Maryland at College Park, College Park, Maryland

Mariam Jean Dreher, PhD, Department of Curriculum and Instruction, University of Maryland at College Park, College Park, Maryland

Liz Fasulo, MA, Department of Curriculum and Instruction, University of Maryland at College Park, College Park, Maryland

Helenrose Fives, MA, Department of Human Development, University of Maryland at College Park, College Park, Maryland

Linda B. Gambrell, PhD, School of Education, Clemson University, Clemson, South Carolina

Steve Graham, PhD, Department of Special Education, University of Maryland at College Park, College Park, Maryland

John T. Guthrie, PhD, Department of Human Development, University of Maryland at College Park, College Park, Maryland

Karen R. Harris, EdD, Department of Special Education, University of Maryland at College Park, College Park, Maryland

Kaeli T. Knowles, PhD, Department of Human Development, University of Maryland at College Park, College Park, Maryland

Diane Henry Leipzig, MEd, Department of Curriculum and Instruction, University of Maryland at College Park, College Park, Maryland

Susan Anders Mazzoni, MEd, Department of Curriculum and Instruction, University of Maryland at College Park, College Park, Maryland

Ann Margaret McKillop, PhD, Department of Curriculum and Instruction, University of Maryland at College Park, College Park, Maryland

Diane Schmidt, MA, Department of Psychology, University of Maryland, Baltimore County, Baltimore, Maryland

Susan Sonnenschein, PhD, Department of Psychology, University of Maryland, Baltimore County, Baltimore, Maryland

Linda Valli, PhD, Department of Curriculum and Instruction, University of Maryland at College Park, College Park, Maryland

Allan Wigfield, PhD, Department of Human Development, University of Maryland at College Park, College Park, Maryland

Preface

What should teachers know to teach reading well? Our answer is that teachers need to know how and why to foster reading engagement. Reading engagement refers to the simultaneous functioning of motivation, conceptual knowledge, strategies, and social interactions during literacy activities. Engaged readers are those who read widely for a variety of purposes and create situations that extend opportunities for literacy. Engagement is essential to long-term achievement. To engage young readers, teachers need to offer a coordinated emphasis on competence and motivation in their reading instruction. Both skill and will are important ingredients.

The underlying message of this book is that many more children can attain high levels of reading achievement if efforts are made to increase engagement. To reach this goal, reading instruction should be reconceptualized in terms of research-based design principles for promoting engagement. The contributors to this book have identified the best practices in their respective areas, and they present research evidence in support of practical recommendations. Each chapter is central to the message of the book as a whole. The chapter titles reflect the active role that the teacher plays in implementing each of the processes that lead to engagement and achievement (e.g., fostering . . ., facilitating . . ., building . . .).

The book opens with an introductory chapter that explains why teachers should promote reading engagement. Chapters 2–13 focus on particular instructional principles that will help a child become an engaged reader. The topics reflect our shared vision of the important elements of effective reading instruction, and go beyond traditional emphases on cognitive processes in reading to include motivational, social, and contextual processes. Specifically, a child needs a good foundation at the word level (Chapter 2), help if he or she is in trouble (Chapter 3), opportunity to read for learning (Chapter 4), ample materials for reading (Chapter

5), opportunities to share in a community of learners (Chapter 6), instructional contexts that are motivating (Chapter 7), a teacher who is familiar
with the child's strengths and weaknesses (Chapter 8), time to read (Chapter 9), coherent instruction that pulls all of the pieces together (Chapter 10),
classrooms that are coordinated with the school as a whole (Chapter 11),
continuities between home and school (Chapter 12), and masterful teaching by teachers knowledgeable about engagement and achievement
(Chapter 13). Finally, the concluding chapter explains why teachers themselves need to be engaged in order to promote student achievement.

The engagement perspective on reading was the cornerstone of the
research mission of the federally funded National Reading Research Center (NRRC), a joint effort of the University of Maryland and the University
of Georgia. The publications arising from the work at the center highlight
the integration of the cognitive, motivational, and social dimensions of
reading and reading instruction. The legacy of the NRRC continues in this
volume. Many of the authors from this interdisciplinary team were principal investigators at the Maryland site of the NRRC. They have a long history of successful collaboration and a shared understanding of engaged
reading.

We would like to thank all of the authors who contributed their time
and intellectual energies toward bringing this book to fruition. Their spir-
ited participation in several planning meetings, and their willingness to
tailor their chapters to our specifications, are very much appreciated. We
also wish to acknowledge the colleagues and professional organizations
that facilitated the development of the ideas expressed in this volume. In
particular, we extend our thanks to our NRRC colleagues at the collaborating institutions: the University of Georgia, the University of Texas at Austin, the University of Washington, the State University of New York at
Albany, Rutgers University, San Diego State University, and Stanford University.

The book is intended primarily for teacher educators and inservice
teachers enrolled in graduate-level courses in reading instruction, and is
written in a style that is accessible to graduate students in reading education. It does not assume extensive familiarity with research methods and
findings, but it assumes some familiarity with classroom teaching of reading. These fresh syntheses of the research literature with an emphasis on
instructional implications are likely to make the book of interest to reading
researchers and other professionals as well.

LINDA BAKER, PHD
MARIAM JEAN DREHER, PHD
JOHN T. GUTHRIE, PHD

Contents

ENGAGING YOUNG READERS

CHAPTER ONE

Why Teachers Should Promote Reading Engagement

LINDA BAKER
MARIAM JEAN DREHER
JOHN T. GUTHRIE

A variety of recent initiatives at the local, state, and federal levels are designed to increase reading achievement in the United States. Many of these focus on teachers' professional development. But what do teachers need to know? The purpose of this book is to answer the following professionally and politically urgent question: What should teachers know to teach reading well? The essence of our response to this question is that teachers need to know how to promote reading engagement. Engagement is essential to long-term achievement. Engaged children read widely for a variety of purposes and create situations that extend opportunities for literacy. In the classroom, promoting reading engagement requires a coordinated emphasis on competence and motivation in reading instruction. If motivation is treated as secondary to the acquisition of basic reading skills, we risk creating classrooms filled with children who can read but choose not to. On the other hand, if motivation is the only focus, we risk that children may love to read but cannot.

In this introductory chapter we set the stage for the book by explaining why teachers should promote reading engagement. We begin by elaborating our definition of engaged reading. We then describe characteristics of successful and less successful young readers to illustrate the challenges that teachers face. Next we consider how well children are achieving in reading in the United States today. The following section offers evidence of critical links between engagement and achievement. Then we describe instructional practices observed in the classrooms of today to demonstrate the need for greater emphasis on engagement. We close by previewing the principles for promoting engaged reading that are explicated in the remainder of this book.

WHAT IS ENGAGED READING?

When we say that someone is *engaged* in an activity, we often use the term to mean that he/she is involved at a deep level. Synonyms include absorbed, engrossed, interested, and involved. Clearly, motivation is inherent in the term. But engaged reading involves more than motivation. How much more depends on the definition of reading engagement under consideration.

In this book "engaged reading" refers to the joint functioning of motivation, conceptual knowledge, strategies, and social interactions during literacy activities (Guthrie & Anderson, 1999). This engagement perspective was the cornerstone of the research mission of the federally funded National Reading Research Center (NRRC). The resulting body of work by NRRC researchers has increased awareness that reading involves more than cognitive skills (Gambrell & Almasi, 1996; Baker, Afflerbach, & Reinking, 1996b; Baumann & Duffy, 1997; Guthrie & Alvermann, 1999; Guthrie & Wigfield, 1997). The engagement perspective has appeal because it integrates the cognitive, motivational, and social dimensions of reading and reading instruction. Indeed, the term "engagement" is being used increasingly by reading researchers, educators, and policy makers. Motivation is now widely recognized as an important outcome of reading instruction, as reflected, for example, in the Reading Excellence Act of 1998 (see also Braunger & Lewis, 1997; Snow, Burns, & Griffin, 1998).

Students are engaged readers when they read frequently for interest, enjoyment, and learning. The heart of engagement is the desire to gain new knowledge of a topic, to follow the excitement of a narrative, to expand one's experience through print. Engaged readers can find books of personal significance and make time for reading them. The investment of time is rewarded by the experience of immersion in the text itself. Engaged readers draw on knowledge gained from previous experiences to construct new understandings, and they use cognitive strategies to regulate comprehension so that goals are met and interests are satisfied. Benefits to readers may also occur through their satisfaction in possessing valued information about a topic that plays a central role in their sense of self. Engaged readers are curious and involved in a literate lifestyle.

To promote engaged reading, instructional contexts must be well designed: "In an engaging classroom, reading lessons are designed to develop long-term motivation, knowledge, social competence, and reading skill" (Guthrie & Anderson, 1999, p. 37). The chapters in this volume describe a variety of instructional contexts that facilitate engagement. If reading instruction is constrained to a limited set of materials (e.g., basal stories) and procedures (e.g., students answering teachers' questions about a text), engaged reading will be less likely than if reading instruction encompasses diverse texts and tasks and abundant opportunities to interact with texts in collaboration with others (Baker et al., 1996b).

It is important to emphasize that engaged reading may occur at all levels of development. As McCarthey, Hoffman, and Galda (1999) put it, "Proficiency levels and expertise may vary but the fundamental processes of engagement are the same" (p. 48). Thus, kindergarten and first-grade teachers, as well as fourth- and fifth-grade teachers, can and should strive to promote engaged reading. Reading engagement is as much a goal for the child struggling to decode words as it is for the proficient reader seeking information for a class project.

WHAT ARE THE CHARACTERISTICS OF SUCCESSFUL AND LESS SUCCESSFUL 9-YEAR-OLD READERS?

To highlight the challenges teachers face in promoting engaged reading, we illustrate the differences in what successful and less successful 9-year-old readers can do. The successes and failures of such children help set the agenda for improved instruction. It is a widely endorsed goal that children should be reading well by age 9, or the end of grade 3. Numerous descriptions of benchmarks in reading progress are available (e.g., America Reads Challenge . . ., 1998; International Reading Association & National Association for the Education of Young Children, 1998; Pressley, 1998; Snow et al., 1998). To describe what successful readers are able to do by the time they leave third grade, we draw on these detailed listings of reading progress.

The U.S. Department of Education's *Checkpoints for Progress in Reading and Writing* (America Reads Challenge . . ., 1998) lists what we can expect from successful readers at each developmental level. The checkpoints for third graders indicate that they are fluent and strategic. They relate what they read to what they already know; they monitor their comprehension; they learn new vocabulary from context; they figure out unfamiliar words with word analysis skills including phonics and context clues; they understand literary elements such as events, characters, and settings and compare these elements across books; they recognize themes; they understand how genres such as fables, poetry, and nonfiction differ and can write examples of these genres; and they communicate in writing in a logical order, with attention to purpose and audience, as well as language conventions. Further, the checkpoints describe successful third graders as children who are motivated to read. They have "favorite authors and types of books"; they read widely across all content areas in diverse types of materials; and they talk and write about what they read. In short, the checkpoints for third grade paint a picture of engaged readers.

Snow et al. (1998) offered a similar list of what third graders can do. Perhaps much of their list might be summarized by their first point: A successful third grader "reads aloud with fluency and comprehension any text that is appropriately designed for grade level" (p. 83). In addition, not only can successful third graders read aloud with fluency and comprehension, they can summarize points from both fiction and nonfiction, they can discuss the themes in fiction, they can reason about hypotheses and opinions in what they have read, and they can combine "information from multiple sources in writing reports" (p. 83).

Checkpoints for Progress includes an excerpt from *Sarah, Plain and Tall* (by Patricia MacLachlan) to illustrate the level of material third graders can read and understand. The document notes that successful third graders can also read books such as *Encyclopedia Brown, Boy Detective* (by Donald Sobel) and *The Boxcar Children* (by Gertrude Chandler Warner). In contrast, Cole (1998) described a child in her classroom: "In September of Jackie's third-grade year, she could only read early first-grade materials independently. That month she read *The Little Red Hen* by Jean Berg with 96% accuracy (four substitutions, omissions, and/or insertions per 100 words of text)" (p. 490).

Although Jackie, the child Cole described, was determined to learn to read and did so thanks to a skilled and dedicated teacher, many children who have not learned to read well in the early grades fail to do so (see Graham & Harris, Chapter 3, this volume). In a longitudinal study following children from first through fourth grades, Juel (1988) found that 88% of the first graders who were poor readers were still poor readers in fourth grade.

Successful 9-year-olds can read and choose to read; they have both competence and motivation. But less successful children struggle. Descriptions of unsuccessful readers abound in books on diagnostic instruction (e.g., McCormick, 1999). A few examples illustrate the problems faced by unsuccessful readers. Isaac, tutored by Caswell and Duke (1998) at a university laboratory, was a bilingual child:

> At the beginning of third grade, Isaac still could not read or write. His uncle indicated in his application to the Lab that Isaac "speaks and understands English but cannot read a single word of it. He knows some of the letters of the alphabet but requires coaching to write even monosyl-

labic words." This situation had improved somewhat by . . . the beginning of his fourth-grade year. . . . as he was reading and writing at approximately a first-grade level. (p. 111)

Isaac's score on a measure of decoding skill was 28%; a successful fourth-grade reader would score at or near 100%. Not surprisingly, his reading comprehension was similarly poor.

As they progress through school, readers like Isaac continue to have difficulty if they do not receive effective intervention. Ivey (1999) described a sixth grader, Katie, who stumbled through her attempts to read and who was not even able to use beginning consonants reliably to decode unknown words. Further, unsuccessful readers often become turned off to reading very early, like Peter, another child described by Caswell and Duke (1998). By the end of first grade, according to his records, Peter took "his reading difficulties very seriously and felt quite ashamed of his problems" (p. 109). After repeating first grade, having a hard time in second, and under peril of repeating second, "Peter was increasingly concerned about his academic difficulties, showing signs of depression, low self-esteem, and anxiety" (p. 110).

Unsuccessful readers typically avoid reading. Hence, they get very little practice. Juel (1988) found that by the time they reached fourth grade, only 5 out of 24 poor readers said they liked to read. In fact, when asked, "Which would you rather do, clean your room or read?" only 5% of good readers but 40% of poor readers chose cleaning their room. Indeed, one poor reader commented, "I'd rather clean the mold around the bathtub than read." Successful readers read many more words each day than poor readers do. Allington (1983) estimated that good readers read 10 times as many words per day as poor readers, with poor readers reading only what they must read during reading instruction. The differences in the amount of out-of-school reading are even greater (Byrnes, Chapter 9, this volume; Stanovich, 1986). When low-achieving students avoid getting engaged in reading, their opportunities to learn decrease.

HOW ARE STUDENTS DOING TODAY
IN READING ACHIEVEMENT?

The benchmarks presented in the previous section indicate that expectations for third-grade readers are quite high. Skills of successful readers go far beyond basic comprehension. How many students are meeting these expectations?

Reading achievement of students in the United States is judged on various criteria by different persons. By far the most frequently used national standard is the National Assessment of Educational Progress (NAEP). Reading comprehension is the central focus of this assessment. At grade 4, students read full stories and complete information texts of 500–1,000 words in length. They answer open-ended questions requiring both short and long written responses. To illustrate students' reading comprehension at grade 4, we will give two examples. The first shows the level of comprehension possessed by the large majority of fourth graders. One text given in 1998 was an 800-word article from *Highlights for Children*. It stated, "Crabs are able to replace their lost limbs. If a leg or claw is seriously injured, the crab drops it off. The opening that is left near the body closes to prevent the loss of blood. Soon a new limb begins growing at the break." Students were asked such questions as, "What is the most interesting thing you learned from this passage about blue crabs?" An acceptable response was "that they can loose [*sic*] a leg and grow it back." Most of the students (87%) at the "Basic" level gave an acceptable response of this kind (Donahue, Voelkl, Campbell, & Mazzeo, 1999). On the NAEP assessment, reading at the Basic level means that a student can answer simple questions related directly to words and literal meanings in the text.

In contrast, higher-level comprehension was much less frequent. To illustrate: Students were also given the question, "Describe the appearance of a female blue crab that is carrying eggs." An acceptable response was, "The egg mass sometimes looks like a [*sic*] orange-brown sponge and carries up to 1 million eggs and the crab has pinchers." Only 29% of the students scoring Basic on the assessment gave a response of this quality. It is evident that the response required students to integrate multiple details into a coherent statement after reading and remembering the information. Comprehension at this level relies on many knowledge construction processes, including understanding the literal meaning of the text, integrating new information with background knowledge, self-monitoring during initial reading, and organizing an effective statement.

Higher-level comprehension can be substantially increased by reading engagement. Successful performance in complex comprehension tasks requires that students are motivated to understand the text, curious to learn the content, and confident in their ability to read well. Further, a single successful performance will not occur by accident. Success depends on the student having a history of many engaged reading events that provide knowledge and fluency in reading skills.

It is unsettling that despite the concerted efforts to increase reading achievement in the elementary grades, relatively few gains in reading achievement were evidenced on the nationwide 1998 NAEP at grade 4 compared to previous years (Donahue et al., 1999). At grade 4, 62% of students were at or above the Basic level. This was up from 60% in 1994, but it was the same as in 1992. The change from 1994 to 1998 was not statistically significant. It is noteworthy that grade 8 and grade 12 students made statistically significant gains between 1994 and 1998. In grade 8, the percentage at or above Basic increased from 70% in 1994 to 74% in 1998. In grade 12, the percentage at or above Basic increased from 75% in 1994 to 77% in 1998.

Consider these achievement trends in relation to trends in engagement. Fourth graders have not changed since 1992 in reading engagement. In 1992, NAEP began collecting indicators of students' engagement in reading from students and teachers. For example, students reported how many pages they read for homework and pleasure. In 1992 56% reported reading 11 or more pages per day, whereas in 1998 57% reported this amount of reading, which was not a significant increase. Students were asked how often they were asked to explain their reading, write extensively, or read books of their own choosing. None of these indicators of reading engagement changed from 1992 to 1998 for fourth graders. However, change did occur for other ages. Middle school students and high school students reported significant increases. They were expected to read more. For example, in 1992 38% of middle schoolers reported reading 11 pages or more daily, whereas in 1998 42% reported this much reading, which was a significant increase. (Note, however, that middle schoolers read less than elementary school students in both years, a point to which we return in the next section.) Middle schoolers were expected to explain more, write longer answers on texts, and read self-selected books more frequently in 1998 than in 1992. Is it coincidental that the middle and high school students increased in both reading engagement and reading achievement while elementary students did not increase in either area? The answer is unknown. However, it appears that for fourth graders, reading engagement has languished. This status quo is addressed in this book. We believe that higher achievement is desirable for all students. At the same time, we believe that increasing reading engagement is the most promising route to increasing achievement.

WHAT ARE THE ADVANTAGES
OF ENGAGED READING?

Engaged Reading Predicts Reading Achievement

We can determine the extent of a student's engaged reading through many avenues. In-depth interviews are a good approach. In addition, diaries, classroom observations, parental reports, and questionnaires have been used to indicate students' levels of engaged reading. These indicators are related statistically to one another (Cipielewski & Stanovich, 1992). This means that a short easy-to-administer questionnaire often can be as revealing about engagement as more extensive measures.

Engaged reading of 9-year-olds can be estimated from responses to the following questions that have been used in NAEP assessments:

1. How often do you read for fun on your own time?
     Daily   Weekly   Monthly
2. How often do you talk with your friends or family about something you have read?
     Daily   Weekly   Monthly
3. How often do you take books out of the library for your own enjoyment?
     Daily   Weekly   Monthly
4. During the past month how many books have you read on your own outside of school?
     5 or more   3 or 4   1 or 2   None
5. What kind of reader do you think you are?
A very good reader   A good reader   An average reader   A poor reader

Using these indicators in a secondary analysis of 1994 NAEP data, Guthrie and Schafer (1999) found that engaged readers have much better text comprehension and reading achievement than do disengaged readers. Beyond that simple fact, however, engaged reading can overcome major obstacles to achievement. For example, low levels of education in the family and low income usually pose obstacles to reading achievement. Students with less-educated mothers nearly always score lower in reading comprehension than students whose mothers have more education. However, Guthrie and Schafer found that engaged readers who had mothers with a low level of education achieved more highly than did disengaged readers who had highly educated mothers. For example, a student with a less-educated mother who reads "almost every day" for enjoyment has better reading achievement and text comprehension than a student who reads "never or hardly ever" but has a mother who is highly educated. A similar relation occurs for engaged reading and income. Low-income students (receiving free or reduced-price lunch) who were engaged readers scored highly on achievement tests. These engaged readers were comparable in text comprehension to students with higher income (not receiving free or reduced-price lunch) but who were disengaged readers.

The same pattern appears for gender. Whereas girls usually have higher reading achievement than boys, engagement can reverse the pattern. That is, boys who are highly engaged readers (who read "almost every day") are much higher achievers than girls who are disengaged readers (reporting that they "never or hardly ever" read). It is clear from these results that engaged reading is a powerful force influencing achievement.

The engaged reader is capable of overcoming obstacles of low parental education and income, as well as preferences and abilities associated with gender (Guthrie & Schafer, 1999).

In addition to these impressive benefits for engaged reading, longitudinal studies have shown that engagement at a young age predicts achievement at an older age. Cunningham and Stanovich (1997) found that children in grade 3 who were highly engaged readers had higher reading achievement in grade 11 than students in grade 3 who were disengaged readers. The dispositions and interests in reading established in the primary grades determine achievement not only in grade 3 or 5 but as far into the future as grade 11. These benefits of engaged reading for achievement are real and cannot be explained away as an artifact of another factor. A range of predictive studies documents that engaged reading increases achievement when such factors as intelligence, home income, ethnicity, and school grades are statistically controlled. In other words, if teachers can enable students to become "self-starters" as readers, they increase the children's chances of success in immediate and distant futures, and this benefit accrues for a wide range of students (Stanovich & West, 1989).

Amount of Engaged Reading among Elementary Students Is Remarkably Low

Because being an engaged reader is important to text comprehension and general reading achievement, we might hope that most students would become engaged readers in the early grades and remain so throughout their lives. However, that hope is all too rarely fulfilled. How often do 9-year-old students read for their own enjoyment? In a national sample of students, 44% answered that question by saying "daily." If daily reading is a sign of engagement in reading, then only a minority of students is reading engaged. Another side of engagement is social interaction around reading. When the national sample of students was asked, "How often do you talk about what you read?" only 29% said "almost every day." A majority of 71% did not talk about their reading with family or friends on a typical day. These data signal low reading engagement across the nation (Campbell, Voelkl, & Donahue, 1997).

Not only is engaged reading relatively rare among 9-year-olds, but it is even rarer among 13-year-olds. In a national sample, only 21% of 13-year-olds stated that they read "daily" for their own enjoyment. Only 13% stated that they talk daily about what they read with family or friends. By these indicators, more than 75% of middle school students are disengaged readers. These findings confirm the reported decline of motivation for reading across the elementary and middle school years (Harter, Whitesell, & Kowalski, 1992; Wigfield et al., 1997). Without classroom experiences that serve to invite students into the community of active readers, disengagement from reading begins by age 9 and progresses dramatically during the later grades.

Engaged Reading Is Equal Parts Competence and Motivation

It has been said that a good reader possesses skill and will (Paris & Turner, 1994). Both the competence and the desire to read undergird a student's decision to read frequently and widely. Many teachers assume that if a student gains competence in reading, he/she will become an active reader. However, teachers are also aware that many students who can read choose not to read. A range of studies verifies the mutual contribution of competence and motivation to engaged reading. For example, Guthrie, Wigfield, Metsala, and Cox (1999) showed that previous achievement predicted the amount of engaged reading with a correlation of .35. Relatively higher achievers were more likely to read frequently than lower achievers. In addition, motivation predicted amount of reading with the same correlation of .35. The more motivated students read more frequently than less motivated students. The impact of motivation on reading amount was substantial. Highly motivated students in grades 3 and 5 read about 30 minutes per day for their own interest and enjoyment. However, less motivated students in these grades read 10 minutes or less for their own interest (Wigfield & Guthrie, 1997).

In discussing motivation for engaged reading, we emphasize long-term interest, deeply held beliefs about the value of reading, and intrinsic motivation. Motivation that influences engaged reading is not based on temporary excitement or a passing whim. Intrinsic aspects of motivation such as curiosity, desire to be immersed in a narrative, and willingness to tackle challenging text are acquired slowly. They develop through successful reading experiences. Low achievers are notoriously disengaged. However, achievement is not sufficient. Students also need a range of supportive experiences. These experiences help promote feelings of competence, autonomy, and relatedness, which Deci, Vallerand, Pelletier, and Ryan (1991) identify as basic needs for all students. For example, students' sense of competence is promoted by providing them with materials to read that are challenging yet manageable; students' sense of autonomy is promoted by encouraging them to choose books of personal interest; and students' sense of relatedness is promoted by giving them the opportunity to discuss what they are reading with others. When these needs are fulfilled through supportive home and classroom environments, intrinsic motivation for reading emerges as a stable trait that supports long-term engagement (Guthrie, 1999). We believe that the classroom teacher cannot neglect the support system for engaged reading.

Benefits of engaged reading point to a new meaning for "balanced instruction." Our message is that teaching students to be competent readers is necessary but not sufficient. Because engaged reading includes equal parts competence and motivation, teachers should allocate attention evenly to each of these twin goals. Neither can be neglected. A balanced program is cognitive and motivational. It teaches the skills of reading, and it also nurtures the disposition for reading. These dual priorities on skill and will, or competence and motivation, can be attained. But without both, reading engagement is unlikely. And without engagement, text comprehension will not increase in the long term. Because the effects of disengagement from reading are so devastating for achievement, we recommend in this book a set of instructional practices capable of ensuring achievement and adequate to attaining the aspiration of engaged reading for all.

WHAT DOES INSTRUCTIONAL PRACTICE LOOK LIKE TODAY?

One way to illustrate the current status of instructional practice is to consider what outstanding teachers do. By examining what exemplary teachers do, we learn by default what does *not* typically occur in current instruction and we gain insight into the best practices that can best serve the needs of all children. One source for such information is the research Pressley and his colleagues have conducted in which they surveyed or observed teachers nominated by their supervisors as effective in promoting their students' literacy.

In one such study, Pressley, Wharton-McDonald, Allington, Block, and Morrow (1998) observed first-grade teachers at five sites across the country who had been nominated by their supervisors as either outstanding or typical. After observing these teachers, Pressley and colleagues identified the most and least effective teachers at each of the sites and compared their instruction. They found marked differences in instruction, and these differences had a demonstrable effect on students' achievement. By the end of first grade, for example, most children in the most effective teachers' classrooms were reading at or above end-of-first-grade level, and they were writing fairly lengthy compositions with good spelling and attention to capitalization and punctuation. A smaller proportion of children in the least effective teachers' classrooms were able to perform at these levels. Interestingly, lower-achieving children in the most effective teachers' classes did as well or better on standardized tests as did the average students in the least effective teachers' classes.

The most effective first-grade teachers' classrooms were characterized by the following: "high academic engagement, excellent classroom management, positive reinforcement and cooperation, explicit teaching of skills, an emphasis on literature, much reading and writing, matching of task demands to student competence, encouragement of student self-regulation, and strong cross-curricular connections" (Pressley, Wharton-McDonald, Allington, et al., 1998, p. iv). In contrast, the classrooms of the least effective first-grade teachers fell short in each of these areas.

Particularly striking was the high level of academic engagement in the classrooms of the most effective teachers. Students in these classrooms were engaged in reading and writing much of the time. Pressley, Wharton-McDonald, Allington, et al. (1998) found that "90% of the students were engaged 90% of the time" (p. 7). They concluded that even on days of relatively low academic engagement in the most effective teachers' classes, students were more engaged in reading and writing tasks than on the days of relatively highest academic engagement in the least effective teachers' classes.

It is important to note that the least effective teachers were not poor teachers; rather they were considered typical teachers. If the contrast is so clear between outstanding and typical teachers, then instructional practice in classrooms of more marginal or poor teachers seems even less likely to promote engagement.

Studies of classroom instruction in the upper elementary grades also provide information on the state of current instructional practice. In an in-depth analysis of fourth- and fifth-grade teachers' instruction, Pressley, Wharton-McDonald, Mistretta Hampston, and Echevarria (1998) found much to praise. Nevertheless, they noted that Durkin's (1978/1979) classic finding of little comprehension instruction but much practice still characterizes today's classrooms. Even with effective teachers (all considered "competent" and a few considered "really exceptional" by their language arts coordinators), the researchers found little evidence of instruction reflecting current knowledge about effective comprehension strategy instruction. They did note that the comprehension tasks being assigned appeared to be better than those Durkin observed 20 years ago: Tasks required children to practice comprehension strategies (e.g., required them to summarize or to self-question), but these strategies were not being taught.

Pressley, Wharton-McDonald, Mistretta-Hampston, et al. (1998) also noted that most of these fourth- and fifth-grade teachers were weak on facilitating children's self-regulation, with children exhibiting dependence on the teacher. Further, there was much variability in the level of engagement in these classrooms. Most teachers had little apparent knowledge of practices that facilitate motivation and interest.

In short, children in the classrooms of outstanding teachers experience classroom environments that facilitate intense literacy engagement. These classrooms are distinguished by the coherence of their instruction

(Guthrie, Cox, et al., Chapter 10, this volume). They feature connections across the curriculum, few disciplinary disruptions, meaningful skills instruction, a positive atmosphere, and instruction tailored to help children develop competency and independence. But the current instructional situation for most children does not rise to this level.

DESIGN PRINCIPLES FOR PROMOTING ENGAGED READING

The underlying message of this book is that many more children can attain high levels of reading achievement if efforts are made to increase engagement. To reach this goal, reading instruction should be reconceptualized in terms of research-based design principles for promoting engagement. The authors of the chapters in this book have identified best practices in their respective areas. The chapters present research evidence in support of practical recommendations, and they include sources of additional useful information. Each chapter focuses on particular instructional principles that will help a child become an engaged reader.

Specifically, a child needs: a good foundation at the word level (Chapter 2), help if he/she is in trouble (Chapter 3), opportunity to read for learning (Chapter 4), ample materials for reading (Chapter 5), opportunities to share in a community of learners (Chapter 6), instructional contexts that are motivating (Chapter 7), a teacher who is familiar with the child's strengths and weaknesses (Chapter 8), time to read (Chapter 9), coherent instruction that pulls all of the pieces together (Chapter 10), classrooms that are coordinated with the school as a whole (Chapter 11), continuities between home and school (Chapter 12), and masterful teaching by teachers knowledgeable about engagement and achievement (Chapter 13).

The final chapter of the book synthesizes the design principles presented in earlier chapters and examines their implications for professional development. It illustrates that not only is it important for students to be engaged readers but teachers must be engaged as well.

RECOMMENDED READINGS

Baker, L., Afflerbach, P., & Reinking, D. (Eds.). (1996). *Developing engaged readers in school and home communities.* Mahwah, NJ: Erlbaum.

This book introduces the engagement perspective that framed the mission of the National Reading Research Center (NRRC). Chapters deal with such topics as social and cultural contexts of reading engagement, motivation and engaged reading, and engaged instruction and learning.

Burns, M. S., Snow, C. E., & Griffin, P. (Eds.). (1999). *Starting out right: A guide to promoting children's reading success*. Washington, DC: National Academy Press.

This volume is based on a lengthier report (see below) edited by Snow, Burns, and Griffin (1998). The authors provide activities that parents can use at home with young children and that teachers can use in the classroom. The book includes checklists of what children should accomplish at each grade from kindergarten to grade 3.

Guthrie, J. T., & Alvermann, D. E. (Eds.). (1999). *Engaged reading: Processes, practices, and policy implications*. New York: Teachers College Press.

This volume is a synthesis of the research conducted at the NRRC from 1992 to 1997. It offers a model of engaged reading and examines engagement within homes, elementary schools, and middle and secondary schools.

Guthrie, J. T., & Wigfield, A. (Eds.). (1997). *Reading engagement: Motivating readers through integrated instruction*. Newark, DE: International Reading Association.

This book provides an introduction to the broader research literature on motivation as it relates to literacy development and offers detailed descriptions of classroom contexts that promote literacy engagement.

Snow, C. E., Burns, M. S., & Griffin, P. (Eds.). (1998). *Preventing reading difficulties in young children*. Washington, DC: National Academy Press.

In this 400-plus-page volume, members of a National Research Council (NRC) panel summarize research relevant to helping all children learn to read well. The book includes information on how children learn to read, predictors of reading difficulty, prevention strategies, and implications for instruction and professional development.

REFERENCES

Allington, R. L. (1983). The reading instruction provided readers of differing ability. *Elementary School Journal, 83*, 549–559.

America Reads Challenge: READ*WRITE*NOW! Partners Group. (1998). *Checkpoints for progress in reading and writing for teachers and learning partners* (ARC 97-4501). U.S. Department of Education. [http://www.ed.gov/inits/americareads/arc-pubs.html]

Baker, L., Afflerbach, P., & Reinking, D. (1996a). Developing engaged readers in school and home communities: An overview. In L. Baker, P. Afflerbach, & D. Reinking (Eds.), *Developing engaged readers in school and home communities* (pp. xiii–xviii). Mahwah, NJ: Erlbaum.

Baker, L., Afflerbach, P., & Reinking, D. (Eds.). (1996b). *Developing engaged readers in school and home communities*. Mahwah, NJ: Erlbaum.

Baumann, J. F., & Duffy, A. M. (1997). *Engaged reading for pleasure and learning: A report from the National Reading Research Center*. Athens, GA: Universities of Georgia & Maryland, National Reading Research Center.

Braunger, J., & Lewis, J. P. (1997). *Building a knowledge base in reading*. Newark, DE: International Reading Association.

Burns, M. S., Snow, C. E., & Griffin, P. (Eds.). (1999). *Starting out right: A guide to promoting children's reading success*. Washington, DC: National Academy Press.

Campbell, J. R., Voelkl, K. E., & Donahue, P. L. (1997). *NAEP 1996 trends in academic progress.* Washington, DC: National Center for Education Statistics.

Caswell, L. C., & Duke, N. (1998). Non-narrative as a catalyst for literacy development. *Language Arts, 75,* 108–117.

Cipielewski, J., & Stanovich, K. E. (1992). Predicting growth in reading ability from children's exposure to print. *Journal of Experimental Child Psychology, 54,* 74–89.

Cole, A. D. (1998). Beginner-oriented texts in literature-based classrooms: The segue for a few struggling readers. *The Reading Teacher, 51,* 488–501.

Cunningham, A. E., & Stanovich, K. E. (1997). Early reading acquisition and its relation to reading experience and ability 10 years later. *Developmental Psychology, 33,* 934–945.

Deci, E. L., Vallerand, R. J., Pelletier, L. G., & Ryan, R. M. (1991). Motivation and education: The self-determination perspective. *Educational Psychologist, 26,* 325–346.

Donahue, P. L., Voelkl, K. E., Campbell, J. R., & Mazzeo, J. (1999). *The NAEP 1998 reading report card for the nation.* Washington, DC: U.S. Department of Education, National Center for Educational Statistics.

Durkin, C. (1978/1979). What classroom observations reveal about reading comprehension instruction. *Reading Research Quarterly, 15,* 481–533.

Gambrell, L. B., & Almasi, J. F. (Eds.). (1996). *Lively discussions: Fostering engaged reading.* Newark, DE: International Reading Association.

Guthrie, J. T. (1999). The young reader as a self-extending system: Motivational and cognitive underpinnings. In J. Gaffney & B. Askew (Eds.), *Stirring the waters: The influence of Marie Clay* (pp. 149–165). Portsmouth, NH: Heinemann.

Guthrie, J. T., & Alvermann, D. E. (Eds.). (1999). *Engaged reading: Processes, practices, and policy implications.* New York: Teachers College Press.

Guthrie, J. T., & Anderson, E. (1999). Engagement in reading: Processes of motivated, strategic, knowledgeable, social readers. In J. T. Guthrie & D. E. Alvermann (Eds.), *Engaged reading: Processes, practices, and policy implications* (pp. 17–45). New York: Teachers College Press.

Guthrie, J. T., & Schafer, W. (1999). *Reading motivation, engagement, achievement and instruction: Policy analyses of NAEP 1994.* Manuscript submitted for publication.

Guthrie, J. T., & Wigfield, A. (Eds.). (1997). *Reading engagement: Motivating readers through integrated instruction.* Newark, DE: International Reading Association.

Guthrie, J. T., Wigfield, A., Metsala, J., & Cox, K. (1999). Predicting text comprehension and reading activity with motivational and cognitive variables. *Scientific Studies of Reading, 3,* 231–256.

Harter, S., Whitesell, N., & Kowalski, P. (1992). Individual differences in the effects of educational transitions on children's perceptions of competence and motivational orientation. *American Educational Research Journal, 29,* 777–808.

International Reading Association & National Association for the Education of Young Children. (1998). Learning to read and write: Developmentally appropriate practices for young children. *The Reading Teacher, 52,* 193–216.

Ivey, G. (1999). Reflections on struggling middle school readers. *Journal of Adolescent and Adult Literacy, 42,* 372–381.

Juel, C. (1988). Learning to read and write: A longitudinal study of 54 children from first through fourth grade. *Journal of Educational Psychology, 80,* 437–447.

McCarthey, S. J., Hoffman, J. U., & Galda, L. (1999). Readers in elementary classrooms: Learning goals and instructional principles that can inform practice. In J. T. Guthrie & D. E. Alvermann (Eds.), *Engaged reading: Processes, practices, and policy implications* (pp. 46–80). New York: Teachers College Press.

McCormick, S. (1999). *Instructing students who have literacy problems* (3rd ed.). Columbus, OH: Merrill.

Paris, S. G., & Turner, J. C. (1994). Situated motivation. In P. R. Pintrich, D. R. Brown, & C. E.

Weinstein (Eds.), *Student motivation, cognition and learning* (pp. 213–237). Hillsdale, NJ: Erlbaum.

Pressley, M. (1998). *Reading instruction that works: The case for balanced teaching.* New York: Guilford Press.

Pressley, M., Wharton-McDonald, R., Allington, R., Block, C. C., & Morrow, L. (1998). *The nature of effective first-grade literacy instruction* (CELA Research Rep. No. 11007). Albany: State University of New York at Albany, The National Center on English Learning & Achievement. [http://cela.albany.edu/1stgradelit/index.html]

Pressley, M., Wharton-McDonald, R., Mistretta-Hampston, J., & Echevarria, M. (1998). Literacy instruction in 10 fourth- and fifth-grade classrooms in upstate New York. *Scientific Studies of Reading, 2,* 159–194.

Snow, C., Burns, M., & Griffin, P. (Eds.). (1998). *Preventing reading difficulties in young children.* Washington, DC: National Academy Press.

Stanovich, K. E. (1986). Matthew effects in reading: Some consequences of individual differences in the acquisition of literacy. *Reading Research Quarterly, 21,* 360–407.

Stanovich, K. E., & West, R. F. (1989). Exposure to print and orthographic processing. *Reading Research Quarterly, 24,* 402–433.

Wigfield, A., Eccles, J. S., Yoon, K. S., Harold, R. D., Arbreton, A. J. A., Freedman-Doan, C., & Blumenfeld, P. C. (1997). Change in children's competence beliefs and subjective task values across the elementary school years: A 3-year study. *Journal of Educational Psychology, 89,* 451–469.

Wigfield, A., & Guthrie, J. T. (1997). Relations of children's motivation for reading to the amount and breadth of their reading. *Journal of Educational Psychology, 89,* 420–432.

CHAPTER TWO

Building the Word-Level Foundation for Engaged Reading

LINDA BAKER

To become engaged readers, children need to get off to a good start in the "basics" of reading—the ability to recognize words and access their meanings. A critical component of effective reading instruction, therefore, is at the word level. Word study need not and should not entail skills instruction divorced from the context of meaningful reading. Direct and explicit study of words, including phonological, orthographic, morphological, and semantic aspects, can be included within a coherent literature-based program. This chapter draws on what we know about word recognition and other aspects of word study to offer a view of instruction that maintains a focus on engaged reading.

Word study is intended to foster a broad range of word-level competencies. Word study includes phonics, as well as spelling patterns (orthography), word structure (prefixes, suffixes, roots), word meanings, and the development of automaticity in word recognition. Research has documented the importance of word study from these multiple angles (Snow, Burns, & Griffin, 1998). For example, we know that children who understand the alphabetic principle (i.e., understand how letters or graphemes relate to speech sounds or phonemes) learn to read more easily than those who do not. We also know that children who have extensive knowledge about words and their parts are able to apply strategies flexibly to help them identify new words and figure out their meanings. We know that learning to spell facilitates learning to read and vice versa. And we know that fluent and accurate word identification (automaticity) is critical to reading comprehension; children who must devote all of their cognitive resources to identifying individual words are not able to construct the meaning of what they are reading.

Of all the different facets of reading instruction, none has generated more dissension than instruction at the word level. The acrimonious debates over how to teach children to read have been widely publicized in the media and will not be revisited in this chapter. We take as a given, based on an extensive body of research, that children need direct and explicit instruction in phonics to help them acquire independence in word recognition, a critical prerequisite to independence in reading (for documentation, see Braunger & Lewis, 1997; Pressley, 1998; Snow et al., 1998; Stahl, Duffy-Hester, & Stahl, 1998). Our concern is that phonics instruction and other aspects of word study are too often divorced from contexts that facilitate engaged reading. Even when word study is advanced as part of a "balanced" curriculum, it may be unconnected to the literature children are reading. We argue that word study itself can be engaging, affording opportunities for enhancing knowledge and skills, strategies and metacognition, motivation, and social interaction.

This chapter is organized as follows. The first section covers the prerequisites for word study, addressing the skills children need to recognize words and the ways teachers can facilitate the development of those skills. The second section focuses on how teachers can promote the skills and strategies children need for independent word recognition. Topics include different instructional approaches, texts that support early reading development, and the importance of creating motivating and socially interactive instructional contexts. Next come sections on promoting the development of reading fluency, vocabulary, and spelling and word analysis. The penultimate section addresses classroom organizational issues. It is followed by closing comments.

HELPING CHILDREN DEVELOP THE SKILLS THEY NEED FOR RECOGNIZING WORDS

What Are the Prerequisite Skills for Word Recognition?

The focus of this book is on what teachers should know to promote engaged reading, but it is important that they be aware of what children should know before formal instruction begins. Research has identified several cognitive prerequisites for learning to read words, without which children likely will experience difficulty. These include phonological/phonemic awareness, knowledge of the alphabet, concepts about print, and an adequate oral vocabulary. Children begin to acquire knowledge about reading and writing through their everyday experiences in the first few years of life; many children already show considerable competence in the cognitive prerequisites before they enter kindergarten (Baker, Fernandez-Fein, Scher, & Williams, 1998).

Phonological awareness refers to a particular kind of language awareness, the awareness that words are composed of smaller units of sound. Children who are able to analyze the sounds of spoken words are more successful in learning to read printed words (Blachman, 1997; Ehri, 1998). This analysis can occur at multiple levels, the easiest of which is the syllable level. Another level of analysis involves the components of single-syllable words known as onsets and rimes. The onset is the initial consonant or consonant cluster, and the rime is the remaining portion of the word. For example, in the word "dust" the sound corresponding to the initial letter is the onset; the remaining sounds constitute the rime. It is not necessary to be able to isolate the individual speech sounds in the rime in order to detect the similarity between "dust" and rhyming words like "rust." The most sophisticated form of phonological awareness is the ability to isolate the individual speech sounds or phonemes of spoken words; this is known as phonemic awareness. A child would demonstrate phonemic awareness if he/she could identify the four separate phonemes in the word dust: /d/, /u/, /s/, and /t/. Most children follow the developmental sequence of first learning to analyze syllables, then rimes, then onsets, then phonemes; however, there are some children who do not follow this pattern (Christensen, 1997).

The evidence is quite clear that phonological awareness is necessary (but not sufficient) for children to learn how to decode words using phonics principles (Adams, 1990). Countless studies have shown that children who score poorly on tests of phonological awareness in kindergarten also score poorly on tests of word recognition in the primary grades (Scarborough, 1998). If they are unable to hear the separate speech sounds in a spoken word, they will not be able to link those speech sounds to letters. This disrupts understanding of the alphabetic principle. The evidence is also clear, however, that phonemic awareness grows as children acquire reading skill. Some rudimentary knowledge is necessary early on, but children become more proficient at phonemic analysis as they learn the spellings that correspond to particular combinations of phonemes (Ehri, 1998).

Children who know the letters of the alphabet before they begin reading instruction are more successful learning to recognize words. Along with phonemic awareness, letter knowledge is a strong predictor of later word recognition ability (Scarborough, 1998). Children who do not know the names of individual letters or the sounds that correspond to the letters will not be able to read new words independently. Young children may appear to recognize words in the environment before they know letter names, but this recognition is typically based on a memorable context or logo (e.g., the red octagon of a stop sign). Knowledge of letter names is necessary for children to be able to read such words outside of their familiar context (Ehri, 1998).

Why are researchers so confident that phonological awareness and letter knowledge contribute to reading? One of the best ways to find out whether a particular skill is important to reading is to identify children who have not yet developed that skill. Some of the children are then given instruction in that skill, and others are not. The two groups of children are later compared to determine whether those who received instruction outperform the others on a test of reading. Many such studies have demonstrated the value of training in phonological awareness, letter knowledge, and spelling–sound correspondence knowledge (see Graham & Harris, Chapter 3, this volume; Snow et al., 1998).

Another important prerequisite to reading is a basic understanding of how print works. Children need to understand the functions of print, the meanings of terms like "word" and "letter," and the directionality of print. Much of this knowledge is acquired incidentally, without formal instructions. Contexts for learning about print include shared storybook reading at home or in preschool, attention to print in the environment, and observation of everyday literacy practices such as list writing and newspaper reading (Baker, Serpell, & Sonnenschein, 1995; Purcell-Gates, 1998). Children who come to school with print concepts in place are more receptive to formal instruction focusing on print (Adams, 1990; Snow et al., 1998).

Finally, children need a well-developed oral vocabulary so that they know the meanings of the words they encounter when they are learning to read. By the time middle-income children enter first grade, they understand as many as 10,000 different words (Anglin, 1993). This puts them in a good position for learning the skills of word recognition without having the double burden of simultaneous vocabulary acquisition. Many low-income children know considerably fewer words on entering school (Hart & Risley, 1995), increasing the risk of reading comprehension difficulties in later years (Beck & McKeown, 1991).

Fostering the Prerequisite Skills

The strong research evidence for the importance of alphabetic and phonological knowledge led two major professional organizations to step into the controversy on early literacy instruction. The International Reading Association (IRA) and the National Association for the Education of Young Children (NAEYC) issued a joint position statement calling for instruction of these prerequisite skills in prekindergarten and kindergarten classrooms (IRA & NAEYC, 1998). Advocating such instruction does not mean that children should be subjected to drills on isolated skills or that they should sit quietly at desks completing worksheets. Rather, the emphasis should be on fostering this knowledge through engaging activities and exposure to interesting literature.

One might worry that the tasks used to promote phonological awareness would be tedious and unmotivating to young children, but there are in fact a variety of enjoyable approaches that can be used. Teachers can promote phonological/phonemic awareness through language play that includes rhymes and beginning sounds, and they can read aloud books with rhyme and alliteration (Fernandez-Fein & Baker, 1997). By the time children reach grade 1, most will have developed some phonological awareness, but instruction should continue if necessary. Many resources are now available that offer explicit guidance and practical suggestions for activities in kindergarten and first-grade classes (e.g., Adams, Foorman, Lundberg, & Beeler, 1996; Ericson & Juliebo, 1998; Strickland, 1998; see also Graham & Harris, Chapter 3, this volume). An annotated bibliography of 44 books in which play with language is an explicit and dominant feature was compiled by Yopp (1995; for an updated listing, see Opitz, 1998).

Teachers should involve children in activities that promote their knowledge of the alphabet, concepts of print, and vocabulary. Children should be able to recognize all of the letters in kindergarten, and they should be learning how to write them. Attention can be directed at learning relations between letters and sounds, again within enjoyable and meaningful contexts (see Schickedanz, 1998, for suggested activities). Literacy play centers are particularly effective for promoting all of the prerequisites of word recognition (Neuman & Roskos, 1997). Concepts about print can be developed as children watch teachers write dictated stories, illustrating how words are represented in print. In addition, teachers can model how they use their knowledge of grapheme–phoneme correspondences as they read aloud or as they write from dictation. Children's vocabulary can be developed through listening to stories (Elley, 1989; Robbins & Ehri, 1994).

Writing is a valuable activity for promoting prerequisite knowledge. Teachers should give children frequent opportunities to write, with the freedom to use whatever knowledge of letters and letter sounds they possess. Controversy exists as to whether children should be encouraged to invent their own spellings if they are not sure how to spell a word, but most teachers of young children today do accept invented spelling (Baumann, Hoffman, Moon, & Duffy-Hester, 1998). Of course, eventually children must be taught to spell conventionally, but such instruction should not be a focus in kindergarten. Evidence is clear that spelling practice promotes children's understanding of the alphabetic principle (Snow et al., 1998; Treiman, 1998; Zutell, 1998). As they try to spell words, children access their knowledge about how words sound and they attempt to represent these sounds with the letters that they know. This provides an excellent window for the teacher on the children's growing phonemic awareness and understanding of the alphabetic principle. Studying children's spelling is therefore a valuable means of ongoing assessment (see Leipzig & Afflerbach, Chapter 8, this volume; Rosencrans, 1998; Temple, Nathan, Burris, & Temple, 1993). Kindergarten children's skills at reading words and writing words are strongly interconnected, as they are for older children; skill in one area contributes to skill in the other (Richgels, 1995).

HELPING CHILDREN DEVELOP SKILLS
AND STRATEGIES FOR INDEPENDENT
WORD RECOGNITION

The Importance of Balance

The research literature on how children learn to read words is tremendous. Dozens of empirical articles are published in professional journals each year, and edited syntheses of the research appear with great regularity (e.g., Blachman, 1997; Metsala & Ehri, 1998). Many researchers have suggested that children develop word recognition skills in a stage-like manner. That is, first children use superficial features of the words (e.g., configuration) or just a few key letters to identify the words. Then they move on to an alphabetic approach, where they apply their emerging knowledge of letter–sound relations to decode words sequentially from left to right. Finally they use a mature approach that draws on orthographic knowledge of units larger than individual letters (Ehri, 1998). Other researchers, however, argue that there are many different pathways to proficient word recognition rather than a fixed sequence of stages. It is beyond the scope of this chapter to review these basic research findings. Highly readable treatments of the topic are available in Pressley (1998), Ehri and McCormick (1998), and Snow et al. (1998). The focus here is on the instructional implications of the basic research for promoting engaged reading. The chapter therefore goes beyond the cognitive aspects of instruction in word recognition to consider the motivational and social aspects.

Our position in this book is that phonics instruction is an important component of beginning reading instruction. However, we concur with the IRA's (1997) position statement on phonics that "phonics instruction, to be effective in promoting independence in reading, must be embedded in the context of a total reading/language arts program." The National Research Council (NRC) similarly concluded in their major report on preventing reading difficulties that children will show good progress in reading if they have systematic code instruction and meaningful reading (Snow et al., 1998). This call for balance is echoed in other recent syntheses by Braunger and Lewis (1997), Pressley (1998), IRA and NAEYC (1998), Freppon and Dahl (1998), and Stahl et al. (1998), among others. It is critical that neither teachers nor students lose sight of the ultimate goals of reading—comprehension, knowledge acquisition, enjoyment—and they need to understand that phonics instruction helps foster the enabling skills of accurate and efficient word recognition.

Reports in the media led to widespread concern that teachers had abandoned phonics instruction in favor of whole-language approaches, but recent surveys indicate that this is not the case. First-grade teachers regarded as highly effective tend to use balanced instruction, as revealed in a survey by Pressley, Rankin, and Yokoi (1996). Teachers provided explicit phonics instruction in formal lessons as well as informal instruction as the need arose during story reading. They encouraged students to reflect on what they were doing and why, promoting metacognitive awareness about reading. They also used a variety of approaches to teach decoding, illustrating that there are multiple routes to word identification.

Explicit phonics instruction combined with meaningful reading and writing is not the exclusive province of expert teachers. Baumann et al. (1998) surveyed approximately 1,200 prekindergarten through grade 5 public school teachers and found that most teachers favored a balanced approach, blending phonics and holistic principles in compatible ways. More than 90% of the kindergarten–grade 2 (K–2) teachers believed it was important or essential to teach phonics, contextual analysis, structural analysis, sight words, and meaning vocabulary. Teachers also recognized the importance of teaching children multiple strategies for reading and pronouncing unfamiliar words.

Approaches to Phonics Instruction

In traditional phonics instruction, children are taught to decode words through synthetic or analytic approaches. In a synthetic approach, children are taught letter–sound correspondences first and then are taught how to decode words through segmentation and blending. In an analytic approach, children are taught some simple regular words by sight and then are taught phonics generalizations from these words, but they do not break the words down into component phonemes. In the Baumann et al. (1998) survey, 66% of the teachers reported synthetic approaches and 40%

analytic. Research suggests there is a slight advantage of synthetic approaches over analytic (Stahl et al., 1998), indicating that explicit attention to phonemes is valuable.

Teachers should be aware that an emphasis on phonics generalizations may be misguided, given that many such rules are not valid most of the time. In a now classic study, Clymer (1963/1996) examined the usefulness of 45 phonic generalizations included in instructional materials for the primary grades. He searched for words that conformed to the generalizations and words that did not, and then calculated the percentage of utility. He selected 75% utility as a cutpoint for when it made sense to teach the generalization. Only 18 of the 45 generalizations met this criterion. The well-known generalization "When two vowels go walking the first does the talking" was valid only 45% of the time!

Traditional approaches have been supplemented with several contemporary approaches, described more fully by Stahl et al. (1998). Spelling-based approaches that capitalize on the well-established reciprocal relations between word recognition and spelling have become popular. These include word sorting (Bear & Templeton, 1998), making words (P. M. Cunningham, Hall, & Defee, 1998), and metaphonics (Calfee, 1998). To illustrate, in the Cunningham et al. approach, children are given sets of letters and are asked to make specific words from them, starting with short words and moving on to longer words within the set. The final task is to use all of the letters to create a word. The words are usually taken from a story that children are reading for instruction. The students then sort the words by semantic properties or letter–sound patterns, as in other approaches involving word sorting. These activities are reportedly very engaging and are appropriate for students at a variety of levels. Even struggling readers can experience success with the shortest, simplest words.

Analogy-based approaches are also becoming increasingly popular, fueled by research evidence that children can learn to recognize new words by analogy with known words (Goswami, 1998). Sixty-six percent of the teachers in the Baumann et al. (1998) survey reported using analogy approaches, typically to supplement explicit traditional phonics. Gaskins and her colleagues (Gaskins, 1998; Gaskins, Ehri, Cress, O'Hara, & Donnelly, 1997) developed a program in which children were provided with an extensive listing of word families or phonograms (e.g., words ending in -at, -in, and -ine) and were taught to use these key words to identify related unknown words. Most children benefited from the program, but there were some who did not learn to identify words independently. Gaskins (1998) therefore added explicit instruction in blending phonemes to her program. This ensured that children would direct enough attention to the individual letters of the key words to store them in memory. It has been shown that such stored memory representations are necessary to use analogies effectively (Ehri, 1998).

Another contemporary instructional approach is embedded phonics. Phonics principles are taught on an as-needed basis during the course of reading and writing, as in many whole language classrooms. Of the K–2 teachers surveyed in the Baumann et al. (1998) study, no more than 19% reported teaching phonics only as needed. A concern with embedded approaches is that whether or not children are taught certain principles depends on whether relevant words are encountered in the course of reading or writing. Children's knowledge may therefore be incomplete.

Research comparing these new approaches in the classroom is limited, as noted by Stahl et al. (1998). However, in a recent study by Foorman, Francis, Fletcher, Schatschneider, and Mehta (1998), first and second graders showed greater gains in word recognition in a direct code instruction program (explicit or synthetic phonics) than did children who learned about the code incidentally through their reading in a more holistic curriculum (implicit or embedded phonics). Students who learned to recognize words through an analogy approach were intermediate in their gains. In addition, students who had low levels of phonemic awareness at the beginning of the study benefited from the direct code approach but not from the other two approaches. These results highlight the importance of explicit attention to phonemes in word recognition instruction for children who do not already possess this knowledge.

So, what approach to phonics instruction should teachers use? Chall (1996) suggested that as long as children are given early and systematic information about the code, it may not matter very much how it is done. Nevertheless, it appears to be highly desirable to teach multiple strategies for recognizing words. The best approach may be to teach children to recognize words by blending phonemes (synthetic phonics) and by analogy. Analogy training may be particularly valuable in helping children identify new irregular words because knowledge of grapheme–phoneme correspondences is less useful for such words (Levy & Lysynchuk, 1997).

It is important to emphasize that systematic phonics instruction need not use the much-maligned worksheets. Indeed, we know that worksheets and rote drills are not very effective for teaching children to recognize words (A. E. Cunningham, 1990), and they can have a negative motivational impact (Turner, 1997). Seventy percent of the teachers in the Baumann et al. (1998) survey said they rarely or never used phonics workbooks. Instead, they taught phonics in the context of stories, writing, spelling, and word families. Many resources for teachers are available that include instructional strategies for promoting children's phonics knowledge in engaging contexts (Bear, Invernizzi, Templeton, & Johnston, 1996; P. M. Cunningham, 1995; Strickland, 1998).

Reading That Supports the Development of Word Recognition

Children learn to read by reading. This truism holds for learning to recognize words as well as learning to comprehend text. Children need to have extensive opportunities to read in order to refine their knowledge of the alphabetic principle and to develop a repertoire of words known automatically by sight. Most of these opportunities should involve reading meaningful text rather than isolated words. Nevertheless, there is a place for attention to isolated words. Although flashcards have acquired a bad reputation as a tool for drilling on skills, some children take great pleasure and pride in constructing banks of words they can read quickly and accurately (Johnston, 1998). Similarly, "word walls" reinforce the learning of important words by sight. In P. M. Cunningham and colleagues' (1998) program, selected words are written on the bulletin board each week. Children chant the letters, clap the letters, and write the words in what is reportedly an enjoyable recurrent group activity. Teachers who offer such word study help children build a store of high-frequency words that they can read and spell automatically.

For maximum gains in word recognition, teachers should have children engage in real reading of meaningful texts on a daily basis (Braunger & Lewis, 1997; Snow et al., 1998). Research has shown that the types of text used by children in their reading instruction influence how they go about recognizing words. Some texts are highly decodable, containing primarily words that children can readily decode using learned phonics principles. Other texts include primarily words that occur with very high frequency in the language, but the words are not necessarily decodable and so must be learned by sight. Juel and Roper/Schneider (1986) found that if first graders used a decodable basal, they developed a phonological strategy based on letter–sound correspondences; if they used a high-frequency basal, they adopted a strategy that was primarily visual.

Instructional materials today are much less contrived than the basals used when Juel and Roper/Schneider conducted their study (Hiebert, 1998; Hoffman et al., 1998); good-quality children's literature is often used. However, concerns have been raised about the use of literature with predictable language patterns, a feature common in texts for beginning readers. Beck (1998) argued that such texts can be "disastrous" for the development of word recognition because their strong contexts and high predictability do not require thorough analysis of all the letters in the words (p. 27). Ehri and McCormick (1998) similarly cautioned that students may simply memorize the story rather than attend to the print.

How much do students in fact learn about words from reading predictable text, relative to what they learn when reading is supplemented with activities that focus attention more explicitly on print? Johnston

(1998) addressed this question by asking three groups of students to read predictable text in repeated readings. One group of students also read the story in sentence context without picture support and rebuilt the story using sentence strips. A second group of students also created word banks in which they selected and practiced reading words from the text written on cards. The third group read the text only. The students learned more words when they used sentence strips and word banks than when they simply reread the text; word banks were most effective. Students with better letter–sound correspondence knowledge learned the most words, attesting once again to the importance of being able to analyze words with respect to their phonological features. Clearly, teachers need to direct children's attention to print; predictable text reading alone is unlikely to promote word recognition skills.

What kinds of texts should be used? Hiebert (1998) analyzed the strengths and weaknesses of three types of texts used in beginning reading instruction. Decodable texts provide children an opportunity to practice newly learned phonics skills independently and refine their understanding of the alphabetic principle. High-frequency texts help children build up a repertoire of important irregular sight words. Predictable texts and other texts selected for literary merit show children that reading is meaningful, that books and stories can entertain and inform. Such texts are most likely to foster reading engagement, but they tend to be demanding for young readers because they lack vocabulary control. Hiebert recommended that teachers select texts for their students to serve all of these different purposes. In other words, the texts should allow children to use their growing knowledge of high-frequency sight words, decodable words, and predictable story structure (Braunger & Lewis, 1997; Snow et al., 1998). The texts should include both meaningful stories and information books (see Dreher, Chapter 4, this volume). Few texts that meet all of these criteria simultaneously are available commercially, however, so teachers likely will need to use different texts for different purposes. Fortunately, it is not necessary to use the contrived texts of older decodable basals to reinforce patterns being learned in phonics instruction (see Trachtenburg, 1990, for a listing of children's trade books that include a high proportion of particular vowel patterns). Chambliss and McKillop (Chapter 5, this volume) provide further discussion and recommended resources for building classroom libraries.

The Role of Metacognitive Knowledge and Strategic Control in Word Recognition

Just as metacognitive knowledge and strategic control contribute to reading comprehension, so too do these play a role in effective word recognition. It is important to teach children when, where, and why particular strategies for recognizing words are advantageous. Students need to be shown strategies for using what they already know about how words work to identify new words. Research has shown that some beginning and less proficient older readers believe that good reading is being able to pronounce all of the words correctly (Baker & Brown, 1984). This impression is considerably more likely to develop in classrooms where there is an emphasis on accurate and fluent decoding rather than comprehension. Contextualizing word study within a larger literature-based framework is important in showing children that word recognition is the means to the end, not the end in itself.

When children self-correct during oral reading, they show meta-cognitive awareness that a word does not make sense in the context of the larger passage. Such self-correction would not occur if children focused only on decoding individual words (Schwartz, 1997). Children should be taught to use the semantic and syntactic cues provided by the surrounding context to help them decide if they have decoded a word correctly. According to the NRC (Snow et al., 1998), it is a reasonable expectation that children begin to monitor their own reading in grade 1. A recent study demonstrated that Finnish first graders (who are a year older than their American counterparts) are in fact capable of monitoring their comprehension while reading, but— as one might expect—children who were struggling with decoding were less likely to recognize that there were inconsistencies in the texts they were reading (Kinnunen, Vauras, & Niemi, 1998). Not only does facility with word recognition enable comprehension, it also enables comprehension monitoring. Because oral reading provides a window on the child's cognitive and metacognitive skills of reading, it is a valuable form of ongoing assessment (see Leipzig & Afflerbach, Chapter 8, this volume).

Teaching children to reflect on the processes and strategies they use to recognize words is effective. The value of such metacognitive awareness training was illustrated in a study by A. E. Cunningham (1990). First-grade children who were given information about when, where, and why to use the knowledge of the phonemes they were acquiring performed better on tests of word recognition than those who received phonemic awareness instruction without the metacognitive component. As a second example, Greaney, Tunmer, and Chapman (1997) combined metacognitive training with instruction in a rime-based strategy for word recognition with positive effects.

For guidance in designing instruction that emphasizes metacognitive knowledge and strategic control, teachers can refer to descriptions of several well-known programs for promoting word recognition. The word study program of Gaskins et al. (1997) emphasizes the development of metacognitive knowledge, as does Calfee's (1998) metaphonics program. Reading Recovery also has a strong metacognitive component, consistent with Clay's (1991) emphasis on "the construction of inner control."

Creating Motivating Contexts for Instruction in Word Recognition

Instruction in word recognition should be embedded within an engaging context. It is important to create an atmosphere in which students are willing to take risks, to make mistakes in applying their growing knowledge to identifying unknown words, figuring out word meanings, and reading to others. Challenge is a powerful motivator for many children. Word study all too often is a dull activity that does not sustain interest. Low interest is especially likely if the tasks are not appropriately tailored to students' needs, either because they are too easy or too difficult.

Evidence in support of careful tailoring was provided by Sacks and Mergendoller (1997), who examined the affect and task involvement of kindergartners in classrooms that differed in their skills orientation. In both skills and whole-language types of classrooms, the higher-ability children demonstrated more positive affective responses than the lower-ability children. Low-ability students demonstrated less task engagement in phonics-oriented classes than in whole-language classes; in the latter type, their task engagement was about the same as that of high-ability students. The above authors suggested that students in whole language classrooms had the opportunity to engage more frequently in literacy tasks appropriately matched to their reading developmental level, thus leading to higher levels of engagement.

Other researchers have also shown that holistic approaches are associated with better motivational outcomes. For example, Turner (1995) found that first graders persisted most when they were engaged in real reading rather than completing worksheets. In general, tasks in which students had choice as to what they would do and how they would do it (open tasks) were more motivating than those in which students had no choice and where there was just one correct answer (closed tasks). Foorman et al. (1998) reported that students in their experimental implicit code classes, which most closely resemble whole-language approaches, had more positive attitudes toward reading than did those in the direct code classes, but they did not differ in the amount of reading they chose to do, nor in perceived self-competence in academics. Freppon and Dahl (1998) also reported more positive affective responses in whole-language classrooms. Hoffman et al. (1998) found that first-grade teachers and students alike were more motivated when high-quality literature was used in beginning reading programs rather than traditional basals with isolated skills instruction.

Teachers should not interpret these findings to mean that explicit instruction in word recognition should be avoided, however. What seems to be critical from a motivational standpoint is the context in which the instruction occurs. To their surprise, McKenna, Stratton, Grindler, and

Jenkins (1995) did not find more positive reading attitudes among students attending schools with a whole-language orientation. This prompted them to observe two first-grade teachers whose instructional approaches were characterized as balanced but whose students differed considerably in their attitudes toward recreational reading. The following contrast is telling: "By meeting the necessity of direct decoding instruction through contextualized lessons geared largely to children's present needs, Teacher A emphasized the utility rather than the abstraction of skills. . . . In contrast by isolating decoding instruction, by mandating it for all children whether or not it was needed . . . Teacher B may have fostered the budding belief that reading is essentially tied to pointless tedium" (p. 40). The students in Teacher A's class were the ones who had more positive attitudes toward reading. Relatedly, McCarthey, Hoffman, and Galda (1999) described a case study showing that students were more willing to take on texts that were challenging for them and were better able to describe the approaches they would use to decode unknown words when they were taught skills within a meaningful and engaging context.

It appears, then, that teachers can and do create motivating contexts for children learning to recognize words. However, such contexts become less common as children progress through school. Tracey and Morrow (1998) reported an observational study in prekindergarten through grade 2 classrooms of lessons designed to teach phonics and phonemic awareness. Explicit instruction was the dominant approach in grades 1 and 2, and few motivating elements were observed. Authentic and balanced lessons had more characteristics considered motivating, but such lessons were less common beyond the preschool level. Tracey and Morrow identified several ways that phonemic awareness and phonics lessons could be made more motivating: (1) provide students choice of materials and experiences for learning; (2) give students more responsibility and control over their learning, such as self-direction and self-pacing; and (3) use more social collaboration during lessons. Collaborative activities involving making words and sorting words (P. M. Cunningham, 1995; Bear et al., 1996) would meet these criteria for student engagement (see also Turner, 1997, and McCarthey et al., 1999).

Promoting Word Recognition Skills through Social Interaction

Children need extensive opportunities to interact with others as they learn to read, not just with proficient adult readers but also with peers whose skills are more closely matched to theirs. As Vygotsky (1978) asserted, learning is a social enterprise. That readers are socially interactive is a key premise of the engagement perspective. Research has in fact shown that social and cooperative literacy experiences motivate independent reading and writing (Morrow & Gambrell, 1998; see Gambrell, Mazzoni, & Almasi, Chapter 6, this volume, for further discussion).

Some may doubt whether beginning readers can work together to good advantage, but research supports the value of peer collaboration even when the focus is on word recognition. Mathes, Howard, Allen, and Fuchs (1998) developed a peer-assisted learning program in which first-grade children worked in pairs on structured word study and reading activities. Evaluation of the program revealed significant benefits to lower-achieving children in word recognition relative to children in comparison classes who received the traditional curriculum. Turner (1997) observed effective peer collaboration when children had been taught by their teachers how to provide assistance in word recognition. For example, partners provided hints about graphophonemic cues and contextual cues rather than simply telling the readers the words they did not recognize. It is clear that simply telling children to work together and help one another is insufficient; teachers need to provide explicit guidance in order for peer collaboration to be productive.

Many commercial reading programs available today recommend shared oral reading, in which the teacher and students read aloud together. This takes the place of round-robin reading, the customary practice in years past in which individual students took turns reading aloud. Eldredge, Reutzel, and Hollingsworth (1996) compared the effectiveness of these two practices in second-grade classrooms over a 4-month period. Students who participated in the shared book approach showed greater gains in word recognition and word analysis, as well as in fluency, vocabulary, and comprehension. Differences were attributable to the mature modeling and scaffolding provided by the teacher, with opportunities for students to take on greater levels of responsibility as their competence increased.

Word recognition skills can be enhanced through shared reading with peers as well as more mature readers (Eldredge et al., 1996). Students can provide support for one another when they encounter difficult words. They can be encouraged to talk with one another not only about what they are reading but about what they do when reading. Children's metacognitive knowledge about reading increases when hearing others talk about their reading processes (McCarthey et al., 1999). Teachers should also encourage shared reading outside of school. Children's reading can improve in the early grades when they read at home to their parents or siblings (Hannon, 1995; see Sonnenschein & Schmidt, Chapter 12, this volume).

HELPING CHILDREN DEVELOP READING FLUENCY

Identification of individual words is a necessary but not sufficient condition for independent reading. Children must be able to identify words quickly enough that they can hold a number of them in working memory simultaneously. Working memory has a short duration, so if a child spends several seconds on each word, he/she will not be able to construct the meaning of larger units of text. If students are encouraged to guess the identity of unknown words from context rather than apply decoding strategies, it will take longer for them to build up a large repertoire of words known automatically by sight (Ehri & McCormick, 1998).

To promote fluency, teachers need to ensure availability of appropriate reading materials (see Chambliss & McKillop, Chapter 5, this volume). The more reading that students do, the more automatic their word recognition becomes. Repeated readings of stories are useful in promoting automaticity and fluency (McCarthey et al., 1999; Samuels, Schermer, & Reinking, 1992), but some children may simply memorize the stories (Johnston, 1998). Repeated readings of several different stories that share many words may be more effective in building fluency for reading new materials than repeated readings of a single story (Snow et al., 1998).

Reading with fluency goes beyond accurate and rapid decoding; it also involves reading with appropriate phrasing and expression. Rasinski (1989) described several methods that teachers can use to help promote fluency: (1) have students engage in repeated readings of the same text; (2) model fluency by having fluent readers read aloud to the students; (3) direct students' attention to what it means to be fluent as they read aloud, thereby increasing their awareness of the process; and (4) provide external support by having students read along orally as a recorded text is played on tape or participate in choral reading with fluent readers.

Research support for such recommendations is available. Stahl, Heubach, and Crammond (1997) showed that their fluency-oriented model of instruction led to benefits not only in children's fluency but also in their word recognition, comprehension, attitude toward reading, and views of themselves as readers. Eldredge et al. (1996) found that shared reading is more effective in promoting fluency than are solitary repeated readings. However, reading with a peer of comparable ability is not as likely to improve fluency as reading with a more able reader (Dixon-Kraus, 1995).

HELPING CHILDREN DEVELOP VOCABULARY KNOWLEDGE

It is not sufficient to decode a word successfully, of course; the reader must also know what the word means. Vocabulary knowledge is not typically considered a critical factor in early reading because most children come to school familiar with the words they will encounter in printed materials intended for beginning readers. But the trend in literature-based instruction is away from strict vocabulary control, so children today may know far fewer of the words they read than would have been true in years past. How might a lack of vocabulary knowledge affect beginning readers' attempts to read on their own? We might well imagine a situation where children struggle to decode a word and are delighted with their success when they realize this new word is "airplane," a concept with which they are highly familiar. Now, in contrast, let us imagine children whose decoding efforts yield words with no meaning to them; they are unlikely to take much delight in breaking the code.

The long-term motivational impact of giving children reading materials that are too difficult for them because of unfamiliar vocabulary is unknown. The lack of vocabulary control in beginning reading materials might put children from low-income and linguistically diverse families at a particular disadvantage because they do not bring the relevant prior knowledge with them to school (Hart & Risley, 1995). Clearly, it is important for teachers to build vocabulary and conceptual knowledge at the same time they provide instruction in the skills of word recognition (see Dreher, Chapter 4, this volume).

As children progress through the primary grades, they are increasingly expected to acquire vocabulary knowledge through their reading. Research on this topic is extensive, but there is still no consensus as to the best ways to teach children to derive word meanings from context (Beck & McKeown, 1991; Fukkink & de Glopper, 1998). Children should be given opportunities to learn vocabulary both through independent reading and explicit instruction. They learn words better if they encounter them in multiple contexts rather than in a single sentence. Teachers should not assume that the age-old advice to "look it up" in the dictionary will be effective as a means of building vocabulary knowledge. Even intermediate students are not very successful in using the dictionary for figuring out the meanings of words and how they should be used in sentences (Scott & Nagy, 1997). Words for vocabulary instruction should come from reading materials rather than from isolated vocabulary lists. As with instruction in word recognition, the context should be meaningful and motivating, with peer collaboration when feasible. It is important that instruction focus on connecting new words with what students already know (Rupley, Logan, & Nichols, 1998/1999). A good source of practical ideas on vocabulary development and instruction is a book by Blachowicz and Fisher (1996).

PROMOTING KNOWLEDGE ABOUT WORDS THROUGH SPELLING AND WORD ANALYSIS

Previous generations of children experienced spelling and reading in separate time blocks, with no connections between the two. It is now recognized that there are important connections between word knowledge in reading and spelling and that it is therefore valuable to deal with both in an integrated fashion (see Cramer, 1998). A number of researchers have described developmental progression in the strategies children use to spell words (Bear & Templeton, 1998; Treiman, 1998; Zutell, 1998). The features a child uses for spelling words and for reading words are similar; they reflect the accuracy and completeness of the representation of the word that is stored in memory. For example, a child who is just beginning to understand that letters correspond to sounds may spell the word "book" as BK. A little later in development of the alphabetic principle, the child adds one vowel per syllable, perhaps now spelling the word as BUK. It is not surprising that children's approaches to spelling predict their reading ability (Ehri, 1998).

Explicit instruction in spelling helps children understand that there is not always a direct correspondence between letters and sounds, and it helps increase their awareness of the underlying regularities of the English spelling, or orthographic, system. Children come to learn that there are good reasons why English is not always spelled the way it sounds. For example, the regular past tense marker *ed* is always spelled the same way, even when it is pronounced differently, as in "walked" versus "painted," because it preserves the meaning: something that happened in the past. The periodic calls to revise our spelling system for greater letter–sound correspondence are misguided; there *is* a "method to the madness" in more cases than not. More complex principles of English orthography can be taught in the intermediate grades when children begin to pay attention to morphology (meaningful units within words) to help them spell (Zutell, 1998). They learn that spelling preserves other kinds of meaning linkages, as in *nature* and *natural*. They no longer match letters and sounds in spelling, but rather the underlying meanings.

An activity that is likely to be engaging for children, especially if it is carried out collaboratively, is word sorting (Bear et al., 1996; Bear & Templeton, 1998; Zutell, 1998). Word learning is not just a matter of rote memorization; it involves recognizing and using similarities and differences in words and word classes. If students engage in an activity where they need to analyze words carefully, their spelling and reading will both improve (Zutell, 1998). Teachers can ask children to sort words into categories based on a number of different dimensions, such as pronunciations, meaning units, spelling patterns, and word origins. The specific words that are used and the criteria for sorting them should be tailored to the developmental level of the students. Students should also be encouraged to study words they encounter in their own readings. As Zutell noted, it is important to have students independently notice and internalize the features of words to help build a large vocabulary.

There are many more words in English than can be taught directly, so word analysis strategies provide an important key to independence. Because so many words are semantically related, if children know one word, they can figure out the meaning of others through their knowledge of suffixes and prefixes (e.g., read, reader, reading, readable, misread, unread). Nagy and Anderson (1984) estimated that 60% of words in English can be predicted from their parts. Clearly, children should be taught to use their knowledge of word parts and morphological relations.

Analyzing the morphological structure of words will help students decode multisyllabic words as well as figure out their meanings. According to the NRC (Snow et al., 1998), children should be able to decode orthographically regular multisyllabic words by grade 2. By grade 3, children should be able to use structural analysis for decoding and infer word meanings from taught roots, suffixes, and prefixes. Even the Reading Recovery program for struggling first-grade readers includes instruction in word affixes, so it is clearly an appropriate area of instruction for all primary-grade children. However, students do not typically receive much instruction to help them decode lengthy multisyllabic words because instruction in phonics usually does not extend beyond the second grade, when the words that are studied are short and simple (P. M. Cunningham, 1998).

Many intermediate-grade students have difficulty identifying long multisyllabic words quickly and accurately even if their decoding of single-syllable words is proficient (P. M. Cunningham, 1998). Limitations in morphological knowledge may be a contributing factor to their poor decoding. P. M. Cunningham (1998) developed guidelines for instruction based on the principle that many words in English are related through their morphology and that this relation is preserved through our orthographic system. Students seldom acquire this insight on their own, so teachers must provide explicit guidance (Bear & Templeton, 1998).

The evidence is compelling that purposeful word study deserves a place in the elementary curriculum, from the primary grades on. However, as Bear and Templeton (1998) asserted, word study can and should be "developmentally appropriate and embedded within the overarching contexts of deeply satisfying engagements with reading and writing" (p. 249).

ORGANIZING WORD STUDY WITHIN THE CLASSROOM

In this section, two organizational issues are considered briefly: time and grouping. How much time should be devoted to word study? Word study should have a separate time of its own within the larger language arts block—at least 15 minutes, no more than 30. This recommendation is consistent with that of Stahl et al. (1998), who suggested that no more than 25% of the language arts instructional block every day should be used for phonics instruction. Many word study programs, like those of Gaskins et al. (1997) and P. M. Cunningham et al. (1998), take 15–20 minutes. The 1,200 teachers surveyed by Baumann et al. (1998) reported a daily average of 2 hours and 23 minutes devoted to reading and literacy; 55 of these minutes were used for teacher-directed skill or strategy instruction (which could include aspects other than word study). Word-level skills are critical, but an overemphasis on them could have the negative effect of undermining children's intrinsic interest in reading for meaning. A brisk pace and a short duration help keep students engaged. Word study can and should occur opportunistically during other reading and writing activities throughout the day. See Byrnes (Chapter 9, this volume) for further discussion of the importance of time spent reading.

Individual seatwork should be minimized for word study, as should whole-group instruction, which is particularly ineffective for early primary students. There can be a 5-year range in children's literacy-related skills in kindergarten, and these initial differences do not disappear over time (IRA & NAEYC, 1998). Within any given classroom, some children may not have mastered certain basic phonics principles whereas others are easily decoding complex multisyllabic words that they have not previously encountered. Small-group work allows for scaffolded instruction that is tailored to students' skill levels. More intensive opportunities for word study can be provided for children who find reading particularly challenging (see Graham & Harris, Chapter 3, this volume), while other students can engage in collaborative reading and writing activities (see Gambrell et al., Chapter 6, and Guthrie et al., Chapter 10, this volume).

CLOSING COMMENTS

The evidence is clear that early word recognition skill is critical to later reading comprehension and achievement. What is less often acknowledged is that early word recognition skill is also critical to later reading motivation and hence reading engagement. Young children generally are very positive about their reading competencies in the early years of schooling regardless of actual ability (Chapman & Tunmer, 1995; McKenna, Kear, & Ellsworth, 1995). However, the relation between reading self-concept and reading ability grows stronger in later years. Chapman and Tunmer (1997) documented that reading ability in the second year of schooling was causally related to self-concept in the third year. What this means is that children who do not develop basic competency in word recognition subsequently come to have weaker self-concepts of themselves as readers.

Evidence such as this illustrates the importance of early intervention. As Pressley (1998) argued, if young children are struggling, what is needed is more effective decoding instruction; it is not yet necessary to work to improve academic self-esteem as well. First graders attribute their failures to lack of effort, so if they are struggling to decode, they will try harder when urged to do so. Older children, in contrast, attribute their failures to lack of ability, so if they are still struggling with decoding in the later grades, they will attribute their struggles to low ability and will lose the motivation to try. This topic is taken up fully by Wigfield (Chapter 7, this volume).

As with all aspects of academic learning, there is a continuum of development with respect to word study. As maintained in the position statement of the IRA and NAEYC (1998), the goals and expectations for elementary school children should be developmentally appropriate, challenging but achievable with sufficient adult support. Teachers need to be knowledgeable about the continuum of development, about individual and cultural variations, and about normal ranges of variation. Several sources include benchmarks that help teachers know what to expect (IRA & NAEYC, 1998; Pressley, 1998; Snow et al., 1998; Strickland, 1998); knowledge of such benchmarks enables intervention as early as possible if children experience difficulty.

It is not usually necessary to offer systematic phonics instruction beyond the second grade (Snow et al., 1998). Once children have caught on to how words work, they become what Clay (1991) has called "self-extending systems," capable of enhancing their own word recognition skills independently. Nevertheless, word study continues to be important beyond the first few years of formal schooling, and word analysis and vocabulary instruction should be given more prominence.

By way of summary, we list 10 features of good phonics instruction identified by Stahl et al. (1998) that in fact extend to word study as more broadly construed in this chapter. Good instruction (1) should develop the alphabetic principle; (2) should develop phonological awareness; (3) should provide a thorough grounding in the letters; (4) should not emphasize rules; (5) need not use worksheets; (6) should not dominate instruction; (7) does not have to be boring; (8) provides sufficient practice in reading words; (9) leads to automatic word recognition; and (10) is one part of reading instruction. These instructional guidelines focus primarily on cognitive processes involved in word study. However, because engaged reading goes beyond the purely cognitive, it is important to provide contexts that support and extend metacognition, motivation, and social interaction. As argued in this chapter, it is entirely possible for children to be engaged even as they learn to recognize and analyze words.

RECOMMENDED READINGS

Allington, R. L. (Ed.). (1988). *Teaching struggling readers: Articles from the Reading Teacher.* Newark, DE: International Reading Association.

This collection of reprints includes many excellent articles on word study that are applicable for all children, not just struggling readers. Included in the collection are articles cited in this chapter by Rasinski (1989), Yopp (1995), and Gaskins et al. (1997).

Ericson, L., & Juliebo, M. F. (1998). *The phonological awareness handbook for kindergarten and primary teachers.* Newark, DE: International Reading Association.

This book reviews the research supporting the importance of phonological awareness in reading and offers practical suggestions for teaching children various aspects of phonological awareness in a context that is playful yet likely to be effective. Appendices include assessments to gauge students' skills, sources of relevant books, and instructional materials.

Rosencrans, G. (1998). *The spelling book: Teaching children how to spell, not what to spell.* Newark, DE: International Reading Association.

This book provides guidance for elementary teachers at all levels in teaching children knowledge and strategies for spelling independently. The emphasis is on teaching spelling as an integrated skill that is part of many everyday tasks.

Strickland, D. S. (1998). *Teaching phonics today: A primer for educators.* Newark, DE: International Reading Association.

This book reviews the evidence for phonics instruction and provides suggestions for how teachers can incorporate phonics instruction into a literature-based curriculum. It includes curriculum frameworks for decoding instruction for grades K–2, instructional strategies, and assessment approaches. Also included are checklists for assessing children's emerging literacy development and knowledge and their use of word recognition strategies for beginning reading.

REFERENCES

Adams, M. J. (1990). *Beginning to read: Thinking and learning about print.* Cambridge, MA: MIT Press.

Adams, M. J., Foorman, B., Lundberg, I., & Beeler, T. (1996). *Phonemic awareness in young children.* Baltimore: Brookes.

Allington, R. L. (Ed.). (1998). *Teaching struggling readers: Articles from The Reading Teacher.* Newark, DE: International Reading Association.

Anglin, J. M. (1993). Vocabulary development: A morphological analysis. *Monographs of the Society for Research in Child Development, 58* (10, Serial No. 238).

Baker, L., & Brown, A. L. (1984). Metacognitive skills and reading. In P. D. Pearson, M. Kamil, R. Barr, & P. Mosenthal (Eds.), *Handbook of research in reading* (pp. 353–395). New York: Longman.

Baker, L., Fernandez-Fein, S., Scher, D., & Williams, H. (1998). Home experiences related to the development of word recognition. In J. Metsala & L. Ehri (Eds.), *Word recognition in beginning literacy* (pp. 263–288). Mahwah, NJ: Erlbaum.

Baker, L., Serpell, R., & Sonnenschein, S. (1995). Opportunities for literacy learning in the homes of urban preschoolers. In L. M. Morrow (Ed.), *Family literacy: Connections in schools and communities* (pp. 236–252). Newark, DE: International Reading Association.

Baumann, J. F., Hoffman, J. V., Moon, J., & Duffy-Hester, A. M. (1998). Where are teachers' voices in the phonics/whole language debate? Results from a survey of U.S. elementary classroom teachers. *The Reading Teacher, 51,* 636–650.

Bear, D., Invernizzi, M., Templeton, S., & Johnston, F. R. (1996). *Words their way: Word study for phonics, vocabulary, and spelling instruction.* New York: Merrill.

Bear, D., & Templeton, S. (1998). Explorations in developmental spelling: Foundations for learning and teaching phonics, spelling, and vocabulary. *The Reading Teacher, 52,* 222–242.

Beck, I. L. (1998). Understanding beginning reading: A journey through teaching and research. In J. Osborn & F. Lehr (Eds.), *Literacy for all: Issues in teaching and learning* (pp. 11–31). New York: Guilford Press.

Beck, I. L., & McKeown, M. G. (1991). Conditions of vocabulary acquisition. In R. Barr, M. I. Kamil, P. S. Mosenthal, & P. D. Pearson (Eds.), *Handbook of reading research* (Vol. 2, pp. 789–814). White Plains, NY: Longman.

Blachman, B. A. (1997). *Foundations of reading acquisition and dyslexia.* Mahwah, NJ: Erlbaum.

Blachowicz, C., & Fisher, P. (1996). *Teaching vocabulary in all classrooms.* Upper Saddle River, NJ: Merrill/Prentice Hall.

Braunger, J., & Lewis, J. P. (1997). *Building a knowledge base in reading.* Newark, DE: International Reading Association.

Calfee, R. (1998). Phonics and phonemes: Learning to decode and spell in a literature-based program. In J. Metsala & L. Ehri (Eds.), *Word recognition in beginning literacy* (pp. 315–340). Mahwah, NJ: Erlbaum.

Chall, J. S. (1996). *Learning to read: The great debate.* New York: McGraw-Hill.

Chapman, J. W., & Tunmer, W. E. (1995). Development of young children's reading self-concepts: An examination of emerging subcomponents and their relationship with reading achievement. *Journal of Educational Psychology, 87,* 154–167.

Chapman, J. W., & Tunmer, W. E. (1997). A longitudinal study of beginning reading achievement and reading self-concept. *British Journal of Educational Psychology, 67,* 279–291.

Christensen, C. A. (1997). Onset, rhymes, and phonemes in learning to read. *Scientific Studies of Reading, 1,* 341–358.

Clay, M. M. (1991). *Becoming literate: The construction of inner control.* Portsmouth, NH: Heinemann.

Clymer, T. (1996). The utility of phonic generalizations in the primary grades. *The Reading Teacher, 50,* 182–187. (Original work published 1963)

Cramer, R. L. (1998). *The spelling connection: Integrating reading, writing, and spelling instruction.* New York: Guilford Press.

Cunningham, A. E. (1990). Explicit versus implicit instruction in phonemic awareness. *Journal of Experimental Child Psychology, 50,* 429–444.

Cunningham, P. M. (1995). *Phonics they use: Words for reading and writing* (2nd ed.). New York: HarperCollins.

Cunningham, P. M. (1998). The multisyllabic word dilemma: Helping students build meaning, spell, and read "big" words. *Reading and Writing Quarterly: Overcoming Learning Difficulties, 14,* 189–218.

Cunningham, P. M., Hall, D. P., & Defee, M. (1998). Nonability-grouped, multilevel instruction: Eight years later. *The Reading Teacher, 51,* 652–664.

Dixon-Kraus, L. A. (1995). Partner reading and writing: Peer social dialogue and the zone of proximal development. *Journal of Reading Behavior, 27*, 45–64.

Ehri, L. C. (1998). Grapheme–phoneme knowledge is essential for learning to read words in English. In J. Metsala & L. Ehri (Eds.), *Word recognition in beginning literacy* (pp. 3–40). Mahwah, NJ: Erlbaum.

Ehri, L. C., & McCormick, S. (1998). Phases of word learning: Implications for instruction with delayed and disabled readers. *Reading and Writing Quarterly: Overcoming Learning Difficulties, 14*, 135–163.

Eldredge, J. L., Reutzel, D. R., & Hollingsworth, P. M. (1996). Comparing the effectiveness of two oral reading practices: Round-robin reading and the shared book experience. *Journal of Literacy Research, 28*, 201–226.

Elley, W. (1989). Vocabulary acquisition from listening to stories. *Reading Research Quarterly, 24*, 174–187.

Ericson, L. , & Juliebo, M. F. (1998). *The phonological awareness handbook for kindergarten and primary teachers.* Newark, DE: International Reading Association.

Fernandez-Fein, S., & Baker, L. (1997). Rhyme sensitivity and relevant experiences in preschoolers from diverse backgrounds. *Journal of Literacy Research, 29*, 433–459.

Foorman, B. R., Francis, D. J., Fletcher, J. M., Schatschneider, C., & Mehta, P. (1998). The role of instruction in learning to read: Preventing reading failure in at-risk children. *Journal of Educational Psychology, 90*, 37–55.

Freppon, P. A., & Dahl, K. L. (1998). Theory and research into practice: Balanced instruction— insights and considerations. *Reading Research Quarterly, 33*, 240–251.

Fukkink, R. G., & de Glopper, K. (1998). Effects of instruction in deriving word meaning from context: A meta-analysis. *Review of Educational Research, 68*, 450–469.

Gaskins, I. W. (1998). A beginning literacy program for at-risk and delayed readers. In J. Metsala & L. Ehri (Eds.), *Word recognition in beginning literacy* (pp. 209–232). Mahwah, NJ: Erlbaum.

Gaskins, I. W., Ehri, L. C., Cress, C., O'Hara, C., & Donnelly, K. (1997). Procedures for word learning: Making discoveries about words. *The Reading Teacher, 50*, 312–327.

Goswami, U. (1998). The role of analogies in the development of word recognition. In J. Metsala & L. Ehri (Eds.), *Word recognition in beginning literacy* (pp. 41–64). Mahwah, NJ: Erlbaum.

Greaney, K. T., Tunmer, W. E., & Chapman, J. W. (1997). Effects of rime-based orthographic analogy training on the word recognition skills of children with reading disability. *Journal of Educational Psychology, 89*, 645–651.

Hannon, P. (1995). *Literacy, home and school.* London: Falmer.

Hart, B., & Risley, T. (1995). *Meaningful differences in the everyday experience of young American children.* Baltimore: Brookes.

Hiebert, E. H. (1998). *Text matters in learning to read* (CIERA Rep. No. 1-001). Ann Arbor: University of Michigan, Center for the Improvement of Early Reading Achievement.

Hoffman, J. V., McCarthey, S. J., Elliott, B., Bayles, D. L., Price, D. P., Ferree, A., & Abbott, J. A. (1998). The literature-based basals in first-grade classrooms: Savior, Satan, or same-old, same-old? *Reading Research Quarterly, 33*, 168–197.

International Reading Association [IRA]. (1997, January). *The role of phonics in reading instruction: A position statement of the International Reading Association* [Brochure]. Newark, DE: Author.

International Reading Association [IRA] & National Association for the Education of Young Children [NAEYC]. (1998). Learning to read and write: Developmentally appropriate practices for young children. *The Reading Teacher, 52*, 193–216.

Johnston, F. R. (1998). The reader, the text, and the task: Learning words in first grade. *The Reading Teacher, 51*, 666–675.

Juel, C., & Roper/Schneider, D. (1986). The influence of basal readers on first grade reading. *Reading Research Quarterly, 20*, 134–152.

Kinnunen, R., Vauras, M., & Niemi, P. (1998). Comprehension monitoring in beginning readers. *Scientific Studies of Reading, 2*, 353–375.

Levy, B. A., & Lysynchuk, L. (1997). Beginning word recognition: Benefits of training by segmentation and whole word methods. *Scientific Studies of Reading, 1*, 359–387.

Mathes, P. G., Howard, J. K., Allen, S., & Fuchs, D. (1998). Peer-assisted learning strategies for first-grade readers: Making early reading instruction more responsive to the needs of diverse learners. *Reading Research Quarterly, 33*, 62–95.

McCarthey, S. J., Hoffman, J. V., & Galda, L. (1999). Readers in elementary classrooms: Learning goals and instructional principles that can inform practice. In J. T. Guthrie & D. E. Alvermann (Eds.), *Engaged reading: Processes, practices, and policy implications* (pp. 46–80). New York: Teachers College Press.

McKenna, M. C., Kear, D. J., & Ellsworth, R. A. (1995). Children's attitudes toward reading: A national survey. *Reading Research Quarterly, 30*, 934–955.

McKenna, M. C., Stratton, B. D., Grindler, M. C., & Jenkins, S. J. (1995). Differential effects of whole language and traditional instruction on reading attitudes. *Journal of Reading Behavior, 27*, 19–44.

Metsala, J., & Ehri, L. (Eds.). (1998). *Word recognition in beginning literacy*. Mahwah, NJ: Erlbaum.

Morrow, L. M., & Gambrell, L. B. (1998). How do we motivate children toward independent reading and writing? In S. B. Neuman & K. A. Roskos (Eds.), *Children achieving: Best practices in early literacy* (pp. 144–161). Newark, DE: International Reading Association.

Nagy, W., & Anderson, R. C. (1984). How many words are there in printed school English? *Reading Research Quarterly, 19*, 304–330.

Neuman, S. B., & Roskos, K. (1997). Literacy knowledge in practice: Contexts of participation for young writers and readers. *Reading Research Quarterly, 32*, 10–32.

Opitz, M. F. (1998). Children's books to develop phonemic awareness—For you and parents, too! *The Reading Teacher, 51*, 526–528.

Pressley, M. (1998). *Reading instruction that works: The case for balanced teaching*. New York: Guilford Press.

Pressley, M., Rankin, J., & Yokoi, L. (1996). A survey of instructional practices of primary teachers nominated as effective in promoting literacy. *Elementary School Journal, 96*, 363–384.

Purcell-Gates, V. (1998). Growing successful readers: Homes, communities, and schools. In J. Osborn & F. Lehr (Eds.), *Literacy for all: Issues in teaching and learning* (pp. 51–72). New York: Guilford Press.

Rasinski, T. V. (1989). Fluency for everyone: Incorporating fluency instruction in the classroom. *The Reading Teacher, 42*, 690–693.

Richgels, D. J. (1995). Invented spelling ability and printed word learning in kindergarten. *Reading Research Quarterly, 30*, 96–109.

Robbins, C., & Ehri, L. C. (1994). Reading storybooks to kindergartners helps them learn new vocabulary words. *Journal of Educational Psychology, 86*, 54–64.

Rosencrans, G. (1998). *The spelling book: Teaching children how to spell, not what to spell*. Newark, DE: International Reading Association.

Rupley, W. H., Logan, J. W., & Nichols, W. D. (1998/1999). Vocabulary instruction in a balanced reading program. *The Reading Teacher, 52*, 336–346.

Sacks, C. H., & Mergendoller, J. R. (1997). The relationship between teachers' theoretical orientation toward reading and student outcomes in kindergarten children with different initial reading abilities. *American Educational Research Journal, 34*, 721–740.

Samuels, S. J., Schermer, N., & Reinking, D. (1992). Reading fluency: Techniques for making decoding automatic. In S. J. Samuels & A. E. Farstrup (Eds.), *What research has to say about reading instruction* (pp. 124–144). Newark, DE: International Reading Association.

Scarborough, H. S. (1998). Early identification of children at risk for reading disabilities: Phonological awareness and some other promising predictors. In B. K. Shapiro, P. J. Accardo, & A. J. Capute (Eds.), *Specific reading disability: A view of the spectrum* (pp. 77–121). Timonium, MD: York Press.

Schickedanz, J. A. (1998). What is developmentally appropriate practice in early literacy?: Considering the alphabet. In S. B. Neuman & K. A. Roskos (Eds.), *Children achieving: Best practices in early literacy* (pp. 20–37). Newark, DE: International Reading Association.

Schwartz, R. M. (1997). Self-monitoring in beginning reading. *The Reading Teacher, 51,* 40–48.

Scott, J. A., & Nagy, W. E. (1997). Understanding the definitions of unfamiliar verbs. *Reading Research Quarterly, 32,* 184–200.

Snow, C. E., Burns, M. S., & Griffin, P. (Eds.). (1998). *Preventing reading difficulties in young children.* Washington, DC: National Academy Press.

Stahl, S. A., Duffy-Hester, A. M., & Stahl, K. A. D. (1998). Theory and research into practice: Everything you wanted to know about phonics (but were afraid to ask). *Reading Research Quarterly, 33,* 338–355.

Stahl, S. A., Heubach, K., & Crammond, B. (1997). *Fluency-oriented reading instruction* (Reading Research Rep. No. 79). Athens, GA: Universities of Georgia & Maryland, National Reading Research Center.

Strickland, D. S. (1998). *Teaching phonics today: A primer for educators.* Newark, DE: International Reading Association.

Temple, C., Nathan, R., Burris, B., & Temple, F. (1993). *The beginnings of writing* (3rd ed.). Newton, MA: Allyn & Bacon.

Tracey, D. H., & Morrow, L. M. (1998). Motivating contexts for young children's literacy development: Implications for word recognition development. In J. Metsala & L. Ehri (Eds.), *Word recognition in beginning literacy* (pp. 341–356). Mahwah, NJ: Erlbaum.

Trachtenburg, P. (1990). Using children's literature to enhance phonics instruction. *The Reading Teacher, 43,* 648–653.

Treiman, R. (1998). Why spelling? The benefits of incorporating spelling into beginning reading instruction. In J. Metsala & L. Ehri (Eds.), *Word recognition in beginning literacy* (pp. 289–314). Mahwah, NJ: Erlbaum.

Turner, J. C. (1995). The influence of classroom contexts on young children's motivation for literacy. *Reading Research Quarterly, 30,* 410–441.

Turner, J. C. (1997). Starting right: Strategies for engaging young literacy learners. In J. T. Guthrie & A. Wigfield (Eds.), *Reading engagement: Motivating readers through integrated instruction* (pp. 183–204). Newark, DE: International Reading Association.

Vygotsky, L. S. (1978). *Mind in society.* Cambridge, MA: MIT Press.

Yopp, H. K. (1995). Read-aloud books for developing phonemic awareness: An annotated bibliography. *The Reading Teacher, 48,* 538–542.

Zutell, J. (1998). Word sorting: A developmental spelling approach to word study for delayed readers. *Reading and Writing Quarterly: Overcoming Learning Difficulties, 14,* 219–238.

CHAPTER THREE

Helping Children Who Experience Reading Difficulties
Prevention and Intervention

STEVE GRAHAM
KAREN R. HARRIS

We were recently introduced to four children in an elementary school in a suburban neighborhood just outside the capital of the United States. Each of the children was experiencing difficulty learning to read. One of the students, Meg,* a third grader, began receiving speech and language services when she was 3 years old as well as resource room services for learning disabilities at the end of first grade. Concerns about reading started to emerge in kindergarten, when her teacher indicated that Meg "has trouble with most of the reading and writing activities we do in class, especially when they involve rhyming or hearing sounds in words." A second grader, Charles Wallace, on the other hand, did not receive any special ser- vices but was referred for special education testing during the middle of second grade. The school psychologist reported that Charles Wallace was indeed reading below grade level but that his reading performance was commensurate with his intellectual capabilities. Like Charles Wallace, the third student, Sandy, another second grader, was reading at a beginning

---

*This is not the child's real name; in all of our writings we substitute real names with the names of fictional characters from popular science fiction or fantasy books.

first-grade level. She began kindergarten with little knowledge of books or even how print works, and her development was further hampered as both her kindergarten and first-grade teacher did little to address her individual needs in learning to read. The fourth student, Denny, was a fourth grader who had a brother, uncle, and two cousins who also experienced problems learning to read. Denny's difficulty sustaining attention and his impulsivity often made it difficult for him to benefit fully from the reading instruction he received at school.

In this chapter, we examine how teachers can help children like Meg, Charles Wallace, Sandy, and Denny become skilled and engaged readers. Our recommendations for prevention and intervention center on the following five principles:

1. Provide exemplary reading instruction to all children.
2. Tailor reading instruction to meet the individual needs of children who experience difficulty learning to read.
3. Intervene early, providing a coherent and sustained effort to improve the literacy skills of children who experience reading difficulties.
4. Expect that each child will learn to read.
5. Identify and address academic and nonacademic roadblocks to reading and school success.

(A checklist for assessing the quality of classroom reading instruction for children experiencing reading difficulties is presented in an appendix at the end of this chapter.) Before examining each principle, we first consider what is known about reading difficulties and the most frequent problems these children experience when learning to read.

"MY CEREBELLUM JUST FUSED"

In a *Calvin and Hobbes* cartoon published a few years ago, Calvin is asked why the Battle of Lexington was important. The "shock" of the question renders him mute for a few seconds, before he is able to respond that it's hard to say, as his cerebellum just fused. When a child encounters difficulty in learning to read, it often is tempting to rely on explanations similar to the one offered by Calvin—namely, it is a neurological problem. The difficulty with this explanation is that it is hard to substantiate in most cases and perpetuates the assumption that the problem resides solely in the child. As our description of Sandy, one of the children introduced earlier, illustrates, children who enter school with little prior exposure to books and the concepts underlying print are at risk for early reading difficulties

(Gelzheiser & Wood, 1998). Still other children are the victims of poor instruction or educational neglect (Pressley, 1998). Factors within the home, school, and social and cultural environment interact with biological factors to influence a child's success in learning to read.

The two most conspicuous biological problems that contribute to a reading difficulty are low general intelligence and language-based difficulties, particularly ones associated with phonological processing of sounds in words (Pressley, 1998). If a child's overall cognitive ability is relatively low, there is a greater likelihood that he/she will not be reading at grade level. This factor potentially influences a considerable number of children, as about 16% of the population has an IQ of less than 85. Because reading makes many language-based demands, children who experience speech and language difficulties are also at increased risk to develop reading problems (Gelzheiser & Wood, 1998). One cluster of language skills that is especially important in the development of reading competence is phonological awareness, or the ability to consciously analyze and manipulate the sound structure of spoken words (see Baker, Chapter 2, this volume). This capability is one of the best predictors of reading attainment (Adams, 1990), and explicitly teaching this skill to young children facilitates reading achievement (Blachman, 1991). Finally, some reading difficulties may be genetically determined, as their co-occurrence is more common in identical twins than fraternal ones (DeFries, Fulker, & LaBuda, 1987), and the correlation between the reading abilities of adopted children and their biological parents is higher than that between adopted children and their adopting parents (Cardon, DiLalla, Plomin, DeFries, & Fulker, 1990).

The earlier descriptions of the four students we met—Meg, Charles Wallace, Sandy, and Denny—suggest that the genesis of their reading difficulties is quite varied. Despite these differences, there is considerable consistency in the types of reading problems experienced by these children. Their most salient problem is that they are not particularly accurate or fluent at deciphering or recognizing many of the words they encounter when reading. Meg, for example, can barely decode at all. When trying to decipher unknown words, she is typically slow and inaccurate, producing incorrect sounds for a variety of letters and letter clusters. Charles Wallace, in contrast, can correctly decipher many of the words he encounters when reading, but decoding does not happen very quickly, as he is relatively slow at sounding out a word and blending the sounds together.

According to their teachers, these four children often bypass their poor decoding skills by using picture cues and information in the material already read to guess the identity of unknown words. Their better-reading classmates, however, are less likely to rely on such strategies, preferring instead to sound out unfamiliar words (probably because this is a more certain strategy for them than simply guessing). Our four students are also more reliant on strategies for determining the identity of unfamiliar words, because they do not recognize automatically as many words in print as their better-reading classmates.

Such decoding and word recognition difficulties are characteristic of early reading problems (Pressley, 1998; Snow, Burns, & Griffin, 1998). In a study by Juel (1988), for instance, 22 of the 24 children classified as poor readers in fourth grade were poor decoders. These children entered first grade with little awareness that words were composed of sequences of somewhat distinct sounds (i.e., phonemic awareness) and did not develop the reading skills of a typical first grader until third grade. Given their poor decoding skills, it is not surprising that these children read much less text than their better-reading counterparts.

In addition to decoding and word recognition difficulties, our four students sometimes have difficulty zeroing in on the correct meaning of a word when they are reading, especially when a word has multiple meanings (e.g., "court"). Their teachers noted that they are not particularly adept at making inferences that link together ideas presented in the text, and they sometimes fail to monitor their understanding of what they are reading. Although one of the students, Charles Wallace, is a very enthusiastic and engaged reader, the attitudes and self-evaluations of the other three students are much less positive. They do little reading outside of school, evidence little confidence in their reading capabilities, and periodically express their dislike for reading. Such comprehension difficulties and motivational attributes are common among children experiencing early reading problems (Pressley, 1998; Snow et al., 1998).

PREVENTION AND INTERVENTION

Provide Exemplary Reading Instruction

In a *Calvin and Hobbes* cartoon poking fun at contemporary society's litigious outlook, Calvin asks his teacher, Miss Wormwood, to sign a contract indicating that she will reimburse him for any job income he might lose as a result of a poor first-grade education. Although Calvin's problems are typically of his own making, this cartoon does highlight the importance of early academic success. This was also apparent in the study by Juel (1988) reviewed earlier: 88% of the children who were poor readers in first grade were still poor readers in fourth grade.

An important tactic in preventing reading difficulties is to provide exemplary reading instruction right from the start, beginning in kindergarten and first grade and continuing throughout the elementary school years (see Pikulski, 1994). Although this approach will not eradicate all reading difficulties, cases of reading failure due to poor instruction can be prevented. Exemplary reading instruction can also help to ameliorate the severity of reading difficulties experienced by other children whose primary problems are not instructional, as well as maximize the reading development of children in general.

What does exemplary reading instruction look like during the elementary school years? To answer this question, Pressley and his colleagues (Pressley, Rankin, & Yokoi, 1996; Pressley, Yokoi, Rankin, Wharton-McDonald, & Hampston, 1997; Wharton-McDonald, Pressley, & Mistretta, in press) conducted a series of studies to determine how outstanding teachers taught reading. In their initial investigation, more than 80 kindergarten through second-grade teachers who were identified by their supervisors as outstanding reading instructors completed questionnaires describing their classroom practices (Pressley, Rankin, et al., 1996). Their responses highlighted the multifaceted nature of effective early reading instruction, as these teachers integrated attractive features of several different approaches to reading, including the following ones:

- A literate classroom environment, where students' literacy work is prominently displayed, chart stories/poems and word lists adorn the walls, and the room is packed with reading material.
- Plenty of opportunities to read, as stories are read, reread, and told daily.
- Regular checks on student comprehension of stories and frequent communication with parents.
- Overt teacher modeling of the process of reading, comprehension strategies, and positive attitudes toward reading.
- Daily practice of reading skills and follow-up instruction to ensure mastery.
- A combination of whole-group, small-group, and individual instruction and individual seatwork, as well as the frequent use of cooperative group arrangements.
- Sensitivity to individual needs through adjustments in teaching style and learning pace, minilessons responsive to current needs, and individually guided reading instruction.
- Integration of reading activities and themes across the curriculum and the use of writing to support reading development.
- Instruction in a broad range of skills, ranging from reading readiness, to concepts of print, to decoding and word recognition, to new vocabulary, to strategies for comprehending and analyzing reading material.
- The use of different types of narrative reading material (e.g., picture books, trade books, pattern) and many types of reading activities

(e.g., choral reading, shared book reading, reading aloud to others, silent reading, and discussion of readings).

• Extensive efforts to enhance students' reading motivation by creating a risk-free environment, setting an exciting mood, selecting materials based on students' interest, encouraging student selection of reading materials, specifying the goal for each lesson, and promoting an "I can do" attitude.

In a second study, Pressley and his colleagues (Wharton-McDonald et al., in press) moved from surveying outstanding reading teachers to observing them in their classrooms. The behaviors of outstanding first-grade reading teachers were contrasted with the practices of more typical first-grade teachers. Most of the instructional practices described above were observed in the classrooms of the best first-grade reading teachers in this follow-up study. In addition to using these practices, the best reading teachers were also masterful at managing classroom behavior and other adult resources, such as in-class help from a resource room teacher. Their classrooms were "jam-packed" with literacy activities and instruction, leading to high rates of student engagement. Students were further encouraged to self-regulate their behavior in that they were often encouraged to work independently or with other children.

In a third study focusing on the upper elementary grades, Pressley et al. (1997) interviewed outstanding fifth-grade reading teachers. Like their counterparts in the primary grades, these teachers provided children with plenty of opportunities to read, employed a variety of grouping patterns, taught both word-level skills and higher-order comprehension and critical thinking processes, regularly evaluated reading skills and progress, and made frequent efforts to increase student engagement and motivation for reading. In addition, the teaching of reading was integrated with content-area instruction.

The impact of instruction that embodies the types of practices just described was illustrated in a study by Englert et al. (1995) with first- through fourth-grade children experiencing reading and writing difficulties. The instructional program, the Early Literacy Project (ELP), was delivered by Special Education teachers to small groups of students within the context of a resource room some 2–3 hours each day. In the ELP curriculum, reading and writing activities are integrated together around thematic units. Both skills and strategies instruction occur within the context of these units. Opportunities to engage in meaningful reading and writing are plentiful; dialogue and modeling are used to promote the development of self-regulated learning; teaching is responsive to individual needs; and a literacy community is created through the use of activities involving sharing and student collaboration. In addition to the decoding and spelling skills taught within the context of the ELP program, the participating students also received more traditional, noncontextualized instruction in phonemic awareness, phonics, and spelling skills.

Students who received ELP instruction from a veteran ELP teacher averaged more than 1 year's reading gain annually. Not surprisingly, some poor readers benefited more from ELP than others (Englert, Mariage, Garmon, & Tarrant, 1998). Children who began the year with the least literacy knowledge made lower gains than children who were more slightly advanced readers, reinforcing the axiom that exemplary reading instruction is not sufficient to overcome the reading difficulties of all children (Gaskins, 1998). In a subsequent study, Englert et al. (1998) tested the effectiveness of ELP in an *inclusive classroom*, that is, one containing students with and without special needs and team-taught by a Special Education teacher and a regular teacher. Similar to the results of the earlier study, both groups of students averaged 1 month or more reading gain for each month of instruction.

Enhancing Phonological Awareness

One of the most important insights into early reading development during the last two decades is that some children experience difficulty learning to read because they do not possess an adequate understanding of how spoken words are segmented into phonemes and how these phonemes are related to print (Blachman, 1991; Snow et al., 1998; see also Baker, Chapter 2, this volume). This has lead to the recommendation that activities designed to promote phonological awareness (i.e., the ability to analyze and manipulate the sound structure of spoken words) be incorporated into the kindergarten and primary curriculum as a preventive measure before children have had the chance to experience reading difficulties (Adams, 1990; Juel, 1988). This recommendation rests upon a considerable body of evidence that demonstrates that explicitly teaching phonological awareness skills to young children facilitates reading achievement (e.g., Ball & Blachman, 1991; Bradley & Bryant, 1985; Castle, Riach, & Nicholson, 1994; Lundberg, Frost, & Peterson, 1988).

A wide array of activities has been used by researchers to teach phonological awareness to young children, including activities for recognizing words that rhyme; segmenting spoken words into syllables; identifying the sound at the beginning, middle, or end of a pronounced word; adding, deleting, or substituting sounds within a word; segmenting pronounced words into phonemes; and blending phonemes into words (see Adams, Foorman, Lundberg, & Beeler, 1998, and Troia, Roth, & Graham, 1998, for examples of activities for teaching phonological awareness). Although explicit instruction in phonemic awareness can be provided as a supplement to existing reading programs (see Ball & Blachman, 1991), it should be considered an integral part of exemplary reading instruction and incorporated directly into the curriculum. One example of such integration was provided in a study by Lundberg et al. (1988). Classroom teachers involved 6-year-old children in daily activity-based group experiences for a period of 8 months. Activities included matching and generating rhyming words, dividing words into syllables, segmenting words into phonemes, and blending phonemes into words. Three years later, these students performed better on reading tasks than children who did not receive instruction in phonemic awareness.

An instructional example with children having more diverse reading skills was provided in a 6-month study by O'Connor, Notari-Syverson, and Vadasky (1996). Teachers integrated phonemic awareness activities into three types of kindergarten classes: general, transition, and Special Education. In the first 2 months, activities stimulated word and syllable awareness. During the next 2 months, rhyming, isolation of the first sound in a word, blending involving onset and rime (e.g., b–oat), and segmenting sounds in words were taught. In the final 2 months, teachers concentrated on representing sounds with letters during phonological activities, matching words on the basis of similar first sounds, and performing more difficult blending activities. Instruction in these skills had a positive effect on reading and writing outcomes for regular kindergarten children, students repeating this grade, and children with special needs.

Phonemic awareness instruction that makes explicit the connections between phonemes and letters is superior to instruction that just concentrates on the sound segments in words (e.g., Bradley & Bryant, 1985; Ball & Blachman, 1988). The power of such instruction can be enhanced further by including discussion about why phonemic awareness is valuable and how phonemic awareness skills, such as segmenting and blending, are used when decoding words (Cunningham, 1990). Finally, some children with especially poor phonemic awareness skills may benefit from the addition of instruction designed to teach them how sounds feel (e.g., position of the tongue and the lips) when they are made (Wise, Ring, Sessions, & Olson, 1997).

Tailor Reading Instruction to Meet the Needs of Children Experiencing Reading Difficulties

In another classroom exchange between Calvin and his teacher, Miss Wormwood, he interrupts class to inform her that his generation doesn't learn this way, so can she please reduce everything to factoids. As usual she ignores his request, leaving him to complain that at least television understands his generation.

Although outstanding reading teachers do not teach "factoids," they recognize the importance of tailoring instruction to meet the individual needs of children experiencing difficulty learning to read. This was evident in both of the studies by Pressley and his colleagues reviewed earlier. They found that outstanding kindergarten through second-grade teachers provided qualitatively similar instruction for all students but that weaker readers received additional teacher support (Pressley, Rankin, et al., 1996). This included devoting more attention to decoding and word recognition (skills that are typically problematic for struggling readers), more explicit teaching of these skills, and more individually guided reading. In the follow-up study with first-grade teachers (Wharton-McDonald et al., in press), the best reading teachers were especially active in providing weaker readers with help when they needed it, monitoring students' performance during reading lessons, and providing guidance and scaffolding as needed. For example, Andy, one of the outstanding reading teachers in this study (Pressley, 1998), scaffolded the learning of the weaker students in his classroom by providing frequent minilessons, helpful hints and prompts to assist understanding during group lessons and individual seatwork, and reading materials and tasks within each child's reach. Weaker readers also received additional assistance from their peers, because Andy assigned them a more proficient reader as a partner.

Selecting Reading Materials

One of the most important aspects of adapting instruction for struggling readers is the use of appropriate reading materials. Too often these children are asked to read texts that are beyond their capabilities (Graham & Johnson, 1989). Not surprisingly, their reading performance is enhanced when they work with more suitable materials, as they not only comprehend more but are more engaged when reading (Armstrong, 1983; Worthy, 1996).

Initially, reading materials selected for struggling readers should be relatively easy, and those introduced thereafter should present increasing levels of challenge (Pikulski, 1994; see also Baker, Chapter 2, this volume). Pattern books are often used early on with struggling readers, as the predictable and repetitive material included in such texts can support the process of word recognition. Some weaker readers, however, will simply memorize the rhythmic, patterned, predictable material presented in such texts, failing to make the connection between the spoken and written word (Cole, 1998). One means for addressing this issue is to apply a whole-to-part strategy. After the child reads the book, practice is provided in reading underlined words in the text or reading specific sentences placed on a chart (F. Johnston, 1998).

Other types of texts that are sometimes recommended for use with struggling readers include materials where vocabulary difficulty is controlled and/or most of the words used in writing the book are easily decodable. Although these types of text are often criticized as being uninteresting and of poor quality, Cole (1998) found that some of the struggling readers she worked with made greater progress when using this type of text versus higher-quality literature, namely, trade books. She hypothesized that some weaker readers may do better with these types of text because they are less complex and easier to read. The print is larger, there are fewer words per page and sentence, vocabulary is more familiar and redundant, the author uses less idiomatic and metaphoric language, and illustrations consistently support the interpretation of unknown words.

Despite the possible advantages and disadvantages of specific types of text, it is difficult to recommend one over another. The reading materials used in effective intervention programs with struggling readers have been quite varied, including pattern books, trade books, and basal readers (Pikulski, 1994; Wasik & Slavin, 1993). Whatever text is used, however, it is important that teachers support or scaffold the reading experience so that the child can successfully read and comprehend the material. One common means for supporting weaker readers is the shared reading approach, where a book is repeatedly reread, moving from the teacher initially reading the book aloud, to reading together, to reading along with a taped version of the text, to reading independently (Eldredge, Reutzel, & Hollingsworth, 1996). Other effective activities for supporting struggling readers include previewing new or difficult words contained in the text; helping children relate their own background knowledge to the reading material; making predictions about upcoming content; setting goals for reading; providing assistance in recognizing words while reading; asking questions to check and extend comprehension of the material just read; and focusing attention on important information, such as text structure or illustrations (Graham & Johnson, 1989; Tancock, 1994).

Finally, care must be taken to select material that the child will be interested in reading. Struggling readers are more likely to make the maximum use of their capabilities when they have a strong interest in what they read (see Chamblis & McKillop, Chapter 5, this volume).

Finding the Right Balance

Another critical aspect of providing personalized and individually tailored assistance to struggling readers is finding the right balance between meaning and decoding and formal and informal instruction. In some classrooms, reading instruction for poorer readers primarily involves the explicit teaching of word attack and word recognition skills, with little time allocated to extended reading and discussion of the text (Palincsar & Klenk, 1992). This stands in stark contrast to other classrooms, where students spend most of their time involved in reading and discussing text, and teachers mostly rely on informal teaching methods, such as incidental learning and capitalizing on teachable moments, to promote the development of decoding and word recognitions skills (Graham & Harris, 1997).

Critics of the first approach, skill-based instruction, argue that such programs are too narrowly focused; they limit struggling readers' opportunities to learn how to use other important skills such as semantic, syntactic, and structural analysis of a text (e.g., Palincsar & Klenk, 1992). Critics also contend that such instruction may lead students to develop an impoverished understanding of the nature of reading, emphasizing decoding (read fast and correctly) rather than meaning as the purpose for reading. They further indicate that this approach can diminish the desire to read and can limit opportunities for acquiring important background information or content knowledge, because both are supported by extended reading and the interactions that occur during discussion (see Gambrell, Mazzoni, & Almasi, Chapter 6, this volume).

Critics of the second approach, reading immersion, contend that the methods used in these programs are not powerful enough to help struggling readers learn all of the knowledge, skills, and strategies they need to become skilled and engaged readers (Graham & Harris, 1997). They indicate that there is a considerable body of evidence demonstrating that many of these children do not acquire a variety of skills and strategies unless detailed and explicit instruction is provided (Brown & Campione, 1990). They further contend that such instruction overemphasizes meaning and fails to adequately address struggling readers' difficulties in deciphering and recognizing words (Graham & Harris, 1997).

A more sensible approach to reading instruction is to combine the best elements of both of these programs, adjusting how much emphasis is placed on meaning and decoding and formal and informal instruction, according to the needs of each individual child. This is just what the outstanding reading teachers did in the studies by Pressley and his colleagues (Pressley, Rankin, et al., 1996; Wharton-McDonald et al., in press). They immersed their students in meaningful reading and writing activities but also actively taught decoding, word recognition, and comprehension, increasing the amount of systematic and explicit coverage of these skills with the weaker readers in their classrooms.

One example of combining explicit decoding instruction with frequent opportunities to read and write for authentic purposes is provided in a study by Uhry and Shepherd (1993). Good, average, and poor first-grade readers who participated in a reading program where trade books were read and discussed received a 10- to 20-minute phonics lesson each day, emphasizing the learning of letter sounds, sounding words out letter by letter, and blending the sounds into words. In addition, words decoded during phonics instruction were included on the weekly spelling test and practiced by writing each from a copy three or four times. Less formally, students were encouraged to use letter cues to read and sound out words when writing. The combination of these procedures led to improvements in reading nonsense words (a measure of decoding) and reading of real words and passages.

A second example focuses on the SAIL Comprehension Strategies Instructional Program (Brown, Pressley, Van Meter, & Schuder, 1996). With this approach, word recognition and comprehension strategies are taught as part of a program emphasizing frequent and extensive reading. Through intensive modeling and coaching support from the teacher, second-grade children reading below grade level learned how to adjust their reading, using specific strategies for dealing with difficult words (e.g., skipping them, rereading for more clues, and so forth) and comprehending and interpreting the text (predicting upcoming events, altering expectations as the text unfolds, generating questions and interpretations while reading, summarizing periodically, visualizing text, and attending to ideas selectively). In comparison to matched students receiving more conventional second-grade reading instruction, the poor readers in the SAIL program made greater improvements on word attack and comprehension measures, and were able to provide more diverse and richer interpretations of the material they read (see McIntyre & Pressley, 1996, and Pressley, 1998, for other examples of explicit instruction within the context of a reading program emphasizing frequent reading and discussion).

A third example involves reciprocal teaching of comprehension strategies within the context of a reading group (Palincsar & Brown, 1984). With this approach, students are taught to make predictions about their reading material, to form questions about the ideas presented in the text, to summarize content, and to identify and clarify difficulties in comprehending the text. Initially, these processes are explained and modeled by the teacher, but responsibility is quickly transferred to students as they rotate responsibility for prompting and supervising the use of these strategies while reading. Such instruction provides explicit instruction of comprehension strategies while students read and has been used successfully with a wide range of students experiencing reading difficulties (Rosenshine & Meister, 1994).

A particularly noteworthy challenge involves the practical issue of providing personalized assistance to struggling readers while continuing to provide quality instruction to the class as a whole. One means for addressing this issue is to reduce the number of students in a class, making it easier for the teacher to be more responsive to children's individual needs. A second option involves increasing the number of teachers and/ or volunteers in the classroom. For example, in many schools, Special Education and regular classroom teachers coteach reading, working together to provide more individualized support for all students. Similarly, a trained volunteer can assume some classroom responsibilities, providing the teacher with added opportunities to instruct struggling readers. Time for delivering personalized help can also be created by structuring the classroom so that students spend some of their time working together or independently.

Taking Account of Diversity

Children who experience difficulty learning to read come from a wide variety of backgrounds and cultures. This diversity should be taken into account when designing and adapting instruction for struggling readers. Teachers need to be especially sensitive to cultural and background differences involving discourse patterns, interaction styles, literacy experiences at home, and views concerning the role of the teacher. Failure to consider these factors can undermine the effects of literacy instruction. This problem was illustrated in a qualitative study by Reyes (1992). When children misspelled a word in their journal writing, their teacher would respond by writing back to the child using the same word but spelling it correctly. The Hispanic children in her classroom valued and expected direct instruction from the teacher, and they failed to realize that she was correcting their spelling miscues, indicating that she should have directly informed them of her intentions.

An example by Au (1980) provides an excellent illustration of how one teacher adapted instruction to the cultural characteristics of her students. She adjusted the discourse pattern in her classroom so that it was more compatible with the ones experienced by her 7-year-old Hawaiian students at home. Common Hawaiian home events have been characterized as having a highly interactive "talk story" pattern, where individuals engage in cooperative production of responses. When conducting reading lessons, she used several discourse structures that were like the talk story pattern, including choral responding and a structure where one child served as the lead speaker and another as a commentator. The use of such patterns with native Hawaiian children has been associated with more productive classroom reading behaviors (Au & Asam, 1996; Au & Mason, 1983).

Intervene Early

Recognizing that he needed some extra help with his homework, our comic strip protagonist, Calvin, constructed a "thinking cap" made out of a kitchen colander, with a grounding string designed to act like a lightning rod for brainstorms so that his ideas would be firmly grounded in reality! Just as Calvin recognized the need for additional assistance, there is an unprecedented agreement among educators that early supplementary instruction or intervention for children experiencing reading difficulties is critical to later success (Gaskins, 1998; Kameenui, 1993; Pikulski, 1994; Snow et al., 1998; Wasik & Slavin, 1993). Unlike Calvin's revelation, however, this belief is firmly grounded in reality, given that it is based on evidence that early intervention programs yield more powerful benefits than do efforts to remediate reading problems in later grades (Slavin, Madden, & Karweit, 1989).

The basic goal of early intervention programs is to help struggling readers catch up with their peers, especially in kindergarten or the primary grades, before their difficulties become more intractable. The basic assumption underlying these efforts is that struggling readers' progress can be accelerated by providing them with additional time receiving quality instruction. The most common vehicle for delivering this additional instruction is small-group or one-on-one tutoring, making it easier for instructors to be responsive to students' individual needs. This supplementary instruction can occur during or after school and is provided by professionals and in some cases by nonprofessionals, such as trained volunteers from the community.

Although there are a number of effective early intervention programs (see Pikulski, 1994; Wasik, 1998; Wasik & Slavin, 1993), perhaps the best known is Reading Recovery (Pinnell, 1989). With this program, specially trained teachers work one-on-one or sometimes in small groups with children who experience difficulty learning to read in first grade. Instruction occurs outside the classroom for 30 minutes a day and consists of repeated readings of short stories, writing to reinforce word recognition, and the application of a variety of strategies for making sense and dealing with print.

Another example of an effective early intervention program is Book Buddies, a one-on-one tutoring program delivered to first-grade children who are having difficulty learning to read (Invernizzi, Rosemary, Juel, & Richards, 1997). In contrast to Reading Recovery, Book Buddies relies on community volunteers who receive continuous training and supervision. Twice a week the tutor works with a child outside the classroom, using a plan that includes repeated reading of a familiar text, instruction in decoding and word recognition, and the reading of a new book.

A third example of an effective early intervention program is the tutoring component from Success for All (Slavin, Madden, Karweit, Livermon, & Dolan, 1990), a comprehensive reading program used mostly in high-poverty schools. The poorest readers in first, second, and third grade receive individual tutoring sessions to supplement the regular program. Unlike the other two programs described above, tutoring sessions focus on the same skills and strategies as those emphasized in the regular classroom. Whenever possible, the child's classroom teacher serves as the tutor.

Critical Features of Effective Early Intervention

Although there is considerable variability in the curriculum and methods used in effective early intervention programs (Wasik & Slavin, 1993), one common feature is an emphasis on quality instruction (Pikulski, 1994; Wasik, 1998). This includes using texts that children can read successfully; instruction that involves explicit explanations, modeling, and scaffolded practice; teaching that focuses on the development of decoding, word recognition, and comprehension strategies; promoting writing activities to support the development of reading skills; and ongoing assessment to monitor progress and adjust instruction as needed (Gaskins, 1998; Pikulski, 1994; Wasik, 1998). These same elements are also features of exemplary general reading instruction, but their application is intensified in effective supplementary programs because students are seen individually or in small groups. Not surprisingly, such programs work best when instructors are adequately trained to carry out the intervention.

For many young children, reading difficulties are a chronic, not a temporary, condition (Juel, 1988). There is no easy or quick inoculation that will make their problems disappear (Pressley, 1998). It is important not only to intervene early with these children but to provide a coherent and sustained effort across the primary grades, and even longer in some cases.

Finally, struggling readers have the best chance for success if they receive exemplary classroom instruction and quality supplementary programs that work together (Gaskins, 1998; Wasik, 1998). Even when the academic progress of struggling readers is accelerated as a result of supplementary instruction, it is difficult to maintain these gains unless there is congruence with the regular reading program (Shanahan & Barr, 1995). The tutoring component in Success for All (Slavin et al., 1990) provides an excellent example of such alignment, because the tutor's primary responsibility is to make sure that the child masters the skills and concepts taught in the regular class.

Expect That Each Child Will Learn to Read

In another *Calvin and Hobbes* cartoon, Miss Wormwood is publicly belittling Calvin for his disgraceful test performance, telling him that our first president was not Chef Boy-AR-Dee and that he should be ashamed of his preposterous answers. Contrast this with the behavior of Andy, the teacher presented earlier, who was one of the outstanding first-grade reading teachers studied by Pressley and his colleagues (see Pressley, 1998). The poorer readers in his classroom are never shown disrespect. Instead, he constantly seeks to maintain and support their participation in the class without stigmatizing them. For example, Andy has worked hard to make sitting next to him a special honor for all students in the class, so when he sits next to a weaker student to support reading, no stigma is attached to time spent interacting with the teacher.

Another outstanding first-grade teacher who participated in this study observed that the poorer readers get the idea in their heads that they are the low ones and they can't do it, so "then they don't put forth much effort" (Pressley, Wharton-McDonald, et al., 1996, p. 257). One way she attempts to counter such beliefs and apathy is to constantly mix up her reading and instructional groups. She tries not to form ability-based reading groups, where children are assigned to work or read with other children of the same capabilities, because this practice can adversely affect the performance of struggling readers (Flood, Lapp, Flood, & Nagel, 1992). She also places considerable emphasis on respecting and trusting each child as a competent learner—one who can learn to work independently and productively in the classroom.

Too often teachers view children with reading difficulties negatively, setting low expectations for their performance and limiting their exchanges with them (Graham & Harris, 1997). During reading instruction, such negative views take the form of less attention and praise, more criticism, briefer and less informative feedback, more interruptions during reading, and fewer interactions with the teacher (P. Johnston & Winograd, 1985). Some teachers view these children as so challenging that a form of pedagogical paralysis occurs; they are uncertain about what to do or they lack confidence in their capabilities to successfully teach these children (Kameenui, 1993).

As the teachers participating in the studies by Englert and her associates (Englert et al., 1995, 1998) cited earlier demonstrated, however, teachers are not powerless—students with severe reading difficulties, even those with special needs, can be taught to read. An essential element in designing an effective reading program for these children is the recognition that they are capable and can succeed. It is also important to set high but realistic expectations for these children's performance; ignore negative expectations (e.g., "Meg is difficult and doesn't try to learn") and perceived group expectations (e.g., "Children with learning disabilities cannot master the regular class curriculum"); monitor and improve the quality of classroom interactions for struggling readers; help them develop an "I can do" attitude; plan lessons so that they can accomplish tasks successfully; and build a positive relationship with each child, accepting each as an individual and showing enthusiasm for his/her interests.

A common instructional arrangement that should be avoided is ability grouping, or the practice of sorting a class into three or four reading groups on the basis of ability. Children are often placed in such groups at the start of first grade, and it is not uncommon for struggling readers to remain in the "bottom" group for the rest of their elementary school years. Ability grouping can undermine the confidence of weaker readers, as they are cast in an often permanent hierarchy where they are labeled as the least successful (Flood et al., 1992; see Wigfield, Chapter 7, this volume).

There are many alternatives to ability grouping, including whole group reading (e.g., choral and shared-book reading), small-group reading (e.g., in book clubs and literature response groups), reading in pairs (e.g., aloud to a peer, the teacher, or a younger child), and independent reading (e.g., reading alone or along with a taped version of the text). Whatever grouping patterns are used, teachers should try to anticipate and minimize any stigmatization that might occur (see Gambrell, Mazzoni, & Almasi, Chapter 6, this volume). For example, teachers often assign a stronger reader to work with a weaker one, anticipating that the better reader will provide needed assistance. A more equitable arrangement, however, would involve each student in helping the other.

Such an arrangement is illustrated in one of the activities included in the Peer-Assisted Learning Strategy (PALS) program (Fuchs, Fuchs, Mathes, & Simmons, 1997). With PALS, the student pair reads a text that is at the instructional level of the weaker reader. During the "partner reading with retell" activity, each student takes turns, reading aloud for a period of 5 minutes. The stronger reader reads first, and the weaker reader serves as tutor, correcting word recognition miscues (e.g., saying the wrong word) and encouraging the correct rereading of any sentence containing an error. The students then switch roles, and the material just read is reread. With this activity both students act as tutors, but the lower-performing child receives additional support, as he/she has the advantage of reading the material after hearing it read by another.

Identify and Address Academic and Nonacademic Roadblocks

The importance of our last principle is illustrated in a final *Calvin and Hobbes* cartoon, where Calvin is sitting quietly at his desk with his eyes closed and his book in front of him. Miss Wormwood repeatedly calls his name, getting louder each time, until she startles him out of his reverie. He apologizes, offering the excuse that his eyes were on screen saver. This is not an unusual scenario for Calvin; he is often daydreaming when class is in session, making himself unavailable for learning.

Like Calvin, many children, especially those with special needs, encounter obstacles that impede their success in learning to read. Children who do not fare well in school, for example, may exhibit one or more maladaptive behaviors, such as a low tolerance for frustration, difficulty activating and orchestrating the elements involved in learning, or attributing success to ability or luck rather than effort (Harris, 1982). Irene Gaskins

(1998), the Director of Benchmark School, a facility that mostly serves children with learning and reading problems, noted that most of the students there had maladaptive learning styles that interfered with their reading and academic success. The teachers in the school identified 32 academic and nonacademic roadblocks to learning. These included difficulties such as poor writing skills, impulsivity, frequent absences, poor home support, disorganization, inflexibility, and lack of persistence. Only 9% of their students were viewed by teachers as having a single roadblock; the remainder had up to 10 roadblocks to learning.

Teachers need to address any roadblocks that struggling readers experience that might interfere with their reading development. For example, children who have difficulty activating and organizing cognitive and motivational resources during reading lessons can learn how to modify this situation through the application of self-regulatory strategies, such as goal setting, self-monitoring, self-instructions, and self-reinforcement (Graham, Harris, & Reid, 1992). Similarly, when struggling readers attribute their failures to uncontrollable factors such as lack of ability or luck and hence are unwilling to exert much academic effort, these attributions can be shifted by teaching them to use strategies to accomplish reading tasks while persuading them that their successes and failures on these tasks are due to their efforts in using these strategies (Carr & Borkowski, 1989).

USING TECHNOLOGY

A first-grade teacher was just starting a lesson on how to read a conventional-style analog clock, explaining the function of the little and big hands, when one of her students said, "I don't need to learn how to do this [he could read his digital watch] . . . and right now it's 10 minutes to 38" (Toth, 1998, p. 85). This anecdote highlights both the promise and challenge of technology for struggling readers.

The promise is that technology can make reading and learning to read easier for these children (see Chambliss & McKillup, Chapter 5, this volume). For example, computers can support reading by pronouncing words highlighted by the reader and by providing immediate access to explanations and elaborations of the information presented on the screen (Reinking, 1994). These tools can increase motivation and time spent reading, as computers and reading software have been shown to hold the attention of struggling readers (Cosden, Gerber, Semmel, Goldman, & Semmel, 1987). They can further provide private instruction, where weaker readers learn and practice critical reading skills, such as phonological awareness (see *Daisy Quest* or *Daisy Castle* from Pro-Ed), word recognition skills (see *Word Munchers* from MECC and *Stickybear's Reading Room* from Weekly Reader Software), and comprehension skills (see *K.C. Clyde in Fly Ball* from Don Johnston and the *Living Book Series* from Broderbund). The benefits of technology are not just limited to computers. Other technology such as television and recording devices can stimulate literacy development. The increasing availability of children's books on tape, for instance, provides more options for children to listen to or read along with books at school or at home, whereas watching captioned television (a capacity on all new TV sets) can improve reading and vocabulary development (Pressley, 1998).

These new technologies also present a challenge, as struggling readers and their teachers often require instruction and assistance to learn how to use these tools fully and effectively. We think the rewards are worth the effort, however. Consider Erica, a 6-year-old with cerebral palsy who could not speak (Erickson & Koppenhaver, 1995). She learned to use a Touch Talker, a dedicated communication device that provides speech output, using a programmable system with a keyboard composed of icons and letters. Initially, a variety of books that Erica liked were programmed into the Touch Talker so that the selection of just two icons produced a reading of a book. Later, the Touch Talker was programmed so that she could use icons to read word by word. Without such technological adaptations, she would have experienced a much smaller range of literacy learning opportunities.

CONCLUSIONS

One of the most pressing questions in reading instruction is what can schools do to reduce the number of children experiencing reading difficulties and to help all students become engaged and skilled readers. In newspapers, state legislatures, and other public forums, this question is often answered by suggesting that we need to do more of this and less of that. A suggestion that is currently popular is that we need more phonics instruction and less whole-language instruction. As the present chapter suggests, however, such simple solutions are not powerful enough. Preventing reading difficulties and intervening successfully when reading problems do occur require a concerted and sustained effort on the part of parents and the school community.

One of the most basic options available to schools for preventing reading difficulties is to provide exemplary reading instruction to all children starting in kindergarten and first grade. This effort can be enhanced by working closely with parents (see Sonnenschein & Schmidt, Chapter 12, this volume) and providing additional support early on, before a child falls significantly behind in reading. Support can involve tailoring classroom instruction to ensure that reading materials as well as instructional emphasis and activities are appropriate for struggling readers. It can also include increasing the amount and/or intensity of reading instruction provided. For example, more classroom time can be devoted to reading instruction; opportunities for individualized attention can be increased by reducing the number of students in a class; trained volunteers or specialists, such as a Special Education teacher, can provide in-class instruction and assistance to struggling readers; and students can participate in supplemental reading programs offered during or after school. We can further maximize our success by identifying and addressing roadblocks, such as attentional and motivational difficulties, that contribute to children's reading problems. Finally, it is critical that teachers maintain an "I can do" attitude when working with struggling readers while treating each child as a capable and competent learner. A program's success can be seriously undermined if the participating teachers have little confidence in their own abilities or those of their students.

APPENDIX: CLASSROOM CHECKLIST FOR WORKING WITH STRUGGLING READERS

Directions: This checklist provides an instrument for assessing the quality of classroom reading instruction for children experiencing reading difficulty. Place a check next to each item that describes a feature of reading instruction *for children experiencing reading difficulties in your classroom*. Determine if the actualization of any unchecked items would improve the quality of reading instruction for struggling readers in your classroom.

Children experiencing reading difficulties in my classroom are provided . . .

_____ Plenty of opportunities to read.
_____ Instruction to improve their phonological awareness skills.
_____ Explicit instruction in word attack and word recognition skills.
_____ Explicit instruction in comprehension strategies.
_____ Extra assistance to help them master reading skills and strategies.

I assist struggling readers in my classroom by . . .

_____ Ensuring that reading materials are at the appropriate level of difficulty.
_____ Capitalizing on students' interest in selecting materials and preparing lessons.
_____ Creating a supportive and risk-free environment.
_____ Using instructional arrangements that do not stigmatize students.
_____ Providing time for individually guided reading.
_____ Using technology to support students' reading and reading instruction.
_____ Specifying the goal for each reading lesson.

_____ Providing an appropriate balance between formal and informal teaching techniques as well as meaning and decoding activities.

_____ Monitoring students' performance during reading lessons and adjusting instruction as needed.

_____ Modeling the processes involved in reading.

_____ Providing follow-up instruction to reinforce previously taught skills and strategies.

_____ Helping students establish an "I can do" attitude.

_____ Teaching children how to help each other during reading.

I make sure that I . . .

_____ Set high but realistic expectations for all students.

_____ Periodically examine my expectations for each student in my class.

_____ Build a positive relationship with each child in my class.

_____ Talk frequently with parents and solicit their advice.

_____ Identify and address any roadblock that may impede a student's success in reading.

_____ Design lessons so that they are responsive to the cultural and background differences of the students in my class.

_____ Organize my class so that time is available for working with struggling readers.

_____ Maintain my belief that I can teach each child in my class how to read.

_____ Coordinate my reading efforts with the efforts of other educators working with a specific child in my class.

ACKNOWLEDGMENT

The development of this chapter was supported by the Center to Accelerate Student Learning, funded by the Office of Special Education Programs (Grant No. H324V98001).

RECOMMENDED READINGS

Erickson, K., & Koppenhaver, D. (1995). Developing a literacy program for children with severe disabilities. *The Reading Teacher, 48*, 676–684.

This article describes a program that combines the use of a variety of technological adaptations to support the reading and writing development of children with severe disabilities. The authors illustrate the use of these supports with two children with severe disabilities.

Tancock, S. (1994). A literacy lesson framework for children with reading problems. *The Reading Teacher, 48*, 130–140.

Tancock presents a literacy lesson framework that combines effective instructional supports with the flexibility needed to address the individual needs of children who experience difficulty learning to read. The lesson involves five components: reading familiar text material, guided reading of new material, writing, word sorting activities, and book sharing.

Troia, G., Roth, F., & Graham, S. (1998). An educator's guide to phonological awareness: Assessment measures and intervention activities for children. *Focus on Exceptional Children, 30,* 1–12.

The authors describe assessment and instructional procedures for teaching a wide range of phonological awareness skills to struggling readers. They explain how these procedures can be applied with published tests as well as instructional materials.

Wasik, B. (1998). Using volunteers as reading tutors: Guidelines for successful practices. *The Reading Teacher, 51,* 562–570.

Wasik presents eight guidelines that are essential to the success of volunteer tutoring programs for young children experiencing reading difficulties. These guidelines focus on both the child and the volunteer tutor.

Worthy, J. (1996). A matter of interest: Literature that hooks reluctant readers and keeps them reading. *The Reading Teacher, 50,* 204–212.

Based on her classroom experience and her research, Worthy suggests books and materials that are interesting and supportive for children who experience difficulty learning to read. She includes examples of repetitive and popular texts, as well as books that support performance activities such as Readers' Theatre.

REFERENCES

Adams, M. (1990). *Beginning to read: Thinking and learning about print.* Cambridge, MA: MIT Press.
Adams, M., Foorman, B., Lundberg, I., & Beeler, T. (1998). *Phonemic awareness and young children: A classroom curriculum.* Baltimore: Brookes.
Armstrong, A. (1983). The effects of material difficulty upon learning disabled children's oral reading and reading comprehension. *Learning Disability Quarterly, 6,* 339–348.
Au, K. (1980). Participation structures in a reading lesson with Hawaiian children: An analysis of a culturally appropriate instructional event. *Anthropology and Education Quarterly, 11,* 91–115.
Au, K., & Asam, C. (1996). Improving the literacy achievement of low-income students of diverse backgrounds. In M. Graves, P. Van den brock, & B. Taylor (Eds.), *The first R: Every child's right to read* (pp. 199–223). New York: Teachers College Press.
Au, K., & Mason, J. (1983). Cultural congruence in classroom participation structures: Achieving a balance of rights. *Discourse Processes, 6,* 145–167.
Ball, E., & Blachman, B. (1988). Phonemic segmentation training: Effects of reading readiness. *Annals of Dyslexia, 38,* 208–225.
Ball, E., & Blachman, B. (1991). Does phoneme awareness training in kindergarten make a difference in early word recognition and developmental spelling? *Reading Research Quarterly, 26,* 49–66.

Blachman, B. (1991). *Getting ready to read: Learning how print maps to speech*. Timonium, MD: York Press.

Bradley, L., & Bryant, P. (1985). *Rhyme and reason in reading and spelling*. Ann Arbor: University of Michigan Press.

Brown, A., & Campione, J. (1990). Interactive learning environments and the teaching of science and mathematics. In M. Gardner, J. Green, F. Reif, A. Schoenfield, A. di Sessa, & E. Stage (Eds.), *Toward a scientific practice of science education* (pp. 112–139). Hillsdale, NJ: Erlbaum.

Brown, R., Pressley, M., Van Meter, P., & Schuder, T. (1996). A quasi-experimental validation of transactional strategies instruction with low-achieving second grade readers. *Journal of Educational Psychology, 88*, 18–37.

Cardon, L., DiLalla, L., Plomin, R., DeFries, J., & Fulker, D. (1990). Genetic correlations between reading performance and IQ in the Colorado adoption project. *Intelligence, 14*, 245–257.

Carr, M., & Borkowski, J. (1989). Attributional training and the generalization of reading strategies with underachieving children. *Learning and Individual Differences, 1*, 327–341.

Castle, J., Riach, J., & Nicholson, T. (1994). Getting off to a better start in reading and spelling: The effects of phonemic awareness instruction within a whole language program. *Journal of Educational Psychology, 86*, 350–359.

Cole, A. (1998). Beginner-oriented texts in literature-based classrooms: The segue for a few struggling readers. *The Reading Teacher, 51*, 488–500.

Cosden, M., Gerber, M., Semmel, D., Goldman, S., & Semmel, M. (1987). Microcomputer uses within micro-education environments. *Exceptional Children, 53*, 399–409.

Cunningham, A. (1990). Explicit versus implicit instruction in phonemic awareness. *Journal of Experimental Child Psychology, 50*, 429–444.

DeFries, J., Fulker, D., & LaBuda, M. (1987). Evidence for a genetic aetiology in reading disability of twins. *Nature, 329*, 537–539.

Eldredge, L., Reutzel, R., & Hollingsworth, P. (1996). Comparing the effectiveness of two oral reading practices: Round-robin reading and the shared book experience. *Journal of Literacy Research, 28*, 201–225.

Englert, C., Garmon, A., Mariage, T., Rozendal, M., Tarrant, K., & Urba, J. (1995). The Early Literacy Project: Connecting across the literacy curriculum. *Learning Disability Quarterly, 18*, 253–275.

Englert, C., Mariage, T., Garmon, A., & Tarrant, K. (1998). Accelerating reading progress in Early Literacy Project classrooms: Three exploratory studies. *Remedial and Special Education, 19*, 142–159, 180.

Erickson, K., & Koppenhaver, D. (1995). Developing a literacy program for children with severe disabilities. *The Reading Teacher, 48*, 676–684.

Flood, J., Lapp, D., Flood, S., & Nagel, G. (1992). Am I allowed to group? Using flexible patterns for effective instruction. *The Reading Teacher, 45*, 608–616.

Fuchs, D., Fuchs, L., Mathes, P., & Simmons, D. (1997). Peer-assisted learning strategies: Making classrooms more responsive to diversity. *American Educational Research Journal, 34*, 174–206.

Gaskins, I. (1998). There's more to teaching at-risk and delayed readers than good reading instruction. *The Reading Teacher, 51*, 534–547.

Gelzheiser, L., & Wood, D. (1998). Early reading instruction. In B. Wong (Ed.), *Learning about learning disabilities* (2nd ed., pp. 311–341). San Diego, CA: Academic Press.

Graham, S., & Harris, K. R. (1997). Whole language and process writing: Does one approach fit all? In J. Lloyd, E. Kameenui, & D. Chard (Eds.), *Issues in educating students with disabilities* (pp. 239–258). Hillsdale, NJ: Erlbaum.

Graham, S., Harris, K. R., & Reid, R. (1992). Developing self-regulated learners. *Focus on Exceptional Children, 24*, 1–16.

Graham, S., & Johnson, L. (1989). Teaching reading to learning disabled students: A review of research-supported procedures. *Focus on Exceptional Children, 21*, 1–12.

Harris, K. R. (1982). Cognitive-behavior modification: Application with exceptional children. *Focus on Exceptional Children, 15*, 1–16.

Invernizzi, M., Rosemary, C., Juel, C., & Richards, H. (1997). At-risk readers and community volunteers: A 3-year perspective. *Scientific Studies of Reading, 1*, 277–300.

Johnston, F. (1998). The reader, the text, and the task: Learning words in first grade. *The Reading Teacher, 51*, 666–675.

Johnston, P., & Winograd, P. (1985). Passive failure in reading. *Journal of Reading Behavior, 17*, 279–301.

Juel, C. (1988). Learning to read and write: A longitudinal study of 54 children from first through fourth grade. *Journal of Educational Psychology, 80*, 437–447.

Kameenui, E. (1993). Diverse learners and the tyranny of time: Don't fix blame; fix the leaky roof. *The Reading Teacher, 46*, 376–383.

Lundberg, I., Frost, J., & Peterson, O. (1988). Effects of an extensive program for stimulating phonological awareness in preschool children. *Reading Research Quarterly, 23*, 263–250.

McIntyre, E., & Pressley, M. (Eds.). (1996). *Balanced instruction: Strategies and skills in whole language.* Norwood, MA: Christopher-Gordon.

O'Connor, R., Notari-Syverson, A., & Vadasky, P. (1996). Ladders to literacy: The effects of teacher-led phonological activities for kindergarten children with and without disabilities. *Exceptional Children, 63*, 117–130.

Palincsar, A. M., & Brown, A. L. (1984). Reciprocal teaching of comprehension-fostering and monitoring activities. *Cognition and Instruction, 2*, 117–175.

Palincsar, A. M., & Klenk, L. (1992). Fostering literacy learning in supportive contexts. *Journal of Learning Disabilities, 25*, 211–225.

Pikulski, J. (1994). Preventing reading failure: A review of five effective programs. *The Reading Teacher, 48*, 30–39.

Pinnell, G. (1989). Reading Recovery: Helping at-risk children learn to read. *Elementary School Journal, 90*, 161–183.

Pressley, M. (1998). *Reading instruction that works: The case for balanced teaching.* New York: Guilford Press.

Pressley, M., Rankin, J., & Yokoi, L. (1996). A survey of instructional practices of primary teachers nominated as effective in promoting literacy. *Elementary School Journal, 96*, 363–384.

Pressley, M., Wharton-McDonald, R., Rankin, J., Mistretta, J., & Yokoi, L. (1996). The nature of outstanding primary-grades literacy instruction. In E. McIntyre & M. Pressley (Eds.), *Balanced instruction: Strategies and skills in whole language* (pp. 251–276). Norwood, MA: Christopher-Gordon.

Pressley, M., Yokoi, L., Rankin, J., Wharton-McDonald, R., & Hampston, J. (1997). A survey of instructional practices of grade-5 teachers nominated as effective in promoting literacy. *Scientific Studies of Reading, 1*, 145–160.

Reinking, D. (1994). *Electronic literacy* (Perspectives in Reading Research No. 4). Athens, GA, & College Park, MD: Universities of Georgia & Maryland, National Reading Research Center.

Reyes, M. (1992). Challenging venerable assumptions: Literacy instruction for linguistically different students. *Harvard Educational Review, 62*, 427–446.

Rosenshine, B., & Meister, C. (1994). Reciprocal teaching: A review of nineteen experimental studies. *Review of Educational Research, 64*, 479–530.

Shanahan, T., & Barr, R. (1995). Reading Recovery: An independent evaluation of the effects of an early instructional intervention for at-risk learners. *Reading Research Quarterly, 30*, 958–966.

Slavin, R., Madden, N., & Karweit, N. (1989). Effective programs for students at risk: Conclusions for practice and policy. In R. Slavin, N. Karweit, & N. Madden (Eds.), *Effective programs for students at risk* (pp. 355–372). Boston: Allyn & Bacon.

Slavin, R., Madden, N., Karweit, N., Livermon, B., & Dolan, L. (1990). Success for All: First year outcomes of a comprehensive plan for reforming urban education. *American Educational Research Journal, 27,* 255–278.

Snow, C., Burns, M., & Griffin, P. (Eds.). (1998). *Preventing reading difficulties in young children.* Washington, DC: National Academy Press.

Tancock, S. (1994). A literacy lesson framework for children with reading problems. *The Reading Teacher, 48,* 130–140.

Toth, S. (1998, July). Time warped. *Reader's Digest,* p. 85.

Troia, G., Roth, F., & Graham, S. (1998). An educator's guide to phonological awareness: Assessment measures and intervention activities for children. *Focus on Exceptional Children, 30,* 1–12.

Uhry, J., & Shepherd, M. (1993). Segmentation/spelling instruction as part of a first-grade reading program: Effects on several measures of reading. *Reading Research Quarterly, 28,* 219–233.

Wasik, B. (1998). Using volunteers as reading tutors: Guidelines for successful practices. *The Reading Teacher, 51,* 562–570.

Wasik, B., & Slavin, R. (1993). Preventing early reading failure with one-to-one tutoring: A review of five programs. *Reading Research Quarterly, 28,* 179–200.

Wharton-McDonald, R., Pressley, M., & Mistretta, J. (in press). Outstanding literacy instruction in first grade: Teacher practices and student achievement. *Elementary School Journal.*

Wise, B., Ring, J., Sessions, L., & Olson, R. (1997). Phonological awareness with and without articulation: A preliminary study. *Learning Disability Quarterly, 20,* 211–225.

Worthy, J. (1996). A matter of interest: Literature that hooks reluctant readers and keeps them reading. *The Reading Teacher, 50,* 204–212.

CHAPTER FOUR

Fostering Reading for Learning

MARIAM JEAN DREHER

Traditionally, learning through reading has been delayed until children have learned the "basics." Indeed, elementary reading instruction has long been parsed into two phases: first children *learn to read*; then, when they can read, they *read to learn*. In the early grades, reading instruction has concentrated on teaching children how to read, using familiar topics in narrative texts. Only later does the focus shift to reading for learning.

But this conception of reading instruction is changing. As Strickland (1995) has argued, even at the kindergarten level, "Establishing an instructional framework within which children can both learn literacy and learn through literacy is critical" (p. 47). Similarly, a National Academy of Sciences committee concluded that by the time children enter fourth grade, they need to be "capable—independently and productively—of reading to learn" (Snow, Burns, & Griffin, 1998, p. 207). If fourth graders are to achieve such a level, they need early experiences that will prepare them to do so. Thus, the National Academy of Sciences committee noted that first, second, and third graders need instruction that will prepare them to read and comprehend "both fiction and nonfiction that is appropriately designed for grade level" (Snow et al., 1998, p. 79). Further, they concluded that early instruction should prepare third graders not only to interpret nonfiction but to combine "information from multiple sources in writing reports" (p. 83), a rather sophisticated accomplishment that many much

68

older students find difficult (Dreher, 1995; Stahl, Hynd, Britton, McNish, & Bosquet, 1996). Others echo these themes, calling for the use of information books with emergent readers (e.g., Guillaume, 1998), for incorporating information books more fully into the entire elementary school curriculum (e.g., Freeman & Person, 1998), and for integrating literacy and the content areas in ways that encourage higher-order thinking and problem solving (e.g., Pappas, Kiefer, & Levstik, 1999).

Thus, expert opinion has converged on the notion of recognizing *learning to read* and *reading to learn* as interwoven processes throughout elementary school. Part of interweaving these two dimensions of reading is to emphasize comprehension from the start, along with skills, rather than adopting a solely skills-based approach (see Baker, Chapter 2, this volume). But, as is documented below, comprehension in elementary school typically involves narrative text. If children are to become effective at reading for learning, they need early instructional experiences that go beyond stories to include non-narrative books and materials that provide information.

Excellent reviews of research have been written about classroom practices that can facilitate comprehension in the elementary school (e.g., Pearson & Fielding, 1991; Pressley, 1998; Tierney & Cunningham, 1984). Further, there are many comprehensive sources on reading for learning (e.g., Vacca & Vacca, 1999). However, reviews such as that of Pearson and Fielding's (1991) survey of intervention studies on improving reading comprehension contain few studies dealing with primary-grade children and, of those few, virtually all involve narrative text. Similarly, research on reading for learning typically involves students from the middle elementary grades through high school. Consequently, this chapter will emphasize research related to comprehension and reading for learning in the early grades, with particular attention to information text because research on such text is scarce at that level.

Because a joint emphasis on learning to read and reading for learning throughout the elementary grades differs from traditional practice, teachers may find themselves needing to make changes in the materials children read and listen to, and changes in the literacy tasks they plan for children. The difficulty of making curricular changes may be exacerbated if teachers are not convinced the changes are needed. Thus, this chapter begins by discussing why we should attend to reading for learning as children learn to read, why we need to focus more attention on the use of information text, and the advantages that may result if we reconceptualize reading instruction in this way. Then this chapter shifts to its main focus: a research-based set of recommendations about what might be done in classrooms so that comprehension and reading for learning are emphasized as children simultaneously learn to read.

ISSUES IN INTERWEAVING LEARNING TO READ
AND READING FOR LEARNING

The need to integrate learning to read and reading for learning can be clarified in terms of the current discussion of "balanced" instruction. In the debate over whether reading instruction should be skills based or holistic, many have called for balance (Braunger & Lewis, 1997; Freppon & Dahl, 1998; International Reading Association & National Association for the Education of Young Children, 1998; Snow et al., 1998). Pressley (1998), for example, characterized both whole-language and skills-based models as incomplete and called for a merger of the two into a balanced model with systematic skills instruction occurring in a print-rich, literature-based environment. Such a balanced model, he argued, would allow for better outcomes than either of the two models alone. Baumann and Ivey (1997), in reviewing their effort to create just such a balanced environment for at-risk second graders, concluded that immersion in literature and systematic strategy instruction were "symbiotic, synergistic" (p. 272): "The literature enhanced students' reading and writing fluency, and their developing literacy abilities promoted their literacy knowledge and appreciation" (p. 272).

Balanced instruction that meshes an emphasis on meaning with effective skills instruction is certainly part of interweaving reading to learn and reading for learning, but it is not enough. Balance needs to include knowledge acquisition through reading. And including knowledge acquisition in the mix necessitates attention to diverse reading materials. Although children can and do learn new information from reading stories, we most often think of reading for learning as occurring in information text. Accordingly, access to and instruction involving information text is very important in a balanced program.

It is well documented that the elementary school reading experience is overwhelmingly narrative. Estimates suggest that narrative materials make up to 90% of what elementary school children read (Trabasso, 1994). Fisher and Hiebert (1990; also Hiebert & Fisher, 1990) analyzed 180 literacy tasks in 40 days of instruction in eight grade 2 and grade 6 classes. Whether they observed literature-based or skills-based classrooms, they found that almost all instruction and materials read or written by students involved narrative text. Similarly, in a recent survey, primary-grade teachers reported that reading in their classrooms involved information text only 6% of the time (Pressley, Rankin, & Yokoi, 1996). Research also indicates that teachers routinely select narrative material to read to their students (Hoffman, Roser, & Battle, 1993). Moreover, writing tasks are overwhelmingly narrative (Daniels, 1990). Not surprisingly, students do better on both reading and writing narratives than on exposition (e.g., Langer, Applebee, Mullis, & Foertsch, 1990).

There appears to be no compelling reason that the elementary school experience should be mainly narrative. Many have assumed that young children prefer narrative or even that exposition is "unnatural" for young children (see Pappas, 1993, for a summary of these arguments). But research suggests that young children respond favorably to non-narrative text. Pappas (1993) found that kindergartners were just as successful in learning new vocabulary and in pretend reading after having listened to an information book as they were with a storybook. They were also equally successful in learning the meaning of new words from each type of book. Similarly, Newkirk (1989) has documented the many types of writing—not limited to stories—that even very young children produce. Further, teachers who have added information text to instructional materials and have expanded their programs to include reading and writing to learn have reported successful experiences even in first grade (Duthie, 1996; Kamil & Lane, 1997).

Interweaving learning to read and reading for learning entails the use of more information text. This balancing of elementary school reading instruction with more information text seems doable even in early grades: teachers have tried it, and research suggests children respond favorably. Further, many would argue that not only is it feasible, it is critically important to make the effort. What is likely to happen if we do? Cases for both engagement and achievement benefits can be made.

Engagement Benefits

Balancing elementary reading instruction with substantial amounts of information text may be very important for motivating some children who have difficulty learning to read when presented with stories that are just not meaningful to them. Caswell and Duke (1998) recently reported case studies of children who failed to learn to read until instructors happened upon information text. Caswell and Duke noted that for these children, information text seemed to serve as a "way in" to literacy that narrative texts did not. Duthie (1996), in a report of her experience teaching first grade, profiled a similar child who was able to succeed because reading instruction accommodated his interest in nonfiction. Like Caswell and Duke, Duthie has argued not for eliminating stories but for balancing children's reading experience by including nonfiction materials.

As McCombs (1997) wrote, "Put simply, what may motivate a particular student to read is not necessarily what may motivate another student to read. In spite of these differences, however, research on student interest shows that, across different students, when interest in reading particular materials is present, it increases attention, use of effective learning strategies, and reading comprehension" (p. 126). By using more diverse materials in reading instruction, we are more likely to arouse children's interests and curiosity. Curiosity is a powerful motivation for reading, strongly related to independent reading activity (Baker & Wigfield, 1999).

Broadening the instructional emphasis to include reading for learning may not only increase the motivation of children who are not fully engaged with reading but may also help to maintain the high levels of motivation typically exhibited by beginning readers. Children's views about reading and their perceptions of themselves as readers are positive in first grade but drop as children progress through school (Chapman & Tunmer, 1997; McKenna, Ellsworth, & Kear, 1995; Wigfield et al., 1997). This decline occurs for all achievement levels but is most pronounced for children of lower reading ability. Effective use of more diverse material, including information books, may help to counteract this drop in motivation to read.

Support for this view comes from Alexander's (1997) argument that "knowledge seeking through exposition" is a neglected aspect of motivation. She noted that, based on reader response theory, "Motivation more often is associated with an aesthetic stance and with narrative text, whereas knowledge-seeking via exposition is linked to the more passive and uninspiring efferent stance" (p. 83). But, as Alexander argued, the act of readers seeking information that is important to them may well be "essential to the development of a reader's knowledge of self or self schemata," because it contributes to goal orientation, interest, and self determination—all aspects of motivation critical to reading (see Wigfield, Chapter 7, this volume). An emphasis on learning from reading may help give children a sense of purpose not fostered by an emphasis on story comprehension.

Achievement Benefits

An achievement case can also be made for balancing reading instruction with more attention to information text. Recent fourth-grade National Assessment of Educational Progress (NAEP) results indicate that diversity of reported reading experience is positively correlated with reading achievement. In other words, fourth graders who reported reading not only stories but also magazines and information books had the highest achievement; achievement scores were lower for children who reported reading only two types of materials; and scores were lowest of all for children who reported reading only stories. The findings also showed that students in the nation's top-third achieving schools reported reading more information books at school than students in the bottom-third schools. However, the figure was low for both groups, with only 39% of children in the top-third schools and 25% in the bottom-third schools reporting that they read information books at school (Campbell, Kapinus, & Beatty, 1995).

Research also suggests that opportunity to interact with information text is likely to be particularly important to "at-risk" children. We know that children from low-income families "tend to perform below norms in literacy on national, state and school assessments. Moreover, the lag in reading becomes greater in later elementary school grades and in high school" (Chall, Jacobs, & Baldwin, 1990, p. 1). What might be revealed if we look at children who seem to get off to a good start even in schools with students from low-income families? Chall et al. (1990) followed children through the grades in schools in high-poverty areas. They found that even those children who had average reading achievement in second and third grades began to lag behind in reading achievement at fourth grade. Chall et al. (1990) pointed out that the performance drop in these children did not occur due to a deficiency in higher-level comprehension skills (as some have suggested), but rather to problems with what they termed academic vocabulary ("difficult, abstract, specialized, and technical words," p. 46). These children had performed adequately in the earlier grades thanks in part to their ability to use context. But as reading tests incorporated more academic vocabulary, these children's lack of complete fluency and their lack of exposure to academic vocabulary converged to cause a lag in reading achievement. A major source of academic vocabulary is, of course, information text and opportunities to read and write for learning.

In a classic article on the importance of having children engage in reading, Allington (1977) asked, "If they don't read much, how they ever gonna get good?" (See Byrnes, Chapter 9, this volume, for a discussion of the importance of time spent reading.) This question certainly applies to opportunities to read and learn from information text. Providing children with opportunities to experience both narrative and information text seems likely to improve both their reading motivation and achievement. Providing such a balance enables children to engage in reading for learning as they simultaneously learn to read. Further, by facilitating young children's experiences with reading for learning, primary-grade teachers will find their classroom practices in agreement with current standards of professional organizations in reading, language arts, early childhood, mathematics, science, and social studies (International Reading Association & National Association for the Education of Young Children, 1996; National Research Council, 1994; National Council for the Social Studies [NCSS], 1994; National Council of Teachers of Mathematics [NCTM] . . ., 1989). These standards are constructivist in nature, emphasizing active learning, inquiry, higher-order thinking, and problem solving throughout elementary school.

CLASSROOM PRACTICES LIKELY TO PROMOTE ENGAGED READING FOR LEARNING

How might teachers promote engaged reading for learning while at the same time helping children learn to read? The eight research-based recommendations offered below should prove helpful.

1. Incorporate Information Books into Daily Read-Alouds

Teachers are routinely advised to read aloud to children every day. This appears to be good advice because we have evidence that children who have been read to at school tend to have higher achievement (e.g., Feitelson, Kita, & Goldstein, 1986; McCormick & Mason, 1986). Rosenhouse, Feitelson, Kita, and Goldstein (1997), for example, found that interactive reading aloud (in which teachers interacted with students before, during, and after reading a story) resulted in improved decoding, reading comprehension, and storytelling ability for at-risk first graders.

Other studies have specifically examined vocabulary growth. When Elley (1989) had teachers read the same book three times in a 7-day period to 7- and 8-year-olds, he found impressive growth in the children's knowledge of vocabulary used in the book. Two facts were particularly noteworthy. First, all the children gained substantially in vocabulary, but poorer readers gained the most. Second, just reading the book produced vocabulary growth, but even more growth resulted when teachers explained word meaning.

Most studies on the effects of reading aloud at school have involved only stories. However, effects like those Elley (1989) found look quite promising for information books, especially if teachers explain new vocabulary and concepts. But are teachers likely to do this with information books? Another study with young children suggests that they will.

Mason, Peterman, Powell, and Kerr (1989) videotaped kindergarten teachers as they read different types of books to children; they found spontaneous and consistent differences in how the teachers handled these books:

> Teachers typically introduced the narrative with comments about the title, author, and setting, and as they read, they asked many questions about vocabulary, characters, and interpretation of events. Their closing remarks dealt with the resolution of the story. With the expository text,

teachers explained and demonstrated text concepts before and during the reading, and arranged follow-up activities that extended some of the book concepts. Also during the reading they had children look at and label the illustrations as a way of helping them understand the text ideas. (p. 114)

Thus, teachers shifted their actions depending on the type of book they read to children.

These spontaneous shifts suggest that if teachers were to read aloud from information books more often, then children would likely benefit from greater exposure to activities and discussions that differ from narrative experiences. These results also suggest that vocabulary learning may occur with repeated read-alouds from information books as in Elley's (1989) study with narratives. Further, because teachers model different ways of thinking and different strategies for varied books, information book read-alouds will help children become aware of different genres, text structures, and purposes for reading. Indeed, Duke and Kays (1998) had kindergartners engage in pretend readings of an information book before and after their teacher read aloud information books almost every day for a 3-month period. They documented rapid growth in characteristic features of information book language. Thus, by changing the materials they read to children, teachers can change their actions and children's experiences.

If children are to become equally proficient in reading in the content areas—if they are to become as least as proficient in expository text as in narratives—then it seems reasonable to argue that approximately 50% of read-aloud selections should be information books. But teachers who are used to reading mainly stories to children may wonder whether they can find appropriate information books for the youngest children. Some years ago, availability was a problem. Since then, publishers have flooded the market with appealing information books so that there is much to select from, even for the earliest grades (see Chambliss & McKillop, Chapter 5, this volume). Further, children's listening comprehension is typically better than their reading comprehension until about sixth or seventh grade (Sticht & James, 1984). Because children can comprehend information books (as well as stories) that they could not read on their own, teachers can take advantage of well-written, appealing expository texts that are above their students' reading level.

Teachers may also wonder whether children will still find "story" time enjoyable if they add a substantial number of information books. Teachers who already use considerable information text find that the switch is not hard to make and that children include information books in their requests for repeat readings of favorite books. Further, as noted above, Pappas (1993) and others have found that children show interest and sometimes even preferences for information texts. Similarly, Horowitz and Freeman (1995) investigated whether children preferred read-alouds from an expository science book or a science book that was written in story form. They found that whether or not the read-aloud was accompanied by pre- and postreading discussion made a difference. With no discussion, kindergarten and second graders preferred a narrative science book. But with discussion, both kindergarten and second graders preferred an expository science book. Interestingly, the second graders preferred the expository book even though they recognized that it was harder and contained more words they did not know.

2. Infuse Information Text into the Materials Used to Teach Reading

Content analyses of reading materials as well as classroom observations indicate that the material typically used for reading instruction is largely narrative. As noted, observations in second and sixth grades, even in literature-based classrooms, showed that reading lessons almost exclusively involved narrative text (Fisher & Hiebert, 1990). Further, Duke (in press) observed virtually no instructional activities involving informational text in first-grade classrooms. When Hoffman et al. (1994) compared five first-grade basal reading series from 1986/1987 to new versions for 1993, they found "substantial changes" in the newer series compared to the older. But one thing that did not change was the percentage of nonfiction in these basals. In both cases it was 12%. Moss and Newton (1998) found similar results for grades 2, 4, and 6 in six recent basal series.

If children rarely read information texts during reading instruction, then no wonder they perform less well on such materials. Thus, including more information texts as part of the materials used to teach reading makes sense. Exposing young children to many types of material during guided reading seems likely to provide them with increased opportunity to develop skill in reading and using diverse texts.

Research indicates that whether teachers are using basal readers, literature-based basals, or trade books, it is likely that more information text is needed (Hiebert & Fisher, 1990; Moss & Newton, 1998). Finding appropriate materials for reading instruction has become easier because publishing companies now offer many information books even at very early reading levels. Often both big books and regular-size books of the same titles are available (e.g., from Children's Press, Rigby, Steck-Vaughn, Scholastic, or the Wright Group).

How much information text is needed during reading instruction? Teachers like Duthie (1996) and researchers like Caswell and Duke (1998) have argued that a substantial amount of information text is very important for some readers who appear to be at risk of failing to learn to read without it. In addition, many have noted that practice in reading information text is important in the early grades if children are to meet expectations later on in school (e.g., Sanacore, 1991). But these calls for "balance" do not indicate a particular proportion. Teachers may want to strive for 50%, as Kamil and Lane (1997) decided to do in their case study.

Some may argue that concern for information text during reading instruction is unnecessary because children are getting experience reading information text during social studies and science. That may be true in some classrooms; but in many classrooms, lecture/discussion-type activities predominate in science and social studies, with little actual reading of content area textbooks or trade books (Armbruster et al., 1991). In fact, studies show that children spend little time reading in general (see Byrnes, Chapter 9, this volume), and even less reading information text (Campbell et al., 1995; Langer et al., 1990). Thus, it is important to include information text in reading instruction or to include reading instruction during content lessons or to do both. Indeed, because there is so much that teachers must "cover," the most efficient approach may be to integrate instruction. That approach is discussed in Recommendation 7, below.

3. Teach Strategies and Text Features That Will Allow Children to Comprehend Both Narrative and Information Text

Recommendation 3 highlights the need not just for exposure to reading information text but for *instruction* on how to read it effectively. Research indicates that elementary school children often receive little comprehension instruction, whether in narrative or expository text. In her classic study, Durkin (1978/1979) showed that children were peppered with questions to assess whether they had comprehended what they read. But she found that children received almost no comprehension instruction either during reading or during social studies. More recent research continues to find similar results (e.g., Armbruster et al., 1991, Neilsen, Rennie, & Connell, 1982; Wendler, Samuels, & Moore, 1989).

Yet, considerable research indicates that reading comprehension is improved by good instruction (see Pearson & Fielding, 1991). Much has been written on comprehension instruction as well as on reading for learning. But, as noted earlier, research relevant to reading for learning in the early grades is scarce. So the focus here is on ways to help young children with information text.

One technique is Ogle's (1986) K-W-L, designed for nonfiction text "at any grade level" (p. 564). Ogle explained that in the K and W parts of this technique, children and teacher brainstorm "what we *k*now," and "what we *w*ant to find out." Then children record their own responses on individual strategy sheets. After reading or as they read, children fill out the L part, for "what I *l*earned." When children have recorded their responses, the class discusses what they have learned. (With young children, teachers may need to start with group strategy sheets, moving toward individual strategy sheets as children's writing skill allows.) By helping children think critically about what they know and don't know, this technique helps children become active processors of information text.

Another approach is reciprocal teaching in which students and their teacher read a text together (silently or aloud together depending on the children's and the text's level). As they read, the teacher and the students take turns leading a discussion of what they are reading. These discussions are guided by four strategies: predicting, generating questions, summarizing, and clarifying. Although most widely researched with upper elementary and older students, reciprocal teaching has been used as early as first grade (Palincsar, Brown, & Campione, 1993).

"Questioning the Author" (QtA) is an approach designed by Beck, McKeown, Hamilton, and Kucan (1997) to help children learn to comprehend what they read in textbooks. Beck and colleagues' book of the same name offers a detailed explanation of QtA, including excerpts from class discussions showing its effectiveness with both narrative and expository text. Teachers help children to interact with the text—or question the author—while they are reading rather than after they read. As the children collaboratively construct meaning, they learn to think of an author as a fallible individual whom they can query. QtA's effectiveness has been documented in fourth grade and up, but the approach appears to be appropriate for younger children as well.

In addition, collaborative strategic reading (CSR), also shown to be effective with upper elementary grades, appears to be promising for younger students. In CSR, small student-led groups help each other apply comprehension strategies as they read expository text. Klingner, Vaughn, and Schumm (1998) found that CSR applied to social studies text improved fourth graders' reading comprehension as well as their social studies content knowledge. These authors noted that CSR improved children's performance even though it occurred in culturally and linguistically diverse, heterogeneous classrooms that included learning disabled children.

K-W-L, reciprocal teaching, QtA, and CSR have in common an emphasis on helping children become active readers who monitor their comprehension. They also have in common the use of discussion and other social interactions among children to help children construct meaning. (A related technique that uses social interaction in the construction of meaning with multiple texts is the idea circle, discussed below in Recommendation 5.) Collaborative instructional approaches appear to be powerful for both learning and motivation; they are discussed in more detail by Gambrell, Mazzoni, and Almasi (Chapter 6, this volume).

Another issue in helping children comprehend what they read is vocabulary instruction. Although vocabulary knowledge and reading comprehension are highly correlated (Beck & McKeown, 1991), Rupley, Logan, and Nichols (1998) noted that vocabulary has slipped out of "hot topic" status. Nevertheless, vocabulary merits instructional attention. Even if they can decode the words, children who do not know the meaning of many of the words they are reading are not likely to comprehend well. Further, as Baker (Chapter 2, this volume) pointed out, if readers' decoding efforts produce words that have no meaning for them, they are not likely to be engaged readers. As a result, teachers need to help children increase their vocabulary knowledge. Because information books, especially textbooks, tend to have a high density of unfamiliar words, vocabulary development is particularly important in reading for learning. Good sources for this effort include Rupley et al. (1998) and Blachowicz and Fisher (1996).

In addition, children's reading comprehension will benefit from instruction on the unique features of information text. Young children can easily learn about such features as the table of contents, index, and glossary. Other features include captions, labels, and boldface. Many information books for young children include these features. A particularly important concept that children need to learn is that they don't need to read all information books from cover to cover. Teachers can help children reach this understanding when they read aloud and when they guide children in reading information text. For example, teachers can point out the table of contents, have children peruse it with them to select an interesting topic, and then read only that selection (Kamil & Lane, 1997).

Text structure knowledge can also facilitate comprehension. Research indicates that young children's comprehension benefits from instruction on the structure of stories (e.g., Baumann & Bergeron, 1993). As teachers provide children with experience in reading different types of information text, they can help children note the different text structures that characterize exposition. Doing so may be difficult for many teachers, however. In a nationwide survey of elementary teachers' views on science reading, Shymansky, Yore, and Good (1991) found that a majority did not believe that "science text required a different structure than other textbooks" (p. 446). Further, a majority also believed that science textbooks could be improved by writing them in a narrative style. Shymansky et al. worried that such results "suggest that elementary teachers know little about the unique language and text structure of expository text" (p. 446). To develop effective techniques for guiding children's text structure knowledge, teachers may benefit from examining resources such as McGee and Richgels's (1985) article.

4. Provide Instructional Activities That Include Writing Information Text

What children read also affects their writing. Eckhoff (1983, 1986) compared the writing of second, third, and fourth graders who were matched on linguistic and comprehension abilities but who were reading in different basal series. Eckhoff found that the children's writing was clearly influenced by the syntactic complexity, style, and format of their basal readers. These results suggest that if children read more information text, their writing patterns may also be influenced by the complexity and format of that material.

However, beyond simply being exposed to information text, children also need simultaneous instructional activities that include writing information text. The rationale for this recommendation is that writing in conjunction with reading can lead to better learning of the content. But the type of writing activity makes a difference. With middle and secondary students, for example, Langer and Applebee (1987) found that writing tasks which led students to reflect and rethink information were best for learning new concepts; short-answer tasks that mainly led to finding isolated information and copying it onto a worksheet helped short-term recall but not understanding of relations among ideas and not long-term retention.

These results also make sense for younger learners. For example, Avery (1993) has used learning logs successfully with first graders. Learning logs are notebooks in which children record their thoughts and findings. As Avery (1993) explained, learning logs are "vehicles that can be used for speculating, predicting, recording, documenting, webbing, charting, listing, sketching, brainstorming, questioning, imagining, hypothesizing, synthesizing, analyzing, and reflecting" (p. 444). These logs can be used to help children engage in strategic processing of material they read and listen to. Children can also use these logs as resources during discussion and when they write about a topic.

In addition to using techniques such as learning logs, teachers need to provide direct instruction relevant to expository writing tasks. There are numerous sources available with suggestions for informational writing; however, most of these deal with older students. One helpful source for young children is Cudd and Roberts's (1989) article that provides examples of simple paragraph frames specifically designed to support primary children's informative writing. Similarly, Lewis, Wray, and Rospigliosi

(1994) offer tips for helping children learn to put material they have learned into their own words.

In considering the need to provide young children with information text writing experience, teachers should keep in mind that although reading and writing influence each other, both reading and writing require instruction. Although they are related processes, the evidence does not support the view that instruction in one will result in improvement in the other. As Shanahan (1997) has noted, "Improved learning is only likely to be the result if reading and writing are combined in appropriate ways" (p. 14). (See Shanahan, 1988, for instructional principles to guide reading–writing combinations.)

5. Help Children Learn to Integrate Information across Multiple Texts

Children today are expected to engage in some fairly sophisticated tasks. In Maryland, for example, a statewide performance assessment in grades 3, 5, and 8 requires even the youngest children to integrate information across more than one text. And, as already noted, the National Academy of Sciences committee concluded that successful third graders should be able to combine "information from multiple sources in writing reports" (Snow et al., 1998, p. 79).

Tasks like these involve discourse synthesis, "a highly constructive act in which readers become writers" (Spivey & King, 1989, p. 9). Reading-to-write tasks with single texts are hard enough; when multiple texts are involved the difficulty is compounded because information must be selected, organized, and combined across sources. Such tasks are challenging even for middle and high school students (Spivey & King, 1989), perhaps because students are likely to have had little relevant instruction (Stahl et al., 1996).

If children are to develop skill at such tasks, they need experience and instruction. Teachers can help children learn to draw intertextual links even before they can read independently. Richgels (1997) found that this can be done even in kindergarten. As a participant observer in a kindergarten class, he documented kindergartners and their teacher interacting in episodes of story and information book read-alouds. He noted that social construction of meaning often involved children referring to multiple texts in a single episode.

Literature discussion groups (see Gambrell et al., Chapter 6, this volume) can help encourage links across multiple pieces of literature. Similarly, idea circles can help third and fifth graders learn to make links as they read multiple information texts. An idea circle, as Guthrie and

McCann (1996) explained, is a "peer-led, small group discussion of concepts fueled by multiple text sources" (p. 88). As Gambrell et al. discuss in detail (Chapter 6, this volume), three to six children collaborate in an idea circle to learn a concept based on various information they have gathered. In contrast to literature discussion groups in which children are encouraged to come away with different conclusions, idea circles aim at helping children converge on understanding a concept. Children learn to draw upon information from multiple books and resources to explain and defend their ideas and to challenge their peers' ideas. In doing so, not only do they acquire a deeper understanding than if they were to read alone, they learn to make intertextual links.

Other instructional activities that are conducive to helping children make intertextual links are inquiry tasks discussed in Recommendation 6 and integrated instruction in Recommendation 7, below.

6. Guide Children to Engage in Inquiry

By the time children reach upper elementary school, we expect them to pose questions, locate information, and write reports. Without appropriate early experiences, upper elementary children will be ill prepared to engage in such tasks. Unfortunately, in addition to receiving little comprehension instruction as noted above, children receive little or ineffective instruction on research skills such as how to find information upon which to base their reports (Armbruster & Gudbrandsen, 1986; Dreher & Sammons, 1994). As a result, research can be an unpleasant experience for both teachers and students, with reports often copied straight out of a book.

Children are motivated by and learn a great deal from effective inquiry tasks. In her book *Making Facts Matter*, Mallett (1992) described many projects in which children as young as 5 years of age showed their enthusiasm for nonfiction. They became young "experts" as they sought information on topics of special interest to them and as they participated in class projects. These students produced reports and other products based on their research that differed considerably from the classic copied report. Similarly, Guthrie et al. (1998) found that children's conceptual learning and reading motivation benefited from inquiry tasks as part of concept-oriented reading instruction. Further, as Mallet (1992) noted, it should not be assumed that only good readers are motivated to become experts; she underscored the point that less able and reluctant readers are often inspired to engage in reading when teachers help them find information books at their level and related to their interests.

The challenge for teachers is to engage children in inquiry in ways that will contribute to their motivation as well as their learning. Many, Fyfe, Lewis, and Mitchell (1996), in a study of 11- and 12-year-olds engaged in research, concluded that "a classroom ethos that encourages autonomy, flexibility, and risk taking will support the development of effective reading–writing–research" (p. 32). Turner's (1995) study with younger children also sheds some light on the nature of tasks children find motivating (see Wigfield, Chapter 7, this volume). She found that it makes a difference whether first graders work on literacy tasks in classroom contexts that are open or closed. In open tasks, "students themselves could select relevant information and/or could decide how to use the information to solve a problem"; in closed tasks, "either the task or the teacher indicated the information to be used . . . as well as the expected solution" (p. 424). Open tasks facilitated higher level cognitive processing by encouraging metacognition and decision making. With open tasks, children exhibited more motivated behavior, as evidenced by more reading strategy use, more persistence, and more attention. Turner's results suggest that classroom contexts that allow for inquiry will influence children's motivation for literacy.

To help children be successful in inquiry tasks, teachers need to teach research skills effectively. One way to do so is to teach new strategies by beginning with familiar contexts and moving to new ones. Korkeamäki, Tiainen, and Dreher (1998) used this notion when they taught second graders to search for information, take notes, and write in their own words using stories, and then to transfer those skills to information text. Research suggests that teaching research skills in the context of meaningful activities is an effective approach (Dreher, Davis, Waynant, & Clewell, 1998; Wray & Lewis, 1992). Dreher and Sammons (1994) found that children often did not think to use research-related knowledge that had been taught in isolation. Instead of separate research skills instruction, children can be provided with instruction related to their ongoing needs as they engage in inquiry tasks.

Children need to learn many things related to the research process, such as how to pose questions, what kinds of resources are available, how to use the information-access features of a resource, how to record the information they find, how to combine information from multiple sources, and how to write their final products. Some of these topics are addressed in other sections of this chapter. Other sources for instructional tips include Hoffman's (1992) explanation of information charts, or I-charts that students can use to record facts they encounter during research. Similarly, Bryan's (1998) K-W-W-L, an extension of Ogle's (1986) K-W-L techniques, is helpful. K-W-W-L adds a W for "where I can learn this," aimed at helping children brainstorm resources for answering their questions. Bryan used this approach to guide children to generate questions from their knowledge, and help children think about resources for answering their questions.

7. Integrate Reading/Language Arts and Content Areas in Thematic Units

In many ways, this recommendation can be seen as tying all the others together. Integration of reading/language arts and the content areas has great potential for maximizing efficiency and learning. By integrating language arts and the content areas in a thematic approach, proponents argue that we can both facilitate students' literacy performance and their content knowledge acquisition. Further, proponents maintain that integrated approaches can help children learn how to learn by involving them in meaningful problem solving in social settings. In this view, knowledge is not just transmitted to children but is instead constructed by children. Because they are active participants in their own learning, children engage in critical thinking and are motivated for learning.

Integration of content areas and literacy is frequently called for in today's methods textbooks and professional literature (e.g., Bredekamp & Copple, 1997). An approach that integrates literacy and the content areas has the potential of providing children with coherent instruction, as discussed in detail by Guthrie, Cox, et al. (Chapter 10, this volume). As Lipson, Valencia, Wixson, and Peters (1993) have argued, "A thematic approach can provide coherence for both teachers and students. The right theme gives the work of the classroom a *focus* and provides a rubric for making decisions about what to teach" (p. 253; their italic). They also argued that this approach can help children better understand why they are doing something, help them see the link between content and process, and raise the likelihood of transfer across different contexts.

Research indicates that the coherence resulting from content integration can lead to improved achievement and motivation. Guthrie et al. (1996, 1998) for example, demonstrated the positive effects of Concept-Oriented Reading Instruction (CORI). CORI, discussed further by Guthrie, Cox, et al. (Chapter 10, this volume), involves literacy instruction rooted in science texts and experiences. CORI has been shown to increase third and fifth graders' literacy engagement and intrinsic motivation for literacy, as well as their reading performance and concept learning.

Similarly, Romance and Vitale (1992) found that fourth graders benefited from integrated science and reading/language arts compared to separate blocks for science and reading/language arts. The children who received integrated instruction scored higher on standardized tests of both reading and science. These children also had more positive attitudes toward both reading and science, as well as greater confidence in their ability to learn science content. Morrow, Pressley, Smith, and Smith (1997) also found positive effects for using both stories and science texts in an integrated reading/language arts program. They contrasted third graders who participated in an integrated reading/language arts approach to children who experienced integrated reading/language arts that included science texts along with stories. The children who experienced both stories and science texts did better on both literacy and science measures than the others.

But an integrated approach can be a challenge to implement effectively. Lipson et al. (1993) concluded that "thematic units" are often fragmented collections of activities instead of focused units that help students learn in depth. In fact, Lipson et al. (1993) found that professional books, methods textbooks, and basal reading/language arts programs offered little helpful information on how to integrate teaching or create thematic units.

If integrating within the language arts is often difficult, then integration across content areas can be even more challenging. Hiebert and Fisher (1990) found that even teachers who integrated the language arts did not integrate content areas:

> Our observations of classroom practices over entire schools days, for example, found the dramatic differences between whole-language and skills-oriented classrooms to be restricted to reading and writing periods. Even after teachers had participated in whole-language practices for several years, mathematics, science, and social studies instruction in their classrooms remained, for the most part, unaffected. Even when the same person taught all subjects, we found relatively crisp subject matter boundaries. (p. 63)

Engaging children in effective thematic units across the content areas takes some teaching expertise (see Alexander & Fives, Chapter 13, this volume). Teachers can find tips for making effective decisions on thematic units in articles by Lipson et al. (1993), Shanahan (1997), and Shanahan, Robinson, and Schneider (1995). They can also take heart that, despite the difficulties, the evidence indicates that well-done content integration pays off in learning and engagement.

8. Encourage Children to Engage in Diverse Independent Reading

In addition to being advised to read to students every day, teachers are also commonly urged to provide time for children to engage in independent reading every day. We know that time spent reading is a predictor of reading achievement. For example, amount of reading correlates with vocabulary development and general knowledge in fourth, fifth, and sixth graders, even when differences in general ability and phonological coding ability are controlled (Cunningham & Stanovich, 1991). But time spent reading is likely to be most beneficial if it occurs in tandem with instructional practices such as those highlighted in Recommendations 1–7, above (see Byrnes, Chapter 9, this volume).

Further, diverse reading is more likely to result in higher performance levels than narrow reading. Because practice in reading is thought to be important for developing fluency, sustained silent reading is popular in elementary school. In most classrooms, however, children appear to read narrative materials during this time. Yet, research supports the importance of encouraging children to add non-narrative material to their independent reading repertoire. As already noted, NAEP data indicate that diverse independent reading, including both stories and information books, is associated with higher reading comprehension (Campbell et al., 1995).

Because sustained silent reading should be a time when children read materials they want to read, teachers should not force children to read things that do not appeal to them. But teachers can take many steps to motivate children to expand their reading choices (Dreher, 1998). Teachers must be sure children know that information books and other non-narrative resources are appropriate during daily silent reading time. By using more information text in daily read-alouds (Recommendation 1, above), teachers signal the appropriateness of this type of book. And because children frequently seek out for their own reading the books teachers read in class, reading aloud from information books will raise the amount of independent information text reading.

In addition, teachers can highlight the appropriateness of diverse reading with reading logs or forms on which children jot down the date, the title they have read, and the category of their book. Children may even color code their entries by type of book. Such forms may differ in complexity by grade level but have in common the purpose of heightening children's awareness of just how much they are reading over a period of time and the diversity of that reading.

Teachers should also encourage more diverse independent reading by showcasing the variety of available books and resources in the media center and the classroom library. As is apparent in Chapter 5 by Chambliss and McKillop (this volume), good library collections at both the classroom and school level are very important to children's reading achievement. The effective use of books and resources includes showing children where to find information books in the school media center. But, even more importantly, teachers need to stock their classroom libraries with lots of information books as well as stories. Duke's (in press) research showed information books to be scarce in first-grade class libraries. Yet Kletzien and Szabo (1998) found that, when given a choice, first, second, and third graders reported that they would chose information books at least as often as stories. If we want to increase the variety of children's reading, then information resources, attractively displayed, must be easily accessible right in the classroom.

CONCLUSION

This chapter has offered recommendations to guide teachers as they seek to interweave learning to read and reading for learning. Specifically, teachers are advised to:

- Incorporate information books into daily read-alouds.
- Infuse information text into the materials used to teach reading.
- Teach strategies and text features that will allow children to comprehend both narrative and information text.
- Provide instructional activities that include writing information text.
- Help children learn to integrate information across multiple texts.
- Guide children to engage in inquiry.
- Integrate reading/language arts and content areas in thematic units.
- Encourage children to engage in diverse independent reading.

Elementary school children must learn to read fluently and capably. Further, they must be able to learn from what they read. But they also need to be motivated to read. By balancing learning to read and reading for learning, teachers increase the likelihood of producing readers who can interact capably with new information and who are also motivated to read.

RECOMMENDED READINGS

Beck, I. L., McKeown, M. G., Hamilton, R. L., & Kucan, L. (1997). *Questioning the Author: An approach for enhancing student engagement with text.* Newark, DE: International Reading Association.

The authors present a detailed explanation of their QtA technique designed to help children learn to comprehend what they read in textbooks. The authors include excerpts from transcripts of class discussions to illustrate how QtA can be used for both narrative and expository text.

Cudd, E. T., & Roberts, L. (1989). Using writing to enhance content area learning in the primary grades. *The Reading Teacher, 42,* 392–404.

This article provides many examples of paragraph frames that teachers can use to help young children write about the new information they are learning in content areas. These frames signal the structure of common expository text structures and help children move from narrative to expository reading and writing.

Doiron, R. (1994). Using nonfiction in a read-aloud program: Letting the facts speak for themselves. *The Reading Teacher, 47,* 616–624.

Doiron presents a detailed argument in favor of adding nonfiction to readalouds. He includes an annotated list of suggested books and closes the article with a list of eight points to remember in reading aloud nonfiction.

Duthie, C. (1996). *True stories: Nonfiction literacy in the primary classroom.* York, ME: Stenhouse.

This easy-to-read book by a first-grade teacher offers lots of examples of how to expand children's literacy instruction to include nonfiction. It includes chapters on nonfiction reading workshops, nonfiction writing workshop, and a special focus on biography. Teachers who want to include more exposition should note that many of the examples, while nonfiction, still tend to be narrative in form.

Horowitz, R., & Freeman, S. H. (1995). Robots versus spaceships: The role of discussion in kindergartners' and second graders' preferences for science texts. *The Reading Teacher, 49,* 30–40.

This study found that discussion can influence children's preference for a science text that they may initially find of limited interest or even unappealing. With discussion, children preferred an expository science book over a narrative science book. This paper contains many specific ideas on using discussion to get children interested and involved in listening to expository text.

REFERENCES

Alexander, P. A. (1997). Knowledge seeking and self-schema: A case for the motivational dimensions of exposition. *Educational Psychologist, 32,* 83–94.

Allington, R. L. (1977). If they don't read much, how they ever gonna get good? *Journal of Reading, 21,* 57–61.

Armbruster, B. B., Anderson, T. H., Armstrong, J. O., Wise, M. A., Janisch, C., & Meyer, L. A. (1991). Reading and questioning in content area lessons. *Journal of Reading Behavior, 23,* 35–59.

Armbruster, B. B., & Gudbrandsen, B. (1986). Reading comprehension instruction in social studies programs. *Reading Research Quarterly, 21,* 36–48.

Avery, C. (1993). *And with a light touch: Learning about reading, writing and teaching with first graders.* Portsmouth, NH: Heinemann.

Baker, L., & Wigfield, A. (1999). Dimensions of children's motivation for reading and their relations to reading activity and reading achievement. *Reading Research Quarterly, 34,* 452–477.

Baumann, J. F., & Bergeron, B. S. (1993). Story map instruction using children's literature: Effects on first graders' comprehension of central narrative elements. *Journal of Reading Behavior, 25,* 407–437.

Baumann, J. F., & Ivey, G. (1997). Delicate balances: Striving for curricular and instructional equilibrium in a second-grade, literature/strategy-based classroom. *Reading Research Quarterly, 32,* 244–275.

Beck, J. L., & McKeown, M. G. (1991). Conditions of vocabulary acquisition. In R. Barr, M. L. Kamil, P. Mosenthal, & P. D. Pearson (Eds.), *Handbook of reading research* (Vol. 2, pp. 789–814). New York: Longman.

Beck, I. L., McKeown, M. G., Hamilton, R. L., & Kucan, L. (1997). *Questioning the author: An approach for enhancing student engagement with text.* Newark, DE: International Reading Association.

Blachowicz, C., & Fisher, P. (1996). *Teaching vocabulary in all classrooms.* Upper Saddle River, NJ: Merrill/Prentice Hall.

Braunger, J., & Lewis, J. P. (1997). *Building a knowledge base in reading.* Portland, OR: Northwest Regional Educational Laboratory's Curriculum & Instruction Services [copublished with the International Reading Association & the National Council of Teachers of English].

Bredekamp, S., & Copple, C. (Eds.). (1997). *Developmentally appropriate practice in early childhood programs* (rev. ed.). Washington, DC: National Association for the Education of Young Children.

Bryan, J. (1998) K-W-W-L: Questioning the known. *The Reading Teacher, 51,* 618–620.

Campbell, J. R., Kapinus, B. A., & Beatty, A. S. (1995). *Interviewing children about their literacy experiences: Data from NAEP's Integrated Reading Performance Record (IRPR) at grade 4.* Washington, DC: U.S. Departent of Education, National Center for Educational Statistics.

Caswell, L. C., & Duke, N. (1998). Non-narrative as a catalyst for literacy development. *Language Arts, 75,* 108–117.

Chall, J. S., Jacobs, V. A., & Baldwin, E. (1990). *The reading crisis: Why poor children fall behind.* Cambridge, MA: Harvard University Press.

Chapman, J. W., & Tunmer, W. E. (1997). A longitudinal study of beginning reading achievement and reading self-concept. *British Journal of Educational Psychology, 67,* 279–291.

Cudd, E. T., & Roberts, L. (1989). Using writing to enhance content area learning in the primary grades. *The Reading Teacher, 42,* 392–404.

Cunningham, A. E., & Stanovich, K. E. (1991). Tracking the unique effects of print exposure in children: Associations with vocabulary, general knowledge, and spelling. *Journal of Educational Psychology, 83,* 264–274.

Daniels, H. (1990). Young readers and writers reach out: Developing a sense of audience. In T. Shanahan (Ed.), *Reading and writing together: New perspectives for the classroom* (pp. 99–124). Norwood, MA: Christopher-Gordon.

Doiron, R. (1994). Using nonfiction in a read-aloud program: Letting the facts speak for themselves. *The Reading Teacher, 47,* 616–624.

Dreher, M. J. (1995). *Sixth-grade researchers: Posing questions, finding information, and writing a report* (Reading Research Rep. No. 40). Athens, GA: Universities of Georgia & Maryland, National Reading Research Center.

Dreher, M. J. (1998). Motivating children to read more nonfiction. *The Reading Teacher, 52,* 414–417.

Dreher, M. J., Davis, K. A., Waynant, P., & Clewell, S. F. (1998). Fourth-grade researchers: Helping children develop strategies for finding and using information. *National Reading Conference Yearbook, 47,* 311–322.

Dreher, M. J., & Sammons, R. B. (1994). Fifth-graders' search for information in a textbook. *Journal of Reading Behavior, 26,* 301–314.

Duke, N. K. (in press). 3.6 minutes per day: The scarcity of informational texts in first grade. *Reading Research Quarterly.*

Duke, N. K., & Kays, J. (1998). "Can I say 'Once upon a time'?": Kindergarten children developing knowledge of information book language. *Early Childhood Research Quarterly, 13,* 295–318.

Durkin, D. (1978/1979). What classroom observations reveal about reading comprehension instruction. *Reading Research Quarterly, 15*, 481–533.

Duthie, C. (1996). *True stories: Nonfiction literacy in the primary classroom.* York, ME: Stenhouse.

Eckhoff, B. (1983). How reading affects children's writing. *Language Arts, 60,* 607–616.

Eckhoff, B. (1986, April). *How basal reading texts affect children's writing.* Paper presented at the American Educational Research Association (EDRS: ED 276 969), San Francisco, CA.

Elley, W. B. (1989). Vocabulary acquisition from listening to stories. *Reading Research Quarterly, 24,* 174–187.

Feitelson, P., Kita, D., & Goldstein, Z. (1986). Effects of listening to series stories on first graders' comprehension and use of language. *Research in Teaching of English, 20,* 339–356.

Fisher, C. W., & Hiebert, E. H. (1990). Characteristics of tasks in two approaches to literature instruction. *Elementary School Journal, 91,* 3–18.

Freeman, E. B., & Person, D. G. (1998). *Connecting informational children's books with content area learning.* Boston: Allyn & Bacon.

Freppon, P. A., & Dahl, K. L. (1998). Theory and research into practice: Balanced instruction: Insights and considerations. *Reading Research Quarterly, 33,* 240–251.

Guillaume, A. M. (1998). Learning with text in the primary grades. *The Reading Teacher, 51,* 476–486.

Guthrie, J. T., & McCann, A. D. (1996). Idea circles: Peer collaborations for conceptual learning. In L. B. Gambrell & J. F. Almasi (Eds.), *Lively discussions! Fostering engaged reading* (pp. 87–105). Newark, DE: International Reading Association.

Guthrie, J. T., Van Meter, P., Hancock, G. R., Alao, S., Anderson, E., & McCann, A. (1998). Does Concept-Oriented Reading Instruction increase strategy use and conceptual learning from text? *Journal of Educational Psychology, 90,* 261–278.

Guthrie, J. T., Van Meter, P., McCann, A., Wigfield, A., Bennett, L., Poundstone, C., Rice, M. E., Faibisch, F., Hunt, B., & Mitchell, A. (1996). Growth of literacy engagement: Changes in motivations and strategies during Concept-Oriented Reading Instruction. *Reading Research Quarterly, 31,* 306–333.

Hiebert, E. H., & Fisher, C. W. (1990). Whole language: Three themes for the future. *Educational Leadership, 47,* 62–64.

Hoffman, J. V. (1992). Critical reading/thinking across the curriculum: Using I-charts to support learning. *Language Arts, 69,* 121–127.

Hoffman, J. V., McCarthey, S. J., Abbot, J., Christian, C., Corman, L., Curry, C., Dressman, M., Elliott, B., Matherne, D., & Stahle, D. (1994). So what's new in the new basals? A focus on first grade. *Journal of Reading Behavior, 26,* 47–73.

Hoffman, J. V., Roser, N. L., & Battle, J. (1993). Reading aloud in classrooms: From modal to a "model." *The Reading Teacher, 46,* 496–505.

Horowitz, R., & Freeman, S. H. (1995). Robots versus spaceships: The role of discussion in kindergartners' and second graders' preferences for science texts. *The Reading Teacher, 49,* 30–40.

International Reading Association & National Association for the Education of Young Children. (1998). Learning to read and write: Developmentally appropriate practices for young children. *The Reading Teacher, 52,* 193–216.

International Reading Association & National Council of Teachers of English. (1996). *Standards for the English language arts.* Newark, DE: International Reading Association.

Kamil, M. L., & Lane, D. (1997, December). *Using information text for first-grade reading instruction.* Paper presented at the meeting of the National Reading Conference, Scottsdale, AZ.

Kletzien, S. B., & Szabo, R. J. (1998, December). *Information text or narrative text? Children's preferences revisited.* Paper presented at the meeting of the National Reading Conference, Austin, TX.

Klingner, J. K., Vaughn, S., & Schumm, J. S. (1998). Collaborative strategic reading during social studies in heterogeneous fourth-grade classrooms. *Elementary School Journal, 99,* 3–21.

Korkeamäki, R., Tiainen, O., & Dreher, M. J. (1998). Helping Finnish second-graders make sense of their reading and writing in science projects. *National Reading Conference Yearbook, 47,* 334–344.

Langer, J. A., & Applebee, A. N. (1987). *How writing shapes thinking.* Urbana, IL: National Council of Teachers of English.

Langer, J. A., Applebee, A. N., Mullis, I. V. S., & Foertsch, M. A. (1990). *Learning to read in our nation's schools: Instruction and achievement in 1988 at grades 4, 8, and 12.* Princeton, NJ: Educational Testing Service.

Lewis, M., Wray, D., & Rospigliosi, P. (1994). ". . . And I want it in your own words." *The Reading Teacher, 47,* 528–536.

Lipson, M. Y., Valencia, S. W., Wixson, K. K., & Peters, C. W. (1993). Integration and thematic teaching: Integration to improve teaching and learning. *Language Arts, 70,* 252–263.

Mallett, M. (1992). *Making facts matter.* London: Chapman Ltd.

Many, J., Fyfe, R., Lewis, G., & Mitchell, E. (1996). Traversing the topical landscape: Exploring students' self-directed reading–writing–research processes. *Reading Research Quarterly, 31,* 12–35.

Mason, J. M., Peterman, C. L., Powell, B. M., & Kerr, B. M. (1989). Reading and writing attempts by kindergartners after book reading by teachers. In J. M. Mason (Ed.), *Reading and writing connections* (pp. 105–120). Boston: Allyn & Bacon.

McCombs, B. L. (1997). Commentary: Reflections on motivations for reading—Through the looking glass of theory, practice, and reader experiences, *Educational Psychologist, 32,* 125–134.

McCormick, C., & Mason, J. M. (1986). *Use of little books at home: A minimal intervention strategy for fostering early reading* (Tech. Rep. No. 388). Urbana: University of Illinois, Center for the Study of Reading.

McGee, L., & Richgels, D. (1985). Teaching expository text structure to elementary students. *The Reading Teacher, 38,* 739–748.

McKenna, M. C., Ellsworth, R. A., & Kear, D. J. (1995). Children's attitudes towards reading: A national survey. *Reading Research Quarterly, 30,* 934–956.

Morrow, L. M., Pressley, M., Smith, J. K., & Smith, M. (1997). The effect of a literature-based program integrated into literacy and science instruction with children from diverse background. *Reading Research Quarterly, 32,* 54–76.

Moss, B., & Newton, E. (1998, December). *An examination of the informational text genre in recent basal readers.* Paper presented at the meeting of the National Reading Conference, Austin, TX.

National Council for the Social Studies [NCSS]. (1994). *Expectations of excellence: Curriculum standards for social studies.* Washington, DC: Author.

National Council of Teachers of Mathematics [NCTM], Commission on Standards for School Mathematics. (1989). *Curriculum and evaluation standards for school mathematics.* Reston, VA: Author.

National Research Council. (1994). *National science education standards: An enhanced sampler.* Washington, DC: National Academy Press.

Neilsen, A. R., Rennie, B., & Connell, B. J. (1982). Allocation of instructional time to reading comprehension and study skills in intermediate social studies classrooms. In J. A. Niles & L. A. Harris (Eds.), *New inquiries in reading research and instruction: Thirty-first yearbook of the National Reading Conference* (pp. 81–84). Rochester, NY: National Reading Conference.

Newkirk, T. (1989). *More than stories: The range of children's writing.* Portsmouth, NH: Heinemann.

Ogle, D. M. (1986). K-W-L: A teaching model that develops active reading of expository text. *The Reading Teacher, 39,* 564–570.

Palincsar, A. S., Brown, A. L., & Campione, J. C. (1993). First-grade dialogues for knowledge acquisition and use. In E. Forman, N. Minick, & C. A. Stone (Eds.), *Contexts for learning: Sociocultural dynamics in children's development* (pp. 43–57). New York: Oxford University Press.

Pappas, C. C. (1993). Is narrative "primary"? Some insights from kindergartners' pretend readings of stories and information books. *Journal of Reading Behavior, 25,* 97–129.

Pappas, C. C., Kiefer, & Levstik, L. (1999). *An integrated language perspective in the elementary school* (3rd ed.). New York: Longman.

Pearson, P. D., & Fielding, L. (1991). Comprehension instruction. In R. Barr, M. L. Kamil, P. B. Mosenthal, & P. D. Pearson (Eds.), *Handbook of reading research* (Vol. 2, pp. 815–860). New York: Longman.

Pressley, M. (1998). *Reading instruction that works: The case of balanced teaching.* New York: Guilford Press.

Pressley, M., Rankin, J., & Yokoi, L. (1996). A survey of instructional practices of primary teachers nominated as effective in promoting literacy. *Elementary School Journal, 96,* 363–384.

Richgels, D. J. (1997, December). *Informational texts in kindergarten: Reading and writing to learn.* Paper presented at the meeting of the National Reading Conference, Scottsdale, AZ.

Romance, N. R., & Vitale, M. R. (1992). A curriculum strategy that expands time for in-depth elementary science instruction by using science-based reading strategies: Effects of a year-long study in grade four. *Journal of Research in Science Teaching, 29,* 545–554.

Rosenhouse, J., Feitelson, D., Kita, B., & Goldstein, Z. (1997). Interactive reading aloud to Israeli first graders: Its contribution to literacy development. *Reading Research Quarterly, 32,* 168–183.

Rupley, W. H., Logan, J. W., & Nichols, W. D. (1998). Vocabulary instruction in a balanced reading program. *The Reading Teacher, 52,* 336–346.

Sanacore, J. (1991). Expository and narrative text: Balancing young children's reading experiences. *Childhood Education, 67,* 211–214.

Shanahan, T. (1988). The reading–writing relationship: Seven instructional practices. *The Reading Teacher, 41,* 636–647.

Shanahan, T. (1997). Reading–writing relationships, thematic units, inquiry learning . . . In pursuit of effective integrated literacy instruction. *The Reading Teacher, 51,* 12–19.

Shanahan, T., Robinson, B., & Schneider, M. (1995). Avoiding some of the pitfalls of thematic units. *The Reading Teacher, 48,* 718–719.

Shymansky, J. A., Yore, L. D., & Good, R. (1991). Elementary school teachers' beliefs about and perceptions of elementary school science, science reading, science textbooks, and supportive instructional factors. *Journal of Research in Science Teaching, 28,* 437–454.

Snow, C. E., Burns, M. S., & Griffin, P. (Eds.). (1998). *Preventing reading difficulties in young children.* Washington, DC: National Academy Press.

Spivey, N. N., & King, J. R. (1989). Readers as writers composing from sources. *Reading Research Quarterly, 24,* 7–26.

Stahl, S. A., Hynd, C. R., Britton, B. K., McNish, M. M., & Bosquet, D. (1996). What happens when students read multiple source documents in history? *Reading Research Quarterly, 31,* 430–458.

Sticht, T. G., & James, J. H. (1984). Listening and reading. In P. D. Pearson, R. Barr, M. L. Kamil, & P. B. Mosenthal (Eds.), *Handbook of reading research* (pp. 293–318). New York: Longman.

Strickland, D. S. (1995). Pre-elementary programs: A model for professional development. In

S. B. Wepner, J. T. Feeley, & D. S. Strickland (Eds.), *The administration and supervision of reading programs* (2nd ed., pp. 41–58). New York: Teachers College Press.

Tierney, R., & Cunningham, J. (1984). Reading comprehension. In P. D. Pearson, R. Barr, M. L. Kamil, & P. B. Mosenthal (Eds.), *Handbook of reading research* (pp. 609–655). New York: Longman.

Trabasso, T. (1994). The power of the narrative. In F. Lehr & J. Osborn (Eds.), *Reading, language, and literacy: Instruction for the twenty-first century* (pp. 187–200). Hillsdale, NJ: Erlbaum.

Turner, J. (1995). The influence of classroom contexts on young children's motivation for literacy. *Reading Research Quarterly, 30*, 410–441.

Vacca, R. T., & Vacca, J. L. (1999). *Content area reading: Literacy and learning across the curriculum.* New York: Longman.

Wendler, D., Samuels, S. J., & Moore, V. K. (1989). The comprehension instruction of award-winning teachers, teachers with master's degrees, and other teachers. *Reading Research Quarterly, 24*, 382–401.

Wigfield, A., Eccles, J. S., Yoon, K. S., Harold, R. D., Arbreton, A., Freedman-Doan, C., & Blumenfeld, P. B. (1997). Change in children's competence beliefs and subjective task values across the elementary school years: A three-year study. *Journal of Educational Psychology, 89*, 451–469.

Wray, D., & Lewis, M. (1992). Primary children's use of information books. *Reading, 19*, 19–24.

CHAPTER FIVE

Creating a Print- and Technology-Rich Classroom Library to Entice Children to Read

MARILYN J. CHAMBLISS
ANN MARGARET MCKILLOP

The effective classroom library provides a print- and technology-rich environment that invites children to read and promotes engaged reading. Print represents a variety of genres including information books, narratives, poetry, references, and multimedia. A variety of cultural backgrounds is represented in the collection. Materials encompass a range of difficulty levels and interests so that they are accessible and appropriate to all students.

The more children read, the better readers they become. Few would argue with this observation. To be sure, educators might disagree on how much direct instruction should accompany extensive opportunities to read, but the truth is that practice leads to improvement (see Byrnes, Chapter 9, this volume). Children who are surrounded by material to read, whether printed on paper, accompanied by audiotape, or dancing across a computer screen, are far more likely to read regularly than children who have little or no access to reading material—another rather obvious observation with which few would quarrel. Well-designed classroom libraries can play an important role in children's reading engagement and achievement. Results from the National Assessment of Educational Progress (NAEP) and several research studies confirm these commonsense notions. Classroom libraries and reading achievement are related. Other research fine-tunes these results. It turns out that how the library is integrated into the overall reading instruction, the number and type of paper and electronic materials in the library, and the library's physical setup affect children's engagement with reading and their achievement. These positive features of classroom libraries are particularly important for children who are at risk for reading difficulties due to their home and neighborhood environments or their proficiency in English.

This chapter reviews research that addresses aspects of effective classroom libraries. It describes a framework for explaining the positive effects of classroom libraries, the characteristics of effective classroom libraries, and practical suggestions for how teachers can create classroom libraries that will enhance the engagement and achievement of all children. The chapter highlights both the use of technology in classroom libraries and the special impact that well-designed classroom libraries can have on children at risk for developing reading difficulties.

THE INFLUENCE OF CLASSROOM LIBRARIES
ON CHILDREN'S ENGAGEMENT AND ACHIEVEMENT

Extensive reading builds children's literacy skills and strategies. If the experience is pleasurable, children come to value reading. A wonderful cycle begins. Children who value reading choose to read, which improves their skills and strategies, which renders reading more pleasurable, which leads them to value reading even more highly. The classroom library can play an important role in this cycle, supporting both children's engagement and their achievement.

The Effect of Classroom Libraries on Children Who Read Well

Using formal assessments, educators have looked at the impact of school libraries on children's achievement. Analyses have revealed not only that school libraries positively affect student reading achievement but that their influence on student engagement is an important aspect of the effect. According to an analysis of NAEP data, fourth-grade reading comprehension scores were associated with the number of books per student in the school library (Krashen, 1995). Another study found that the size of the library media center in schools was strongly related to student scores on a standardized reading assessment (Lance, 1994). In both studies, the larger the number of books, the higher were children's reading scores.

Other analyses suggest that the most important factor is not the number of books per se but whether the library enhances children's engagement with reading. As Wigfield (Chapter 7, this volume) explains, children seek to do whatever increases their feeling of competence and self-determination and shun whatever makes them feel incompetent or coerced. Being able to choose what and when to read enhances children's feelings of competence and self-determination. Obviously, the greater the number of resources in a library, the greater the number of possible choices. A second analysis of fourth-grade NAEP scores showed that better school and public libraries were related to greater library use, which was related to more free reading, which was related to higher reading scores (Krashen, 1997/1998). This analysis also showed that fourth graders who reported choosing to read during free time had higher reading achievement scores than those who reported otherwise. These results supported an earlier study in which children in the 90th percentile on a standardized reading test chose to read 200 times as many minutes per day outside of school as did children at the 10th percentile (R. C. Anderson, Wilson, & Fielding, 1988). The classroom library, so much more readily accessible to children than the school or neighborhood library, could powerfully affect children's engagement with books and reading achievement.

Classroom libraries may well be most effective when embedded within a community of readers who recommend and share materials with one another. Educators have noted that avid readers often belong to communities of readers, typically originating at home, but including teachers and peers at school (Hiebert, Mervar, & Person, 1990). Indeed, across research studies (e.g., Elley, 1991; Neuman, in press) successful media centers and school or classroom libraries were found within literate communities where children and teachers read together and talked with one another about what they read.

The Effect of Classroom Libraries on Children at Risk
for Developing Reading Difficulties

The positive effects of classroom libraries are particularly valuable for children at risk for developing reading difficulties. Two important risk factors for children are the extent to which they come from literacy-impoverished environments or from families whose primary language is something other than English (Snow, Burns, & Griffin, 1998). In both of these cases, the classroom library may be the only setting within which children can choose from an abundance of children's materials and share their reading with adults and other children.

Socioeconomic status is typically linked to the type of literacy experiences children have outside of school (Sonnenschein & Schmidt, Chapter 12, this volume; Snow et al., 1998). It has been estimated that preschool children from low-income families start school with an average of 25 hours of shared reading with an adult in contrast to approximately 1,000 hours for children from middle-class families (Adams, 1990). Researchers have found that children in a neighborhood that they described as working class and "underclass" had an average of 0.4 age-appropriate books at home and approximately 110,000 books in their neighborhood public library, in contrast to children from an upper-middle-class neighborhood who had an average of 199.2 age-appropriate books at home and 200,595 books in their neighborhood public libraries (Smith, Constantino, & Krashen, 1997). A well-designed classroom library could provide resources unavailable in children's homes or neighborhoods.

Access to a classroom library may be even more important for children learning English as a second language (Elley, 1991; Pucci, 1994). Ideally, young second language learners have opportunities to read in both their primary language and English. The development of literacy in children's primary language is strongly related to their literacy in English (Pucci, 1994). As they read in the language that they know, children develop literacy skills that they can use when they read less familiar English. Furthermore, one powerful way for children to learn English as a second language is to read extensively in English (Elley, 1991). In the United States, the average Spanish-speaking family with a limited-English-proficient student has been found to have only 22 books of all kinds in its home (Ramirez, Yuen, Ramey, & Pasta, 1991). Even in heavily Spanish-speaking Los Angeles, elementary school libraries and public libraries in Spanish-speaking neighborhoods can have quite small collections of books for children in Spanish (Pucci, 1994). Classroom libraries with a selection of books for each of the languages represented in the classroom could provide children with important resources unavailable to them anywhere else.

Children at risk for never learning to read well have benefited from what educators have called classroom "book floods." A book flood brings a large collection of children's books into a classroom. Neuman (in press) found that a book flood positively affected concepts of print, letter knowledge, concepts of writing, and narrative competence for economically disadvantaged preschoolers. Strikingly, these differences held up 6 months later for children who entered kindergarten the following year. A series of studies summarized by Elley (1991), most of which were conducted in the South Pacific, focused on elementary school children learning to read a second language. The effects of the book floods were measured by Elley using reading comprehension, listening comprehension, word recognition, vocabulary, sentence syntax, written composition, and oral language measures in English, the children's second language. Children encountering book floods consistently scored higher on all measures than did children in control groups (Elley, 1991).

The cumulative results from these studies are impressive. However, imbedding the library in a community of readers is particularly important for children who are at risk of never reading well. Besides a large increase in available books, children in book flood studies also heard books read by their teacher (Elley, 1991; Neuman, in press), listened to books on tape as they read (Elley, 1991), and engaged in whole-class and small-group discussions around what they were reading (Elley, 1991; Neuman, in press). An important facet of both Neuman's (in press) work with child care centers and many of Elley's (1991) South Pacific studies was the professional development and support offered to child caregivers and teachers as they learned to provide a literate community for the children in their classes.

In summary, research suggests that the well-designed classroom library can be the centerpiece for a community of readers, motivating children to read and engaging them in a cycle that promotes the development of literacy. The classroom library provides children easy access to books. The books are at hand—not down the hall, although the school library can be a wonderful resource for the classroom library; not outside the building, although the public library can be another rich resource. However, children must have free access to the books and be able to choose whatever they want to read, and the teacher must integrate opportunities to interact with the children over their books.

THE CHARACTERISTICS OF WELL-DESIGNED CLASSROOM LIBRARIES

Well-designed libraries have two critical features: quality reading materials and an inviting environment. The following subsections describe reading materials that can enhance children's literacy, types of materials that children choose to read, and classroom environments that encourage children to read.

Principles for Choosing Materials to Enhance Children's Literacy

This section discusses the characteristics of quality narrative and expository writing. It fine-tunes this discussion by presenting criteria for selecting the optimum "fit" between the children in a classroom and the materials in the library.

Children have much to gain in reading literature written specially for them by able writers and illustrators (Guthrie, 1996; International Reading Association [IRA] & National Council of Teachers of English [NCTE], 1996). In creating an effective classroom library, teachers will want to choose narratives such as picture books, fairy tales, and contemporary stories that exemplify the characteristics of good literature. Good literature is aesthetic, giving pleasure and stirring the imagination (Rosenblatt, 1978). It is thematic, and the themes are universal, important themes that weave throughout literature (love, danger, betrayal, and so on). Good literature has a compelling plot, intriguing characters, and an interesting setting, all carefully chosen to communicate the theme. Consider *Charlotte's Web* by E. B. White. The story of the relationship between a pig facing slaughter and a spider with the natural life span of a season develops the themes of friendship and love, all in the setting of a barnyard and a pen at the state fair. The compelling story is communicated through the use of literary devices: metaphor, imagery, rhyme, and other figures of speech (IRA & NCTE, 1996). Every word has been chosen to advance the theme and enhance the reader's literary experience.

Good literature offers a greatly expanded world to children, transporting young readers across time and space. When children enter the world of a story, they are drawn into the lives of the characters and experience whatever joy, sorrow, fear, or peace that the characters experience (Wolf & Heath, 1992). They learn that literature can connect with their own experiences, but also offers new, contrasting views of the world (IRA & NCTE, 1996). In the process children increase their reading competence. They learn about the word, sentence, and plot patterns used by good writers as well as important literary themes. They gain expertise, not only becoming more fluent, but also increasingly able to enjoy and appreciate the special literary devices that the author and illustrator have built into the text. The word patterns in predictable stories, nursery rhymes, and other poetry intended for children can support children's developing print skills and help them enjoy the musical rhythms of literary language (IRA & NCTE, 1996). Through reading fairy tales, as well as well-designed contemporary stories, young children learn the different patterns by which narratives develop.

Traditionally, classrooms for elementary school children have focused far more on literature than information text, and classroom libraries have had more narratives, or storybooks, than exposition, the kind of writing prevalent in information text (Dreher, Chapter 4, this volume). Educators believed that young children could quite naturally and easily read stories but would struggle with the far more formal patterns in expository writing (Chambliss & Calfee, 1998). It is true that young children beg their parents to tell them stories and often seem quite comfortable with simple story patterns by the time they reach school. After all, even if they have not been read to, young children have typically watched untold hours of narrative on television. However, children are curious about the world around them, too. Unless their early questions have consistently gone unanswered, they continue frequently to ask "why" and "how" well into elementary school and beyond. Exposition can answer their questions and introduce them to the vast, intriguing world of information texts.

Unfortunately, exposition written for young children tends to be far less well crafted than are storybooks. Perhaps authors believe that children do not know the rhetorical patterns used by good writers to design exposition and therefore that it is pointless, or maybe confusing, to adhere to a pattern. Whatever the reason, information books for young readers often are not very coherent, presenting bits and pieces of information that do not relate with one another. Even page formats can be confusing: a melange of captioned pictures, graphics, and boxed-off factlets. Not surprisingly, comprehension research with exposition has consistently shown that all readers, young and old, proficient and struggling, are negatively affected by confusing, incoherent writing (see Chambliss & Calfee, 1998). Even excellent readers can feel incompetent when trying to understand poorly designed text.

The well-designed classroom library gives children free access to reading materials that will increase their sense of efficacy. Therefore, it is crucial that teachers choose comprehensible exposition that does not needlessly confuse young readers. Three characteristics have been shown consistently to enhance children's comprehension of exposition: familiarity (e.g., Freebody & Anderson, 1983), structural coherence (e.g., Beck, McKeown, Sinatra, & Loxterman, 1991), and interest value (Hidi & Baird, 1988). Teachers should choose information text that links unfamiliar content to the familiar, is well organized, and has an engaging style.

Snow Is Falling, by Franklyn M. Branley, and illustrated by Holly Keller, can demonstrate this point. This small book is intended for early readers. It is a picture book with one paragraph of several short sentences in large type per page. The book begins by describing for several pages the experience of being in the snow. The middle of the book addresses the questions, What does snow do? Is it good for plants? Is it good for animals? Is it good for you and me? The book ends by reviewing what has been covered: snow is fun to run, roll, and ski in; snow gives us water; snow is good for plants and animals; snow is good for people; snow is good for you and me. This example connects new content about snow with children's familiar experiences (even children who live where it never snows undoubtedly have watched movies and television shows where people are experiencing snow). It is well organized, considering one major topic at a time and progressing logically. Each page has pictures that match the written content. Examples have been chosen to pique children's interest. To describe what can happen when snow melts too fast, the text tells children, "There is more water than streams can carry. The streams overflow. There may be floods" (Branley, 1986, p. 26). The accompanying picture shows children in a rowboat looking with concern at two partially submerged houses, one of which has a cat on the roof, a predicament that should attract young children's interest.

As well written as a piece of literature or an exposition may be, it is important that the content, the reading level, and the language "fit" the particular readers in the class. The primary purpose of the classroom library is to encourage children to choose freely and to read independently.

Content is a tricky issue. Of course teachers will want to choose content that they would like their students to know. As children study about the world around them in science, social studies, and math, they will raise questions. Ideally the classroom library would include books that addressed at least some of their questions, introduced them to intriguing puzzles considered by experts, and added to the knowledge children were gaining during instruction. The content of information materials in the classroom library should be matched to children's curiosity in general and not limited to the classroom curriculum.

If children are to experience success when reading materials from the classroom library, it is important for the library to include materials that match the levels at which children in the class can read independently. Depending on the variety of reading levels in the class, elementary school teachers should consider including picture books, both narrative and expository (Martinez, Roser, Worthy, Strecker, & Gough, 1997), as well as longer books with chapters (Fractor, Woodruff, Martinez, & Teale, 1993), and children's magazines (Morrow, 1991). So that children can learn to appreciate and become comfortable with different types of reading, the classroom library should provide a variety of genres including stories, exposition, and poetry (Fractor et al., 1993; Guthrie, 1996; Morrow, 1991).

Being able to decode the squiggles on the page into meaningful text automatically is the first, although certainly not the only, requisite for proficient reading. Teachers of beginning readers would want to include materials that enhance children's ability to decode. One solution is to include books with read-along tapes (and books on CD–ROMs) that give less able readers decoding support (McKenna, 1998). Not surprisingly, children's favorite choices often include books with some sort of verbal accompaniment (Allen & Eisele, 1990; Elley, 1991). Another solution is to provide decodable and predictable stories, two different types of written materials that support decoding ease, although educators disagree on the relative effectiveness of these text types (see also Baker, Chapter 2, and Graham & Harris, Chapter 3, this volume). Decodable texts include words with phonemic similarity to those the children already know or have been taught by the teacher prior to reading a new selection. Predictable stories repeat story or format elements such as questions and answers or repeated conversational patterns. One group of educators (Beck, 1997, 1998; Kameenui

& Simmons, 1997) believes that children who have not made the connection between print and speech are unlikely to improve their reading skills without the help of decodable text. Another group (Allington, 1997; Moustafa, 1997) maintains that decodable text stories, in contrast to predictable stories, are contrived and unnatural and do not allow young readers to use what they already know about language and their knowledge of the world to learn more about the letter–sound correspondences that they do not know. Both types of text are valuable for different reasons. Depending on the decoding proficiencies of the children in a classroom, teachers should consider including materials that support children's reading, employing both predictable and decodable stories if necessary.

It is also important that materials reflect the cultural backgrounds of children in the class. Perhaps of even greater importance, all class libraries, whether the children come from many cultures or only one, should have collections of books that reflect the cultural and ethnic diversity of society so that all children can learn to appreciate our shared human literary heritage (Fractor et al., 1993; IRA & NCTE, 1996).

Finally, in classrooms where children's primary language is not English, the library should include at least a few children's books per child in the child's native language as well as an extensive collection in English to enhance students' proficiency in both their primary language and English. It is not uncommon to find close to 20 separate primary languages in a single California classroom, for example, and other states (e.g., Maryland) may not be far behind (Cohn & Constable, 1998). Classroom libraries that include children's books in each language represented in a classroom would enhance both children's literacy development and their content knowledge (Pucci, 1994).

Children's Actual Selections

Quality children's literature and well-crafted exposition—who could argue with giving children access to such materials? Perhaps not surprisingly, however, children, when given the choice, may select on different bases than their teachers might wish. Asked to choose among two children's classics, two popular books that one might find at the supermarket, and a text anthology that was part of a published basal reading series, second graders chose the "popular" books—one was about Popeye (Hiebert et al., 1990). First graders selecting freely from their classroom library frequently chose books with exaggerated print size, complete paragraphs on a page or double page, familiar vocabulary, close correspondence of pictures and text, and consistent placement of the text on the page (Lysaker, 1997). When asked, they explained that they chose these books because they thought they could read them and avoided books without these features because they judged them to be too difficult. Interestingly, they also tended to choose more difficult books without these features, alternating between easy and more challenging books (Lysaker, 1997), a pattern that second graders seemed to follow as well (Martinez et al., 1997). First graders explained that they also tried to choose books that they thought would help them to become better readers. Lysaker (1997) noted that when the first graders chose to read together, they worked with one another to identify words rather than to share their aesthetic experiences.

Elementary school students who are considered good readers choose differently than less able readers. First graders already on the road to proficiency have been found to choose books with developed narrative structures as well as books with humor, apparently coming to value reading for the aesthetic experience it provides beyond the enjoyment of learning to read. Less able first-grade readers, in contrast, chose books with informative pictures that required no text reading and did not compel them to engage with print (Lysaker, 1997). Other work has shown fourth- and fifth-grade low achievers to choose books at the same readability level and length as chosen by high achievers but to be far less likely to finish the books than were the able readers (G. Anderson et al., 1985). Whether it is less able first-grade readers choosing picture books because decoding is painful and laborious or fourth- and sixth-grade readers choosing books that are too difficult for them to finish, the outcome is the same. Poorer readers are not choosing books that allow them to engage and practice with print.

Children's choices present some problems, particularly for those children who avoid print by choosing either picture books or materials that are far too difficult for them to read. Free choice alone is not going to improve the reading of less able readers who are choosing not to engage with the text. Even for more able readers, free choice may not lead to as much improvement as could occur if they were choosing more often for "literary" reasons. Surrounding children with great materials will not, on its own, lead to extensive reading of those materials, particularly for young readers who struggle to read. As we discussed above, children are more likely to use the classroom library effectively if it is part of a classroom reading community.

Embedding the Classroom Library in a Reading Community

Children can learn to select well if they are part of a reading community where teacher and children alike use literary standards to evaluate what they read. During whole-class and small-group discussions, children gain a literary lens that they can use to select what to read (Hiebert et al., 1990). Having heard a story or information text read out loud by their teacher supports children's efforts to decode and subsequently comprehend it on their own. Young readers who are already familiar with a book are likely to choose to try to read it independently (Hiebert et al., 1990). Apparently, they choose what they have already heard because they believe that they can read it. Because less able readers often choose material that they are unable to read independently, it is particularly important that teachers read at least some books that less able readers can successfully decode (G. Anderson et al., 1985).

Being members of such a reading community helps elementary school children choose more appropriately than children in textbook-based classrooms, as shown in a study by Hiebert et al. (1990). The literature-based reading communities had an abundance of trade books that were used as a part of the classroom routine. Teachers read from these books at least once a day. During the read-aloud, the teacher and children together discussed styles of authors and illustrators, content of books, and ways of selecting books by topic and difficulty level. Children who were asked if a book was the right level for them gave elaborated reasons for selecting particular books from the school library, referring to particular authors, illustrators, and topics that they like. In contrast, second graders in textbook-based classrooms explained that they were searching for books that "looked" exciting and interesting. These children did not select books as competently as children from literature-based reading communities. The books they chose were approximately one-half grade level more difficult than those chosen by children in classes that were reading communities.

Creating an Enticing Reading Environment

To be sure, having a collection of well-chosen materials within a reading community can have an impact on children's engagement and achievement. However, the physical features of the library are important as well. In the well-designed classroom library, children have easy access to all of the books, a comfortable place to read, room to discuss what they are reading with other children, and a place to interact imaginatively with what they are reading. Indeed, children will be more likely to choose to read during free time if the physical features of the classroom library are well designed (Morrow & Weinstein, 1982).

Not surprisingly, children gravitate toward classroom libraries that are physically attractive, highly visible, and an important part of the classroom (Morrow, 1991; Morrow & Weinstein, 1982). These libraries are clearly set apart from the rest of the room. They are large enough to accommodate several children and are carpeted, have large pillows, or have upholstered chairs for comfortable seating. In the primary grades, effective classroom libraries provide props such as flannel boards and puppets that children can use to act out and retell what they have read (Morrow, 1991).

Effective libraries for intermediate grades have art materials and costume boxes so that children can draw or act out their responses to their readings. At all grade levels, library areas promote children's access to reading. They include space for listening posts where children can listen to and read books on audiotape and for computers on which they can read materials on CD–ROM and explore the World Wide Web (WWW). Books are displayed both on open-faced shelving, so that children can see book covers, and on shelving that shows only the spines but can accommodate more books. Materials are catalogued so that books, tapes, and CDs are easy to locate.

Well-designed classroom libraries also provide a large choice for children. We have already discussed the variety of genres, cultures, and languages that teachers should consider. More specifically, educators recommend five to eight books per child (Fractor et al., 1993; Morrow, 1991) and suggest that some of the books be available in more than one copy so that several children can read and discuss the same text together (Fractor et al., 1993; Guthrie, 1996). Teachers should at least consider including some materials that do not necessarily reflect high literary standards. Particularly for less adept readers, research suggests that it is crucial to find written text with which they are willing to engage. Middle school children given subscriptions to two magazines related to their interests scored higher after 2 years on a standardized reading test than did a control group (Rucker, 1982). Middle school boys who reported heavy comic book reading also reported spending more time reading for pleasure than middle school boys who did not read comic books (Ujiie & Krashen, 1996). Neither of these types of reading materials met high literary standards. As an aside, it is important to note that even comic book stories develop some important literary themes, such as the conflict between good and evil.

THE PRACTICALITIES OF CREATING A WELL-DESIGNED CLASSROOM LIBRARY

Elementary schools are often cramped for space, with too many children in too small an area. These schools are customarily strapped for funds, with too many needs and too little money. Classroom libraries suffer. The researchers in one study (Fractor et al., 1993) surveyed 183 classrooms representative of the diverse socioeconomic and ethnic populations of a large metropolitan area in south Texas. They found that more than one-half of the classrooms had no area that could be identified as a library center. Of the classrooms that had libraries, most of them had too few books and were too cramped to have room for several children to act out stories with puppets or flannel boards. Compared with the requirements outlined above, these library centers fell short. The following subsections address how teachers can identify books that would enhance children's engagement and achievement, acquire a large range of books even with limited budgetary resources, design a classroom library given the reality of small space, and handle the logistics—keeping the books in order, responding to book destruction, and handling book loss.

Choosing Reading Materials to Enhance Children's Engagement and Achievement

To choose children's literature, teachers can consult several references. *The Reading Teacher*, the journal of the IRA that focuses on elementary school reading, periodically publishes reviews of exemplary children's books (e.g., IRA, 1998, 1999). Cullinan (1989) has written *Literature and the Child*. Huck, Hepler, and Hickman (1987) have written *Children's Literature in the Elementary School*. Another valuable resource is *The Reading Teacher's Book of Lists* (3rd ed.), prepared by Fry, Kress, and Fountoukidis (1993). This reference has a "Picture Books" list, a "Predictable Books" list, and a "Books to Read Aloud" list. It also lists the recipients of the Caldecott Medal and the Newbery Medal. Named for Randolph Caldecott, a famous English illustrator of books for children, the Caldecott Medal is awarded annually to the artist of the most distinguished American picture book for children published during the preceding year. The Newbery Medal, named after John Newbery, an 18th-century publisher of quality children's books, is awarded each year to the author of the most distinguished contribution to American literature for children.

These lists are only a starting point, however. To tailor the library to the interests and needs of the children in the classroom, the teacher's own judgment is invaluable. By reading prospective materials, the teacher can assess reading levels, coherence, familiarity, and interest. Teachers also can rely on recommendations from school and public librarians, as well as from the children themselves. Educators have noted that members in communities of readers, young and old alike, recommend books to one another and rely on one another's recommendations in making book choices. Indeed, all of the second-grade reading communities described by Hiebert et al. (1990) had systems for children's recommendations, such as file boxes for comments about books. By collecting children's recommendations and through shared reading with children, teachers will become progressively more familiar with their preferences.

Gathering a Large Collection of Books

Textbook publishers, who for decades have produced basal reader series, in the last several years have packaged classroom literature sets. Teachers can be drawn to these sets as the core of their classroom libraries. School systems, accustomed to spending money on published materials, may well feel more comfortable buying packaged materials from textbook publishers than appropriating budget lines to reimburse teachers for their own purchases.

Allen and Eisele (1990) examined publisher sets and conducted case studies of children and teachers as they put the sets to use in literature-based classrooms. The researchers found that while the collections differed somewhat by grade, each set contained 80–85 paperbacks, including 30–35 copies of one book for whole-class reading; three small-group books of 10 copies each; 5–10 "buddy" books for grades 2–6, two copies each; and 10–20 individual paperbacks for reading aloud in kindergarten and first grade. The publisher libraries also included book and author posters, individual bookmarks, cassette tapes for kindergarten through second grade, a lesson plan book, information about the authors, individual response logs, and a teacher's resource book. Each set was packaged in cardboard boxes with drawers. Books in the sets appear on recognized lists of good children's literature, including several that have been awarded Caldecott Medals or Newbery Medals. While the total number of books in these sets falls far short of the six to eight books per child recommended for a well-designed classroom library, publisher literature sets could serve as the base for a classroom library. The teachers trying out the sets were pleased with how well they lent themselves to literature-based instruction.

Cost is, of course, an important factor. Elementary school teachers typically use their own funds to buy most of the books in their classroom libraries (Allington, Guice, Baker, Michaelson, & Li, 1995). They keep the cost down by haunting garage and yard sales, asking the students in their classes to donate books that they are no longer reading, collecting points for bonus books by encouraging their students to order books through book clubs, and asking local businesses and parents to contribute books to the classroom library (Fractor et al., 1993). Newspapers, too, can provide assistance. For example, the *New York Times Magazine* (August 23, 1998) ran a notice requesting donations from the public of $250.00 to support the classroom library in a third-grade classroom.

Officially, the decision-making power for spending tax money on books rests at the local level in most states (Valli, Chapter 11, this volume). In some cases, local school systems have recognized the importance of classroom libraries, are prepared to spend money on trade books for the libraries, and have prepared both guidelines and book lists that restrict how the public funds can be spent (Pucci, 1994). Teachers in those systems can seek out funds as long as they adhere to the guidelines and book lists. Other school systems have no policy and no provision to spend money on classroom libraries. In such cases, teachers might well band together to submit a formal request to the appropriate administrators asking that some portion of the school or district budget, such as that currently used to purchase consumable materials like workbooks or worksheets, be reallocated to purchasing trade books for classrooms (Fractor et al., 1993). Research results that suggest the positive effects of classroom libraries should be a powerful persuasive tool that teachers could use to influence administrators.

Finally, school and public libraries offer invaluable resources to supplement the teacher's classroom collection. By bringing in books from outside libraries, teachers can provide a dynamic flow of books by new authors, on new topics, for new purposes (Allen & Eisele, 1990). Besides providing resources, however, libraries beyond the walls of the classroom can extend children's reading experiences to the school and neighborhood, providing children with a more extensive community within which to discuss authors, illustrators, topics, and genres (Hiebert et al., 1990).

Compromising When Lack of Space Is a Problem

The teacher in a crowded classroom will have to compromise. Researchers have identified the essential features of effective classroom libraries (Fractor et al., 1993). First, because book choice makes such a difference, teachers should do whatever they can to gather a large number of quality books according to the principles discussed in this chapter. A second feature that is critical is the open display of books. Kindergarten children, for example, are more likely to choose books on open-faced shelving than on shelves where books are arranged with spines outward (Fractor et al., 1993). Teachers will have to be creative in figuring out how to store and display the books in a crowded space. Third, creating a community of readers within the classroom encourages children to use the library and to make thoughtful selections of what to read. Fortunately, a community of readers takes no more space than a group of young children who are unmotivated, nonparticipatory readers.

Publishers generally ship their classroom libraries in boxes with drawers. The packaging works well for storing the books and could be particularly useful for the teacher with minimal space. However, in classes where teachers did not remove books from cardboard boxes, children did not read them (Allen & Eisele, 1990; Neuman, in press). Displaying books so that children can see the covers is consistent with what both bookstores and public libraries do. The covers are attractive and "sell" the books, whether to a potential buyer in a bookstore or a child in a classroom library. The teacher who has no room for open shelving can display books on chalk trays, window sills, small tables, and even children's desks.

Promoting Access to the Books

For a classroom library to function well, children must be able to locate and use the books with ease. Teachers must find ways to organize the 180–240 books, must devise ways to keep the books in good repair while not hampering children's enjoyment, and must decide what to do about allowing children to take books home, a particularly important issue for children who own few books.

Brooks (1995) has described the system she devised to keep books from being strewn from one end of the bookshelves to the other where neither she nor the children knew what books were in the library or where they were located. She divided the books into sections (e.g., reference, history, biography, fiction, and fact, further subdivided into topics). She marked each book with the first three letters of the author's last name and alphabetized within sections accordingly. As children chose a book, they listed the title in a spiral notebook to check the book out. Each child had a cardboard marker with the child's name on it. As children removed a book, they replaced it with their personalized cardboard marker, which "marked the spot" until they returned the book. Student librarians returned books to their proper spots at the end of each day. Brooks (1995) also prepared a computer database that listed fields for author, title, subject, and section of the library. She entered each book in the library into the database. Not every teacher will want to create such an extensive system. Other teachers organize books into bins of similar topics and have children return a book to its bin when they are finished (Fractor et al., 1993). (Remember, though, the drawbacks to having books stored in boxes or bins.) Regardless, it is important to organize the books, to have a recording system for children to use to check out books, and to have a method for returning the books to their proper place in the library when children are finished.

The books in a classroom library are an expensive resource. In their enthusiasm, young children can be hard on books. Teachers may be tempted to keep the books safe and to control their use tightly, thereby limiting children's access to the library (Neuman, in press). Other strategies can protect the library while fostering children's access to and enjoyment of the library books. The most important strategy is to teach young children how to care for books. Preschool children can be taught to personify books; to think of the book cover as a face ("You wouldn't want to write on *The Giving Tree's* face, would you?") and the book pages as arms ("You wouldn't want to bend the pages back just like you wouldn't want your own arms bent back. A book gets hurt when you bend its pages."), and so on (Neuman, in press). Older children could discuss different ways of damaging books and what the negative effects on the library would be.

Children who are learning to value reading will be likely to value the classroom books as well.

A second strategy is to repair damaged books. Teachers can identify a specific spot for children to put books that need to be repaired. Neuman's (in press) book flood child care centers had a "book hospital" stocked with invisible tape, glue, an eraser for crayon marks, and cleaner for book covers. Children were encouraged to do some of the fixing of books in the hospital.

A third strategy is to think of trade books, particularly paperbacks, as consumables analogous to basal workbooks (Allen & Eisele, 1990). If paperbacks were considered at least partially consumable, whether children damaged or returned them would be less important an issue. Children could even be allowed to keep a certain number of books every year. Other children could trade one of their own books for a paperback from the classroom library. Of course, this third strategy only works if teachers are not having to fund the classroom library from their own pockets.

INTEGRATING INTERNET AND CD–ROM READING MATERIAL INTO THE CLASSROOM LIBRARY

The chapter to this point has only hinted at the power of including technology in the classroom library. Two primary vehicles of electronic texts are the Internet and CD–ROM books. This section highlights ways in which teachers can integrate these two types of texts into their classroom libraries, responding to the twin pressures of bringing technology into the classroom and increasing children's reading achievement. Such integration will also enhance engagement.

Extending the Library with Electronic Texts

Both the World Wide Web (WWW) and CD–ROMs offer children's texts, often with graphics, sound, and video included. A variety of internet sites have complete texts by authors such as James M. Barrie, Frank L. Baum, Rudyard Kipling, Robert Louis Stevenson, and Mark Twain. Table 5.1 lists gateway sites, each of which catalogs and provides multiple pathways to individual sites. Most often, the text is in the public domain; thus, anyone with WWW access can download documents free from these sites for use in the classroom. Unfortunately, the texts are not visually appealing because they generally are downloaded in text format. Other WWW sites include texts that are offered chapter by chapter similar to the serialization in a newspaper or magazine. These sites tend to be more visually pleasing, with graphics, sounds, and video included, often created by other chil-

TABLE 5.1. Resources on the World Wide Web That Teachers and Children Can Use to Build an Electronic Classroom Library

Addresses	Gateways to related sites	Resources for parents	Resources for children	Resources for teachers	Reviews	Texts to download	On-line reading
http://yahooligans.com/School_Bell/Language_Arts	X	X	X	X			
http://www.childrenslit.com/	X	X		X	X		
http://www.parentsplace.com	X	X		X			
http://www.acs.ucalgary.ca/~dkbrown/index.html	X	X	X	X			X
gopher://lib.nmsu.edu:70/11/.subjects/Education/.childlit	X	X	X	X	X	X	
http://palmdale.lib.ca.us/youthlib/childteen.html	X	X	X				
http://207.237.120.51/reviews.html	X	X	X	X		X	X
http://www.ala.org/book1	X	X	X		X		
http://www.carolhurst.com/index.html	X	X	X	X	X	X	
http://avatar.lib.usm.edu/~degrum/	X	X	X	X	X	X	X

dren. Some of these sites present both a read-alone version of a story and a second version with a child's voice reading the text aloud. The WWW can also enhance classroom libraries through the diverse number of information-rich sites designed for the younger audience. Daily the WWW has new entries of beautiful, easy-to-read sites for children's reading and research needs. Sites of particular interest to help motivate student reading include children's author home pages where students can e-mail the authors of some of their favorite books and book report/review sites written by children for children. Over the past decade a growing market for CD–ROM books has developed. With superior sound quality, enticing graphics, and video capabilities, these books have quickly found an audience.

Texts accompanied by sound and video should entice even reluctant readers to read. However, teachers sometimes worry about what are typically (and often derisively) termed "bells and whistles," that is, texts such as quicktime movies, video clips, graphics, and sound bytes. But, in what Myron C. Tuman (1992) has labeled a "Word Perfect world," these other texts can broaden and support children's literacy gains. Children who become active seekers of literacy do not limit themselves to one type of text (Lemke, 1998; Myers, Hammett, & McKillop, 1998).

As motivating as electronic texts may be, children need to learn to use them within the larger classroom reading community. Without instruction, children may "surf the net" or view enticing electronic stories without actually reading. Anyone who has surfed the Internet understands how quickly information can pass by and how little reading may actually take place. Children can watch the video and listen to a story being read without actually reading themselves. Teachers will need to spend time helping children "read" electronic texts so that mere viewing does not become the norm. Children who know how to read all forms of texts are less likely to be mindlessly entranced by them (Lemke, 1998). In addition, through instruction and supervision, teachers can eliminate surfing of questionable Internet sites, a concern that has raised questions about the appropriateness of the WWW as a learning tool in the classroom.

Learning to surf the Internet is unique to the computer world and needs its own set of instructional strategies. The prudent teacher will provide at least some structure and ask students to be responsible for their reading on the Internet. Classroom Web card catalogs (Leu & Leu, 1996) divided into topics (Rudo, 1998) are easy to keep and act as both locators and site reviews. Children fill out index cards detailing the site address and content and then rate salient features that the class has chosen as worth knowing. Such features might include stylistic concerns such as graphics and ease of navigation or more content-driven features such as quality of information. To help children learn to choose appropriate web sites, teachers and children can discuss the different ways people and events are portrayed in the media. These lessons can be accompanied by guided lesson sheets to focus and support student exploration. Yahooligans (Yahoo's site designed specifically for children and children's issues) helps teachers to pinpoint well-designed, child-friendly sites. If teachers wish to supervise children's surfing more closely, they can limit Internet access by bookmarking sites and directing children to them or downloading sites to store on their own hard drives instead of having children actually explore the WWW. Software is now available to help teachers "snap" sites to keep on their computers. Finally, programs such as NetNanny act as the computer version of the "V" chip. Teachers would do well to investigate their school district's policies to see what precautions may be required.

Choosing Quality Electronic Reading Materials

In its present state, much of the reading material on the WWW is analogous to comics and magazines. As the Internet grows, more reputable child-centered sites are being developed by universities, publishers, and others who have a stake in children's reading development. Knowing how to buy and select electronic books can also pose problems. Marilyn Courtot (1998), publisher and editor of *Children's Literature*, a web site dealing with electronic texts and the issues surrounding their use with children, and the author of *Children's Multimedia*, a review of electronic texts, detailed a number of these difficulties:

> If selecting good books for young readers is a dilemma, then selecting electronic books and educational software is a real quandary. At least with a book the object is familiar, you can touch it, open it up, read a few pages, look at the illustrations, read reviews and make your decision. It is not quite that easy with an electronic book or educational software product. For the most part, there are not many reviews readily available, and it is frequently not possible to do more than read the packaging to learn about the product. (p. i)

To determine the educational value of the material, teachers should use their own good judgment and the criteria mentioned earlier in this chapter.

The Practicalities of Integrating Electronic Texts into the Classroom Library

Teacher expertise, computer access, and expense are three practical issues that affect how well electronic texts can be integrated into the classroom library. Teachers can easily download books on the Internet in text format. But it takes time and technological knowledge to download audio plug-in programs such as RealAudio so that texts accompanied by sound can be heard. To play media clips, teachers must also know how to access the appropriate plug-ins. A teacher's technological expertise will make a difference.

Available computers must have sufficient power and capability. Courtot (1998) cautioned that color monitors and good speakers are essential if students are to get the full value of electronic books. Computers and modems must be powerful enough to access the Internet without so much lag time that students get bored waiting. Because many child-oriented sites are replete with graphics, the wait time may be considerably longer than normal. CD–ROM books require a computer that includes a CD–ROM drive as well as enough power to avoid lag time. Texts with media clips require computers with sufficient memory for the necessary plug-ins. Teachers should check the technical specifications that come with the CD–ROM to make sure that the computer and the software are compatible. Finally, teachers need to consider computer access and available time for students. A teacher who has a computer on a cart in her classroom for an hour a day will have more difficulty coordinating student access than one who has unlimited computer availability.

Finally, expense is an important consideration. Electronic books are almost always more expensive than print books (although technology advancements may change that). Computers (and printers) are expensive, and constant upgrades in software and operating systems may mean that libraries have to be updated every few years—at considerable expense.

Despite these knotty practical issues, electronic texts can be a valuable addition to the classroom library. Charles Hohmann has stated, "We found that the computer's capacity to create highly interactive settings (like games, puzzles, and creative environments with accessible tools) gives it the potential to stimulate in young children the mental actions of transforming, comparing, organizing, and symbolizing. In this sense, then, computer learning is active learning" (cited in Courtot, 1998, p. i). And computer reading can be active, engaged reading.

CONCLUDING THOUGHTS

The well-designed library situated within a classroom reading community can be a powerful aspect of classroom life. Whether children are curled in a corner turning the pages of a book or sitting at a computer screen exploring an electronic world, the library can offer them hours of pleasure and the opportunity to roam through time and space. At the same time, they painlessly acquire extensive practice reading. Although all children can benefit from a well-designed classroom library, children who are at risk for never learning to read well can reap the most rewards. Only if the library encourages these children to engage with print will it meet high standards. Within the constraints of limited funds and crowded classrooms, teachers must find ways to gather large collections of children's books, choose materials that fit the needs of their particular students, create an attractive physical environment, and place the library within a community of enthusiastic readers. The goal is for all children to love to read, to choose to read often, and to reach the highest levels of achievement possible.

RECOMMENDED READINGS

Courtot, M. (1998). *Children's multimedia: The good, bad, and the ugly of children's software and multimedia*. Bethesda, MD: Children's Literature.

This is a wonderful collection of CD–ROM multimedia reviews written by experts in children's reading and development. Besides including pertinent information about computer requirements, the reviews also give detailed descriptions of the multimedia and the target ages.

Fractor, J. S., Woodruff, M. C., Martinez, M. G., & Teale, W. H. (1993). Let's not miss opportunities to promote voluntary reading: Classroom libraries in the elementary school. *The Reading Teacher, 46*, 476–484.

This paper describes in detail the features of classroom libraries that have proven to be effective in promoting children's use of library materials. It also presents case studies of four teachers who have established successful libraries in their classrooms.

Hiebert, E. H., Mervar, K. B., & Person, D. (1990). Research directions: Children's selection of trade books in libraries and classrooms. *Language Arts, 67*, 758–763.

This paper compares classrooms that are reading communities with classrooms that are textbook based. It describes the types of analytical conversations within a reading community that can enhance children's selection and use of books.

Reinking, D., McKenna, M. C., Labbo, L. D., & Kieffer, R. D. (Eds.). (1998). *Handbook of literacy and technology: Transformations in a post-typographic world*. Mahwah, NJ: Erlbaum.

This collection covers a wide range of computer technology-related issues. The book is divided into areas that are "transformed" by technology, and numerous chapters deal with reading and young children's reading development as related to technology issues.

REFERENCES

Adams, M. (1990). *Beginning to read*. Cambridge, MA: MIT Press.

Allen, J. B., & Eisele, B. (1990). Yelling for books without losing your voice. *The New Advocate, 3*(2), 117–130.

Allington, R. (1997, August/September). Overselling phonics. *Reading Today*, pp. 15–16.

Allington, R., Guice, S., Baker, K., Michaelson, N., & Li, S. (1995). Access to books: Variations in schools and classrooms. *Language and Literacy Spectrum, 5*, 23–25.

Anderson, G., Higgins, D., & Wurster, S. R. (1985). Differences in the free-reading books selected by high, average, and low achievers. *The Reading Teacher, 39*, 326–330.

Anderson, R. C., Wilson, P. T., & Fielding, L. G. (1988). Growth in reading and how children spend their time outside of school. *Reading Research Quarterly, 23*, 285–303.

Beck, I. (1997, October/November). Response to "overselling phonics." *Reading Today*, p. 17.

Beck, I. L. (1998). Understanding beginning reading: A journey through teaching and research. In J. Osborn & F. Lehr (Eds.), *Literacy for all: Issues in teaching and learning* (pp. 11–31). New York: Guilford Press.

Beck, I. L., McKeown, M. G., Sinatra, G. M., & Loxterman, J. A. (1991). Revising social studies text from a text-processing perspective: Evidence of improved comprehensibility. *Reading Research Quarterly, 26*, 251–276.

Branley, F. M. (1986). *Snow is falling*. New York: HarperCollins.

Brooks, H. (1995). "I know that book's here somewhere!" How to organize your classroom library. *The Reading Teacher, 48*, 638–639.

Chambliss, M. J., & Calfee, R. C. (1998). *Textbooks for learning: Nurturing children's minds*. Malden, MA: Blackwell.

Cohn, D., & Constable, P. (1998, August 30). Lives transplanted, a region transformed. *Washington Post*, pp. A1, A20–A21.

Courtot, M. (1998). *Children's multimedia: The good, bad, and the ugly of children's software and multimedia*. Bethesda, MD: Children's Literature.

Cullinan, B. (1989). *Literature and the child*. San Diego, CA: Harcourt Brace Jovanovich.

Elley, W. (1991). Acquiring literacy in a second language: The effect of book-based programs. *Language Learning, 41*, 375–411.

Fractor, J. S., Woodruff, M. C., Martinez, M. G., & Teale, W. H. (1993). Let's not miss opportunities to promote voluntary reading: Classroom libraries in the elementary school. *The Reading Teacher, 46*, 476–484.

Freebody, P., & Anderson, R. C. (1983). Effects of vocabulary difficulty, text cohesion, and schema availability on reading comprehension. *Reading Research Quarterly, 18*, 277–294.

Fry, E. B., Kress, J. E., & Fountoukidis, D. L. (1993). *The reading teacher's book of lists* (3rd ed.). Englewood Cliffs, NJ: Prentice Hall.

Guthrie, J. T. (1996). Educational contexts for engagement in literacy. *The Reading Teacher, 49*, 432–443.

Hidi, S., & Baird, W. (1988). Strategies for increasing text-based interest and students' recall of expository texts. *Reading Research Quarterly, 23*, 465–483.

Hiebert, E. H., Mervar, K. B., & Person, D. (1990). Research directions: Children's selection of trade books in libraries and classrooms. *Language Arts, 67*, 758–763.

Huck, C., Hepler, S., & Hickman, J. (1987). *Children's literature in the elementary school* (4th ed.). New York: Holt, Rinehart & Winston.

International Reading Association [IRA]. (1998). Teachers' choices for 1998. *The Reading Teacher, 51*, 271–277.

International Reading Association [IRA]. (1999). 1998 notable books for a global society: A K–12 list. *The Reading Teacher, 52*, 498–504.

International Reading Association [IRA] & National Council of Teachers of English [NCTE]. (1996). *Standards for the English language arts.* Newark, DE, & Urbana, IL: Authors.

Kameenui, E., & Simmons, D. (1997, October/November). Decodable texts and the language of dichotomy: A response to Allington. *Reading Today,* p. 18.

Krashen, S. (1995). School libraries, public libraries, and the NAEP reading scores. *School Library Media Quarterly, 23,* 235–238.

Krashen, S. (1997/1998). Bridging inequity with books. *Educational Leadership, 55,* 18–22.

Lance, K. C. (1994). The impact of school library media centers on academic achievement. In C. Kuhlthau (Ed.), *School Library Media Annual* (Vol. 12, pp. 188–197). Englewood, CO: Libraries Unlimited.

Lemke, J. L. (1998). Metamedia literacy. In D. Reinking, M. McKenna, L. Labbo, & R. Kieffer (Eds), *Handbook of literacy and technology: Transformations in a post-typographic world* (pp. 283–301). Mahwah, NJ: Erlbaum.

Leu, D. J., & Leu, D. D. (1996). *Teaching with the Internet: Lessons from the classroom.* Norwood, MA: Christopher-Gordon.

Lysaker, J. T. (1997). Learning to read from self-selected texts: The book choices of six first graders. In C. K. Kinzer, K. A. Hinchman, & D. J. Leu (Eds.), *Inquiries in literacy theory and practice* (Forty-sixth yearbook of the National Reading Conference, pp. 273–282). Chicago: National Reading Conference.

Martinez, M. G., Roser, N. L., Worthy, J., Strecker, S., & Gough, P. (1997). Classroom libraries and children's book selections: Redefining "access" in self-selected reading. In C. K. Kinzer, K. A. Hinchman, & D. J. Leu (Eds.), *Inquiries in literacy theory and practice* (Forty-sixth yearbook of the National Reading Conference, pp. 265–272). Chicago: National Reading Conference.

McKenna, M. (1998). Electronic texts and the transformation of beginning reading. In D. Reinking, M. McKenna, L. Labbo, & R. Kieffer (Eds.), *Handbook of literacy and technology: Transformations in a post-typographic world* (pp. 45–59). Mahwah, NJ: Erlbaum.

Morrow, L. M. (1991). Promoting voluntary reading. In J. Flood, J. M. Jensen, D. Lapp, & J. R. Squire (Eds.), *Handbook of research on teaching the English language arts* (pp. 681–690). New York: Macmillan.

Morrow, L. M., & Weinstein, C. S. (1982). Increasing children's use of literature through program and physical design changes. *Elementary School Journal, 83,* 131–137.

Moustafa, M. (1997, October/November). Bravo to Allington. *Reading Today,* p. 18.

Myers, J., Hammett, R., & McKillop, A. M. (1998). Opportunities for critical literacy and pedagogy in student-authored hypermedia. In D. Reinking, M. McKenna, L. Labbo, & R. Kieffer (Eds), *Handbook of literacy and technology: Transformations in a post-typographic world* (pp. 63–78). Mahwah, NJ: Erlbaum.

Neuman, S. (in press). Books make a difference: A study of access to literacy. *Reading Research Quarterly.*

New York Times Magazine. (1998, August 23). Notice, p. 52.

Pucci, S. (1994). Supporting Spanish language literacy: Latino children and free reading resources in the schools. *Bilingual Research Journal, 18,* 67–82.

Ramirez, D., Yuen, S., Ramey, D., & Pasta, D. (1991). *Final report: Longitudinal study of structured English immersion strategy, early-exit and late-exit bilingual education programs for language minority students* (Vol. 1). San Mateo, CA: Aguirre International.

Rosenblatt, L. M. (1978). *The reader, the text, the poem.* Carbondale & Edwardsville: Southern Illinois University Press.

Rucker, B. (1982). Magazines and teenage reading skills: Two controlled field experiments. *Journalism Quarterly, 59*(1), 28–33.

Rudo, A. K. (1998). *Reflections on Internet use in the classroom.* Unpublished manuscript.

Smith, C., Constantino, R., & Krashen, S. (1997, March/April). Differences in print environment for children in Beverly Hills, Compton and Watts. *Emergency Librarian*, pp. 8–9.

Snow, C. E., Burns, M. S., & Griffin, P. (Eds.). (1998). *Preventing reading difficulties in young children*. Washington, DC: National Academy Press.

Tuman, M. C. (1992). *Word perfect: Literacy in the computer age*. Pittsburgh, PA: University of Pittsburgh Press.

Ujiie, J., & Krashen, S. (1996). Comic book reading, reading achievement, and pleasure reading among middle class and Chapter 1 middle school students. *Reading Improvement*, *33*, 50–54.

Wolf, S. A., & Heath, S. B. (1992). *The braid of literature: Children's worlds of reading*. Cambridge, MA: Harvard University Press.

CHAPTER SIX

Promoting Collaboration, Social Interaction, and Engagement with Text

LINDA B. GAMBRELL
SUSAN ANDERS MAZZONI
JANICE F. ALMASI

Research suggests that collaborative literacy experiences promote peer interaction and engagement in learning (Almasi, 1996; Eeds & Wells, 1989; Johnson & Johnson, 1989; Slavin, 1990). The type of interaction that occurs during collaborative literacy experiences may play an important role in shaping students' perceptions of the purposes and goals of reading and writing. Collaborative literacy experiences provide opportunities for students to engage in the construction of meaning as they share ideas about text in what Fish (1980) calls an "interpretive community." As interpretive communities interact, students must reconsider and update their own interpretations of text as new interpretations coalesce from the divergent views that are brought forth by group members. In this chapter, the word "text" is used to describe text that children read as well as text that they produce or write. Accordingly, reading and writing are viewed as meaning-making processes within the social context of literacy learning.

Currently, there is a resurgence of interest in the role of collaboration in learning, largely in response to Vygotsky's (1978) theory that social interaction shapes intellectual growth. His theory stressed the impor-

119

tance of language in the development of thought. Vygotsky examined students' learning within specific contexts and examined the gap between what children are able to accomplish independently and what they might be able to do with the support of more knowledgeable others. Vygotsky defined the zone of proximal development as the distance between a child's actual developmental level (as determined by independent problem-solving ability) and the child's level of potential development (as determined through problem solving under adult guidance or in collaboration with more capable peers). This suggests that, under the right conditions, collaborative social interaction among peers can promote and support cognitive growth as children model for each other more advanced thinking and language skills than those they could perform as individuals. Many researchers and theorists support increased use of collaborative learning in elementary classrooms because interaction among students leads to improved student engagement and achievement (Almasi, 1996; Eeds & Wells, 1989; Raphael & McMahon, 1994). According to Slavin (1995), significant learning will occur in collaborative experiences because "in the discussions of the content, cognitive conflicts will arise, inadequate reasoning will be exposed, and higher-quality understanding will emerge" (p. 18). Thus, it is through increased verbalization and language use during collaborative discussions of text that children share their emergent interpretations.

This theoretical lens suggests that collaborative learning has much to offer in the realm of literacy development with regard to providing opportunities for creating classroom cultures that support students' thinking and engagement with text. In socially interactive learning experiences children develop higher-level skills such as logical memory, selective attention, decision making, and comprehension as they use language within a social context. Collaborative learning provides young children with opportunities to use language to construct and communicate meaning and engage in higher-order, literate thinking.

The terms "collaborative learning" and "cooperative learning" both reflect an emphasis on social interaction. Collaborative learning is a broad term used to refer to the group dynamics that are desirable within any learning context. Collaborative learning provides students with opportunities to actively and substantively engage in an exchange of ideas that results in the co-construction of meaning. Collaborative learning focuses on the quality of social interaction and higher-level thinking among students. According to Vygotsky (1978), social interaction is the primary means by which children arrive at new understandings. It is through the exchange of ideas and subsequent agreements and disagreements that students challenge one another's ideas as well as their own. This social dynamic enables meaning to be constructed within the event. Verbal and cognitive processes related to higher-level thinking are revealed as students interact to express ideas in speaking and writing.

The term cooperative learning, on the other hand, describes a specific type of collaborative experience where small groups or teams of students are provided with opportunities to socially interact and work together to achieve a common goal. The primary characteristic of cooperative learning is that students take responsibility for their teammates' learning as well as their own. In cooperative learning experiences, team goals, team success, and individual responsibility are emphasized.

In addition to providing a theory base for social interaction and collaborative learning, this chapter presents relevant research demonstrating the efficacy of using collaborative learning strategies, including cooperative learning, to foster literacy development. The chapter also describes collaborative and cooperative reading and writing instructional practices that enhance social interaction and engagement with text. The chapter concludes with a section devoted to how social interaction supports the development of children's critical thinking and extended learning.

COLLABORATIVE LEARNING AND SOCIAL INTERACTION

Current theories of motivation recognize that literacy learning is facilitated by social interactions with others (Gambrell, 1996; McCombs, 1989; Oldfather, 1993). Indeed, collaborative learning has received a great deal of attention during the past two decades as researchers and teachers have recognized the important role of social interaction in the development of higher-level literacy skills. A number of recent studies have indicated that social collaboration promotes achievement, higher-level cognition, and the intrinsic desire to read and write (Almasi, 1996; Guthrie, Schafer, Wang, & Afflerbach, 1993; Slavin, 1990; Wood, 1990). Collaborative literacy learning opportunities can also help students develop social insights and creativity as well as literacy skills (Bruffee, 1993).

Researchers have explored a number of specific ways to encourage collaborative interactions among peers. For example, there is evidence to suggest that the way in which teachers respond to students' comments affects whether and how children will participate in an exchange of ideas with one another. Orsolini and Pontecorvo (1992) found that when a teacher repeated or rephrased 5- and 6-year-old children's remarks, students usually responded by elaborating upon the topic. Other children usually followed suit by making additional remarks, reacting to the previous speakers' comments. Furthermore, when the teacher requested an explanation for a disputable claim, children usually responded by making justifying remarks; then, at least two other students reacted to the child's comments by making further claims, justifying their remarks. Dillon (1985, 1990) found that teachers can encourage collaborative discourse by asking fewer questions or by using nonquestioning techniques such as rephrasing or restating students' comments or by simply refraining from speaking. Specifically with respect to students learning from text, a number of researchers and educators have suggested that the traditional classroom interaction pattern of *teacher question–student response–teacher evaluation* is insufficient for developing deeper meanings of text (Cazden, 1986; Eeds & Wells, 1989; Mehan, 1979; Saunders & Goldenberg, 1992). Furthermore, there is evidence to suggest that there are important linkages between peer discussions about text and improved reading comprehension (Gavelek, 1986; Morrow & Smith, 1990; Short & Pierce, 1990), word learning (Ruddell, 1994), long-term memory (Alvermann, Dillon, & O'Brien, 1987), engagement with text (Almasi, 1996; Gambrell & Bobola, 1996; Oldfather & Dahl, 1995, Turner, 1995), self-regulated learning (Almasi, 1996), and complexity of response to teacher-generated questions (Saunders & Goldenberg, 1992). *Peer-led discussions, idea circles, reader reaction circles and reciprocal teaching* are examples of collaborative teaching and learning strategies that foster social interactions among students.

Peer-Led Discussion Groups

Many educators and researchers advocate "decentralized" small-group participation structures during discussions of text so that children will develop social interaction skills as well as strategies for interpreting text (e.g., O'Flahavan, Stein, Wiencek, & Marks, 1992). For example, Almasi (1996) found that in peer-led discussions of literature, students were more likely to recognize and resolve their own misunderstandings about text because in a group setting "cognitive unrest" is more likely to be shared and exposed; conversely, in teacher-led discussions, teachers tended to assume the role of exposing students' inconsistencies. Almasi suggested that relying on the teacher to serve as the interpretive authority may cause students to become passive learners and that in order for children to become active, self-regulated readers and thinkers, they need to recognize and resolve their own discrepancies with text. Almasi's research indicates that one way to encourage this process is to provide children with opportunities for collaboratively exploring the meaning of text through small-group peer-led discussions.

Creating the Classroom Climate for Discussion

Vygotskian theory (Vygotsky, 1978) suggests that literacy development is enhanced when children work together to discuss and reflect on what they are reading and writing. Research conducted by O'Flahavan (1989) revealed that successful discussion groups first focus on developing rules for engaging in dialogue. The teacher plays a very important role in helping students to build positive and supportive rules of engagement. These rules can be developed and discussed as children focus on the topic of how to have a good discussion. The rules can then be prominently displayed in the classroom to help remind the students of important discussion behaviors. For example, the list shown below, "How to Have a Good Discussion," was developed in a teacher–researcher peer-led discussion project at Severna Park Elementary School in Maryland (Gambrell, 1996):

How to Have a Good Discussion
1. Listen carefully to the ideas of others.
2. Contribute at least one idea to the discussion.
3. Use text ideas and language in your comments.
4. Use the ideas of others and add to them.
5. Look at the speakers.
6. Treat others with respect.
7. Keep to the topic.
8. Let others have a turn.

During the process of developing a chart that included these items, the students brainstormed ideas about how to have a good discussion. The teacher recorded the ideas that were generated on a piece of paper. The teacher then organized and incorporated all the important ideas in a master list. A teaching chart was posted in the classroom with just the title, "How to Have a Good Discussion." Each day one important rule was added to the chart, and class members spent 5–8 minutes discussing and reviewing the importance of this rule in fostering good discussions. This process continued until all eight rules had been posted on the chart and discussed by the students. The teacher in this classroom often referred the students to the chart and asked them to review and think about how to have a good discussion prior to having the students participate in discussion groups.

Teaching charts like "How to Have a Good Discussion" can be a reference for students as they participate in discussion group and can cue them to ways they can display appropriate discussion behaviors. Such teaching charts can also be adapted as self-evaluation tools that help children become more metacognitive about their learning strategies and behaviors. The "How to Have a Good Discussion" teaching chart is easily adapted to a self-evaluation instrument that students can use at the conclusion of discussion groups to reflect on their discussion skills and participation behaviors. Following each discussion group, children can evaluate their discussion skills by checking off all the behaviors they engaged in during the discussion. After self-evaluating several discussion sessions, students can look across their self-evaluation sheets to determine behaviors that they always engage in, as compared to behaviors that they rarely or never use. Providing a space for comments on the self-evaluation form encourages children to think about what they did well and to reflect on discussion behaviors they would like to add to their repertoire.

Peer-Led Discussion Groups: Introduction, Discussion, and Debriefing

The purpose of peer discussion groups is to allow students to engage in discussions of text and explore topics that interest them. Whether students are reading a core piece of literature, multiple texts, or a selection from a basal reader, they can gather in groups of six to eight to engage in peer discussion. Research suggests that in peer-led discussion groups, as compared to teacher-led discussion groups, students are more likely to question, clarify, consider alternate points of view, and engage in higher-level thinking about the ideas suggested by the text (Almasi, 1996; Wiencek, 1996).

It is important that students bring some form of response to the discussion so that they have discussion topics available. Journal writing is one form of response that seems to foster discussion. Prior to participating in a discussion group, students read a story or part of a story and write a response in their journal. Students bring their journals to the discussion group, and the entries provide the stimulus for the peer discussion group.

O'Flahavan's (1989) research indicated that there are three phases of the peer discussion group: introduction, discussion, and debriefing. Throughout these three phases the role of the teacher is perhaps best described as one of being a coach or facilitator.

Introduction. In the introduction phase, the teacher typically calls the group together; however, the teacher is not seated within the circle of peers. The teacher reminds students of important discussion behaviors that the group has decided characterize good discussions. Additionally, the teacher and the group can create teaching charts that support children in thinking of ways to interpret text such as comparing and contrasting characters and asking questions to clarify understanding. Various prompts or ways of talking about text can be brainstormed and then developed into a teaching chart with items such as the following:

Ways to Talk about Text

- Look in your journal for ideas.
- Tell about what you liked or disliked.
- Ask a question you had about the story.
- If you don't understand something, ask about it.
- Compare characters.
- Compare the story events to events in your life.
- Talk about the author's style of writing.
- Talk about reasons why the author wrote the story.
- Say whether you agree or disagree with someone's comment and tell why.

Such a chart should be displayed near the discussion group so that students can refer to the chart if the discussion stalls. This chart can also be adapted as a self-assessment tool by converting it to a checklist. Students can then self-assess the variety of strategies they use to interpret and talk about text.

The teacher can support children in getting started with the discussion in a variety of ways. For example, the teacher can provide one or two high-level interpretive questions for the group, students can share their reactions and interpretations from their journals, or students can come with questions they have prepared for discussion. As the group gets started with the discussion, the teacher leaves the group, but lingers nearby in order to provide support and assistance as needed. When the teacher physically moves away from the discussion circle, children are more likely to interact and respond with their peers rather than having the interactions flow through the teacher.

Discussion. Discussion, by definition, is free flowing, decentralized, and leaderless (Wiencek, 1996). During the discussion phase, the teacher limits his/her talk and assumes the role of observer and scaffolder. The teacher contributes to the group when students need assistance, focusing, or support as they explore a topic. For example, as a discussion is coming to a close, the teacher might move near the group to remind students of a particular topic or idea that was not covered in the discussion.

Debriefing. The debriefing phase allows for the culmination of the discussion and can focus on interpretive dimensions of the discussion and/or discussion strategies and behaviors. The teacher may assume leadership at this stage as the focus shifts to debriefing. There are several ways that debriefing can engage children in reflecting on what was learned during the discussion. The teacher can invite one of the group members to summarize by describing the most important ideas that emerged during the discussion. The teacher might also want to have the children reflect on the discussion behaviors demonstrated during the discussion. Self-evaluation tools can also provide a way of having children debrief and reflect on the discussion.

In the peer discussion model presented here (see Almasi, 1996, for a fuller description), the teacher plays a dominant role in the initiating and debriefing phase. During the discussion phase, the students talk without the teacher as a central member of the discussion group. According to Wiencek (1996), the most important role of the teacher is to ensure that students continue to learn, develop, and apply interactive and interpretive strategies during discussions.

O'Flahavan et al. (1992) examined how four different peer discussion structures influenced the interpretive responses of fourth graders. One major finding was that all groups in which the teacher exerted some influence generated a greater variety of interpretive foci (e.g., author based, text based, or reader based) over time than did the control, non-teacher-intervention group. They concluded that fourth graders need teacher influence in order to develop diversity of response and that "lack of teacher participation leads to interpretive stasis" (p. 23). McGee (1992) reported that students who participated in peer-led discussions (with the teacher present) and who were asked a single interpretive question by the teacher tended to provide many more interpretive responses than did the peer-led group that was not asked the question. Wiseman, Many, and Altieri (1992) reported that teacher-guided discussion which focused third graders' attention on thinking and talking about aesthetic and literary responses was a more effective instructional context for enriching students' experiences of a literary work than were non-teacher-guided discussions.

Teachers can support and influence peer-led discussions in a variety of ways. In one study, the teachers provided questions for children to respond to in response journals, and the children's entries were later used as catalysts for discussion (McGee, 1992). In a study conducted by Martinez, Roser, Hoffman, and Battle (1992), response journals substantially improved the quality of children's discussions about literature. McMahon (1992) reported that when the teacher asked more open-ended questions (which children responded to in logs and used as prompts for discussion), fifth graders tended to interact with each other more often than when the teacher provided text-based prompts. Short (1992) reported that by employing text sets, or conceptually related books, third and sixth graders made intertextual connections through peer-led discussions without teachers specifically involving students in lessons to practice making such connections. Taken together, these studies suggest the need for a degree of teacher support and influence in order to stimulate collaborative discussions that are instructional, conversational, and support the development of higher-level thinking skills.

Idea Circles

Guthrie and McCann (1996) have defined *idea circles* as peer-led, small-group discussions of concepts based on the reading of multiple text sources. Idea circles engage children in theorizing, questioning, and challenging information in text. Whereas literature discussion groups are often used to foster discussion about a particular story or book, idea circles focus on intertextuality, the ability to integrate information from multiple sources. The goal of group discussion in idea circles is to foster conceptual learning. In literature discussion children typically focus on a particular text, whereas in idea circles, they focus on a single concept, using multiple texts to learn about it (Guthrie & McCann, 1996). For example, children might study the concept of trees by exploring information on different types of trees, where they are located, the effect of climate on tree growth, the uses of products derived from trees, and the role of trees in the global ecosystem, or biosphere.

In idea circles, children gather specific information, details, and data from multiple text sources as they build conceptual understandings (Chi, DeLeeuw, Chiu, & Lavancher, 1994; Ng, Guthrie, Van Meter, McCann, & Also, 1998). One important feature of idea circles is an evolving consensus among the participants as they engage in collaborative learning. As children contribute information to the idea circle, a conceptual framework evolves. This contrasts with the typical literature discussion group where "conflicting interpretations about theme and diversity of viewpoint are encouraged. . . . Although both literature discussion groups and idea circles depend on text-based information, literature circles encourage the possibility of different conclusions, whereas idea circles promote the participants' convergence of conceptual understanding" (Guthrie & McCann, 1996, p. 89).

According to Guthrie and McCann (1996), the most successful idea circles are made up of three to six students. These teams of children may need time and experience working together to build group cohesion. Developing and using rules for discussion can help foster the interaction skills that will be required for children to meet the challenge of conceptual learning in a team.

In idea circles, each student researches and brings unique information to the discussion. This information may be based on a variety of sources such as previous experience, trade books, reference books and materials, films, television programs, or discussions with other students. To deepen and extend conceptual learning, the students must work together in order to integrate the information in meaningful ways. Students should be encouraged to check the accuracy of all information and to ask for verification and explanations from their peers. This continual quest for verification of information encourages students to search for documentation, read, comprehend, and synthesize information from a variety of sources. The ultimate goal of an idea circle is to support students in using a variety of cognitive strategies to interact with multiple texts for the purpose of new learning (Guthrie & McCann, 1996; Ng et al., 1998).

The conceptual aim of an idea circle needs to be clear for all members of the group. Guthrie and McCann (1996) suggest starting with a question such as "What is a river?" as an overarching aim. The teacher should choose conceptual topics carefully. Topics should be broad rather than narrow and have an extensive information base. The concept should be interesting, expansive, and one that will lead to further questions. When students work toward answering the conceptual question, they should be expected to provide facts, examples, and explanations. For example, they should be asked how a river differs from a creek, a lake, or a waterfall; also, how a river is affected by rainfall, and how both relate to the oceans.

The goal of the idea circle also needs to be clear and explicit. The products of an idea circle can be varied. For example, appropriate products might include simply participating in a group discussion, a written record of points made during the discussion, an artistic presentation, or a dramatized presentation of the information. Graphic organizers such as webs, think-links, and compare–contrast charts are also very appropriate products for communicating conceptual information.

Clearly, it is important that a variety of resources be available for students. Trade books at various levels of difficulty, as well as resources such as encyclopedias and other reference materials, provide a base for information searches (see Chambliss & McKillop, Chapter 5, this volume). Students should also be encouraged to contribute materials to the classroom resources as they come across them in the school or public library or when they find materials at home that contain information on the topic, such as newspaper articles, *Ranger Rick* magazines, or *National Geographic*.

Guthrie and McCann (1996) suggested that the most important benefit of using idea circles is student strategy learning. First, idea circles provide meaningful opportunities for students to search for information and become more comfortable in using a variety of books to gather information. In searching for information, they continually engage in decision making as they learn to distinguish important information from irrelevant details. Second, idea circles provide opportunities for students to develop a set of strategies related to understanding and comprehending text (see Guthrie, Cox, et al., Chapter 10, this volume). These strategies include use of prior knowledge, understanding technical words as they appear in context, and evaluating and summarizing significant information. Third, idea circles provide opportunities for students to integrate information in meaningful ways. Students learn to incorporate information they have gathered through their reading and research with the information gathered by other group members. According to Guthrie and McCann (1996), idea circles support students in learning to see that reading is more than a technical skill, but rather is "an avenue for the pursuit of information and the discovery of ideas. They learn that books are reservoirs they can tap for their own purposes" (p. 98).

Reader Reaction Circles

Sociocognitive theories of learning suggest that learning is enhanced when children have opportunities to share and discuss what they are reading with others. *Reader reaction circles*, a discussion strategy developed by Gambrell (1995), engage children in reading, listening, and speaking experiences about the books and stories they are reading. The primary objective of reader reaction circles is to help children develop ownership of strategies for entering into and engaging in discussions about text they have read. When reader reaction circles are used, the teacher should always emphasize that children are learning three important ways that they can enter discussions: (1) you can always comment on what you like or agree with; (2) you can always comment on something you would like to know more about; and (3) you can always ask a question. Teaching these strategies for entering conversations and discussions empowers students as they develop independence in participating in collaborative learning. Reader reaction circles provide children with opportunities to read aloud from a familiar text and listen to the reactions of their group to the ideas in the text. They also have an opportunity to respond to text that is read aloud by other group members and to practice specific discussion strategies.

One important aspect of reader reaction circles provide a motivating context for children to share books they are reading for pleasure. In developing and initiating reader reaction circles, the teacher first establishes discussion tasks for the groups. There must be a specific task for each child in the reader reaction circle. For example, the tasks for a four-member group might include the following: student 1, read a brief selection from your book; student 2, tell what you liked best about what student 1 read; student 3, tell what you would like to know more about concerning student 1's book; and student 4, ask a question about what student 1 read.

One important aspect of reader reaction circles is that the "reader" (child 1), should be encouraged to respond as each of the other children respond to what he/she has read by providing some additional information or elaboration. This activity helps children practice discussion skills such as listening and responding to others. In most elementary classrooms it takes only about 4–6 minutes for all four tasks to be completed by the group. The next step is to shift roles so that child 2 takes task 1, child 3 takes task 2, child 4 takes task 3, and child 1 takes task 4. This process continues until every child has had an opportunity to take each task. If reader reaction circles are being conducted with the entire class in groups of four, the entire process take approximately 30–35 minutes.

Children should also practice reading aloud from the familiar text they are reading in preparation for reading aloud to their group. On days when children are going to participate in reader reaction circles, the teacher might put an announcement on the board and as children enter the classroom they can select and practice what they will share from their book.

Reader reaction circles have many benefits because of the collaborative nature of the activity. Research suggests that children most often engage in reading books they know a little bit about (Gambrell, 1996). As children share information about books in their reader reaction circles, the likelihood that group members will be motivated to read those books increases.

Reciprocal Teaching

Reciprocal teaching is a technique in which students learn under the guidance of the teacher to take turns leading peers through four comprehension activities: summarizing, asking questions, clarifying, and predicting. According to Palincsar and Brown (1984, 1985), the primary goal of the discussion is the application of strategies for the purpose of having the students come to a shared sense of the meaning of the text.

Reciprocal teaching has been researched in elementary classrooms, yielding positive results for children in grades 2–6. Research by Palincsar and Brown (1985) revealed that comprehension performance, as well as comprehension monitoring, improved for students participating in the reciprocal teaching groups. Reciprocal teaching involves a great deal of peer interaction and dialogue exchange as the teacher and the children read a piece of common text. The reading may be done as a read-along, silent reading, or an oral reading by the teacher, depending on the reading abilities of the children and the level of the text. The children and the teacher take turns leading the discussion of segments of the text, using the summarizing, questioning, clarifying, and predicting strategies. Students are asked to (1) summarize the paragraph that was read in a simple sentence, (2) generate a question about the paragraph that was read to ask a fellow student, (3) ask for clarity of anything in the text that was unclear, and (4) make a prediction about what will happen next in the text. In research by

Palincsar and Brown (1985) and Palincsar (1986), students were shown how to engage in this process through teacher modeling. Adult support was withdrawn gradually as students developed independence. Palincsar (1986) reported that students participating in reciprocal teaching made gains of 35% and more on comprehension assessments after only 20 days of instruction.

COOPERATIVE LEARNING AND SOCIAL INTERACTION

As noted earlier, cooperative learning is a specific type of collaborative learning in which small groups or teams work together to achieve a common goal. This type of collaborative learning has been widely researched. A number of researchers have investigated student competence in conversing with peers as an important aspect of cooperative learning (e.g., Johnson & Johnson, 1990; Sharan & Sharan, 1992). Johnson and Johnson (1990) posited that placing socially unskilled students in a group and telling them to discuss a topic or work together will not necessarily produce higher achievement and positive social outcomes. Teaching students interpersonal and small-group social interaction skills produces greater learning, retention, and critical thinking than when students are not taught these critical skills (Calonico & Calonico, 1972; Johnson & Johnson, 1989). Research has also clearly demonstrated that both learning and the quality of relationships among students improve when group members are given the opportunity to engage in discussion as compared to groups that do not engage in discussion (Johnson, Johnson, Stanne, & Garibaldi, 1989).

The research literature has provided evidence and insights about the value of diversity in cooperative groups. Most researchers who advocate cooperative learning suggest that the group members should differ in terms of ethnicity and social class so that individuals can share differing perspectives and challenge one another's point of view (Bruffee, 1993) as well as improve cross-ethnic and cross-racial relationships (Aronson & Sikes, 1977; Johnson & Johnson, 1981; Sharan & Shachar, 1988; Slavin & Oickle, 1981). According to Slavin (1983), cross-ethnic and cross-racial collaboration appears to have positive effects on intergroup relations.

However, there is a continuing debate over the extent to which mixed-ability groups should be used in collaborative learning contexts (see Allan, 1991; Slavin, 1991). The concern is that high-ability students may be held back in their own learning. However, in Slavin's (1991) review of the research on grouping, he asserted that high-, middle-, and low-achieving students showed greater gains in achievement than students in control classrooms that did not use cooperative grouping. In describing the advantages of mixed-ability grouping, Johnson, Johnson, Holubec, and Roy (1984) maintained that "more elaborative thinking, more frequent giving and receiving of explanations, and greater perspective in discussing material seem to occur in heterogeneous groups, all of which increases the depth of understanding, the quality of reasoning, and the accuracy of long-term retention" (p. 27). Peer-Assisted Learning Strategy (PALS) and Jigsaw are examples of cooperative teaching and learning strategies that foster social interactions among students.

Peer-Assisted Learning Strategy for First Grade

PALS, developed by Mathes, Howard, Allen, and Fuchs (1998), was designed as a tool for improving the reading performance of first-grade students, particularly low-achieving students. First-grade PALS helps teachers to accommodate diverse learners by (1) decentering instruction through the use of peer mediation, (2) integrating phonological and alphabetic skills into the decoding of words in connected text, and (3) providing extensive exposure to a variety of children's literature. In the Mathes et al. (1998) study, teachers implemented PALS three time a week for 35-minute sessions for 16 weeks. Each teacher assigned students to pairs that consisted of a stronger and weaker reader. The more capable student was referred to as the "Coach," while the less capable student was called the "Reader." This allowed the stronger reader to take on a teacher-like role and the weaker student to benefit from a model good reader. After pairing students, the teacher assigned each pair to one of two class teams for which they earned points. Each teacher in PALS also used bonus points to foster academic and social development as well as to motivate students to accomplish goals. At the end of every week, the teacher totaled up the points for each team. The winning team was introduced, and they stood and took a bow while the second place team clapped. The second-place team was acknowledged in a like manner in recognition of its good effort.

First-grade PALS is composed of two sets of routines: *sounds and words*, which is a code-based activity based on the principles of *direct instruction*, and *partner read-aloud*, a literature activity. The first 10 minutes of instruction are devoted to the sounds and words routine and include the following activities: letter sounds, hearing sounds, sounding out, and stories. Daily lesson sheets based on these activities are completed by each team. The partner read-aloud routine immediately follows the sounds and words activity. There are three activities included in the 20 minutes devoted to the partner read-aloud: pretend-read, partner read-aloud, and retell. During pretend-read, the Coach reads the title and then the Reader reads the title. Next, the Coach guides the Reader through the story, page by page, and the Reader predicts what is happening in the story. During the partner read-aloud activity, the Coach and Reader take turns reading each sentence in the story, with the Coach always reading first to provide a model for the Reader. In the final activity, retell, the Coach prompts the Reader to retell the story.

Mathes and her colleagues (1998) compared the performance of children in 10 classrooms that implemented PALS with 10 classrooms that served as a comparison group. The results of the study revealed that PALS positively affected the reading performance of all learner types (low, average, and high ability). Low-ability students appeared to make the most substantial gains, based on measures of word attack, word identification, oral reading rate, concepts of print, and phonological segmentation.

Peer-Assisted Learning Strategies in Grades 2–6

A program similar to the first-grade PALS has also been shown to be effective in increasing the reading performance of students in grades 2–6. In a study conducted by Fuchs, Fuchs, Mathes, and Simmons (1997), students of all ability levels participated in PALS that focused on comprehension strategy instruction. PALS for grades 2–6 includes three activities: *partner reading with retell, paragraph summary,* and *prediction relay.* The primary goal of partner reading with retell is to increase students' oral reading fluency. The stronger reader reads connected text for 5 minutes, and then the weaker reader reads the same text. The weaker reader then retells in sequence what has been read. During paragraph summary, students take turns reading aloud one paragraph at a time and attempt to identify the subject and main idea. Prediction relay is introduced during the fifth week of PALS after students are comfortable with procedures and have become better at summarizing and identifying the main idea. In this activity the student makes a prediction about what will be learned on the next page, reads aloud from the page, confirms or disconfirms the prediction, summarizes the just-read text, makes a new prediction, and turns to the next page to continue to process. Each student follows this routine for 5 minutes, with the stronger reader always modeling for the weaker reader.

The teacher assigns each pair of students to one of two teams, giving PALS a competitive as well as a cooperative dimension. Students earn points for their team by reading sentences without error in partner reading, trying to do their best during retellings of the story, identifying the correct subject and main idea during paragraph summary, making reasonable predictions, and summarizing the main idea during prediction relay. The winning team is acknowledged at the end of each week. The points do not earn the winning team material benefits or anything that might be construed as a material reward.

Jigsaw

Jigsaw is a cooperative learning strategy first developed by Aronson and Sikes (1977) and later adapted by Slavin (1986). This strategy can be used whenever the material to be learned is in either written narrative or informational form. Materials such as stories, chapters in social studies and science books, biographies, or descriptive text can be used. Students are placed in teams that are mixed in reading level, gender, and ethnicity. There are five phases of the Jigsaw strategy: (1) *reading*, (2) *expert-group discussion*, (3) *team report*, (4) *test*, and (5) *team recognition*. During the reading phase, students receive expert sheets, with different topics for each team member to focus on while reading. In the expert-group discussion phase, students with the same expert topics meet to discuss them in expert groups. During the team report phase, the experts return to their teams to teach their topics to their teammates. In the test phase, students take individual quizzes covering all topics. Finally, during the team recognition phase, the team scores are computed and the winning team is rewarded with certificates or other recognition. Students are motivated to study and learn the material so that they can help their team do well. In Jigsaw every student depends on his/her teammates to do well on the assessments.

In a study conducted by Ziegler (1981) with sixth-grade students representing at least five different ethnic groups, Jigsaw students learned more and retained their knowledge better than did students in the control group. Lucker, Rosenfield, Sikes, and Aronson (1979) implemented Jigsaw with fifth- and sixth-grade Anglo, Mexican American, and African American students. The Jigsaw method resulted in superior performance for minority students as compared with the control group, which received traditional whole-class instruction. There were no significant differences for the Anglo students. Other studies have reported positive effects of Jigsaw on attitudes toward classmates and school, as well as on self-esteem (e.g., Blaney, Stephan, Rosenfield, Aronson, & Sikes, 1977; Geffer, 1978).

CONCLUSION: SOCIAL INTERACTION AND ENGAGEMENT WITH TEXT

Collaborative literacy experiences provide students with cognitive and social benefits by placing them within an environment in which they must remain cognitively and socially engaged. Students enter these collaborative literacy experiences knowing that they must actively participate and contribute to the group's endeavor. This places the responsibility on participants for making their contributions worthy of respect (Bridges, 1979). Thus, the culture that emerges with collaborative groups is one in which the interactions among group members involve recursive actions and reactions that are influenced by and influence one another as they engage with text (Gall & Gall, 1976).

In collaborative learning strategies, including cooperative learning, the teacher helps create a decentralized classroom culture. The teacher sits on the periphery, carefully noting the group's progress. By relinquishing authority for asking questions, determining who may talk and when, and evaluating responses, the teacher forces the students to take on these roles. When students begin asking questions of interest to them, negotiating meaning with peers, and learning how to navigate within a social system, they *must* be more engaged. There is no room for passivity, for relying on others to answer questions, or for waiting for the teacher to call on you. Collaboration requires active social participation and active cognitive processing.

RECOMMENDED READINGS

Blumenfeld, P. C., Marx, R. W., Soloway, E., & Krajcik, J. (1996). Learning with peers: From small group cooperation to collaborative communities. *Educational Researcher*, 25(8), 37–40.

This brief paper describes variations in purposes and types of group work, detailing factors such as group norms, tasks, group composition, accountability, and methods that influence group processes.

Bridges, D. (1979). *Education, democracy, and discussion*. Windsor, UK: National Foundation for Educational Research.

This theoretical text provides readers with the foundations and guiding principles that underlie discussion. It provides an overview of the learning possibilities in discussion, what is involved in open discussion, and an examination of how discussion can be used in teaching.

Gambrell, L. B., & Almasi, J. F. (Eds.). (1996). *Lively discussions: Fostering engaged reading*. Newark, DE: International Reading Association.

This edited volume is ideal for practitioners. The 18 chapters are dedicated to sharing research-based information about the benefits of engaging students in peer discussions of text, how to create classroom cultures that foster such discussions, and how to assess such discussions.

Webb, N. M., & Palincsar, A. S. (1996). Group processes in the classroom. In D. C. Berliner & R. Calfee (Eds.), *Handbook of educational psychology* (pp. 841–873). New York: Macmillan.

This chapter provides an overview of the history of group processes in classrooms, theoretical perspectives on the manner in which students learn in group contexts, and a practical collection of contemporary approaches to peer-based learning in the classroom.

REFERENCES

Allan, S. D. (1991). Ability-grouping research reviews: What do they say about grouping and the gifted? *Educational Leadership, 48*, 60–65.

Almasi, J. F. (1996). The nature of fourth graders' sociocognitive conflicts in peer-led and teacher-led discussion of literature. *Reading Research Quarterly, 30*, 314–351.

Alvermann, D. E., Dillon, D. R., & O'Brien, D. G. (1987). *Using discussion to promote reading comprehension.* Newark, DE: International Reading Association.

Aronson, E., & Sikes, J. (1977). Interdependence in the classroom: A field study. *Journal of Educational Psychology, 69*, 121–128.

Blaney, J., Stephan, S., Rosenfield, D., Aronson, E., & Sikes, J. (1997). Interdependence in the classroom: A field study. *Journal of Educational Psychology, 69*, 121-128.

Bridges, D. (1979). *Education, democracy, and discussion.* Windsor, UK: National Foundation for Educational Research.

Bruffee, K. (1993). *Collaborative learning: Higher education, interdependence, and authority of knowledge.* Baltimore: Johns Hopkins University Press.

Calonico, J., & Calonico, B. (1972). Classroom interaction: A sociological approach. *Journal of Educational Research, 66*, 165–169.

Cazden, C. B. (1986). Classroom discourse. In M. C. Wittrock (Ed.), *Handbook of research on teaching* (pp. 432–463). New York: Macmillan.

Chi, M. T. H., DeLeeuw, N., Chiu, M., & Lavancher, C. (1994). Eliciting self-explanations improves understanding. *Cognitive Science, 18*, 439–477.

Dillon, J. T. (1985). Using questions to foil discussion. *Teaching and Teacher Education, 1*, 109–121.

Dillon, J. T. (1990). Conducting discussions by alternatives to questioning. In W. Wilen (Ed.), *Teaching and learning through discussion* (pp. 79–96). Springfield, IL: Thomas.

Eeds, M., & Wells, D. (1989). Grand conversations: An exploration of meaning construction in literature study groups. *Research in the Teaching of English, 23*, 4–29.

Fish, S. (1980). *Is there a text in this class: The authority of interpretive communities.* Cambridge, MA: Harvard University Press.

Fuchs, D., Fuchs, L. S., Mathes, P. G., & Simmons, D. C. (1997). Peer-assisted learning strategies: Making classrooms more responsive to diversity. *American Educational Research Journal, 34*, 174–206.

Gall, M. D., & Gall, J. P. (1976). The discussion method. In N. L. Gage (Ed.), *The psychology of teaching methods* (pp. 166–216). Chicago: University of Chicago Press.

Gambrell, L. B. (1995). Motivation matters. In W. M. Linek & E. G. Sturtevant (Eds.), *Generations of literacy* (Seventeenth yearbook of the College Reading Association, pp. 2–24). East Texas, TX: College Reading Association.

Gambrell, L. B. (1996, May). Creating classroom cultures that foster reading motivation. *The Reading Teacher, 50*, 14–25.

Gambrell, L. B., & Bobola, K. (1996). *Discussion: What matters most?* Paper presented at the annual meeting of the International Reading Association, New Orleans, LA.

Gavelek, J. R. (1986). The social context of literacy and schooling: A developmental perspective. In T. E. Raphael (Ed.), *The contexts of school-based literacy* (pp. 3–26). New York: Random House.

Geffner, R. (1978). *The effects of interdependent learning on self-esteem, interethnic relations, and interethnic attitudes of elementary school children: A field experiment.* Unpublished doctoral dissertation, University of California, Santa Cruz.

Guthrie, J. T., & McCann, A. D. (1996). Idea circles: Peer collaborations for conceptual learning. In L. B. Gambrell & J. F. Almasi (Eds.), *Lively discussions!: Fostering engaged reading* (pp. 87–105). Newark, DE: International Reading Association.

Guthrie, J. T., Schafer, W., Wang, Y.Y., & Afflerbach, P. (1993). Relationships of instruction to amount of reading: An exploration of social, cognitive, and instructional connections. *Reading Research Quarterly, 30*, 8–25.

Johnson, D. W., & Johnson, R. T. (1981). Effects of cooperative and individualistic learning experiences on interethnic interaction. *Journal of Educational Psychology, 73*, 444–449.

Johnson, D. W., & Johnson, R. T. (1989). *Cooperation and competition: Theory and research.* Edina, MN: Interaction Book Co.

Johnson, D. W., & Johnson, R. T. (1990). Social skills for successful group work. *Educational Leadership, 47*, 29–33.

Johnson, D. W., Johnson, R. T., Holubec, E. J., & Roy, P. (1984). *Circles of learning: Cooperation in the classroom.* Washington, DC: Association for Supervision and Curriculum Development.

Johnson, D.W., Johnson, R. T., Stanne, M., & Garibaldi, A. (1989). The impact of leader and member group processing on achievement in cooperative groups. *Journal of Social Psychology, 130*(4), 507–516.

Lucker, G., Rosenfield, D., Sikes, J., & Aronson, E. (1979). Performance in the interdependent classroom: A field study. *American Educational Research Journal, 13*, 115–123.

Martinez, M., Roser, N. L., Hoffman, J. V., & Battle, J. (1992). Fostering better book discussions through response logs and a response framework: A case description. In C. K. Kinzer & D. J. Leu (Eds.), *Literacy research, theory, and practice: Views from many perspectives* (Forty-first Yearbook of the National Reading Conference, pp. 303–312). Chicago: National Reading Conference.

Mathes, P. G., Howard, J. K., Allen, S. H., & Fuchs, D. (1998). Peer-assisted learning strategies for first grade readers: Responding to the needs of diverse learners. *Reading Research Quarterly, 33*, 62–94.

McCombs, B. L. (1989). Self-regulated learning and academic achievement: A phenomenological view. In B. H. Zimmerman & D. H. Schunk (Eds.), *Self-regulated learning and achievement: Theory research, and practice* (pp. 51–82). New York: Springer-Verlag.

McGee, K. G. (1992). An exploration of meaning construction in first graders' grand conversations. In C. K. Kinzer & D. J. Leu (Eds.), *Literacy research, theory, and practice: Views from many perspectives* (Forty-first Yearbook of the National Reading Conference, pp. 177–186). Chicago: National Reading Conference.

McMahon, S. L. (1992). Book club: A case study of a group of fifth graders as they participate in a literature-based reading program. *Reading Research Quarterly, 28*, 292–294.

Mehan, H. (1979). *Learning lessons.* Cambridge, MA: Harvard University Press.

Morrow, L. M., & Smith, J. K. (1990). The effects of group size on interactive storybook reading. *Reading Research Quarterly, 25*, 213–231.

Ng, M. M., Guthrie, J. T., Van Meter, P., McCann, A., & Also, S. (1998). How classroom characteristics influence intrinsic motivations for literacy. *Reading Psychology, 19*(4), 319–398.

O'Flahavan, J. F. (1989). *An exploration of the effects of participant structure upon literacy development in reading group discussion.* Unpublished doctoral dissertation, University of Illinois, Urbana–Champaign.

O'Flahavan, J. F., Stein, S., Wiencek, J., & Marks, T. (1992). *Interpretive development in peer discussion about literature: An exploration of the teacher's role.* Final report to the trustees of the National Council of Teachers of English, Urbana, IL.

Oldfather, P. (1993). What students say about motivating experiences in a whole language classroom. *The Reading Teacher, 46*, 672–681.

Oldfather, P., & Dahl, K. (1995). *Toward a social constructivist reconceptualization of intrinsic moti-*

vation for literacy learning (Perspectives in Reading Research No. 6). Athens, GA: Universities of Georgia & Maryland, National Reading Research Center.

Orsolini, M., & Pontecorvo, C. (1992). Children's talk in classroom discussions. *Cognition and Instruction, 9,* 113–136.

Palincsar, A. S. (1986). The role of dialogue in providing scaffolded instruction. *Educational Psychologist, 21,* 73–98.

Palincsar, A. S., & Brown, A. L. (1984). Reciprocal teaching of comprehension fostering and monitoring activities. *Cognition and Instruction, 2,* 117–175.

Palincsar, A. S., & Brown, A. L. (1985). Reciprocal teaching activities to promote reading with your mind. In E. J. Cooper (Ed.), *Reading, thinking, and concept development: Interactive strategies for the class* (pp. 181–192). New York: The College Board.

Raphael, T. E., & McMahon, S. I. (1994). Book club: An alternative framework for reading instruction. *Reading Teacher, 48,* 102–116.

Ruddell, M. R. (1994). Vocabulary knowledge and comprehension: A comprehension-process view of complex literacy relationships. In R. B. Ruddell, M. R. Ruddell, & H. Singer (Eds.), *Theoretical models and processes of reading* (2nd ed., pp. 414–447). Newark, DE: International Reading Association.

Saunders, W., & Goldenberg, C. (1992, April). *Effects of instructional conversations on transition students' concept development.* Revised version of paper presented at the annual meeting of the American Educational Research Association, San Francisco, CA.

Sharan, S., & Shachar, C. (1988). *Language and learning in the cooperative classroom.* New York: Springer Verlag.

Sharan, Y., & Sharan, S. (1992). *Expanding cooperative learning through group investigation.* New York: Teachers College Press.

Short, K. G. (1992). Intertextuality: Searching for patterns that connect. In C. K. Kinzer & D. J. Leu (Eds.), *Literacy research, theory, and practice: Views from many perspectives* (Forty-first Yearbook of the National Reading Conference, pp. 187–198). Chicago: National Reading Conference.

Short, K. G., & Pierce, K. J. (1990). *Talking about books creating literate communities.* Portsmouth, NH: Heinemann.

Slavin, R. E. (1983). *Cooperative learning.* New York: Longman.

Slavin, R. E. (1986). *Using student team learning* (3rd ed.). Baltimore: Johns Hopkins University, Center for Research on Elementary & Middle Schools.

Slavin, R. E. (1990). *Cooperative learning: Theory, research, and practice.* Englewood Cliffs, NJ: Prentice Hall.

Slavin, R. E. (1991). Are cooperative learning and "untracking" harmful to the gifted? *Educational Leadership, 48,* 68–71.

Slavin, R. E. (1995). *Cooperative learning* (2nd ed.). Boston: Allyn & Bacon.

Slavin, R. E., & Oickle, E. (1981). Effects of cooperative learning teams on student achievement and race relations: Treatment by race interactions. *Sociology of Education, 54,* 174–180.

Turner, J. C. (1995). The influence of classroom contexts on young children's motivation for literacy. *Reading Research Quarterly, 30,* 410–441.

Vygotsky, L. S. (1978). *Mind in society.* Cambridge, MA: Harvard University Press.

Webb, N. (1982). Peer interaction and learning in cooperative small groups. *Journal of Educational Psychology, 74,* 642–655.

Wiencek, B. J. (1996). Planning, initiating, and sustaining literature discussion groups: The teacher's role. In L. B. Gambrell & J. F. Almasi (Eds.), *Lively discussions!: Fostering engaged reading* (pp. 208–223). Newark, DE: International Reading Association.

Wiseman, D. L., Many, J. E., & Altieri, J. (1992). Enabling complex aesthetic responses: An examination of three literary discussion approaches. In C. K. Kinzer & D. J. Leu (Eds.), *Literary research, theory, and practice: Views from many perspectives* (Forty-first Yearbook of the National Reading Conference, pp. 283–290). Chicago: National Reading Conference.

Wood, K. (1990). Collaborative learning. *The Reading Teacher, 43,* 346–347.

Ziegler, S. (1981). The effectiveness of cooperative learning teams for increasing cross-ethnic friendship: Additional evidence. *Human Organization, 40,* 264–268.

CHAPTER SEVEN

Facilitating Children's Reading Motivation

ALLAN WIGFIELD

Students' motivation (or the lack thereof) is a major concern of many teachers. Indeed, researchers at the National Reading Research Center found that stimulating children's interest in reading was teachers' number-one concern (O'Flahavan, Gambrell, Guthrie, Stahl, & Alvermann, 1992). Teachers who have been recognized as outstanding frequently utilize strategies to facilitate children's motivation (Pressley, Yokoi, Rankin, Wharton-McDonald, & Mistretta-Hampston, 1997). Motivation has a strong impact on children's reading; recent research confirms that students of elementary school age with stronger motivation spend substantially more time reading than do students with lower motivation (Guthrie, Wigfield, Metsala, & Cox, 1999; Wigfield & Guthrie, 1997). Research thus documents the importance of motivation to the likelihood that children will become engaged readers. Even very skilled readers may not read if they are not motivated to do so.

Despite the importance of motivation, its study in the field of reading has been rather limited. Most reading researchers have focused on the cognitive aspects of reading. Because reading is an effortful activity that involves choice (e.g., "Am I going to read or watch television?"), motivation is involved in reading, along with cognition (Guthrie & Wigfield, in press). Motivation deals with the *whys* of behavior, in that motivation researchers study motivation to understand the choices individuals make about which activity to do or not to do, their degree of persistence at the chosen activities, and the amount of effort they put forth as they do the activity (Eccles, Wigfield, & Schiefele, 1998; Pintrich & Schunk, 1996). Purely cognitive models of reading do not deal with these sorts of issues and so do not provide a complete picture of reading (see Baker, Dreher, & Guthrie, Chapter 1, this volume).

The topic of motivation is especially important for young readers. As is discussed later in this chapter, many children come to school optimistic about their skills, excited about being in school, and eager to learn to read. These beliefs and feelings change for many children during the first few years of elementary school, and in fact some children come to have doubts about their abilities in reading and other areas, and they lose their excitement for school.

The focus of this chapter is the nature and development of children's reading motivation. I begin by discussing current views on motivation and reading motivation. I then discuss the development of motivation over the early school years, and also discuss gender differences in reading motivation. The next section focuses on links of reading motivation to the frequency of children's reading and their reading achievement. The final section presents ways in which teachers can facilitate children's reading motivation in order that they may become lifelong, self-directed readers.

DEFINING MOTIVATION

Researchers have identified many crucial components of students' motivation. Eccles et al. (1998), Pintrich and Schunk (1996), and Wigfield, Eccles, and Rodriguez (1998) provided detailed reviews of this work. The focus in this chapter is on three aspects of motivation that are central to reading motivation (Baker & Wigfield, 1999; Wigfield & Guthrie, 1997): (1) intrinsic and extrinsic motivation, (2) competence and efficacy beliefs, and (3) social motivation. Definitions for each term are provided, and different children's approaches to reading are used to exemplify each term.

When individuals are intrinsically motivated, they do activities for their own sake and out of interest in the activity. Cheryl's approach to reading illustrates what is meant by intrinsic motivation to read. She is a third-grade student who reads avidly in class and grabs a book when there are breaks in classroom activities. She often reads after she goes to bed at home, because she says she becomes very involved in the characters in books she is reading and the plot of the stories. This excitement sparked by books keeps Cheryl reading even when other activities are available to her.

When extrinsically motivated, individuals do activities for instrumental or other reasons, such as receiving a reward. For example, James is a student whose motivation for reading is extrinsic. He will read when others around him are reading. But once the support of peers is removed, his reading often stops. His teacher reports that much of the work he begins does not get finished because he does not get very personally involved with his work. James rarely sticks with his reading unless directed to or rewarded by his teacher. Although many children are motivated for both extrinsic and intrinsic reasons, many motivation researchers argue that intrinsic motivation is more beneficial to long-term learning than is extrinsic motivation (Deci & Ryan, 1985). Recent research on teachers' beliefs about motivation showed that teachers see their high-achieving students as more intrinsically motivated (Sweet, Guthrie, & Ng, 1998).

Competence and efficacy beliefs refer to individuals' assessments of their ability at different activities. Researchers have shown that children's competence beliefs relate to and predict their achievement in different school subjects such as mathematics and reading (e.g., Bandura, 1997; Meece, Wigfield, & Eccles, 1990; Nicholls, 1979). Jamal is a reader with a strong sense of his competence in reading. He reads a wide range of books in his free time, from books about sports stars to books about nature. When asked about his reading, he said that unfamiliar and difficult words sometimes slow him down and disrupt his reading, but he continually strives to improve his reading. When he understands the new words and phrases, his sense of his reading competence grows stronger. His sense of competence helps him continue to pursue his reading interests.

Social motivation concerns individuals' motivation to relate to others (Wentzel, 1996). This kind of motivation is crucial to reading, because reading often is a social activity. Children read together in class, and families read together at home. For example, Miss Ryan attempts to foster children's social motivation to read. She has a reading corner in her classroom where students can sit and read books and share what they are reading. She allots time each day for the children in her class to read in this corner, and it is one of the highlights of the children's day. Sharing reading materials in this way can strengthen the child's sense of reading competence and stimulate intrinsic motivation to read.

One important implication of this conceptualization of motivation is that it is multifaceted: there are different aspects of children's motivation (Wigfield, 1997). It therefore is not appropriate to think of children as motivated or unmotivated, but rather as motivated in a variety of ways. Some of these aspects of motivation are more beneficial to learning than are others: children who are intrinsically motivated, have positive competence beliefs, and relate well to others often are more committed to learning. These children will persist longer, choose more challenging activities, and show a higher level of engagement in different activities (Ames, 1992;

Wentzel, 1996). Thus, children who are intrinsically motivated, have positive competence beliefs, and enjoy sharing in reading activities with others should be more likely to become self-directed readers.

DEVELOPMENTAL AND GENDER DIFFERENCES IN READING MOTIVATION

Because this book focuses on promoting engaged reading during the elementary school years, it is important to consider the development of motivation during these years. In this section, developmental differences in children's reading motivation are explored. In addition, because boys' and girls' experiences in reading often differ, gender differences in reading motivation are discussed.

The Development of Reading Motivation

How does children's motivation change during elementary school? Most children come to school expecting to do well, are curious about learning, and have a desire to interact with others. However, children's competence beliefs and intrinsic motivation for learning tend to decline across the elementary school years, especially in academic subject areas like reading and math (see Eccles et al., 1998, for a detailed review of the research showing these declines). For instance, researchers studying the early development of children's competence beliefs and intrinsic motivation for different subjects found that both decrease during the early elementary school years (Wigfield et al., 1997). Children's extrinsic motivation often increases throughout elementary school and into middle school, sometimes at the expense of their intrinsic motivation (Harter, 1981; Maehr & Midgley, 1996).

Page's experiences in school can be used to illustrate these points. She came to first grade eagerly, excited to learn more about reading and numbers. The first few weeks of school went well for her. She fit in with her classmates and enthusiastically completed her work. As the year went on, however, she began to experience some difficulty. Although she could decode some words, she had a hard time with other ones. She became hesitant to read aloud in class or at home with her parents. She was placed in the low-reading group, where she continued to struggle with her reading. Her excitement about attending school gradually was replaced by apprehension, and she sometimes resisted the work given to her to do. Page would respond to rewards given to her by increasing her efforts, but she would not often pick up a book in her free time. She was relieved when the school year finally was over. As the new school year approached, Page was much less eager to return to school. How would she handle the more difficult work in second grade?

Such changes in children's motivation have been explained in two main ways. One explanation focuses on children's increasing capacity to understand their own performance. Children become much more sophisticated at understanding the evaluative feedback they receive, and for some children this leads to a growing realization that they are not as capable as other children. For instance, even first-grade children are quite aware of which groups they are assigned to and what that means regarding their capabilities (see Weinstein, 1989). The realization that one is not as capable as others can decrease motivation (see Bandura, 1997). A second explanation focuses on how teaching practices may contribute to a decline in some children's motivation. Practices that emphasize social comparison between children and too much competition between them may lead children to focus too much on how their skills compare to those of others. Such practices can deflate many children's competence beliefs. Instruction that makes few attempts to spark children's interests in different topics and relies too much on extrinsic rewards can lead to declines in children's intrinsic motivation (see Brophy, 1998; Wigfield, Eccles, & Pintrich, 1996, and Stipek, 1996, for more detailed discussion). Teaching practices that can facilitate children's competence beliefs and intrinsic motivation are discussed later.

Do these general declines in motivation occur for reading motivation? The evidence on this point is somewhat mixed. Wigfield et al. (1997) reported that children's competence beliefs and interest in reading declined across the elementary school years, and also that the decline in interest in reading was strongest across grades 1–4. Marsh (1989) reported that older elementary school children had lower self-concepts of ability in reading than did younger children. McKenna, Kear, and Ellsworth (1995), in a national study of how much children liked recreational and school reading, found that children's liking of both kinds of reading was higher in younger children than in older children. Chapman and Tunmer (1995) also reported that younger elementary school children's liking of reading was greater than that of older children.

Other researchers have found fewer age differences. Gottfried (1990) did not find age differences in 7- to 9-year-old children's intrinsic motivation for reading. Wigfield and Guthrie (1997) and Baker and Wigfield (1999), using the Motivation for Reading Questionnaire (MRQ; see below) found relatively few age differences in the different aspects of children's reading motivation measured by that instrument. Their studies were with fourth-, fifth-, through sixth-grade students. Although they found age differences in children's liking of reading, Chapman and Tunmer (1995) found no age differences in children's beliefs about their reading competence.

The somewhat conflicting results may be due to the different ages of children in these studies. The largest decreases in reading motivation seem to occur across grades 1– 4. The observed differences also may be tied to differences in instructional practices in reading. Some teachers may foster reading motivation, whereas perhaps others do not; we return to this point later.

Gender Differences in Reading Motivation

Evidence indicates that boys have more difficulty learning to read than girls do, although the differences are small (Hyde & Linn, 1988). Boys more often are held back in school and diagnosed with various learning disabilities. There are a variety of explanations offered for these findings. These include boys not being as mature as girls when they start school, the lack of male teachers in the early grades, and the sex-typing of reading as an activity more appropriate for girls than for boys (Brophy, 1985).

Another factor in the reading performance differences could be differences between girls and boys in their reading motivation. Researchers have found that girls often have more positive motivation for reading than do boys. Wigfield et al. (1997) reported that even at first grade, girls had higher competence beliefs and expressed greater interest in reading than did boys. Marsh (1989) reported similar findings for boys' and girls' self-concepts of ability in reading. McKenna et al. (1995) found that the mean level of girls' liking of reading was higher than that of boys at each grade level from 1 to 6. This gap widened across the grades for recreational reading. Wigfield and Guthrie (1997) reported sex differences favoring girls on several aspects of reading motivation assessed by the MRQ; the only difference favoring boys was in how much children liked competitive activities in reading. The one exception to this general pattern is Gottfried's (1990) study of intrinsic motivation; she found no sex differences in young children's intrinsic motivation for reading.

The overall pattern is that there are sex differences in reading motivation in children as young as first grade. In fact, the differences in reading motivation actually may be larger than the observed differences in reading performance during the early elementary school years. These differences should be kept in mind when educators are considering instructional practices to facilitate reading motivation. Some of the differences, such as boys' preference for competitive activities in reading, suggest that different instructional practices may be needed to facilitate boys' and girls' reading motivation.

LINKING READING MOTIVATION TO READING
FREQUENCY AND ACHIEVEMENT

How does reading motivation relate to the amount of reading children do and their reading achievement? The amount of reading children do is important to consider because reading amount relates strongly to children's text comprehension and achievement (Baker, Dreher, & Guthrie, Chapter 1, this volume; Campbell, Voelkl, & Donahue, 1997; Cunningham & Stanovich, 1997). Wigfield and Guthrie (1997) developed a questionnaire called the MRQ to measure different aspects of reading motivation, including the aspects discussed in this chapter: intrinsic and extrinsic motivation, reading efficacy, and social aspects of reading motivation. They looked at how these aspects of reading motivation related to the amount of reading children did in their free time. They found that both intrinsic and extrinsic reading motives related to children's reading amount, although overall it appeared that aspects of intrinsic motivation for reading related more strongly to the outcomes than did the extrinsic motivation. Children's sense of reading efficacy also related to the amount of their reading. Baker and Wigfield (1999), in a study of urban fifth- and sixth-grade students, obtained similar relations between aspects of reading motivation and reading amount.

Wigfield and Guthrie (1997) also looked at how children with different levels of intrinsic and extrinsic motivation differed in the amount of reading they did. The results showed strong differences in amount of reading across the high, middle, and low intrinsically motivated groups. Children higher in intrinsic motivation read much more than did children who were medium and low in intrinsic motivation. In contrast, the three groups of extrinsically motivated children did not differ as greatly in the amount of reading that they did. Baker and Wigfield (1999) extended this work by looking at how children's reading motivation related to their reading achievement. They found that children's reading motivation related to their achievement in reading, although these relations were weaker than those between children's reading motivation and amount of reading.

In summary, both intrinsic and extrinsic aspects of children's reading motivation relate positively to children's reading amount. Reading motivation also relates directly to achievement in reading. Reading amount relates strongly to reading achievement, and itself is predicted by children's reading motivation (see also Guthrie et al., 1999). Therefore, children's reading motivation has an important role both in the amount of reading children do and their achievement in reading.

INSTRUCTIONAL PRACTICES THAT FACILITATE READING MOTIVATION

There are many different classroom practices that can facilitate reading motivation. Researchers and teachers have collaborated to develop instructional programs to facilitate the development of children's reading skills and motivation. A number of these programs are discussed by other authors in this book (e.g., see Chapter 3 by Graham & Harris, Chapter 4 by Dreher, and Chapter 10 by Guthrie, Cox, et al.). What is discussed in this section is research coming out of the motivation and reading research fields on how different kinds of teaching practices can facilitate, or sometimes debilitate, students' motivation. The presentation of this work is organized around the aspects of motivation focused on in this chapter: intrinsic motivation, extrinsic motivation, self-efficacy, and social aspects of motivation. Interested readers should consult Brophy (1998), Guthrie and Wigfield (in press), Stipek (1996), and Wigfield et al. (1998) for further discussion of work on instructional practices and student motivation.

Intrinsic Motivation and Self-Directed Reading

Student Choice

Researchers have argued that as students learn to value learning, they become intrinsically motivated and self-directed (Deci & Ryan, 1985; Ryan & Stiller, 1991). When students are self-directed learners, they choose to be involved in learning and they like to have some control over what they learn. The classroom contexts that students are in greatly influence students' intrinsic motivation and engagement; the degree of teacher versus student control is one crucial part of this. Deci, Ryan, and their colleagues have discussed how teachers who are overly controlling and do not provide students with control over their own learning can undermine their students' intrinsic motivation and engagement (see Ryan & Stiller, 1991, for a review). Giving students some control over their learning, by providing them choices, can foster intrinsic motivation.

A study of young children's reading illustrates this point. Turner (1995, 1997) studied how classroom contexts influence different aspects of young students' motivation for literacy activities. She distinguished between open and closed literacy activities, or tasks. Open activities are ones that allow students choice, require strategy use, and facilitate student involvement and persistence. Because students choose the activities, they often are more interested in them. In contrast, closed activities are more constrained, both in terms of students' choices about whether and how to engage in them and the cognitive demands of the activity. Turner (1995) found that in classrooms where tasks were more open, students were more engaged in literacy activities, used more elaborate strategies, and were much more interested in literacy activities than were students in classrooms where closed tasks were used more frequently.

Building choice into the reading curriculum, then, is a good way to facilitate children's intrinsic motivation in reading and sense of ownership over their reading. Young children of course will need guidance in what kinds of books to choose. Teachers can provide an appropriate range of choices of reading materials for students and let them make choices within that range (see Chambliss & McKillop, Chapter 5, this volume). Choice of materials is an important part of reading instructional programs like Concept Oriented Reading Instruction (CORI; see Guthrie et al., 1996; Guthrie, Cox, et al., Chapter 10, this volume).

Interesting Texts and Challenging Tasks

Children's motivation to read can be enhanced when interesting texts and materials are used in class. Examples of interesting texts include trade books, electronic reading sources, and lively reference materials featuring pictures and activities (see Dreher, Chapter 4, this volume; Guthrie & Alao, 1997). These books can be used to supplement, or possibly replace, basal reading series. These interesting texts can be a powerful influence on children's intrinsic motivation, particularly when children also have some choice about which texts to read.

Motivation theorists have discussed how to present tasks and activities in order to facilitate children's intrinsic motivation (Brophy, 1998; Guthrie & Alao, 1997; Guthrie & Wigfield, in press; Stipek, 1996). There are several important principles that can be taken from their work. First, tasks should be moderately difficult for children so that they face some challenges in accomplishing them. Tasks that are too easy—or too hard— decrease intrinsic motivation. Second, giving children a variety of tasks and activities and presenting them in novel ways maintains motivation. Changes in the daily classroom routine are important. Third, the use of hands-on activities in science and other subjects is an especially important way to stimulate children's intrinsic motivation. These activities can be paired with reading materials to supplement the learning that occurred during the activity. Such activities are an important part of programs like CORI (Guthrie & Alao, 1997; Guthrie et al., 1996). Finally, including tasks that are personally meaningful to children stimulates their intrinsic motivation (Stipek, 1996). Not every task or activity needs to be novel or personally meaningful, but efforts should be made to include many of these kinds of tasks into the reading curriculum.

Extrinsic Rewards and Self-Directed Reading

The use of rewards by teachers to stimulate motivation is a common practice in many schools. The rewards can be tangible ones like extra privileges, or verbal ones like praise. A number of early reading programs, such as the All-American Reading Challenge, Book It!, Bucks for Books, and

RUNNING START, rely on giving children incentives for reading a certain number of books. The incentives range from receiving free books, free pizza, or money (see Gambrell & Marinak, 1997, for review). These programs have been successful in promoting children's engagement in reading activities, at least over the short term. The effective use of praise has been documented in many studies. Praise that is given for specific accomplishments, is sincere, and is tied to effort and achievement can enhance student motivation and achievement (Brophy, 1998).

Yet, many motivation theorists, particularly those who believe intrinsic motivation has positive effects on students' learning, have argued that under certain conditions the overuse of reward and praise can undermine students' sense of control over their achievement outcomes and reduce their intrinsic motivation (e.g., Deci & Ryan, 1985; Lepper, 1988; Ryan & Stiller, 1991). This is particularly true when children already are doing the activity because they are intrinsically motivated to do it. Lepper, Greene, and Nisbett (1973) used the compelling phrase "turning play into work" to describe such effects. In addition to the "turning play into work" issue, Ryan and Stiller (1991) discussed how extrinsic rewards can change students' sense that they control their own achievement outcomes to the sense that the teacher is controlling them. In Ryan and Stiller's view, this change undermines students' motivation to engage in the activity. These researchers thus have advocated that extrinsic rewards be used with care in classroom settings. Others, however, have argued that extrinsic rewards do not undermine intrinsic motivation (Cameron & Pierce, 1994).

A balanced perspective on this debate perhaps is the best way to resolve it. Children appear to be motivated to read for a variety of reasons. Some are motivated to read for extrinsic reasons, and some are intrinsically motivated to read (Baker & Wigfield, 1999; Wigfield & Guthrie, 1997). Many children likely need encouragement to engage in reading, and the incentives that teachers provide, as well as those that are built into some early reading programs, could provide that encouragement. Acquiring the basic skills needed for reading (e.g., word recognition) may not be intrinsically motivating for many children, and some incentives may be needed to keep children working on them. This may be particularly true for children struggling with reading. As children become involved with books and reading, the incentives should be less necessary and children should become more self-directed in their reading engagement.

Reading Self-Efficacy

Grouping Practices

As discussed earlier, it is crucial that students develop a strong sense of their reading competence if they are to become self-directed readers. One classroom practice that has an influence on children's developing sense of competence or efficacy is ability grouping for different subjects. Students are grouped by ability in two main ways. In elementary schools, children are often grouped by ability within classrooms for instruction in subjects such as reading and mathematics. In middle school and high school, between-classroom ability grouping, or tracking, is used more frequently. These practices are controversial and have attracted much attention (see Oakes, 1985). A major concern is that children in the lower-ability tracks will perceive they are not very able. Children often are very aware of their group membership and what it means, despite the best efforts not to label the groups in obvious ways (Weinstein, 1989). However, Pallas, Entwisle, Alexander, and Stluka (1994) found no evidence that within-class ability grouping in reading affected children's competence beliefs and performance expectations during the early elementary school years.

Research on ability grouping, although not providing completely clear-cut results, shows it may have benefits for higher-ability students' motivation but may weaken the motivation of children in the lower-ability groups (Fuligni, Eccles, & Barber, 1995; Oakes, 1985). Because of the potential negative effects of ability grouping, especially on children in the low groups, such grouping should be used with care. Teachers should reevaluate group membership on a regular basis. Children should know they have the opportunity to move into different reading groups.

Fostering Ownership

Another way to enhance reading self-efficacy is to facilitate children's sense that they have control over what they learn. As discussed earlier, this control also can enhance intrinsic motivation. Au and her colleagues (Au, 1997; Au, Scheu, Kawakami, & Herman, 1990) used the term "ownership" in discussing students' sense of control over their learning. They argued that student ownership of the activities they do is a crucial contributor to students' developing literacy skills, especially for many minority students. These authors developed reading curricula in Hawaii to help foster the development of literacy skills in native Hawaiians, a group that traditionally has done poorly in school. The reading and writing activities in the Kamehameha Elementary Education Program (KEEP) curricula have student ownership as a major goal. One way this goal is accomplished is through making the materials culturally relevant to the children. Evaluations of the program have shown that students are strongly engaged in the literacy activities and have a strong sense of ownership of these activities. Initially, improvement in the children's reading performance was not dramatic, but in more recent evaluations some 80% of the students in the KEEP program were at or above grade level in reading.

Classroom Goal Structures, Competition, and Social Comparison

Ames (1984) discussed various goal structures used in classrooms and how they impact students' motivation. She focused on three different goal structures. *Individualized* structures occur when each student is judged on his/her own performance. In this structure all students can succeed if each works hard. The performance of other students does not impact the evaluation of any given student. *Competitive* structures mean that some students are winners and others losers; that is the essence of competition. Ames noted that competition makes social comparison and judgments of ability especially salient. She and other motivation researchers have argued against the use of too many competitive activities in school. In competition only a few children can win, and that means the motivation of the students not winning likely will suffer. *Cooperative* structures mean that group members share in the rewards or punishments; the overall group's performance is key (although individuals often are accountable as well).

What are the implications for children's competence and efficacy beliefs of these different structures? In general, according to Ames (1984), students are most likely to focus on evaluating their ability under competitive goal structures. Winners' ability beliefs are enhanced, and losers' are diminished. Overall, differences in competence beliefs are heightened under competitive conditions, which can be detrimental to the motivation of those children not often winning. With individualistic structures, each student's main focus is on improving his/her own skills. Competence beliefs likely are less salient, because the focus is on effort and improvement. Cooperative goal structures foster an emphasis on shared effort and interdependence, rather than ability. This also means there is less emphasis on the individual's competence. Ames and other motivation theorists like Brophy (1998) recommend that individualistic and cooperative goal structures be used more frequently than competitive goal structures in classroom settings.

Evaluation Practices

Another influence on self-efficacy is evaluation practices. When these practices are public, comparative, and competitive, children's self-efficacy may be reduced. Motivation theorists recommend that assessments and evaluations be focused on providing students feedback on what they have learned and what else they need to learn. Assessments should be seen as part of the curriculum rather than solely as evaluations of relative performance (see Leipzig & Afflerbach, Chapter 8, this volume; see also Brophy, 1998; Stipek, 1996).

Self-Efficacy Training

Teachers can enhance children's self-efficacy by helping them succeed at different classroom tasks and activities. Sometimes, however, children lacking a sense of efficacy in reading need individualized programs to boost their self-efficacy. Schunk and his colleagues have conducted several intervention studies designed to improve elementary school children's reading and writing performance through skill training, enhancement of self-efficacy, and training children how to set goals (e.g., Schunk, 1983; Schunk & Rice, 1987, 1989; Schunk & Swartz, 1993). Modeling successful performance often is an important aspect of the training. Schunk and his colleagues have found that the training increases both children's performance and their sense of self-efficacy (e.g., Schunk & Rice, 1989). Also, training children to set short-term, specific, and somewhat challenging goals enhances both their self-efficacy and performance.

Social Motivation and Reading Engagement

Individualistic, competitive, and cooperative goal structures have different influences on relations among students (Ames, 1984). When the goal structure focuses on the individual, there may be little concern for others because each individual determines his/her own achievement. In competitive goal structures, children are quite concerned about how others do. Sometimes the competition can make relations among different group members difficult. Some children will be seen as winners, some as losers. If some children consistently are viewed as losers, both their motivation and relations with other children in the class can suffer. In cooperative goal structures, the social group also is emphasized. Because the group outcome is especially salient, children's social interactions and motivation may be enhanced. Individuals' own competence beliefs become less crucial; rather, the group's performance is emphasized. Thus, cooperative goal structures, with their emphasis on students working together, should enhance collaboration, thereby facilitating student motivation. As mentioned earlier, reading often is a social activity, and so reading activities that allow social interaction should facilitate reading motivation.

Cooperative Learning

A major approach to instruction that utilizes cooperative goal structures is cooperative learning. Generally, cooperative learning involves students working together in groups rather than on their own or competing with others. There are a variety of types of cooperative learning; these are described by Gambrell, Mazzoni, and Almasi (Chapter 6, this volume),

Slavin (1995), and Webb and Palincsar (1996). For instance, in Jigsaw each student in a group is given part of the material that he/she needs to learn, and each shares this material with the other members of his/her group. In Teams Games Tournaments, students form into groups to learn some material, and then they compete against other groups to earn points for their team.

An extensive literature now documents cooperative learning's positive effects on children (see Johnson & Johnson, 1994, and Slavin, 1995, 1996, for reviews). When teachers adopt a cooperative instructional and reward structure in their classrooms, achievement often improves, social relations are more positive, and students' motivation is enhanced (see Sharan & Shaulov, 1993). Learning and motivation appear to be highest in cooperative learning situations that are characterized by both group goals and individual accountability (Slavin, 1995). Such situations appear to create positive interdependence and stimulating group inquiry, which in turn arouse social and academic motivational goals and prevent the "free-rider effect." This effect refers to children receiving good evaluations because their group does well, even though they did not contribute to the group (Stevens & Slavin, 1995).

Different aspects of student motivation are affected by cooperative learning. For example, Stevens and Slavin (1995) assessed students' beliefs about their competence in different subject areas along with their liking of the subjects. They found that students in cooperative elementary schools did have higher perceived competence in reading and mathematics than did students in "traditional" schools; however, there were no differences in students' liking of the different subjects at the two schools.

Another benefit of cooperative learning and collaboration with peers is that peers can help each other understand and learn the material through group discussion, sharing of resources, modeling academic skills, and interpreting and clarifying the tasks for each other (Gambrell, Mazzoni, & Almasi, Chapter 6, this volume; Schunk & Zimmerman, 1997). Each of these characteristics should influence achievement through its impact on children's expectations for success, their valuing of the activity, and their focus on improving their skills.

Peers can play important facilitating roles even in early reading. Turner (1995, 1997) noted that one of the many benefits of open literacy tasks is that they allow opportunities for social collaboration. The social activities she observed included modeling, peer tutoring, and discussion of the materials being read. These activities enhanced not only the products that students produced but also the processes of learning. It is important for the classroom to work together to create a community of literacy learners, rather than being either unconnected or competing individuals (Turner & Paris, 1995).

Collaboration with peers to facilitate students' skills and thematic understandings also will facilitate student motivation. This is a key premise of Guthrie and his colleagues' CORI program (Guthrie et al., 1996; Guthrie & McCann, 1997). Time is set aside each day for children to discuss what they are reading and learning, and to engage with other children around books.

Although cooperative learning and collaboration have many desirable outcomes, they do pose challenges for teachers. Structuring activities cooperatively takes extensive planning, and record keeping can be challenging as well. Another important issue in cooperative learning is how groups are set up. Slavin (1995) and other researchers generally recommend that groups be heterogeneous, in terms of children's ability level as well as other characteristics such as race and gender. There is a growing body of research showing how group composition influences student interaction in the group (see Webb & Palincsar, 1996, for a review). Webb and Palincsar noted that children with middle levels of ability may get ignored in heterogeneous groups; high-ability children benefit by being leaders and teachers, and low-ability children benefit from the high-ability children's teaching. Further, mixed-race groups can be dominated by white children, and mixed-sex groups dominated by boys. At the least, care must be taken in constructing groups, and teachers are advised to change groups frequently.

SUMMARY AND CONCLUSION

Children's motivation is crucial to their reading engagement. Motivation can be conceptualized as multifaceted, consisting of several different aspects. These aspects include intrinsic and extrinsic motivation, efficacy beliefs, and social motivation. Children who are intrinsically motivated, have positive efficacy beliefs, and are motivated to interact with others tend to be more engaged in learning. However, children's sense of competence and intrinsic motivation to learn often declines across the early school years. There are a variety of instructional practices that can alleviate these declines, and increase children's motivation. The use of these practices will help all children become self-directed readers and lifelong literacy learners.

RECOMMENDED READINGS

Brophy, J. E. (1998). *Motivating students to learn.* New York: McGraw-Hill.

This book provides a review of current work on motivation in theory and in practice. It includes many good suggestions for how teachers can encourage students' motivation.

Pintrich, P. R., & Schunk, D. H. (1996). *Motivation in education: Theory, research, and applications*. Englewood Cliffs, NJ: Merrill/Prentice Hall.

This book provides a comprehensive overview of motivation theory and research. It includes a good balance of motivation theory and educational applications of motivation theory.

Turner, J. C., & Paris, S. G. (1995). How literacy tasks influence children's motivation for literacy. *The Reading Teacher, 48*, 662–673.

This paper provides a very readable summary of Turner's work on different kinds of literacy tasks used in the early grades and the impact of such tasks on children's motivation.

Wigfield, A., Eccles, J. S., & Rodriguez, D. (1998). The development of children's motivation in school contexts. In. A. Iran-Nejad & P. D. Pearson (Eds.), *Review of research in education* (Vol. 23). Washington, DC: American Educational Research Association.

This chapter provides a detailed review of the nature of children's motivation and its development. It also presents information on classroom influences on motivation. Suggestions for promoting children's motivation are provided.

Wigfield, A., & Guthrie, J. T. (1997). Relations of children's motivation for reading to the amount and breadth of their reading. *Journal of Educational Psychology, 89*, 420–432.

This paper presents information about the development of the Motivation for Reading Questionnaire (MRQ), and describes the first study done using that questionnaire. The items in the MRQ are presented in the paper and can be adapted for classroom use.

REFERENCES

Ames, C. (1984). Competitive, cooperative, and individualistic goal structures: A cognitive-motivational analysis. In R. E. Ames & C. Ames (Eds.), *Research on motivation in education* (Vol. 1). San Diego, CA: Academic Press.

Ames, C. (1992). Classrooms: Goals, structures, and student motivation. *Journal of Educational Psychology, 84*, 261–271.

Au, K. H. (1997). Ownership, literacy achievement, and students of diverse cultural backgrounds. In J. T. Guthrie & A. Wigfield (Eds.), *Reading engagement: Motivating readers through integrated instruction* (pp. 168–182). Newark, DE: International Reading Association.

Au, K. H., Scheu, J. A., Kawakami, A. J., & Herman, P. A. (1990). Assessment and accountability in a whole literacy curriculum. *The Reading Teacher, 43*, 574–578.

Baker, L., & Wigfield, A. (1999). Dimensions of children's motivation for reading and their relations to reading activity and reading achievement. *Reading Research Quarterly, 34*, 452–477.

Bandura, A. (1997). *Self-efficacy: The exercise of control*. New York: Freeman.

Brophy, J. E. (1985). Interactions of male and female students with male and female teachers. In L. Wilkinson & C. Marett (Eds.), *Gender influences in classroom interaction* (pp. 115–142). Cambridge, MA: Abt.

Brophy, J. E. (1998). *Motivating students to learn.* New York: McGraw-Hill.

Cameron, J., & Pierce, W. D. (1994). Reinforcement, reward, and intrinsic motivation: A meta-analysis. *Review of Educational Research, 64,* 363–423.

Campbell, J. W., Voelkl, K. E., & Donahue, P. L. (1997). *NAEP 1996 trends in academic progress* (National Center for Educational Statistics Publication No. 97-985). Washington, DC: U.S. Department of Education.

Chapman, J. W., & Tunmer, W. E. (1995). Development of young children's reading self-concepts: An examination of emerging subcomponents and their relationship with reading achievement. *Journal of Educational Psychology, 87,* 154–167.

Cunningham, A. E., & Stanovich, K. E. (1997). Early reading acquisition and its relation to reading experience and ability 10 years later. *Developmental Psychology, 33,* 934–945.

Deci, E. L., & Ryan, R. M. (1985). *Intrinsic motivation and self-determination in human behavior.* New York: Plenum Press.

Eccles, J. S., Wigfield, A., & Schiefele, U. (1998). Motivation to succeed. In W. Damon (Series Ed.) & N. Eisenberg (Vol. Ed.), *Handbook of child psychology* (5th ed., Vol. 3). New York: Wiley.

Fuligni, A. J., Eccles, J. S., & Barber, B. L. (1995). The long-term effects of seventh-grade ability grouping in mathematics. *Journal of Early Adolescence, 15,* 58–89.

Gambrell, L. B., & Marinak, B. A. (1997). Incentives and intrinsic motivation to read. In J. T. Guthrie & A. Wigfield (Eds.), *Reading engagement: Motivating readers through integrated instruction* (pp. 205–217). Newark, DE: International Reading Association.

Gottfried, A. E. (1990). Academic intrinsic motivation in young elementary school children. *Journal of Educational Psychology, 82,* 525–538.

Guthrie, J. T., & Alao, S. (1997). Designing contexts to increase motivation for reading. *Educational Psychologist, 32,* 95–106.

Guthrie, J. T., & McCann, A. D. (1997). Characteristics of classrooms that promote motivations and strategies for learning. In J. T. Guthrie & A. Wigfield (Eds.), *Reading engagement: Motivating readers through integrated instruction* (pp. 128–148). Newark, DE: International Reading Association.

Guthrie, J. G., Van Meter, P., McCann, A., Wigfield, A., Bennett, L., Poundstone, C., Rice, M. E., Faibisch, F., Hunt, B., & Mitchell, A. (1996). Growth in literacy engagement: Changes in motivations and strategies during Concept-Oriented Reading Instruction. *Reading Research Quarterly, 31,* 306–325.

Guthrie, J. T., & Wigfield, A. (in press). Engagement and motivation in reading. In M. L. Kamil & P. D. Pearson (Eds.), *Handbook of reading research* (Vol. 3.). New York: Longman.

Guthrie, J. T., Wigfield, A., Metsala, J., & Cox, K. (1999). Predicting text comprehension and reading activity with motivational and cognitive variables. *Scientific Studies of Reading, 3,* 231–256.

Harter, S. (1981). A new self-report scale of intrinsic versus extrinsic orientation in the classroom: Motivational and informational components. *Developmental Psychology, 17,* 300–312.

Hyde, J. S., & Linn, M. C. (1988). Gender differences in verbal ability: A meta-analysis. *Psychological Bulletin, 104,* 53–69.

Johnson, D. W., & Johnson, R. T. (1994). *Learning together and alone: Cooperative, competitive, and individualistic learning* (4th ed.). Boston: Allyn & Bacon.

Lepper, M. R. (1988). Motivational considerations in the study of instruction. *Cognition and Instruction, 5,* 289–310.

Lepper, M. R., Greene, D., & Nisbett, R. E. (1973). Undermining children's intrinsic interest with extrinsic rewards: A test of the "overjustification" hypothesis. *Journal of Personality and Social Psychology, 28,* 129–137.

Maehr, M. L., & Midgley, C. M. (1996). *Transforming school cultures*. Boulder, CO: Westview Press.

Marsh, H. W. (1989). Age and sex effects in multiple dimensions of self-concept: Preadolescence to early adulthood. *Journal of Educational Psychology, 81*, 417–430.

McKenna, M. C., Kear, D. J., & Ellsworth, R. A. (1995). Children's attitudes toward reading: A national survey. *Reading Research Quarterly, 30*, 934–956.

Meece, J. L., Wigfield, A., & Eccles, J. S. (1990). Predictors of math anxiety and its consequences for young adolescents' course enrollment intentions and performances in mathematics. *Journal of Educational Psychology, 82*, 60–70.

Nicholls, J. G. (1979). Development of perception of own attainment and causal attributions for success and failure in reading. *Journal of Educational Psychology, 71*, 94–99.

Oakes, J. (1985). *Keeping track: How schools structure inequality*. New Haven, CT: Yale University Press.

O'Flahavan, J., Gambrell, L. B., Guthrie, J. T., Stahl, S., & Alvermann, D. (1992, April). Poll results guide activities of research center. *Reading Today*, p. 12.

Pallas, A. M., Entwisle, D. R., Alexander, K. L., & Stluka, M. F. (1994). Ability-group effects: Instructional, social, or institutional? *Sociology of Education, 67*, 27–46.

Pintrich, P. R., & Schunk, D. H. (1996). *Motivation in education: Theory, research, and applications*. Englewood Cliffs, NJ: Merrill/Prentice Hall.

Pressley, M., Yokoi, L., Rankin, J., Wharton-McDonald, R., & Mistretta- Hampston, J. (1997). *A survey of the instructional practices of grade-5 teachers nominated as effective in promoting literacy* (Reading Research Rep. No. 85). Athens, GA: Universities of Georgia & Maryland, National Reading Research Center.

Ryan, R. M., & Stiller, J. (1991). The social contexts of internalization: Parent and teacher influences on autonomy, motivation, and learning. In M. L. Maehr & P. R. Pintrich (Eds.), *Advances in motivation and achievement* (Vol. 7, pp. 115–149). Greenwich, CT: JAI Press.

Schunk, D. H. (1983). Ability versus effort attributional feedback: Differential effects on self-efficacy and achievement. *Journal of Educational Psychology, 75*, 848–856.

Schunk, D. H., & Rice, J. M. (1987). Enhancing comprehension skills and self-efficacy with strategy value information. *Journal of Reading Behavior, 19*, 285–302.

Schunk, D. H., & Rice, J. M. (1989). Learning goals and children's reading comprehension. *Journal of Reading Behavior, 21*, 279–293.

Schunk, D. H., & Swartz, C. W. (1993). Goals and progress feedback: Effects on self-efficacy and writing achievement. *Contemporary Educational Psychology, 18*, 337–354.

Schunk, D. H., & Zimmerman, B. J. (1997). Developing self-efficacious readers and writers: The role of social and self-regulatory processes. In J. T. Guthrie & A. Wigfield (Eds.), *Reading engagement: Motivating readers through integrated instruction* (pp. 34–50). Newark, DE: International Reading Association.

Sharan, S., & Shaulov, A. (1993). Cooperative learning, motivation to learn, and academic achievement. In S. Sharan (Ed.), *Cooperative learning: Theory and research*. New York: Praeger.

Slavin, R. E. (1995). *Cooperative learning: Theory, research, and practice* (2nd ed.). Boston: Allyn & Bacon.

Slavin, R. E. (1996). Research on cooperative learning and achievement: What we know, what we need to know. *Contemporary Educational Psychology, 21*, 43–69.

Stevens, R. J., & Slavin, R. E. (1995). The cooperative elementary school: Effects on students' achievement, attitudes, and social relations. *American Educational Research Journal, 32*, 321–351.

Stipek, D. J. (1996). Motivation and instruction. In D. C. Berliner & R. C. Calfee (Eds.), *Handbook of educational psychology* (pp. 85–113). New York: Macmillan.

Sweet, A. P., Guthrie, J. T., & Ng, M. M. (1998). Teacher perceptions and student reading motivation. *Journal of Educational Psychology, 90*, 210–223.

Turner, J. C. (1995). The influence of classroom contexts on young children's motivation for literacy. *Reading Research Quarterly, 30*, 410–441.

Turner, J. C. (1997). Starting right: Strategies for engaging young literacy learners. In J. T. Guthrie & A. Wigfield (Eds.), *Reading engagement: Motivating readers through integrated instruction* (pp. 183–204). Newark, DE: International Reading Association.

Turner, J. C., & Paris, S. G. (1995). How literacy tasks influence children's motivation for literacy. *The Reading Teacher, 48*, 662–673.

Webb, N. M., & Palincsar, A. S. (1996). Group processes in the classroom. In D. C. Berliner & R. C. Calfee (Eds.), *Handbook of educational psychology* (pp. 841–873). New York: Macmillan.

Weinstein, R. S. (1989). Perception of classroom processes and student motivation: Children's views of self-fulfilling prophecies. In R. E. Ames & C. Ames (Eds.), *Research on motivation in education* (Vol. 3, pp. 187–221). New York: Academic Press.

Wentzel, K. R. (1996). Social goals and social relationships as motivators of school adjustment. In J. Juvonen & K. R. Wentzel (Eds.), *Social motivation: Understanding school adjustment.* New York: Cambridge University Press.

Wigfield, A. (1997). Reading motives: A domain-specific approach to motivation. *Educational Psychologist, 32*, 59–68.

Wigfield, A., Eccles, J. S., & Pintrich, P. R. (1996). Development between the ages of eleven and twenty-five. In D. C. Berliner & R. C. Calfee (Eds.), *Handbook of educational psychology* (pp. 148–185). New York: Macmillan.

Wigfield, A., Eccles, J. S., & Rodriguez, D. (1998). The development of children's motivation in school contexts. In A. Iran-Nejad & P. D. Pearson (Eds.), *Review of research in education* (Vol. 23, pp. 73–118). Washington, DC: American Educational Research Association.

Wigfield, A., Eccles, J. S., Yoon, K. S., Harold, R. D., Arbreton, A., Freedman-Doan, K., & Blumenfeld, P. C. (1997). Changes in children's competence beliefs and subjective task values across the elementary school years: A three-year study. *Journal of Educational Psychology, 89*, 451–469.

Wigfield, A., & Guthrie, J. T. (1997). Relations of children's motivation for reading to the amount and breadth of their reading. *Journal of Educational Psychology, 89*, 420–432.

CHAPTER EIGHT

Determining the Suitability of Assessments
Using the CURRV Framework

DIANE HENRY LEIPZIG
PETER AFFLERBACH

This chapter introduces the CURRV framework for evaluating reading assessment. The CURRV can be used by teachers, administrators, or curriculum coordinators to examine the following concepts: (1) *c*onsequence and (2) *u*sefulness of reading assessment; (3) *r*oles and responsibilities of teachers and students in relation to reading assessment; and (4) *r*eliability and (5) *v*alidity of reading assessment. Thus, the CURRV framework may prove helpful in designing assessment programs, choosing between various assessments, or developing new assessments.

In this chapter we first describe the five elements of the CURRV framework enumerated above. We then explicate these elements further by applying and pairing each with a form of reading assessment, including norm- and criterion-referenced tests, portfolios, oral reading measures, and performance assessment. Finally, we demonstrate how the CURRV framework can be used by a teacher of engaged reading to examine a particular assessment program. Although the CURRV framework is applied to engaged reading in this chapter, it can be used to evaluate reading assessment in relation to any view of reading.

THE CURRV FRAMEWORK

The CURRV framework is based upon the premise that good reading assessment should be developed and evaluated in relation to the five separate but closely intertwined concepts of consequences, usefulness, roles of teachers and students, reliability, and validity. For clarity, these five concepts are discussed separately in this chapter. Each of the five concepts is a critical element of successful assessment, and each influences the other in various ways. Many researchers have argued that these concepts overlap and should be considered together. Points of intersection have been identified between validity and consequences (Moss, 1998; Shepard, 1997); usefulness and reliability (Wainer & Thissen, 1996); validity, usefulness and roles (Messick, 1989a; Tittle, 1989); and validity and reliability (McBee & Barnes, 1998; Moss, 1994). Each of the concepts of the CURRV framework should be carefully considered as reading assessments are developed, chosen, or adapted for particular audiences and purposes.

Consequences of the Assessment

The consequences of reading assessment are an important consideration (Shepard, 1997). Both the consequences of using particular test scores and the effects of reading assessment in general on teachers, students, and instruction should be anticipated when assessment is planned and evaluated when assessment is used (Afflerbach, 1996). The consequences of reading assessment must be examined in the local context, for the consequences of using standardized reading test scores are best understood in relation to what meaning the scores have for parents, teachers, and students, what these audiences believe about reading and reading tests in general, and what they have learned about the usefulness and importance of this particular test (Moss, 1998). The local context also plays a role in determining consequences of reading assessment in general. For example, when teachers play more active roles in school or district assessment decision making, negative consequences of external testing may be lessened and teacher agency increased (Stephens et al., 1995).

An assessment that helps policy makers may have negative impact on students or teachers, so it is important to specify to whom the consequences apply. There may be different consequences for school districts than there are for individual classrooms, and different consequences for teachers than for students (Lane, Parke, & Stone, 1998). For example, under conditions where assessment is not used to inform instruction, teachers often have little detailed knowledge about their students' reading behaviors and abilities (Johnston, Afflerbach, & Weiss, 1993). Reading assessment may help students come to know the culture of assessment, and it may help determine whether a student is an insider or outsider to this assessment culture. A hallmark of successful independent readers is the ability to self-assess (Baker & Brown, 1984). For those students who do not have considerable experience and ability with self-assessment, a dire consequence is often that they fail to attain true independence as readers.

It is helpful to specify the intended consequences of assessment. Similarly, the unintended consequences must be predicted based upon past experiences with reading assessment. Teaching to the test is an intended consequence when assessment is created to change instruction. However, teaching to the test can have unintended consequences, including the curriculum being narrowed to instruction on tested skills and performances, a lack of emphasis on understanding concepts underlying instruction (Shepard, 1989), test preparation practices that increase scores without increasing achievement, or unethical practices (Popham, 1991). These consequences can occur on a broader level as well: what is regularly tested in large-scale assessments can become what is regularly taught in schools (Frederiksen, 1984). Intended consequences of reading assessment may include tracking or promotion (Taylor & Walton, 1997), curricular changes, changes in the content and format of classroom assessments, and increased student or teacher motivation and effort (Lane et al., 1998). Unintended consequences may include teacher alienation from assessment (Smith, 1991; Stiggins & Conklin, 1992), student alienation and demotivation (Taylor & Walton, 1997), unfair use of scores, and test bias for different subgroups of students. Whether these consequences arise from proper test use or from test misuse (Shepard, 1997), they should be revealed through careful study of reading assessment use in classrooms. The consequences of particular reading assessments are potentially far reaching, and the assessments themselves wield potential power and influence over classroom practice.

Usefulness of the Assessment

The complex context of reading assessment initiatives and agendas may blur the most critical aspect of reading assessment: its utility. Usefulness is defined as the extent to which a test can yield information valuable to people who are centrally involved in teaching and learning processes. The first criterion of a reading assessment program should be usefulness for teachers and students. However, usefulness is often determined by policy makers and administrators who hold considerable power.

The usefulness of an assessment is contingent upon the particular purpose and particular audience for which it is being used. These audiences and purposes are many, and part of the task of creating an effective reading assessment program is determining exactly who the audiences are, what information they need, and what assessments will provide this information. Useful assessments are geared to the needs of individuals within the array of consumers of test information. These consumers may include teachers, students, parents, administrators, school board members, state legislators, and taxpayers. An important component of utility of assessment information is its comprehensibility to its intended audiences. Assessment information is not useful if it is not understood well enough to be acted upon (Afflerbach, 1993).

Useful assessments can often efficiently serve various purposes and audiences simultaneously (Valencia, 1990; Winograd, Paris, & Bridge, 1991). However, assessments should not serve such diverse purposes that, in so doing, they are unable to serve any of those purposes well. In attempting to be useful to all audiences, an assessment may prove useful to none. Shepard (1989) argued that the purposes of accountability and of informing instruction are so different that they might be better met with separate assessments. Utility, considered a component of an assessment's validity (Messick, 1989a; Tittle, 1989), has traditionally being appraised in terms of the accuracy with which scores can be predicted. The purposes the results will serve determine the level of error in prediction to be tolerated (Messick, 1989a). For example, if a running record is being used to place a student in an ability-based reading group, it should have a much smaller margin of error than a criterion-referenced reading test that is being used with other indicators to determine a student's eligibility for the honor roll: testing for purpose of informing classroom instruction is a "high-stakes" matter (as we discuss later).

A recent focus is reading assessments' usefulness for informing instruction and improving learning (Black & Wiliam, 1998). We focus here upon usefulness from a classroom perspective—the extent to which an assessment can inform teachers and students about ongoing progress in (1) using comprehension strategies, (2) demonstrating intrinsic motivation for reading, (3) building prior knowledge related to text content, (4) providing broad exposure and appreciation for the uses of reading, and (5) becoming active participants in the culture of reading assessment. When used effectively by teachers, informal assessments paint an ongoing, ever-developing portrait (Johnston, 1992) of students as engaged readers. There is no more useful assessment than that which informs the daily instruction and learning routines of teachers and students. Reading instruction and assessment should go hand in hand in the classroom. Reading assessment should be used to focus students' efforts upon desired goals in reading, and reading instruction should continuously provide teachers and students with assessment information (Henk, 1993).

Roles of Teachers and Students in the Assessment

Each reading assessment requires that teachers and students assume particular roles and responsibilities. When teachers exercise their prerogative to develop classroom assessment programs, they should strive to achieve balance between mandated and chosen informal and formal measures (Afflerbach & Kapinus, 1993). They must balance the use of assessments for summative and formative purposes (Black & Wiliam, 1998). Although teachers do not always select every assessment to be used in the classroom, they should take responsibility for the overall program of assessment (Johnston, 1992). Teachers must be skillful users of informal assessments, but they must also be comfortable with using formal assessments like standardized testing (Taylor & Walton, 1997). They must administer assessments, interpret their results, and sometimes develop them—roles that require teacher expertise in assessment. Unfortunately, teacher preparation for assessment is frequently inadequate (Schafer & Lissitz, 1987; Stiggins & Conklin, 1992). Teachers must become more familiar with psychometric concepts like validity and reliability (Lambert, 1991) and must learn to apply their understandings of assessment to the instructional context (Taylor & Nolen, 1996).

Teachers are ideally situated to assess students' reading in the course of everyday instruction (Afflerbach, 1996). They should collect assessment information from several data sources, using multiple methods in systematic ways (Calfee & Hiebert, 1991; Wolf, 1993). For example, teachers might determine their students' strengths in reading each quarter by examining records of their oral reading, surveys of their reading attitudes and habits, logs of their reading selections, and the results of a basal unit test of reading comprehension.

Teachers use reading assessment information for diagnosis of instruction (Johnston, 1992), but they also play an important role in facilitating students' ability to use and understand reading assessment. When teachers construct and communicate learning goals with students, they enable students to take an active role in self-assessment (Black & Wiliam, 1998; Taylor & Nolen, 1996).

A most authentic purpose of assessment is to encourage and enable student self-assessment, particularly if the goal for instruction is to develop strategic readers who monitor their own performance and who are truly independent (Winograd et al., 1991). Unfortunately, this is not a frequent focus of reading assessment (Bol, Stephenson, O'Connell, & Nunnery, 1998). Students engaged in self-assessment practices display independence and increased control over their decision making about reading (Afflerbach, 1996): They are the ultimate users of assessment information (Black & Wiliam, 1998). The importance of the roles teachers and students

play in transforming assessment information into opportunities for learning cannot be overstated. Assessment information, like any other text,
must be "read" and understood by those who use it, primarily teachers
and students (Tittle, 1989). We believe that reading assessment should be
evaluated in terms of the precedent set for teacher and student involvement, with each in roles more active than that of assessment givers and assessment takers.

Reliability of the Assessment

Reliability of reading assessment is defined as how consistently a test of
reading is administered and scored. Results are reliable if the same person
would get the same score were he/she to retake the test. The term has
come to refer to the amount of faith that can be placed in an assessment's
results (Farr & Carey, 1986). Reading assessments that are used reliably
have objective scoring criteria and yield results subject only to the variability that comes from students' performance. If test administrators do not
have a shared understanding of how to administer, score, and interpret the
findings of the assessment, the resulting scores will not be reliable. A
shared understanding of the underlying construct to be measured is also
important. Moss (1994) argued that reliability is fundamentally a question
of communication: it relies upon the extent to which the audiences involved develop shared understandings of reading and the purposes of
reading assessment. For example, a teacher who believes that reading is a
set of separate subskills may not reliably score a reading assessment that
conceptualizes reading as the use of several skills and strategies in conjunction with one another. Any approach to measuring reliability reflects
implicit theories about the construct of reading to be measured. Even the
ways that we measure reliability of reading assessment are guided by particular constructs of reading which should be acknowledged (Nichols &
Smith, 1998). For example, traditional reliability measures that rely upon
large numbers of items may not be well suited to measuring the reliability
of performance assessments containing few numbers of items. Reliability
of reading assessment, combined with strong construct validity, can increase our faith in the usefulness and relevance of assessment results.

  Assessment in the reading classroom relies on consistency of administration and scoring by the teacher, a consistency that is difficult to establish
(Stiggins & Conklin, 1992). The consistency of teacher administration relies
upon the complexity of the assessment type. It is easier to establish the
consistency of administration and scoring of a standardized test (e.g.,
through a paragraph of directions to be read aloud by the teacher and machine scoring) than it is to establish teachers' consistent use and scoring of
portfolios, for example. However, Valencia and Au (1997) found that they

were able to establish consistency of scoring when teachers from two different sites evaluated portfolios across the sites using different sets of criteria. They attributed the strong inter-rater reliability to the teachers' agreement with the general underlying construct of reading.

Assessments must also be reliable in terms of scoring student responses. The task of assessment may become increasingly difficult as the complexity of the student behavior increases or as the focus of assessment becomes broader. For example, the determination that a first-grade student has mastered the consonant blend "cl" may be a relatively easy and highly reliable classroom assessment task. The determination that the same student successfully applies comprehension strategies to read a persuasive essay is a much more demanding assessment task.

Validity of the Assessment

Validity of a reading assessment is the extent to which a test measures the construct of reading it is meant to measure. Validity must be reevaluated for each testing application, for a test might be used validly in one setting but not in another, or for one purpose but not for another (Messick, 1989a). For example, the score a student receives on a standardized, norm-referenced test may be validly used by an administrator to infer a broad view of the student's reading achievement, but this same score would be invalidly used by a teacher to identify the child's use of reading strategies. Thus, validity refers to the adequacy and appropriateness of inferences and actions based upon assessment information (Messick, 1989a). The interpretations made of test scores are to be validated—not the tests themselves. One does not measure the validity of running records but the validity of the student reading level that results from scoring a running record.

Validity of a testing application also depends upon the local context in which the test is used and the audience for which the scores are intended (Tittle, 1989). Ecological validity, the degree to which assessment procedures and materials reflect practice in elementary schools, plays an important role (Valencia, 1990). Good assessment tasks often resemble (or are part of) good instructional activities. A valid task of reading might require students to integrate information from multiple sources about recycling in order to write a letter to their school board arguing for a school recycling program. In this case, "real" reading involves students in a variety of integrated tasks (Calfee & Hiebert, 1991) for a social purpose (Johnston, 1992).

Validity theory has evolved from a fragmented set of validity types to a unitary concept (Jonson & Plake, 1998). Three main types of validity traditionally have been identified: content validity, criterion-related validity, and construct validity (Messick, 1989b). If a reading assessment has content validity, the material included in the test adequately covers the test's purposes. If a reading assessment has criterion-related validity, its results identify and predict the reading achievement that students exhibit on other measures of reading. If a reading assessment has construct validity, its scores serve as indicators of "real" reading, because the cognitive demands of the test are similar to the cognitive demands of real reading. Thus, differences in scores represent real differences in reading achievement. Construct validity has been considered the unitary concept that subsumes the other two types of evidence about validity (Messick, 1989b).

An assessment with construct validity can be used in invalid ways, if reading as measured by the assessment is conceptualized differently than it is taught in the classroom. For example, a particular oral reading inventory might define reading achievement as perfect word-by-word reading and may validly award scores based upon this criterion. However, for a teacher who taught students that reading fluently sometimes meant making meaningful substitutions, this particular reading test would not be a valid test of reading achievement. Thus, valid inferences about scores of particular assessments can only be made at the local level by teachers (Tittle, 1989). Reading assessment is a values statement; it reflects aspects of reading that a particular person or group of people has designated worthy of assessing and evaluating. In examining validity, it is essential to identify the ways in which the values statement implicit in assessment aligns with the values implicit in classroom reading.

Traditionally, reading assessment has been evaluated in terms of its validity and reliability. We have argued that an examination of usefulness, roles and responsibilities of teachers and students, and consequences of reading assessment must also be considered central to the evaluation process. Some key questions to guide teachers, administrators, and curriculum specialists in their use of the CURRV are presented in Table 8.1. The CURRV framework is a tool teachers can use to evaluate individual assessments or assessment programs to identify strengths and weaknesses, psychometric qualities and practical uses.

ILLUSTRATING THE CURRV FRAMEWORK
WITH DIFFERENT FORMS OF ASSESSMENT

The complex domain of reading assessment may include tests, checklists, portfolios, performance assessment, and reading inventories that are mandated or chosen by particular teachers, schools, districts, or states. Faced with this wide array of assessment, teachers must develop assessment programs that adequately provide them with as complete a picture of students as readers as is possible to obtain from available measures. Such a program must consist of a variety of assessments that sample broadly from the view of reading that undergirds classroom instruction. In order to explore the meaning of each dimension of the CURRV framework while providing evaluative information about particular reading assessments, the following subsections pair each dimension with a form of reading assessment, chosen to shed light upon this dimension. Norm-referenced and criterion-referenced tests, portfolios, oral reading measures, and performance assessments are described to illustrate the five dimensions of the CURRV framework. Throughout, examples demonstrate how these reading assessments can be used in effective ways.

Norm-Referenced "High-Stakes" Reading Assessments and the Consequences of Such Assessments

Although consequential validity is most often discussed in relation to the consequences of use of reading assessment results and scores, we conceptualize the consequences of reading assessment more broadly. We believe that the consequences of reading assessment are not restricted to those resulting from the use of test results and scores. There are potentially powerful consequences for teachers and students when reading assessment is mandated rather than chosen, when reading assessment is done to and for the student rather than by and with the student, and when reading assessments co-opt teachers' professional prerogative and good judgment.

What are the consequences for teachers and students in a society that values single test scores above all else as indicators of reading achievement? Norm-referenced tests (allowing for the description and interpretation of a student's score in reference to a particular group) are the most powerful and widely used indicators of reading achievement outside the classroom. These tests are labeled "high stakes" because of their potential to influence education funding, public perception, public support, and teachers' professionalism. Such norm-referenced reading tests may consist of machine-scored, multiple-choice items or items that demand complex student performances and human scoring. Norm-referenced test results are often the most public information related to the lives and accomplishments of teachers and students. Because of their psychometric makeup, norm-referenced tests provide scores that designate one-half of the test takers as below average.

Norm-referenced test scores are valued and trusted by many because standardized tests are believed to be fair, objective, scientific, and efficient (Afflerbach, 1990). Tests are believed to be fair because all students take the same test, such as a statewide or districtwide reading test. Tests are perceived to be objective because of the belief that standardization renders them immune to bias that may be introduced by teachers and others during the test administration process. And tests are seen as scientific because they reduce the complexity of reading achievement to a single score or a small set of scores. Finally, norm-referenced reading tests are considered efficient because they provide reading achievement data for individual students in one or two testing sessions that often can be quickly scored by a machine. Given the general public's perception of norm-referenced large-scale assessments as impartial and scientific, they often serve as an ersatz standard of reading assessment against which other assessments are judged. As many people value norm-referenced reading tests and their scores, they may place less faith in other reading assessments, including teachers' classroom-based assessments of reading.

The consequences of standardized, norm-referenced reading test scores include punishing or rewarding schools, teachers, and students. School funding may be increased or decreased based on test performance. Schools may gain widespread recognition and approval based on norm-referenced test scores, or they may be sanctioned and taken over by a district or state education department. They may gain or lose community support as a consequence of test scores. Norm-referenced high-stakes assessments influence teaching and curriculum in the classroom. Because of their focus on cognitive skills and strategies, these high-stakes tests most often ignore the other aspects of engaged reading, including motivation and increased purposes for reading. In many high-stakes assessment situations, teaching to the test is a regular temptation or mandate, and the narrowing of the reading curriculum is the result. This may lead to diminution of teaching and learning related to aspects of engaged reading that are not encountered on such high-stakes tests.

The media regularly report on large-scale norm-referenced reading tests. In a recent week, the *Washington Post* carried two articles (Mathews, 1999; Rusakoff, 1999) that described consequences of such high-stakes testing. Each article focused on the clear and present influence and consequences of tests, and the two articles demonstrated the diversity of consequences of testing. "P. S. 123 Pumps Up for the Big Test" (Rusakoff, 1999) described teachers at one school who adopted an unquestioning "jump on the bandwagon" approach to test preparation. The entire school united to teach to the test by training students in test-taking skills and by restricting the reading curriculum to test-like materials and procedures. In contrast, "No Fanfare at Fairfax School Over Success on Statewide Tests" (Mathews, 1999) described one school that performed well on the high-stakes tests, yet the teaching corps generally lamented the influence of the statewide test on the curriculum. The teachers felt their teaching was negatively impacted and constrained as a result of the test.

We note that the term "high stakes" is used most often to describe standardized, norm-referenced large-scale state and district reading assessments. The consequences of these assessments include public reward or sanction, and increase or decrease in school, teacher, and student self-esteem. We prefer a much broader conceptualization of the term "high-stakes assessment." An assessment that helps a teacher understand a student as the student reads aloud, define a teachable moment, and scaffold a needed reading strategy certainly seems a high-stakes event. Any assessment that involves students and their reading development is truly a high-stakes effort. If it is not, it is probably not worth the resources spent on developing the assessment, gathering the assessment information, and interpreting it.

Criterion-Referenced Assessments and Their Uses

Criterion-referenced tests provide measures of student performance in relation to a learning goal. In the reading classroom, the goal may be a student demonstrating knowledge of a sound–symbol correspondence (e.g., a criterion measure is student knowledge that the letter *b* says "buh") or demonstrating the ability to use knowledge gained from reading to perform a complex task (e.g., a criterion measure is the use of knowledge constructed from reading history to build a diorama of an historical event). Having designated a particular learning goal, criterion-referenced assessment allows for a detailed examination of student learning in relation to the goal. Criterion-referenced tests allow for comparison of individual students' knowledge and performance with the designated and defined reading knowledge and performance. One advantage of criterion-referenced assessment is that it does not force comparisons among students. This limits the practice of designating some students as "below average," regardless of their accomplishment in relation to their actual achievement in reading. For example, a student may make substantial progress across the school year and move from the 5th percentile to the 45th percentile in a nationally normed test. The fact that the student made monumental gains may be lost with a vocabulary that describes reading gains only in terms of this normed, percentile ranking and that continues to label the student as "below average."

The criterion-referenced test can provide both formative and summative information related to students' reading achievement. Formative information may be gathered as students attempt to meet a target criterion. For example, if text comprehension is the goal, a criterion-referenced measure may help show that a student is quite capable of answering factual questions that contain information explicitly stated in the text. The same criterion-referenced assessment might indicate developing readers who are encountering difficulty with answering inferential comprehension questions. In this sense, criterion-referenced tests can provide formative, diagnostic information to shape subsequent instruction. A teacher may make immediate use of information gathered during a criterion-referenced assessment task and use that information to inform the next day's lesson, or the next teachable moment in which an inference is modeled and explained by the teacher. Criterion-referenced tests can also provide summative assessment information. Should a teacher, school, or district want detailed information on how well each student can meet a grade-level benchmark performance (e.g., comprehend a complex science or history passage) and want to use the information to make decisions about promotion or retention, criterion-referenced tests can provide this information.

Using criterion-referenced assessment in this manner demands that the assessment include detailed descriptions of a desired, capstone achievement as well as descriptions of the growth that is expected of developing readers on their way to this achievement. Criterion-referenced assessments may include checkpoints that represent anticipated points of achievement and progress within the more complex criterion. For example, student demonstration of understanding of key vocabulary words might be a checkpoint prior to the student being asked to undertake the complex criterion-referenced assessment of describing the difference between mammals and reptiles. Criterion-referenced assessment may describe student achievement related to both the process and content of reading.

Criterion-referenced assessments can be used to measure and describe a range of student achievement across the many facets of reading. An important goal for young readers is learning and overlearning sound–symbol correspondences, and criterion-referenced assessment can help determine if students are reaching this goal. When teachers circulate among young readers and listen to them read, they may apply a criterion-referenced assessment and evaluation routine. For example, running records may provide information related to criteria of fluency, oral reading accuracy, and decoding. Teachers' mental notes, checklists, and observations are often tied to such criteria. The criteria may not be as formally stated as in a year-end criterion-referenced test, and a key task is to make the criteria explicit and to use them consistently.

Performance assessments are a form of criterion-referenced test that assess complex learning criteria or goals. As performance assessments are developed, the benchmark performances that are expected of students meeting specific reading criteria may be detailed and made public. For example, using comprehension strategies to comprehend text and using decoding strategies to identify words that are unfamiliar in print are performances that lend themselves to the development of rubrics. Rubrics present general characteristics of student performance and their relation to specific levels of achievement. A scoring rubric might give five samples of student response on a score scale from 1 to 5. The detail of description that is built into good rubrics help make the assessment public and transparent (Popham, 1991). That is, teachers and students may have clear examples and descriptions of what they need to accomplish in relation to a particular criterion-referenced reading assessment.

In summary, criterion-referenced reading assessments have several uses. They may inform classroom instruction when used in a formative manner, and they may offer summative descriptions of students' accomplishments. These accomplishments are varied, reflecting the ongoing growth of individual students and the challenges they meet in becoming increasingly engaged readers. Because of their relationship to benchmarks and rubrics, criterion-referenced assessments may inform instruction while measuring learning. In addition, criterion-referenced assessment may serve to clarify and explain curriculum and instruction to students, making the assessment situation familiar and less threatening. It also represents a more direct link between assessment and instruction. To the extent that criterion-referenced assessments tap valued and necessary aspects of reading achievement, they may have beneficial influence on curriculum. Teaching to the criterion-referenced assessment may be entirely suitable. Finally, criterion-referenced assessments do not require labeling certain students "below average." It is expected that different students will need varying amounts of instruction, time, and practice to meet the range of learning goals that criterion-referenced assessments measure. Teachers need not label as "underachieving" those children who are meeting increasingly complex reading goals and increasingly complex criteria.

Portfolios and the Roles of Teachers and Students

The reading portfolio is a purposeful collection of work and reflections upon that work which tells the story of a learner's progress over a period of time. Portfolio assessment can provide a multifaceted portrait of a student's interactions with various tasks, events, and individuals in different environments (Jochum, Curran, & Reetz, 1998), through the use of several forms of evidence. The purpose for portfolio use is an important determinant of its contents and character. For example, *showcase portfolios* consist of a student-chosen collection of best work, whereas *evaluation portfolios* are prespecified and scored with the aim of comparing them to one another. *Documentation portfolios* are richly descriptive collections providing evidence of growth, while *process portfolios* capture the ongoing nature of the learning process itself (Valencia & Place, 1994). Portfolio use began with grassroots efforts by teachers for more learner-centered assessment. Although portfolios are gaining acceptance for accountability purposes at the school, system, state, and national levels, their beginnings highlight the centrality of teacher and student roles in portfolio assessment (Tierney & Clark, 1998).

Effective portfolio use is a team effort that may involve learners, teachers, parents, and peers. It requires a shared understanding of literacy goals, portfolio purposes, and criteria for quality to be used in evaluation. These shared understandings are achieved through collaborative planning, decision making, and evaluation, particularly by teachers and students (Jochum et al., 1998). Teachers and students must determine together what goals portfolios should target (e.g., increased motivation for reading) and what purposes portfolios are meant to serve (e.g., to document progress in motivation across the year) in order to bring meaning to what would otherwise just be a folder of student work. Portfolios have the potential both to support and inform instruction and to help teachers and students alike define reading as a meaningful and enjoyable activity (Valencia & Place, 1994). LeMahieu, Gitomer, and Eresh (1995) found that teachers embraced the added responsibility of portfolio assessment because they welcomed the accompanying restructuring of teacher and student roles in assessment.

Students play the most central roles in portfolio assessment—the locus of portfolio control is to reside with them. Students' active engagement in the portfolio process helps them develop the capacity for metacognition and goal setting, and helps them gain facility with use of reading strategy (Jochum et al., 1998). The student's role in selecting and presenting portfolio artifacts allows for the development of voice (Hebert, 1998). LeMahieu et al. (1995) found that when students were given categories for artifact selection (a satisfying piece, an important piece, etc.) and were taught about the purpose of portfolios, they could control the selection process without sacrificing psychometric rigor. Although student control created variability in the contents of portfolios, the reliability of scoring remained high (LeMahieu et al., 1995).

What students select to be included in a portfolio (i.e., what they value) sheds light upon their understandings about literacy processes and products and reflects their strengths and weaknesses as readers. However, these understandings about reading development can only be constructed when students' roles in selection and design are balanced with students' roles in portfolio analysis and self-assessment: "portfolios are tools, and efforts to implement a portfolio program should be equitably divided between helping students build the tool and helping them use it effectively" (Afflerbach, 1996, p. 201). For example, in reviewing the reading logs contained within her portfolio, a student might discover that she consistently chooses to read mysteries, and might subsequently set the goal to read a variety of genres. Another student, if he can't think of something to write about, might review past writing samples in his portfolio in order to find a topic that invites further development.

In using portfolios as tools, students can reflect upon skill development, present progress to other audiences, and evaluate their personal and instructional growth (Jocham et al., 1998). By identifying patterns across the body of work included in a portfolio, students can articulate their strengths in literacy and can set specific goals for literacy improvement (Tierney & Clark, 1998). A study by Valencia and Place (1994) found that students felt using portfolios increased their ability to evaluate their own progress and recognized the increased opportunity such portfolios provided their teachers for assessing progress as well. Students' participation in building and using a portfolio can help initiate them into the culture of reading assessment.

The benefits of portfolio use for students hinge upon the roles their teachers play in establishing portfolio purposes and procedures. Teachers model for students and serve as participant observers in the portfolio process, guiding student learning, choices, and reflections (Tierney & Clark, 1998). The most important role a teacher can play in portfolio assessment is that of collaborator with students, developing portfolio purposes, scoring criteria, and shared reading goals (LeMahieu et al., 1995). However, when teachers overdetermine portfolio contents and limit student choice, they mediate against student ownership over the portfolio process (Hebert, 1998). Flood, Lapp, and Monken (1992) found that teachers emphasized the role portfolios played in their own evaluation of students (they used the information to report to parents) but did not see the potential for instructional use (through student conferences or diagnosing student needs). Most teachers surveyed felt that the teacher alone should determine the design and contents of the portfolio and that the categories for artifacts should be predetermined. The potential for student self-assessment was unrealized (Flood et al., 1992). Although teachers may well opt to prescribe the contents of one part of a student's portfolio, or to keep a separate file for their own anecdotal records, conference reports, tests, or inventories (Tierney, Carter, & Desai, 1991), they should not forget that the most important potential benefit of portfolio use is developing students' capacity for self-assessment.

Oral Reading Measures and Their Reliability

The reliability of oral reading measures stems from the fact that they are direct measures of real reading and are often more grounded in classroom activities and instruction than norm-referenced tests. Oral reading measures highlight the importance of local contextual factors, including genre, the reader's prior knowledge, text familiarity, use of illustrations, passage length, and linguistic features. These factors contribute to a more complex, textured characterization of reading (Murphy, 1998). Oral reading measures, including informal reading inventories (IRIs; Farr & Carey, 1986), miscue analysis (Goodman, 1982), and running records (Clay, 1993), share the purpose of collecting in-depth information about an individual student's processes of reading. These measures can be administered and scored quite reliably by assessors experienced with their use. These oral reading measures are administered in a one-to-one setting: a child reads a passage aloud to an assessor, usually the classroom teacher. Whether these passages are from children's books chosen from the classroom context (for running records) or are developed commercially to link to basal levels for the purpose of assessing oral reading (for IRIs), they are identified by a particular level of reading difficulty. Whereas running records were designed to assess emergent literacy in the context of Reading Recovery (a first-grade intervention for struggling readers), IRIs contain leveled passages that range from preprimer through eighth grade or above. While a student reads aloud, the assessor takes note of the differences between the text as read and the text as written, coding these differences as omissions, reversals, substitutions, and so forth (Farr & Carey, 1986). These coding systems are slightly different for IRIs, running records, and miscue analysis.

Whatever coding scheme is used must be used consistently if it is to yield reliable and comparable results across students. Depending upon the percentage of words read correctly (and the percentage of comprehension questions answered correctly for IRIs), the passage level is labeled *independent* (i.e., easy), *instructional* (i.e., just right), or *frustrational* (i.e., too challenging) for the student (Wiener & Cohen, 1997). For IRIs, the departures from the text that change the meaning of what is read are coded as errors and are counted to determine level of reading accuracy. Goodman (1982) proposed that differences between the text as read and the text as written be called miscues rather than errors because meaning may be maintained when the text is not read exactly as written. Miscue analysis and running records are used to examine what cuing systems (graphophonic, syntactic, or semantic) and strategies are being used by the reader for each miscue. In miscue analysis, the description of oral reading is kept separate from the interpretations about strategy use; in running records, on the other hand, description and interpretation are conducted concurrently (Murphy, 1998). If a child reads "the girl saw tires" and then correctly changes it to "the girl was tired," an IRI would simply not count this as an error, for self-corrections are not considered errors. An assessor using miscue analysis or a running record might attribute the child's initial miscue to knowledge of the structure of the English language ("the girl saw tires" is a legitimate sentence), while attributing the self-correction to increased visual attention to the letters of the words read within the meaning-laden context of the text. Finally, a running record would count this self-correction in determining the child's self-correction rate (or the pro-portion of times a reader corrects errors in relation to the number of errors made)—an indicator of how well a child monitors his/her own compre-hension (Johnston & Clay, 1997).

The reliability of IRIs has been well documented in the literature, par-ticularly in their determination of reading grade level (see Farr & Carey, 1986). However, IRIs have been criticized for their tendency to quantify reading processes instead of describing them (Pikulski & Shanahan, 1982) and for their focus upon error-free reading as the mark of a good reader (Allington, 1984). Miscue analysis adds an interpretive element to the characterization of oral reading in order to identify miscue patterns and determine instructional implications, a use that constitutes a threat to reli-ability (Pikulski & Shanahan, 1982). In miscue analysis, the descriptive and interpretive systems are kept separate, because the interpretive system constitutes a greater threat to reliability. Often, the most meaningful, instructionally informing statements are the most difficult to make reliably. Allington (1984) asserted that there was strong consistency in raters' abil-ity to classify errors as either omissions, additions, substitutions, mispro-nunciations, repetitions, self-corrections, or other such categories. Hence, there is widespread agreement between raters about what constitutes an error. However, when assessors move from counting errors to identifying the qualitative features of these errors and interpreting what these features signify about the student's reading habits and implications for instruction, reliability between raters can break down (Pikulski & Shanahan, 1982).

Running records employ a procedure highly consistent with miscue analysis. Unlike an IRI, taking a running record requires only a blank piece of paper on which to make notations about the text as read. This allows for flexibility in recording oral reading at any time from any text (Johnston & Clay, 1997). Thus, running records are well suited to the regular classroom context (Hiebert, 1994). Interpretations about patterns in reading behavior and strategies are meant to be made using at least three running records across different texts (Pinnell, DeFord, & Lyons, 1988), yielding for more reliable interpretations than those produced by oral reading measures that rely upon one text. These three reading samples often include different levels of passage difficulty for the child, including independent and in-structional selections (Wiener & Cohen, 1997). Tindal and Marston (1996) investigated the reliability of classroom teachers' use of oral reading mea-sures, including running records, finding moderate-to-high correlations with the criterion measures of teacher judgments and a standardized test in reading.

Oral reading measures have greater potential for reliable use when teachers conduct multiple administrations and ongoing observations (Pikulski & Shanahan, 1982). The more a behavior is observed, the more faith can be put in the reliability of the observation (Farr & Carey, 1986). Because reading achievement varies according to the reading situation and the text read, it is to be expected that oral reading assessment results should vary according to the situation and the text as well (Farr & Carey, 1986). Thus, no single measurement of oral reading behaviors should be used to make important instructional decisions.

Performance Assessments and Their Validity

Performance assessments are designed to allow students to demonstrate their competency by creating a response or a product from tasks that resemble classroom activities. Performance assessments may involve students in sustained or collaborative work, in higher-order thinking, and in interaction with materials and naturalistic settings (Valencia, Hiebert, & Afflerbach, 1994) in order to measure and describe process as well as product (McBee & Barnes, 1998). Performance assessments in reading acknowledge that reading is often not an end unto itself but a precursor to some real-world application of what is read (Afflerbach, 1996). The similarity of assessment tasks to classroom instructional activities is cited in asserting the validity of performance assessment over that of standardized tests. The validity of the link between instruction and assessment has led teachers to call for and develop performance assessment programs to supplant the use of standardized tests in certain school systems (Ervin, 1998; Hoffman et al., 1996). However, this validity should not be assumed; performance-based assessment must be accompanied by performance-based instruction (McTighe, 1997). For example, having a group of students read a passage about haiku poetry and write a collaborative poem in haiku format for a performance task is only valid if, in the course of classroom instruction, students regularly read and write collaboratively.

Statewide performance assessment programs have been developed to preserve the link to instruction while obtaining information to be used for accountability purposes. Performance assessments are being used to bridge the gap between the purposes and audiences that standardized tests serve and the purposes and audiences that classroom assessments serve (Hoffman et al., 1996). The PALM (Primary Assessment of Language Arts and Mathematics), developed by a team of teachers in Austin, Texas, is a good example of an assessment that serves various purposes simultaneously. The PALM uses three types of tasks: curriculum-embedded (e.g., a classwork assignment), individualized (e.g., a running record), and on-demand assessments (e.g., a reading attitudes survey). A developmental profile that reflected teachers' beliefs and values related to early reading was developed to serve as the framework of reading behaviors to be addressed by the three types of assessments. Hoffman et al. (1996) found that "the psychometric properties of the PALM model are at least as strong as those of the standardized test, and provide data that are more informative and equally valid to a wide variety of external audiences" (p. 110).

In order to be valid, performance tasks must adequately represent the content domain of reading, test processes in authentic ways, and hold up under comparison to other measures or settings. Valid performance tasks allow score users to make inferences about reading achievement based on specific task performance. For example, a task for which students read a nonfiction passage about cats would ideally yield similar results if the passage were about another topic, and it would allow test users to understand something about how the reader comprehends nonfiction in general. Performance tasks must be developed to ensure that low scores are neither the result of inadequate coverage of reading skills and behaviors nor the outgrowth of nonreading behaviors and factors (Messick, 1995). Performance tasks are direct indicators of achievement and can represent the full range of complex learning outcomes, resulting in strong content validity (Shepard et al., 1996). Performance assessment is also considered to have more "cognitive validity" (Baxter & Glaser, 1998), in that the cognitive complexity of real reading is reflected in the cognitive complexity of reading performance tasks. Performance tasks can capture the interactions between content knowledge and process skills. Performance assessments that incorporate hands-on activities are valid because they reflect classroom activities, but the tasks that are included are often so different from one another that it is difficult to establish validity in terms of what they demonstrate about reading achievement (Shavelson, Baxter, & Pine, 1992).

Characteristics of particular tasks can create differences in scores that do not stem from differences in reading achievement. While task variety makes for broad coverage of reading behaviors (i.e., content validity), it limits the inferences that can be made about general reading achievement (i.e., construct validity) (McBee & Barnes, 1998). For example, if one task requires students to read two fairy tales and compare them using a Venn diagram, and another task requires students to read an article about Mars and use evidence from this article to write an essay about life on Mars, it is difficult to compare the results. The students' familiarity with Venn diagrams, prior knowledge about Mars, and essay-writing ability are all nonreading factors that may influence the scores students receive on each task. The lengthy nature of the tasks on performance assessments usually means that scores are based upon fewer examples of student work, limiting the validity of the inferences to be made about the construct being measured. The challenge to validity that task limitations constitute is largely dependent upon the level of inference to be made from the scores. For example, validity of a performance task that requires students to orally retell a fable may be easy to achieve if the goal is simply to infer how well a student retells stories. However, if the goal is to determine how well a student comprehends a variety of genres, validity would be more difficult to establish (Mehrens, Popham, & Ryan, 1998). Efforts have been made to increase the validity of performance assessment by making tasks more similar to one another or by identifying certain task "types" (Solano-Flores & Shavelson, 1997).

The nature of validity evidence is complex because performance assessments collect information about how students apply skills and strategies in particular contexts (Baxter & Glaser, 1998). Some authors argue that traditional validity is not a construct sophisticated enough to be used for evaluating performance assessments. The concept of validity is not as useful "as one moves from narrowly defined domains with large samples of items to more broadly defined and complex domains that must be represented by relatively few tasks" (McBee & Barnes, 1998, p. 183). Performance assessments hold great promise for serving different purposes and various audiences, and therefore must be subjected to scrutiny with regards to validity.

Having described the CURRV framework by discussing several types of reading assessments, we return to the notion of engagement. Engagement can be used to describe not only readers but teachers of reading (see Guthrie, Dreher, & Baker, Chapter 14, this volume). Engaged teachers of reading are at the heart of the development and maintenance of effective reading assessment programs.

ENGAGED ASSESSMENT
AND THE TEACHING OF READING

Engagement is a compelling perspective for assessing and teaching reading. Good assessment and teaching are skillful and strategic, and good teachers are motivated. There is no doubt that successful teaching involves skills and strategies. Good teachers are proficient decision makers. They can use assessment information to identify teachable moments and meet students at instructionally appropriate points to facilitate learning. Skillful teachers strategize: they plan instruction and assessment concomitantly, creating environments that are best suited to their instructional goals. Skillful teachers use a variety of strategies to gather information that can be used to address both the needs of diverse students and the diverse needs of individual students. These teachers collect, interpret, and use reading assessment information to improve teaching and learning. The engaged teacher is motivated. Through personal commitment, reflection, and effort engaged teachers continuously challenge themselves. They set goals for self-improvement and are motivated to meet these goals. They receive satisfaction from the job well done—the efficient reading assessment practice that provides information for crafting the successful lesson that boosts student self-esteem and furthers student learning. This satisfaction provides further motivation to continue on the path of excellence in the assessment and teaching of reading.

The engaged teacher regularly uses prior experiences and professional knowledge to meet the immediate and long-term demands of teaching reading well. Through a variety of sources that include professional development opportunities, teacher preparation courses, discussions with colleagues, and attendance at professional meetings, teachers construct and enhance understandings that inform classroom decision making, lesson planning, and interactions with students. Engaged teachers regularly reflect on their knowledge, examining how they assess and teach, make decisions, and interact with their students and the curriculum. Finally, engaged reading teachers seek and gain personal fulfillment from helping students with a job well done. Engaged teachers make connections between their professional lives and their lives outside of the classroom, and they avidly pursue reading for purposes of personal fulfillment.

Gloria: An Engaged Teacher

The case of Gloria, a first-grade teacher, will now be discussed to illustrate the active and intentional use of the CURRV framework by an engaged teacher when the perspective of engaged reading guides classroom practice. Gloria's students are developing competencies of engaged reading in highly individualized ways. Her students' performance varies from one task and context to another. Her students vary widely in their abilities to decode, use vocabulary, use comprehension skills and strategies, exhibit self-confidence and motivation for reading, bring prior knowledge to texts, and read for several different purposes. Because Gloria envisions her students as engaged readers with individual differences, she wants to develop a reading assessment program that provides information related to the different facets of their development as engaged readers. An assessment well-suited to Gloria's classroom would provide information about students' use of comprehension strategies, motivation, prior knowledge, and appreciation of the uses of reading. Such an assessment program would have exceptional construct validity for Gloria's classroom because it would provide information related to several different aspects of engaged reading.

Gloria evaluates a particular reading assessment, the Kamehameha Literacy Portfolio Assessment, by holding it up to her notion of engaged reading and the dimensions of the CURRV framework, including related beliefs about what should be assessed and how it might be assessed. As a teacher in a Kamehameha Elementary Education Program (KEEP) school (see Au, 1994), Gloria is required to use this portfolio program. As an engaged teacher, she must be able to recognize the aspects of reading that this assessment measures so that she can identify the role it plays in her overall reading assessment program. She notes the strengths and weaknesses in this assessment's ability to provide information for her classroom so that she may supplement its use with other assessments that measure aspects of engaged reading not assessed by the portfolios. Gloria is an engaged teacher, for she is skillful, strategic, knowledgeable, and motivated to evaluate the effectiveness of her reading assessment program given the view of reading to which she subscribes.

KEEP: Consequences

What are the consequences of using the KEEP portfolio system as a means to assess engaged reading in Gloria's classroom? Unlike many portfolio systems designed primarily for teachers, portfolio system was created expressly for the purpose of program evaluation, that is, accountability (Seda, 1994). Administrators supported this portfolio system and many were willing to accept the data it offered in place of standardized test scores. Because KEEP portfolio data are summarized on data collection forms and then aggregated by grade level and across schools, they can serve the purposes of administrators and policy makers as they serve the needs of teachers and students (Au, 1994).

However, from Gloria's perspective, the role that portfolios play for accountability carries with it implications for student self-assessment with which she is not comfortable. Portfolios are formally evaluated in terms of grade-level benchmarks, which could alienate students from the evaluation process. In explaining and sharing data collection forms with her students, Gloria is able to adapt and monitor the nature of portfolios to better reflect her goals for instruction: her students are motivated to take on the responsibility of self-assessment; they are able to monitor and document reading habits, skills, and strategies; and they have a forum for discussing and reporting individual goals and development.

KEEP: Usefulness

The portfolios assess the six main aspects of KEEP's whole literacy curriculum: student ownership of literacy (assessed with student surveys and written teacher observations), the writing process (assessed with written teacher observations and student writing samples), voluntary reading (assessed with voluntary reading logs and written teacher observations), reading comprehension (assessed with written responses to literature), student language and vocabulary knowledge (assessed with written responses to literature as well), and word-reading strategies (assessed with running records). These information sources in the portfolio are used to determine a student's standing in relation to KEEP's grade-level benchmarks (Au, 1994). Because these benchmarks are used across all KEEP schools, student achievement can be compared across grade levels and across schools. Thus, the portfolios are useful for accountability purposes.

However, the portfolios also have the potential to be useful for instruction in Gloria's classroom. A feature of KEEP portfolios which is quite useful for a classroom that reflects the engaged reading perspective is the multidimensionality of products related to reading included in the portfolio. Gloria analyzes and has students analyze portfolios more often than the required twice a year as a means to diagnose individual students' needs in her classroom. KEEP portfolios are highly individualized in nature, but Gloria guides the collection of reading artifacts even further with her students (e.g., by collecting information about several types of texts read for different purposes, with differing levels of student knowledge) in order to obtain the data that will enable her to effectively teach them.

KEEP: Teacher and Student Roles

The Kamehameha Literacy Portfolio Assessment was developed by teachers within a single school district. KEEP's portfolio program demands that Gloria take on certain responsibilities. Gloria has to consistently monitor and assess student development across the many areas that represent a developing engaged reader; indeed, she has to become an evaluation expert (Johnston, 1992). Furthermore, the KEEP portfolios have the potential, more than many other types of assessment, to involve students and require them to play the important role of self-assessors. This potential was recognized but not realized in the early stages of the KEEP portfolio project. In 1994, pilot studies were being conducted using portfolios to aid in student goal-setting (Au, 1994), and involving students became the focus of attention after teacher involvement was more firmly established. Although a concern for creating assessment that would involve and serve the needs of teachers and students was a central priority in the conception of the KEEP project, the needs of accountability and program evaluation were addressed first.

Gloria's use of portfolios in her classroom reflects her belief that students must become self-assessors. She uses the section of the portfolio for student ownership as an opportunity to assess how well they monitor their own progress in reading. Gloria has students choose pieces to include in the portfolio because she values how motivated they are to represent their interests and progress in reading. A comprehensive assessment of engaged reading demands that students become centrally involved in assessing their reading processes and products.

KEEP: Reliability

The reliability of KEEP's portfolio program, centered around the purpose of making cross-school comparisons, is tied to the use of grade-level benchmarks for evaluation. Benchmarks are set for the six aspects of literacy, and portfolios are evaluated in light of these benchmarks to determine whether students are performing at, below, or above grade level for each of these aspects. Although portfolio contents are collected on an ongoing basis, portfolios are formally evaluated twice a year with the benchmarks. Gloria disagrees with the use of benchmarks that disregard contexts or different purposes for reading. Although she uses the benchmarks for accountability purposes, she always appends narrative descriptions of students in different reading situations to these results and uses narrative descriptions to report to parents and students. These adaptations make the use of portfolios more reliable for her classroom. Gloria recognizes that reliability for her classroom is found in the multiple measures themselves. The portfolios provide a sense of how students respond to different kinds of tasks. Data on each student are triangulated by several sources. Thus, for classroom purposes, Gloria avoids condensing this rich information into scores that are less meaningful to her and her students.

KEEP: Validity

Gloria must examine the validity of KEEP's portfolio program in terms of its ability to measure her own view of engaged reading. There are many features of KEEP's underlying view of whole literacy that are consistent with Gloria's model of engaged reading. This makes KEEP portfolios a relatively valid measure of engaged reading: students are seen as strategic and motivated; they have ownership over their reading; and their development is seen as individualized and multifaceted. Gloria appreciates the portfolio's ability to represent the contextualized nature of reading, as evidenced by its reliance upon authentic classroom artifacts. However, there are some differences between the two views. Whereas KEEP's view subsumes reading under the larger umbrella of literacy, Gloria's view focuses upon engaged reading. Thus, KEEP's portfolios are not always able to assess engaged reading in ways that are not confounded with writing achievement. Gloria collects audiotapes of students' oral reading and book discussions with a variety of genres in order to supplement portfolio assessment information. Her view of engaged reading is also reflected in her greater attention to students' varying purposes and levels of prior knowledge for different texts they read. Consequently, Gloria builds into her assessments prereading activities like tapping prior knowledge and identifying purposes for reading. The use of KEEP portfolios in Gloria's classroom allows for sampling a relatively broad range of engaged reading behaviors.

CONCLUSION

Effective assessment is critical for children's early and ongoing reading development. Quality classroom reading assessment involves teachers and students in collecting valid, reliable, and useful information in ways that maximize the potential benefits and minimize the potential harmful consequences to its central audiences. It provides information that informs educational practice and helps create opportunities for students' reading achievement. However, navigating the terrain of reading assessment can be extremely challenging. The field of reading is flooded with assessments that represent diverse purposes for assessment, that are designed to meet the needs of several different audiences, and that represent varying views of reading and levels of quality and suitability for classroom use. Recognizing the challenges associated with choosing among or developing quality reading assessments, we have introduced the CURRV framework as a tool which can be used to develop comprehensive reading assessment programs that are well-suited for the classrooms in which they are used. Engaged teachers must be at the heart of this process. They must reflect upon and characterize their own views of reading and accompanying values and beliefs about reading assessment. This enables them to examine the suitability of potential reading assessments in terms of their consequences, usefulness, roles and responsibilities of teachers and students, reliability, and validity. By designing a reading assessment program that adequately and appropriately measures the types of reading students in their classrooms are expected to do, teachers are tapping into the power of assessment as a means for promoting student reading achievement.

RECOMMENDED READINGS

Johnston, P. (1997). *Knowing literacy: Constructive literacy assessment.* York, ME: Stenhouse.

This book examines literacy assessment practice in light of current conceptualizations of learning to read and learning to be literate. The book focuses on the overuse of standardized testing and the promising use of teacher-centered, classroom-based assessments of reading.

Lipson, M., & Wixson, K. (1996). *Assessment and instruction of reading and writing disability: An interactive approach* (2nd ed.). Boston: Addison-Wesley.

This book contains a vast amount of useful information related to classroom-based reading assessments and commercially published assessments that can be used to inform the different audiences and purposes of assessment.

Valencia, S. W., Hiebert, E. H., & Afflerbach, P. P. (1994). *Authentic reading assessment: Practices and possibilities*. Newark, DE: International Reading Association.

This edited volume provides nine case studies of states, school districts, and schools creating useful reading assessment in response to specific assessment needs. Each case study is critiqued by an assessment expert.

REFERENCES

Afflerbach, P. (1990). *Issues in statewide reading assessment*. Washington, DC: American Institutes for Research.

Afflerbach, P. (1993). Constructing meaning from diagnostic assessment texts: Validity as usefulness. In R. M. Joshi & C. K. Leong (Eds.), *Reading disabilities: Diagnosis and component processes* (pp. 63–69). Dordrecht, The Netherlands: Kluwer.

Afflerbach, P. (1996). Engaged assessment of engaged reading. In L. Baker, P. Afflerbach, & D. Reinking (Eds.), *Developing engaged readers in school and home communities* (pp. 191–214). Mahwah, NJ: Erlbaum.

Afflerbach, P., & Kapinus, B. (1993). The balancing act. *The Reading Teacher, 47,* 62–64.

Allington, R. L. (1984). Oral reading. In P. D. Pearson, R. Barr, M. L. Kamil, & P. Mosenthal (Eds.), *Handbook of reading research* (pp. 829–864). White Plains, NY: Longman.

Au, K. (1994). Portfolio assessment: Experiences at the Kamehameha elementary education program. In S. W. Valencia, E. H. Hiebert, & P. P. Afflerbach (Eds.), *Authentic assessment: Practices and possibilities* (pp. 103–126). Newark, DE: International Reading Association.

Baker, L., & Brown, A. (1984). Metacognitive skills in reading. In P. Pearson, M. Kamil, P. Mosenthal, & R. Barr (Eds.), *Handbook of reading research* (pp. 353–394). New York: Longman.

Baxter, G., & Glaser, R. (1998). Investigating the cognitive complexity of science assessments. *Educational Measurement: Issues and Practice, 17*(3), 37–45.

Black, P., & Wiliam, D. (1998). Inside the black box: Raising standards through classroom assessment. *Phi Delta Kappan, 80,* 139–148.

Bol, L., Stephenson, P., O'Connell, A., & Nunnery, J. (1998). Influence of experience, grade level, and subject area on teachers' assessment practices. *Journal of Educational Research, 91,* 323–330.

Calfee, R., & Hiebert, E. H. (1991). Classroom assessment of reading. In R. Barr, M. L. Kamil, P. B. Mosenthal, & P. D. Pearson (Eds.), *Handbook of reading research* (Vol. 2, pp. 281–309). White Plains, NY: Longman.

Clay, M. (1993). *An observation survey of early literacy achievement*. Portsmouth, NH: Heinemann.

Ervin, R. (1998). Assessing early reading achievement: The road to results. *Phi Delta Kappan, 80,* 226–228.

Farr, R., & Carey, R. (1986). *Reading: What can be measured?* Newark, DE: International Reading Association.

Flood, J., Lapp, D., & Monken, S. (1992). Portfolio assessment: Teachers' beliefs and practices. In C. K. Kinzer & D. J. Leu (Eds.), *Literacy research, theory, and practice: Views from many perspectives.* Chicago: National Reading Conference.

Frederiksen, N. (1984) The real test bias: Influences of testing on teaching and learning. *American Psychologist, 39,* 193–202.

Goodman, K. S. (1982). A linguistic study of cues and miscues in reading. In F. V. Gollasch (Ed.), *Language and literacy—The selected writings of Kenneth S. Goodman: Vol. 1. Process, theory, and research* (pp. 115–120). Boston: Routledge & Kegan Paul.

Hebert, E. A. (1998). Lessons learned about student portfolios. *Phi Delta Kappan, 79,* 583–585.

Henk, W. (1993). New directions in reading assessment. *Reading and Writing Quarterly, 9,* 103–120.

Hiebert, E. H. (1994). Reading Recovery in the United States: What difference does it make to an age cohort? *Educational Researcher, 23*(9), 15–25.

Hoffman, J., Worthy, J., Roser, N., McKool, S., Rutherford, W., & Strecker, S. (1996). Performance assessment in first-grade classrooms: The PALM model. In D. J. Leu, C. K. Kinzer, & K. A. Hinchman (Eds.), *Literacies for the 21st century: Research and practice* (pp. 100–111). Chicago: National Reading Conference.

Jochum, J., Curran, C., & Reetz, L. (1998). Creating individual educational portfolios in written language. *Reading and Writing Quarterly, 14,* 283–306.

Johnston, P. (1992). Nontechnical assessment. *The Reading Teacher, 46,* 60–62.

Johnston, P., Afflerbach, P., & Weiss, P. (1993). Teachers' evaluation of teaching and learning of literacy. *Educational Assessment, 1,* 91–117.

Johnston, P., & Clay, M. (1997). Recording oral reading. In P. Johnston, *Knowing literacy: Constructive literacy assessment* (pp. 192–211). York, ME: Stenhouse.

Jonson, J., & Plake, B. (1998). A historical comparison of validity standards and validity practices. *Educational and Psychological Measurement, 58,* 736–753.

Lambert, N. (1991). The crisis in measurement literacy in psychology and education. *Educational Psychologist, 26*(1), 23–35.

Lane, S., Parke, C., & Stone, C. (1998). A framework for evaluating the consequences of assessment programs. *Educational Measurement: Issues and Practice, 17*(2), 24–28.

LeMahieu, P., Gitomer, D., & Eresh, J. (1995). Portfolios in large-scale assessment: Difficult but not impossible. *Educational Measurement: Issues and Practice, 14*(3), 11–28.

Mathews, J. (1999, January 16). No fanfare at Fairfax school over success on statewide tests. *Washington Post,* pp. B1, B4.

McBee, M., & Barnes, L. (1998). The generalizability of a performance assessment measuring achievement in eighth-grade mathematics. *Applied Measurement in Education, 11,* 179–194.

McTighe, J. (1997). What happens between assessments? *Educational Leadership, 54*(4), 7–12.

Mehrens, W. A., Popham, W. J., & Ryan, J. M. (1998). How to prepare students for performance assessments. *Educational Measurement: Issues and Practice, 17*(1), 18–22.

Messick, S. (1989a). Meaning and values in test validation: The science and ethics of assessment. *Educational Researcher, 18*(2), 5–11.

Messick, S. (1989b). Validity. In R. Linn (Ed.), *Educational measurement* (3rd ed., pp. 13–103). Phoenix, AZ: Oryx.

Messick, S. (1995). Standards of validity and the validity of standards in performance assessment. *Educational Measurement: Issues and Practice, 14*(4), 5–8.

Moss, P. (1994). Can there be validity without reliability? *Educational Researcher, 23*(2), 5–12.

Moss, P. (1998). The role of consequences in validity theory. *Educational Measurement: Issues and Practice, 17*(2), 6–12.

Murphy, S. (with Shannon, P., Johnston, P., & Hansen, J.). (1998). *Fragile evidence: A critique of reading assessment.* Mahwah, NJ: Erlbaum.

Nichols, P., & Smith, P. (1998). Contextualizing the interpretation of reliability data. *Educational Measurement: Issues and Practice, 17*(3), 24–36.

Pikulski, J., & Shanahan, T. (1982). Informal reading inventories: A critical analysis. In J. Pikulski & T. Shanahan (Eds.), *Approaches to the informal evaluation of reading* (pp. 94–116). Newark, DE: International Reading Association.

Pinnell, G., DeFord, D., & Lyons, C. (1988). *Reading Recovery: Early intervention for at-risk first graders.* Arlington, VA: Educational Research Service.

Popham, W. J. (1991). Appropriateness of teachers' test-preparation practices. *Educational Measurement: Issues and Practice, 10*(4), 12–15.

Rusakoff, D. (1999, January 14). P. S. 123 pumps up for the big test. *Washington Post,* pp. A6, A7.

Schafer, W., & Lissitz, R. (1987). Measurement training for school personnel: Recommendations and reality. *Journal of Teacher Education, 38,* 57–63.

Seda, I. (1994). Commentary on Portfolio Assessment: Experiences at the Kamehameha Elementary Education Program. In S. Valencia, E. H. Hiebert, & P. Afflerbach (Eds.), *Authentic assessment: Practices and possibilities* (pp. 127–133). Newark, DE: International Reading Association.

Shavelson, R., Baxter, G., & Pine, J. (1992). Performance assessments: Political rhetoric and measurement reality. *Educational Researcher, 21*(4), 22–27.

Shepard, L. (1989). Why we need better assessments. *Educational Leadership, 46*(7), 4–9.

Shepard, L. (1997). The centrality of test use and consequences for test validity. *Educational Measurement: Issues and Practice, 16*(2), 5–24.

Shepard, L., Flexer, R., Hiebert, E. H., Marion, S., Mayfield, V., & Weston, T. (1996). Effects of introducing classroom performance assessments on student learning. *Educational Measurement: Issues and Practice, 15*(3), 7–18.

Smith, M. (1991). Put to the test: The effects of external testing on teachers. *Educational Researcher, 20*(5), 8–11.

Solano-Flores, G., & Shavelson, R. (1997). Development of performance assessments in science: Conceptual, practical, and logistical issues. *Educational Measurement: Issues and Practice, 16*(3), 16–25.

Stephens, D., Pearson, P. D., Gilrane, C., Roe, M., Stallman, A., Shelton, J., Weinzierl, J., Rodriquez, A., & Commeyras, M. (1995). Assessment and decision-making in schools: A cross-site analysis. *Reading Research Quarterly, 30,* 478–499.

Stiggins, R., & Conklin, N. (1992). *In teachers' hands: Investigating the practices of classroom assessment.* Albany: State University of New York Press.

Taylor, C., & Nolen, S. (1996). A contextualized approach to teaching teachers about classroom-based assessment. *Educational Psychologist, 31,* 77–88.

Taylor, K., & Walton, S. (1997, September). Co-opting standardized tests in the service of learning. *Phi Delta Kappan, 79,* 66–70.

Tierney, R., Carter, M., & Desai, L. (1991). *Portfolio assessment in the reading–writing classroom.* New York: Christopher-Gordon.

Tierney, R., & Clark, C. (with Fenner, L., Herter, R., Simpson, C., & Wiser, B.). (1998). Portfolios: Assumptions, tensions, and possibilities. *Reading Research Quarterly, 33*(4), 474–486.

Tindal, E., & Marston, D. (1996). Technical adequacy of alternate reading measures as performance assessments. *Exceptionality, 6,* 201-230.

Tittle, C. (1989). Validity: Whose construction is it in the teaching and learning context? *Educational Measurement: Issues and Practice, 8,* 5–13.

Valencia, S. (1990). Alternative assessment: Separating the wheat from the chaff. *Reading Teacher, 44,* 60–61.

Valencia, S., & Au, K. (1997). *Portfolios across educational contexts: Issues of evaluation, teacher de-*

velopment, and system validity (Reading Research Rep. No. 73). Athens, GA: Universities of Georgia & Maryland, National Reading Research Center.

Valencia, S., & Place, N. (1994). Literacy portfolios for teaching, learning, and accountability: The Bellevue Literacy Assessment Project. In S. Valencia, E. H. Hiebert, & P. Afflerbach (Eds.), *Authentic assessment: Practices and possibilities* (pp. 134–156). Newark, DE: International Reading Association.

Wainer, H., & Thissen, D. (1996). How is reliability related to the quality of test scores? What is the effect of local dependence on reliability? *Educational Measurement: Issues and Practice, 15*(1), 22–29.

Wiener, R., & Cohen, J. (1997). *Literacy portfolios: Using assessment to guide instruction.* Upper Saddle River, NJ: Prentice Hall.

Winograd, P., Paris, S., & Bridge, C. (1991). Improving the assessment of literacy. *Reading Teacher, 45,* 108–116.

Wolf, K. (1993). From informal to informed assessment: Recognizing the role of the classroom teacher. *Journal of Reading, 36,* 518–523.

CHAPTER NINE

Using Instructional Time Effectively

JAMES P. BYRNES

Over the years, three important findings have appeared in the literature on reading. The first is that children tend to read very little at home or school (e.g., Greany, 1980; R. C. Anderson, Wilson, & Fielding, 1988). The second is that most children in the fourth, eighth, and twelfth grades are not reading at their appropriate grade levels (e.g., Donahue, Voelkl, Campbell, & Mazzeo, 1999). The third is that there is a positive correlation between frequent reading and reading achievement (i.e., children who read frequently tend to have higher test scores than children who read less frequently). Collectively, these findings seem to invite the following two inferences: (1) test scores could be raised by getting students to read more often, and (2) teachers should allocate more time to silent reading during their reading/language arts lessons.

The primary goal of this chapter is to consider whether such inferences follow from the evidence. It will be shown that the correlation between frequent reading and reading achievement is credible, plausible, and practically significant. Hence, there is reason to think that increased reading would benefit students. However, it will also be shown that teachers could not enhance student achievement simply by allocating more time to silent reading. Instead, teachers need to think about ways to foster *diverse* reading and provide scaffolds for children as they practice their reading skills (especially during the first few grades of elementary school).

In what follows, these ideas will be explored in greater detail. In the first section, the focus is on developing a proper understanding of the correlation between frequent reading and reading achievement. In the two parts of the second section, the focus is on understanding the instructional implications of this correlation. The final section briefly summarizes the conclusions of this chapter.

READING ACHIEVEMENT IS POSITIVELY CORRELATED WITH FREQUENT READING

As noted above, studies have consistently shown that students who read frequently tend to have higher scores on reading achievement tests than students who read less frequently (e.g., Cipielewski & Stanovich, 1992; Greany, 1980; Greany & Hegarty, 1987; Nell, 1988; Walberg & Tsai, 1984). How should this finding be interpreted? One approach would be to accept the correlation at face value, assume a causal relationship between frequent reading and reading achievement, and infer that a good way to raise test scores is to have students read more often. Another approach, however, would be to examine the evidence more critically before drawing any instructional implications from it. The latter approach is adopted here.

More specifically, the evidence will be evaluated by considering answers to four important questions:

1. How credible is the correlation between frequent reading and reading achievement?
2. Are there sound theoretical reasons for thinking that an increase in reading will lead to higher test scores?
3. Is the correlation between frequent reading and reading achievement large enough to justify wholesale changes in current practices?
4. Is there experimental evidence that suggests that an increase in reading will translate into an increase in achievement?

The Credibility Question

The issue of credibility is important to consider because instructional decisions should not be made on the basis of illusory or misleading evidence. One way to test the credibility of a correlation is to see whether it is *spurious*. To get a sense of what a spurious correlation is, consider the fact that there is high correlation between the number of doctors in a geographic area and the infant mortality rate in that area (i.e., the more doctors in an area, the higher the infant mortality rate). Such a correlation makes very little sense until we learn that lots of doctors work in cities and that cities have lots of low-income people who tend to have inadequate prenatal care. Hence, poverty is the main reason for the high infant mortality rate, not the number of doctors.

What about the correlation between frequent reading and reading achievement? How could that correlation be due to some other variable that tends to be associated with both frequent reading and high test scores? One obvious "other variable" would be reading ability (Cipielewski & Stanovich, 1992). Motivation theorists recognize that people are more likely to engage in some activity if they feel self-efficacious (Pintrich & Schunk, 1996). (See a discussion of efficacy beliefs in Wigfield, Chapter 7, this volume.) Moreover, they have shown that talented individuals tend to feel more self-efficacious than their less talented peers. If so, then it would be expected that good readers would tend to read more than poor readers. In addition, good readers, by definition, have higher test scores than poor readers. Hence, it is entirely possible that the correlation between frequent reading and reading achievement is spurious.

Statistically, researchers determine whether a correlation is spurious by seeing if it maintains its numerical value (ranging between 0 and 1.0) when the effects of other variables that might be involved are mathematically eliminated. For example, let us say that the correlation between frequent reading and reading achievement is $r = .30$. If this correlation shrinks down to a figure close to zero (e.g., $r = .05$) when the effects of reading ability are subtracted out, it is probably a spurious correlation. However, if it stays roughly the same size after the effects due to reading ability are subtracted out (e.g., $r = .27$), then it is probably not spurious (at least with respect to the variable of ability). Studies have shown that the correlation between frequent reading and reading achievement does shrink somewhat when the effects of reading ability and other possible factors (e.g., socioeconomic status) are subtracted out, but it does not shrink to zero (R. C. Anderson et al., 1988; Cipielewski & Stanovich, 1992; Heyns, 1978; Taylor, Frye, & Maruyama, 1990; Walberg & Tsai, 1984). Thus, the correlation between frequent reading and higher test scores does not appear to be spurious.

However, another way of looking at the issue of credibility relates to the notion of causal directionality. In showing that the correlation between frequent reading and higher test scores is not spurious, researchers have not shown that frequent reading causes higher test scores. To see this, consider the following possibility. Imagine that two parents are concerned about the fact that their child is not in the top reading group in her classroom. So, they hire a tutor who helps their child after school. The next year when the child is retested, the school finds that the child has test scores that warrant her placement in the top reading group. After being placed in the top group, the child reads more often because, in her school, children in the top group are given more time to read silently than are children in the lower groups. Thus, it is the increase in achievement scores that causes increased reading, not the other way around.

The Theory Question

Issues such as those regarding the direction of causality lead to the second question above regarding the theoretical reasons for thinking that frequent reading would lead to higher test scores. Statistics alone cannot determine the meaning of a mathematical relationship or the direction of causality. There has to be a well-regarded theory to lend further support to an assumed connection between two factors. It turns out that there are theoretical grounds for assuming that frequent reading will promote the development of reading skills. However, the links between frequent reading and skill development are more complicated than they would first appear.

Contemporary theories of cognition suggest that one of the best ways to become more proficient in some activity is to practice regularly and extensively (J. R. Anderson, 1995; Ericsson & Smith, 1991). In fact, some studies show that a minimum of 4 hours per day of practice is required for someone to attain the highest level of expertise in domains such as tennis, piano, or chess. However, research on the so-called Power Law of Learning suggests that practice is particularly important during the earliest stages of skill acquisition (J. R. Anderson, 1995). After a certain point in time, practice provides diminishing returns. To illustrate, consider the case of a first grader who makes pronunciation mistakes about 30% of the time in September but only 15% of the time after 9 months of regular reading in school (a 50% reduction in errors). During the second and third grades, however, she may find that her error rate reduces down further from 15% to just 10% and 8%, respectively, after two more years of practice. The latter pair of rates represent reductions of only 33% and 20% in her error rate, respectively. Thus, the notion of diminishing returns suggests that increased practice would be most beneficial to individuals who are in the earliest stages of learning to read (e.g., first through third graders) and least beneficial to individuals who are in the latter stages (e.g., ninth through twelfth graders). If so, then a uniform policy that mandates an increase in reading for all students (e.g., all students should read 15 minutes more per day) would have a greater effect on younger readers than on older readers.

In a related way, the idea of diminishing returns suggests that there would be a higher correlation between frequent reading and test scores in younger children (e.g., second and third graders) than in older children (e.g., fifth and sixth graders). It is notable that most of the studies that have investigated the role of frequent reading have focused on children in the fifth grade or older (presumably because many younger children are not yet fluent, independent readers). However, if practice has its strongest effects early in the process, then the correlations generated from studies of fifth graders may underestimate the potential value of frequent reading for younger children.

One further theoretical point relates to so-called Matthew effects (Stanovich, 1986; the origin of this term is discussed later in this subsection). Cognitive psychologists have shown that the comprehension of sentence-length constructions requires the ability to process and hold in working memory the meaning of all of the words in the sentence (Just & Carpenter, 1987). As one's eyes fixate on each word in a sentence, all preceding words in that sentence must be retained and maintained in working memory before this information fades. If any obstacle to comprehension is encountered before the information starts to fade (in about 2 seconds), comprehension processes usually falter (Baddeley, 1990). One such obstacle is the presence of an unfamiliar word. Whereas highly familiar words can be processed in a quarter of a second or less, unfamiliar words can take considerably longer to process. With only 2 seconds to process all of the words, then, unfamiliar words pose quite a problem. However, if a person reads many different types of works and does so on a regular basis, he/she tends to convert words that used to be unfamiliar into familiar words (in the same way that unfamiliar faces can become quickly recognized through repeated encounters). Over time, the troublesome words soon become processed nearly as quickly as other words and comprehension processes are no longer disrupted (Perfetti, 1985).

The most significant consequence of this increase in processing speed is that the reader now has better access to the knowledge contained in the texts that he/she is reading. Acquiring more knowledge, in turn, helps the reader make new inferences that further enhance the comprehension process (Pearson & Fielding, 1991). Other benefits of wide reading include (1) the acquisition of new vocabulary words and grammatical constructions that are normally not acquired in conversation (Stanovich & Cunningham, 1992), and (2) enhanced phonemic awareness that can be used in the decoding process (Stanovich, 1986).

Thus, regular reading has the potential to increase one's reading speed, vocabulary, knowledge, and phonemic awareness. Such changes, in turn, make one a better reader still. In effect, reading skills tend to "snowball" over time. This analysis implies that if two individuals were to start out at roughly the same place in the first grade but only one were to read extensively, it would be expected that the extensive reader would show faster growth in reading skills than the less extensive reader. Moreover, if we were to plot their reading scores as a function of time, we would see a widening gap between their respective "learning curves" over time.

Stanovich (1986) labeled this phenomenon the "Matthew effect" after the Gospel in which reference is made to the rich getting richer and the poor getting poorer (i.e., Matthew 25:29).

However, it is important to note that the Matthew effect would not be expected to occur if children were to read exactly the same (unchallenging) works again and again. Similarly, little growth would be expected if children were to read new books each time but select books that contain many of the same words and ideas. Thus, researchers would tend to find a higher correlation between extensive reading and reading achievement in a study if they asked questions such as "How many different books did you read last year?" than if they asked, "How many minutes do you spend reading each day?" In addition, the idea of a Matthew effect suggests that the causal relationship between frequent reading and reading achievement is more appropriately viewed as reciprocal than unidirectional (i.e., frequent reading causes higher achievement, which in turn promotes more frequent reading). But, in general, there does appear to be a solid theoretical basis for assuming that frequent reading will promote higher levels of reading achievement.

The Magnitude Question

The next issue that should be raised by a reflective practitioner concerns the size of the correlation between frequent reading and reading achievement. If frequent reading is authentically connected to reading achievement but the relationship is relatively weak, why should a teacher allocate more instructional time to silent reading (or assign more of it as homework)? Researchers who focus on such issues have approached the idea of magnitude in several ways. One approach consists of assigning the label "small" to correlations in the range of $r = 0$ to .30, "moderate" to correlations between .30 and .80, and "large" to correlations greater than .80 (Cohen, 1992). Then, greater weight is given to correlations in the moderate and large ranges than to correlations in the small range.

Studies show that the correlations between frequent reading and reading achievement typically range between $r = .10$ and $r = .40$ (e.g., R. C. Anderson et al., 1988; Cipielewski & Stanovich, 1992; Greany, 1980; Greany & Hegarty, 1987; Heyns, 1978; Nell, 1988; Taylor et al., 1990; Walberg & Tsai, 1984). According to the labeling approach above, these correlations would be considered "small" and perhaps not given very much consideration in instructional decisionmaking.

In recent years, however, it has been argued that the conventional labeling approach is not especially helpful when the practical value of some sort of intervention is under consideration. A better approach is to convert the correlation to something called a *binomial effect size display* (Rosenthal,

1994). The details of this conversion are less important than the bottom line that so-called small correlations (e.g., those found in studies of reading frequency) can be shown to have nontrivial practical implications. For example, let us assume that the average correlation between frequent reading and reading achievement is $r = .24$. Expressed in the form of a binomial effect size display, a correlation of .24 suggests that an intervention designed to increase reading would tend to produce growth in reading skills in 62% of students as opposed to just 38% of students who do not increase their reading. At the school level, this difference in success rate would mean that a school of 500 students would show growth in 310 students instead of 190 students (i.e., 120 additional students). At the aggregate level across all of the schools in the United States, this analysis suggests that additional reading would have a noticeable effect that would be clearly worth the effort.

But a reflective practitioner might still wonder why the correlations seem to vary so much across studies. Which of the respective values is closest to the truth? One reason for the variability was alluded to earlier. Some researchers subtracted out the effects of other important variables such as reading ability and socioeconomic status, whereas others did not. Uncorrected, the correlations are closer to $r = .40$. With the corrections, they drop down into the range of $r = .10$ to .25.

A second important reason for the variability is the varying degrees of precision and accuracy with which reading frequency has been assessed in each study. If someone asked, "How many books did you read last month?" or "How often do you read books?" you might give a less accurate answer than if you kept a daily journal of your reading for a month. Imprecise measurement tends to lead to smaller correlations than precise measurement, so one would expect that the journal approach would generate higher correlations than the questions approach. Studies generally confirm this expectation. Whereas researchers who used the journal approach have tended to find uncorrected correlations in the .30–.40 range (e.g., R. C. Anderson et al., 1988; Greany, 1980; Greany & Hegarty, 1987; Nell, 1988; Taylor et al., 1990), those using the questionnaire approach have found much smaller correlations (e.g., Walberg & Tsai, 1984).

In the same way, one would also expect that the journal approach would be more precise than an observational technique in which a researcher periodically visits classrooms to see how often individual children seem to be reading in class. Consistent with this expectation, researchers who have used the observational approach (e.g., Leinhardt, Zigmond, & Cooley, 1981; Wilkinson, Wardrop, & Anderson, 1988) tend to report lower correlations than those using the journal approach.

However, the journal approach is not without its problems. Apart from the fact that it is labor intensive, there is also the issue of social desirability. People (especially children) may be inclined to report more reading than they actually do in order to make a favorable impression on researchers. In addition, although the journal approach taps into current reading habits, it does not assess children's prior reading habits that contributed to their current level of skill. Further, in most studies that utilized the journals approach, researchers chose to focus on the average number of minutes per day spent reading. As noted earlier, the amount of time spent reading may matter less than the type and diversity of books read. To address all of these problems, Keith Stanovich and his colleagues have recently come up with a new technique that taps into a variable called *print exposure* (Cipielewski & Stanovich, 1992; Cunningham & Stanovich, 1991; Stanovich & West, 1989). In this technique, people are presented with names of authors (e.g., Stephen King), books (e.g., *The Grapes of Wrath*), and magazines (*Cosmopolitan*) and are asked to say if they recognize these names. Mixed within the list of actual names are foils (e.g., names of the consulting editors of journals in educational psychology). Note that this measure seems to tap into both the extent of reading *and* the diversity of reading. That is, someone who never reads or who only reads the same three authors would tend to recognize fewer names than someone who reads widely. Also, people who are inclined toward social desirability would tend to check more names, even the foils. Researchers can use the selection of foils to adjust scores down to a more accurate figure.

Aware of the fact that any correlation between print exposure and reading skills might be spurious (e.g., smart people tend to read more and also know more names of authors), Stanovich and colleagues were careful in each of their studies to control for general intelligence (using IQ tests) and aptitude (using various measures of reading comprehension and reading-specific skills such as decoding). Across a series of studies from 1989 to 1995, results showed that print exposure was highly predictive of the following: (1) college students' orthographic (i.e., spelling) knowledge (Stanovich & West, 1989); (2) children's phonological coding, spelling, vocabulary, verbal fluency, and general knowledge (Cunningham & Stanovich, 1991); (3) college students' vocabulary, reading comprehension, knowledge of history and literature, spelling ability, and verbal fluency (Stanovich & Cunningham, 1992); (4) children's reading comprehension and reading rate (Cipielewski & Stanovich, 1992); and (5) college students' and older adults' cultural knowledge (Stanovich & Cunningham, 1993; Stanovich, West, & Harrison, 1995). On average, the corrected correlations clustered near the value of $r = .28$, suggesting that extensive and diverse reading is associated with growth in reading skills and knowledge. In addition, these studies illustrate how a more precise measurement technique can yield a higher and more accurate indication of the degree of relationship between two factors than can less precise techniques.

One final way to address the magnitude question is to consider the likely consequences of increasing reading by a certain amount each day. An interesting aspect of correlational studies is that mathematical formulas can be created that allow researchers to say how much one factor might increase if another factor were increased by a certain amount. In the case of reading, several researchers have attempted to determine how much test scores would increase if children were to read a certain amount more. In one study, for example, R. C. Anderson et al. (1988) showed that a unit increase in minutes of book reading would be associated with a 4.9 percentile gain in reading comprehension as measured by a standardized test. To illustrate such an increase, a child at the median for book reading in their study (i.e., about 5 minutes per day) would have to increase his/her reading by just 9 minutes more per day (i.e., 13 minutes per day) to show a 4.9 percentile gain. Another interesting aspect of R. C. Anderson and colleagues' (1988) data was that increases in book reading time produced diminishing returns. For example, a child who went from no reading per day to 6 minutes per day would move from the 40th percentile for reading comprehension to the 60th percentile. In contrast, a comparable 6-minute shift from 6 minutes per day to 12 minutes per day would move a child from the 60th percentile to just the 64th percentile.

The Experimental Evidence Question

One way to summarize the arguments so far is to say that there is good reason to assume that the correlation between frequent reading and achievement is both credible and plausible. It might still be argued, however, that no instructional implications should be drawn from this correlation until researchers demonstrate the causal connection between frequent reading and reading achievement in multiple well-designed experiments. Is there evidence to suggest that children who are asked to read more often show larger gains in achievement than do children in control groups?

At present, the experimental evidence is somewhat sparse, but a few relevant studies have been conducted. In one study, for example, Carver and Liebert (1995) considered whether a 6-week summer program would improve children's vocabulary and reading rate. Half of the children were allowed to select library books that were, according to the publishers, relatively easy for children in the study (group A), and half were allowed to select books that were designated to be somewhat harder (group B). Children were given approximately 1 hour to read each day at the library, and they were also given prizes and rewards for passing comprehension tests on the books. Results showed that children in group A read an average of 41 books over the 6 weeks, whereas those in group B read an average of 23 books. Nevertheless, neither group seemed to experience a significant increase in their vocabulary or reading rate by the end of the program. Carver and Liebert (1995) explained these results by suggesting that the intervention was probably too short to have had an effect. In addition, they showed that the publishers' definitions of easy and hard were not entirely accurate. Hence, the books selected by the children may not have exposed them to a sufficiently wide selection of new vocabulary words.

In another line of studies, researchers examined the relative effectiveness of a program called Uninterrupted Sustained Silent Reading (USSR). This approach is described in detail later in this chapter, but for now it can be said that children in the USSR program are asked to spend extended periods of time engaged in silent reading. Across 10 studies, researchers found significant differences favoring USSR over the traditional approach in five studies (i.e., Aranha, 1985; Langford & Allen, 1983; Milton, 1973; Pfau, 1966, cited in Wiesendanger & Birlem, 1984; Wiesendanger, 1982) but no significant differences or even a negative effect for USSR in the remaining five studies (i.e., Evans & Towner, 1975; Oliver, 1976; Vacca, 1976, cited in Wiesendanger & Birlem, 1984; Reed, 1977, cited in Wiesendanger & Birlem, 1984). One factor that seemed to relate to the effectiveness of USSR was the length of the intervention (Wiesendanger & Birlem, 1984). When USSR was implemented for 5 months or less, no significant differences emerged between treatment and control classrooms in four out of five studies. In contrast, when it was implemented for 6 months or more, significant differences emerged in every case. This finding converges with Carver and Liebert's (1995) explanation of their results. A second factor that related to the effectiveness of USSR was the use of explicit skill instruction. When teachers combined USSR with skills instruction, children showed more growth than when teachers did not combine USSR with skills instruction.

Summary

The literatures pertinent to the four questions of credibility, theory, magnitude, and experimental evidence all support the inference that frequent reading does seem to make an independent and nontrivial contribution to growth in reading skills. Although there are inconsistencies in the literature, these inconsistencies have prompted researchers to refine their theoretical approaches and methodological designs instead of abandoning their assumption that frequent reading promotes growth in reading skills. In all, the suggestion that children should be reading more often seems to be well justified.

Nevertheless, it is not enough to convince someone of the connection between frequent reading and achievement. Knowing how to translate this finding to the needs of the classroom requires some additional reflection on the best way to promote additional reading in students. It is to the latter issue that we turn to next.

CERTAIN TYPES OF READING AND INSTRUCTION MAY BE MORE LIKELY TO AFFECT THE FREQUENCY–ACHIEVEMENT RELATION THAN OTHERS

In the present section, implementation processes will be explored at two levels of analysis. The first level consists of general issues that teachers should consider when they are in the midst of considering ways to foster increased reading in students. The second level consists of specific, contemporary approaches that exemplify the general issues to greater or lesser degrees.

General Issues

Although theories of skill acquisition support the idea that practice is generally a good way to promote increased skill (J. R. Anderson, 1995), there are different *types* of practice that would be expected to be more or less related to skill improvement. As suggested earlier, children who read diverse and challenging books would be expected to show more growth than children who read as much as the former children but select the same less challenging books each time. To make an analogy to music, a pianist's skills would be expected to show more improvement if he/she played multiple classical pieces during 4 hours of practice than if he/she repeatedly played "Chopsticks" or mainly worked on isolated drills (e.g., scales). Although Carver and Liebert's (1995) relatively brief study seems to contradict the idea that challenging materials will promote more growth, the literature on print exposure is entirely consistent with this idea. As such, teachers, parents, and librarians need to play an active role in monitoring the types of reading performed by children when they are given more time to read.

   Similarly, even when people know that they are not very good in some aspect of a skill (e.g., serving in the case of tennis), they often need expert advice to help them understand how they *should be* executing that aspect (e.g., a tennis instructor). Very few people could induce the right "fix" on their own. This analysis suggests that *guided* practice in reading (in which someone observes mistakes, corrects them, and provides "scaffolds" for children to induce the right answer on their own) might lead to faster growth than unmonitored independent reading at home or school (Ericsson, 1996). In support of this claim, Juel (1996) found that struggling readers in the first grade benefited more from scaffolded tutoring than from opportunities to read children's literature on their own. Whereas the number of scaffolded experiences correlated around $r = .60$ with growth in reading comprehension, the number of minutes of reading literature was *negatively* correlated with growth, $r = -.43$ (i.e., children who read more on their own showed *less* growth).

Another issue concerns the difference between *allocated time* and *engaged time* (Guthrie, 1980; Karweit & Slavin, 1981). Even when two teachers seem to be allocating the "right" amount of time to skill-enhancing activities (e.g., both allocate 30 minutes of a 45-minute period to silent reading and just 10 minutes to isolated drills), they may differ in their ability to get children to stay "on task." Depending on the instructional approach used and a teacher's classroom management skills, children given the same amount of time for an activity might well spend differing amounts of time engaged in that activity (e.g., 50% of the time vs. 75% of the time).

Yet another issue has to do with the construct of aptitude. Educational psychologists differ in terms of whether they think talents are largely unalterable traits of individuals (i.e., people are born with a fixed amount of reading ability) or modifiable through practice. Regardless of which stance one prefers, both of these perspectives suggest that, in any classroom, there will always be children who need a lot of time to master some skill as well as children who need less time. The children who need less time are said to have more aptitude than those who need more time (Gettinger, 1984). If so, then it follows that there may be no relationship between the time allocated to reading and reading achievement because the same 45-minute period may be too much time for high-aptitude children but too little time for low-aptitude children. Thus, researchers should not simply consider the amount of time given to reading in different classrooms. Instead, they should consider whether children in the two classrooms are given the time *they need* to acquire reading skills (Carroll, 1963; Gettinger, 1984). Note that if teachers allocate the right amount of time to both high- and low-aptitude children (e.g., 30 minutes of silent reading to the former vs. 45 minutes to the latter), allocated time should be *negatively* correlated with achievement; that is, higher scores on a reading achievement test should be associated with shorter allocated times, and lower scores on the reading test should be associated with longer allocated times. On the other hand, if teachers allocate roughly the same amount of time to all students, then one would expect a zero correlation between time allocated and reading achievement.

It turns out that most research has found either a zero correlation between allocated time and reading achievement, or only a small effect for increased time. Karweit (1976), for example, conducted a secondary analysis of the Equality of Educational Opportunity Report (EEOR) database and other databases to examine the effect of time in reading achievement. In the case of the EEOR database, she focused on the performance of sixth graders from 944 metropolitan schools. After controlling for degree of urbanism and several background factors, she found that a combination of three time variables (i.e., average daily attendance of students in the school, length of the school day, and days in the academic year) was a significant predictor of reading comprehension scores. Inspection of the predictive equation suggested that a unit of change in the time variable would produce an increase in reading comprehension scores of 1.23. However, the amount of time that would be required for such a modest change would be unrealistic, to say the least. To illustrate, imagine a school that had an average daily attendance of 85%, a school day that was 6 hours long, and an academic year of 180 days. To increase comprehension scores by 1 unit (e.g., average scores increasing from 68.2 to 69.2), Karweit's formula suggests that students would have to have perfect attendance, go to school for 264 days a year (no holidays and only weekends off), and stay in school for 9.4 hours a day!

In a similar way, Kiesling (1977/1978) examined the effect of time allocation on the reading achievement of fourth, fifth, and sixth graders from four New York State school districts ($N = 2{,}400$ students). Unlike Karweit (1976), Kiesling focused on the amount of time devoted to reading instead of the amount of time spent in school. He found that, with the exception of the poorest readers, all children received essentially the same number of minutes of reading instruction per week (i.e., about 125 minutes). The poorest performers (i.e., those who were two or three levels below grade for reading) received an average of 182 minutes of reading instruction. The lack of appreciable variability in time for better readers may partly explain why the results showed no significant relation between minutes of large- or small-group instruction and reading achievement in 84% of the analyses that he conducted. Interestingly, the few effects that were significant occurred for students who were at or below grade level for reading. Kiesling (1977/1978, pp. 572–573) argued that such results strongly support the idea that "high ability children may have the capacity for 'getting on,' whether or not they receive large allotments of instruction."

In a follow-up study, Kiesling (1984) controlled for pretest scores (and other variables) and found that the number of minutes of small group instruction predicted growth in vocabulary scores on the California Achievement Test but not growth in comprehension scores. Also, he found that whereas the number of minutes of large-group instruction was unrelated to growth in scores, the number of minutes of individualized instruction was related to growth in both vocabulary and comprehension scores. But, once again, the effects were stronger for children who were below grade level for reading than for children who were above grade level. Overall, Kiesling's data can be interpreted as implicating the role of aptitude and time-on-task as factors in degree of growth. Note that low-ability students tend to get more individualized instruction than high-ability students and that students are more likely to be on task in small-group or individualized settings than they are in large-group instruction (Brophy & Good, 1986).

As one further illustration of the finding that allocated time does not seem to matter that much, the present author recently conducted a secondary analysis of the 1992 National Assessment of Educational Progress (NAEP) database for reading proficiency. In the midst of exploring the possible role of a variety of time variables, I found that the amount of time teachers allocated to reading instruction was correlated only $r = -.02$ with fourth graders' proficiency scores ($N = 4,534$). If we examine the scores for just the bottom third of scorers, children who were given 30 minutes of reading instruction had a mean proficiency score of 175. For the lowest scorers who had 60 minutes of instruction, the mean is extremely similar at 172. Thus, doubling the amount of allocated time had apparently no effect! For the top third and middle third of scorers, the findings were extremely similar.

Overall, the findings across studies suggest that increased allocation time either has no effect or only a modest effect on reading achievement. In light of earlier arguments, these findings are to be expected. Allocated time should only be related to reading achievement if there is reason to suspect a positive correlation between allocated time and time spent reading diverse materials. If children are no more likely to read in this way during a 60-minute period than in a 30-minute period, then allocated time would not be expected to relate to reading achievement in a consistent way. Similarly, if they are not provided with feedback on errors, they should not be expected to improve as well.

One final general issue concerns whether it would be better for children to read more often at home or at school. Studies that have investigated this issue have produced somewhat discrepant results. For example, Taylor et al. (1990) asked 195 students in grades 5 and 6 to keep daily reading logs from mid-January through mid-May (17 weeks). Students completed their logs at the end of each 50-minute reading class on a total of 47 days. In addition to recording the amount and type of reading at school, children also recorded their at-home reading behavior for the day before. Results showed that children read for an average of 16 minutes in their reading class (i.e., 32% of the time allotted) and an average of 15 minutes at home. In addition, whereas the uncorrected correlation between minutes of reading in school and reading achievement was $r = .37$, the uncorrected correlation between minutes of reading at home and reading achievement was $r = .16$. The difference between these two correlations remained after corrections, so the results of this study suggest that reading in school is more important to growth than reading at home.

However, the present author reached a different conclusion when I reanalyzed the data from the 1992 NAEP. Here, I considered the correlations between proficiency scores in reading and the following variables: (1) student responses to the item, "How often do you read for fun in your own time?" (almost every day, once or twice a week, once or twice a month, never or hardly ever); (2) student responses to the item, "How often does your teacher give you time to read books you choose?" (almost every day, etc.); (3) student responses to the item, "How often do you take books out of the library for your own enjoyment?"; (4) teacher responses to the item, "How often do your students read silently in reading class?"; (5) teacher responses to the item, "How much time do you spend per day on reading instruction?"; (6) student ethnicity (white, black, or Hispanic); (7) student gender; and (8) parent education. Results showed that all of these variables except for the two teacher items were significantly correlated with reading proficiency. As a set, the three indices of out-of-school reading yielded a corrected correlation of about $r = .28$ (here, the effects of ethnicity, gender, and parent education were subtracted out). Using the data to create a predictive equation, I found that a unit increase in any of the three indices of out-of-school reading (e.g., reading for pleasure once or twice a week instead of once or twice a month) would be associated with rises in proficiency scores of 4.2, 4.3, and 5.7 points, respectively. A unit increase in all three indices would be associated with a rise in proficiency scores of 14.2 points (e.g., from 200 to 214.2). Note, however, that I could not control for prior reading achievement in this analysis, so the actual magnitude of the out-of-school reading effect may be smaller than what I found. However, as noted earlier, the NAEP methodology of asking questions is a less precise way to measure reading frequency than other approaches, so perhaps the correlation is not so inflated. Either way, my findings conflict with those of Taylor et al. (1990). As a result, the issue of whether children should read more at home or at school is not yet resolved.

Specific Approaches to Reading Instruction

Another way to think about the best way to increase reading is to apply the aforementioned general issues to several existing approaches to reading instruction. For the sake of brevity, we shall only consider three approaches as an illustrative exercise: (1) Uninterrupted Sustained Silent Reading (USSR), (2) Concept-Oriented Reading Instruction (CORI), and (3) traditional small-group oral reading.

The general approach of USSR is as follows (Wheldall & Entwistle,

1988): (1) students read silently in a quiet reading atmosphere, free from distractions and interruptions; (2) the teacher also reads recreational materials (not schoolwork), thereby providing an adult model; (3) students are free to read a wide variety of books or magazines (these need to be made available in the classroom), but students need to select materials that will take the entire allotted time to avoid getting up and distracting other readers; and (4) children's comprehension of their selected materials is not to be evaluated in any way (e.g., by making them write a book report).

As described, it would seem that USSR would clearly foster extended periods of engaged reading at school. In addition, the motivation to read would presumably be intrinsic, given the fact that children choose their reading materials and are not graded (Deci & Ryan, 1985). Intrinsic motivation and positive attitudes, in turn, would be expected to spill over to increased reading in out-of-school contexts. In addition, there is an emphasis on diverse reading, but there does not appear to be opportunities for teacher feedback on reading errors (as would occur with oral reading), nor for teacher scaffolding of skills. Further, the fact that children are not evaluated after reading implies that they are not getting feedback on their comprehension attempts as well. Overall, however, USSR is fairly consistent with the general issues discussed in the previous subsection. As a result, one would expect it to promote growth in reading achievement (especially if it is implemented for a long time and combined with skills instruction; see the earlier discussion of experimental evidence).

In CORI, the instructional framework involves four phases (Guthrie et al., 1996): (1) observe and personalize (e.g., students find a bird's nest and brainstorm in small groups about questions they want to explore with additional observations or reading); (2) search and retrieve (e.g., teaching children how to find the answers they seek); (3) comprehend and integrate the materials retrieved (e.g., teaching and modeling reading strategies such as summarizing and fix-up strategies such as rereading); and (4) communicate to others (e.g., write a report or class-authored book). Similar to USSR, then, intrinsic motivation is enhanced by giving children freedom to choose, but reading is also directed toward finding out information. In USSR, in contrast, students could choose to limit their reading to narrative texts to satisfy goals related to pleasure reading (e.g., diversion). Moreover, although both involve adult modeling, CORI gives a sense of a busy, energized environment whereas USSR seems to foster a calmer setting. In addition, whereas CORI involves instruction on fix-up strategies and teachers catching mistakes, teachers in USSR would not catch students' silent reading mistakes. Both approaches, however, are designed to create positive attitudes toward reading that should, it is hoped, lead to greater out-of-school reading as well.

USSR and CORI can be distinguished from the more traditional approach of teachers circulating through small groups of children who are matched for reading level. While the teacher is working with one group (e.g., asking each child to read aloud from a text), the children in the other groups are usually working by themselves on exercises in workbooks. In such a classroom setting, then, there often is no teacher modeling, very little silent reading, and children are not free to choose the selections that they are reading. Moreover, the children who are working on workbooks (away from the teacher) are likely to be off task and occasionally disruptive (Brophy & Good, 1986). Even when the teacher is present, however, studies have shown that children disengage their attention when they have to listen to their peers read aloud and make mistakes (e.g., Imai, Anderson, Wilkinson, & Yi, 1992). The primary positive feature of the traditional approach (from the standpoint of the general issues discussed earlier) is that teachers can catch the reading mistakes of students and engage in either modeling or scaffolding.

Of course, there is no reason to think that teachers would have to choose just one of these approaches. In fact, teachers could very easily implement all three in the course of a day. For example, children could engage in USSR during homeroom period, read aloud in small groups during reading period, and then engage in CORI during science period. The point is not that one approach should be favored over others, but rather that certain approaches are more likely to lead to extended periods of engaged reading than others. It should also be noted that the assignments given to children for homework could also require extended periods of free reading as well. Thus, there are many ways to foster increased reading in children that do not have to supersede other instructional goals.

CONCLUSIONS

The primary goals of the present chapter were to (1) evaluate the claim that teachers should implement strategies to increase the amount of reading that children do, and (2) describe instructional issues that teachers should consider when they commit themselves to the goal of fostering additional reading in their students. A positive correlation between frequent reading and reading achievement was shown to be credible, plausible, and practically significant. In addition, the evidence suggested that teachers could not enhance student achievement simply by allocating more time within language arts lessons to silent reading. Instead, teachers need to think about ways to foster *diverse* reading and provide scaffolds for children as they practice their reading skills (especially during the first few grades of elementary school).

In closing, three additional features of the literature are worth noting.

The first is that researchers are still a long way from understanding the precise connection between reading frequency and reading achievement. In particular, there are a number of practical questions that still lack answers. For example, should children be reading more often at home or school? What kinds of books are most likely to give them the diversity they need? Until researchers find answers to these questions, it is likely that some programs to enhance reading will produce disappointing results. The second feature of the literature worth noting is that the benefits that accrue from increased reading generally take several years to manifest themselves. As such, little change would be expected during the first year in which a program to increase reading is implemented. The third feature is that the best predictors of growth in reading have been found to be (1) prior reading achievement, (2) indicators of socioeconomic status, and (3) extensive reading, in that order. In fact, the predictive power of the first two factors is anywhere from two to eight times as much as that of frequent reading. In other words, a school system that targeted early reading skills (but did not specifically promote increased reading) would show far greater gains than a school system that limited its focus to increasing the amount of reading in fifth graders. But there is no reason why a system could not target all of the factors that predict reading achievement. The other chapters in this book provide clues as to how to this might be done.

RECOMMENDED READINGS

Gambrell, L. B. (1978). Getting started with Sustained Silent Reading and keeping it going. *Reading Teacher, 32,* 328–331.

This paper describes how to implement USSR in the classroom.

Guthrie, J. T. (1996) Educational contexts for engagement in literacy. *Reading Teacher, 49,* 432–445.

This paper written for a practitioner audience, provides a good description of Concept-Oriented Reading Instruction (CORI) and its effects on children's motivation to read and reading skills.

Guthrie, J. T., Anderson, E., Alao, S., & Rinehart, J. (1999). Influences of Concept-Oriented Reading Instruction on strategy use and conceptual learning from text. *The Elementary School Journal, 99,* 343–365.

This research report provides details on how the CORI research was conducted. It shows how CORI increased strategy use, conceptual learning, and text comprehension more than traditional instruction did, even after background variables were controlled.

Juel, C. (1996). What makes literacy tutoring effective? *Reading Research Quarterly, 31,* 268–289.

This paper provides a number of examples of how teachers and tutors can use scaffolds effectively to teach beginning reading skills. Teachers can utilize some of the techniques when providing instruction to small reading groups.

Stanovich, K. E. (1986). Matthew effects in reading: Some consequences of individual differences in the acquisition of literacy. *Reading Research Quarterly, 21,* 360–407.

In this paper, Stanovich gives the original and most complete exposition of Matthew effects. He shows how the gap between good and poor readers grows over time due to grouping practices and other instructional decisions.

REFERENCES

Anderson, J. R. (1995). *Learning and memory: An integrated approach.* New York: Wiley.

Anderson, R. C., Wilson, P. T., & Fielding, L. G. (1988). Growth in reading and how children spend their time outside of school. *Reading Research Quarterly, 23,* 285–303.

Aranha, M. (1985). Sustained Silent Reading goes East. *The Reading Teacher, 39,* 214–217.

Baddeley, A. D. (1990). *Human memory: Theory and practice.* Needham Heights, MA: Allyn & Bacon.

Brophy, J., & Good, T. (1986). Teacher behavior and student achievement. In M. C. Wittrock (Ed.), *Handbook of research on teaching* (pp. 328–375). New York: Holt, Rinehart & Winston.

Carroll, J. B. (1963). A model of school learning. *Teachers College Record, 64,* 723–733.

Carver, R. P., & Liebert, R. E. (1995). The effect of reading library books at different levels of difficulty upon gain in reading ability. *Reading Research Quarterly, 30,* 26–48.

Cipielewski, J., & Stanovich, K. E. (1992). Predicting growth in reading ability from children's exposure to print. *Journal of Experimental Child Psychology, 54,* 74–89.

Cohen, J. J. (1992). A primer on power. *Psychological Bulletin, 112,* 155–159.

Cunningham, A. E., & Stanovich, K. E. (1991). Tracking the unique effects of print exposure in children: Associations with vocabulary, general knowledge, and spelling. *Journal of Educational Psychology, 83,* 264–274.

Deci, E., & Ryan, R. (1985). *Intrinsic motivation and self-determination in human behavior.* New York: Plenum Press.

Donahue, P. L., Voelkl, K. E., Campbell, J. R., & Mazzeo, J. (1999). *NAEP 1999 Report Card for the Nation and the States.* Washington, DC: National Center for Education Statistics, U.S. Department of Education.

Ericsson, K. A. (1996). *The road to excellence.* Mahwah, NJ: Erlbaum.

Ericsson, K. A., & Smith, J. (1991). *Toward a general theory of expertise: Prospects and limits.* Cambridge, UK: Cambridge University Press.

Evans, H. M., & Towner, J. C. (1975). Sustained Silent Reading: Does it increase skills? *The Reading Teacher, 29,* 155–156.

Gettinger, M. (1984). Achievement as a function of time spent in learning and time needed for learning. *American Educational Research Journal, 21,* 617–628.

Greany, V. (1980). Factors related to amount and time of leisure time reading. *Reading Research Quarterly, 15,* 337–357.

Greany, V., & Hegarty, M. (1987). Correlates of leisure-time reading. *Journal of Research in Reading, 10,* 3–20.

Guthrie, J. T. (1980). Time in reading programs. *The Reading Teacher, 34,* 500–502.

Guthrie, J. T., Van Meter, P., McDann, A. D., Wigfield, A., Bennett, L., Poundstone, C. C., Rice,

M. E., Faisbisch, F. M., Hunt, B., & Mitchell, A. M. (1996). Growth of literacy engagement: Changes in motivations and strategies during Concept-Oriented Reading Instruction. *Reading Research Quarterly, 31*, 306–332.

Heyns, B. (1978). *Summer learning and the effects of schooling.* New York: Academic Press.

Imai, M., Anderson, R. C., Wilkinson, I. A. G., & Yi, H. (1992). Properties of attention during reading lessons. *Journal of Educational Psychology, 84*, 160–173.

Juel, C. (1996). What makes literacy tutoring effective? *Reading Research Quarterly, 31*, 268–289.

Just, M. A., & Carpenter, P. A. (1987). *The psychology of reading and language comprehension.* Boston: Allyn & Bacon.

Karweit, N. (1976). A reanalysis of the effect of quantity of schooling on achievement. *Sociology of Education, 49*, 236–246.

Karweit, N. L. (1981). Time in school. *Research in Sociology of Education and Socialization, 2*, 77–110.

Karweit, N. L., & Slavin, R. E. (1981). Measurement and modeling choices in studies of time and learning. *American Educational Research Association, 18*, 157–171.

Kiesling, H. (1977/1978). Productivity of instructional time by mode of instruction for students at varying levels of reading skill. *Reading Research Quarterly, 4*, 554–582.

Kiesling, H. J. (1984). Assignment practices and the relationship of instructional time to the reading performance of elementary school children. *Economics of Education Review, 3*, 341–350.

Langford, J. C., & Allen, E. G. (1983). The effect of USSR on students' attitudes and achievement. *Reading Horizons, 23*, 194–200.

Leinhardt, G., Zigmond, N., & Cooley, W. W. (1981). Reading instruction and its effects. *American Educational Research Journal, 18*, 343–361.

Milton, M. J. (1973). The effect of sustained silent reading upon comprehension. *Reading Improvement, 10*, 16–18.

Nell, V. (1988). The psychology of reading for pleasure: Needs and gratification. *Reading Research Quarterly, 23*, 6–50.

Oliver, M. E. (1976). The effect of high intensity practice on reading achievement. *Reading Improvement, 13*, 226–228.

Pearson, P. D., & Fielding, L. (1991). Comprehension instruction. In M. Barr, M. L. Kamil, P. B. Mosenthal, & P. D. Pearson (Eds.), *Handbook of reading research* (Vol. 2, pp. 815–861). New York: Longman.

Perfetti, C. A. (1985). *Reading ability.* New York: Oxford University Press.

Pfau, D. W. (1966). *An investigation of the effects of planned recreational reading programs in first and second grade.* Unpublished doctoral dissertation, State University of New York at Buffalo.

Pintrich, P. R., & Schunk, D. H. (1996). *Motivation in education: Theory, research, and applications.* Englewood Cliff, NJ: Merrill/Prentice Hall.

Reed, K. (1977). *An investigation of the effect of sustained silent reading on reading comprehension skills and attitude toward reading of urban secondary school students.* Unpublished doctoral dissertation, University of Connecticut, Storrs.

Rosenthal, R. (1994). Parametric measures of effect size. In H. Cooper & L. V. Hedges (Eds.), *The handbook of research synthesis* (pp. 231–244). New York: Russell Sage Foundation.

Stanovich, K. E. (1986). Matthew effects in reading: Some consequences of individual differences in the acquisition of literacy. *Reading Research Quarterly, 21*, 360–407.

Stanovich, K. E., & Cunningham, A. E. (1992). Studying the consequences of literacy within a literate society: The cognitive correlates of print exposure. *Memory and Cognition, 20*, 51–68.

Stanovich, K. E., & Cunningham, A. E. (1993). Where does knowledge come from? Specific associations between print exposure and information acquisition. *Journal of Educational Psychology, 85*, 211–229.

Stanovich, K. E., & West, R. F. (1989). Exposure to print and orthographic processing. *Reading Research Quarterly, 24*, 402–426.

Stanovich, K. E., West, R. F., & Harrison, M. R. (1995). Knowledge growth and maintenance across the lifespan: The role of print exposure. *Developmental Psychology, 31*, 811–826.

Taylor, B. M., Frye, B. J., & Maruyama, G. M. (1990). Time spent reading and reading growth. *American Educational Research Journal, 27*, 351–362.

Vacca, R. T. (1976, December). *An exploration of holistic and subskills centered instruction in a reading program for students in grades 7–8.* Paper presented to the meeting of the National Reading Conference, Atlanta, GA.

Walberg, H. J., & Tsai, S. (1984). Reading achievement and diminishing returns to time. *Journal of Educational Psychology, 76*, 442–451.

Wheldall, K., & Entwistle, J. (1988). Back in the USSR: The effect of teacher modeling of silent reading on pupil's reading behavior in the primary school classroom. *Educational Psychology, 8*, 51–66.

Wiesendanger, K. D. (1982). Sustained Silent Reading: Its effect on comprehension and word recognition skills when implemented in a university summer reading clinic. *The Reading Professor, 8*, 33–37.

Wiesendanger, K. D., & Birlem, E. D. (1984). The effectiveness of SSR: An overview of the research. *Reading Horizons, 24*, 195–201.

Wilkinson, I., Waldrop, J. L., & Anderson, R. C. (1988). Silent reading reconsidered: Reinterpreting reading instruction and its effects. *American Educational Research Journal, 25*, 127–144.

CHAPTER TEN

Building toward Coherent Instruction

JOHN T. GUTHRIE
KATHLEEN E. COX
KAELI T. KNOWLES
MICHELLE BUEHL
SUSAN ANDERS MAZZONI
LIZ FASULO

What do we mean by coherent instruction? Coherent instruction is teaching that connects. It connects the student's reading skills to writing. It connects reading and writing to content. It links the content of learning to student interests. Coherent teaching makes it easy for students to learn because it combines the strange–new with the familiar–old. When the classroom is coherent, teachers help students make connections among reading, writing, and content.

Coherence of instruction fosters engagement because engaged reading is a process of linking. Engaged learners find time to read interesting books. By following their motivations for reading, they learn the skills that make them better readers. Engaged readers connect their reading with their friendships and their leisure time. Reading is a way to share and build a social life. In brief, engagement is a network of bonds among skills, strategies, knowledge, and motivation, in the social community. As engaged reading is a weave of many threads, it is best developed in a classroom that connects. A coherent classroom affords students abundant opportunities to become and stay engaged.

Coherent instructional processes make engagement possible. We depict these instructional processes in an ellipse at the outside of Figure 10.1. All of these aspects of the classroom have been shown through empirical and theoretical arguments to impact engagement processes and learning outcomes (see Guthrie & Alao, 1997; Guthrie, Cox, et al., 1998). When they work together, we say instruction is coherent. Instructional processes include (1) learning and knowledge goals, (2) real-world interactions, (3) autonomy support, (4) interesting texts, (5) reading strategy instruction, (6) collaboration support, (7) praise and rewards, (8) evaluation, and (9) teacher involvement. Coherence is the linkage network among these instructional elements. Closer to Figure 10.1's center are processes of engaged reading, which include strategies, aspects of motivation, conceptual knowledge, and social interactions. These engagement processes enable students to attain the outcomes of instruction (see Baker, Dreher, & Guthrie, Chapter 1, this volume). At the center of Figure 10.1 are the outcomes of achievement, knowledge, and reading practices. Reading practices include the time spent reading preferred contents and the contexts for reading activities.

We first discuss the engagement processes. After defining motivation, cognitive strategies, and conceptual knowledge, we describe how they work together during engaged reading. Social interaction is not discussed here, as it is the main emphasis in Chapter 6 by Gambrell, Mazzoni, and Almasi (this volume). Next, we present each instructional process (e.g., autonomy support) briefly. We devote considerable space to portraying the importance of coherence, or the interconnections among the instructional processes. We close with a teacher's guide for planning coherent instruction.

PROCESSES OF ENGAGED READING

Strategies for Engaged Reading

Engaged readers use a wide range of strategies. Using prior knowledge and posing questions as they explore their environment, engaged readers are involved in a process of searching. They read multiple texts, examine a variety of documents, and extract critical details (Guthrie, Weber, & Kimmerly, 1993). As engaged readers succeed in searching, they use strategies for integrating information (Dole, Duffy, Roehler, & Pearson, 1991) from expository and narrative texts (Graesser, Golding, & Long, 1991). Engaged learners also utilize strategies for communicating and representing their understanding. This may entail drawing, charting, note taking, and

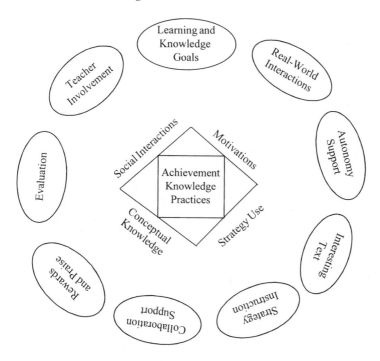

FIGURE 10.1. Model of instructional contexts for reading engagement.

composing in narrative, expository, or persuasive rhetorical structures (Flower et al., 1990).

Cognitive strategies are procedures that can help students succeed at higher-order tasks such as reading comprehension. Research suggests that children's reading comprehension is improved by instruction in strategies such as activating prior knowledge, self-questioning, comprehension monitoring, and summarizing. We describe these selected strategies briefly and present some instructional processes that promote them.

Activating Prior Knowledge

Teaching children to activate relevant background knowledge before and during reading helps them form cognitive links between prior knowledge and text-based ideas. A broad research base suggests that readers' prior knowledge about a topic interacts with text information to aid readers in drawing inferences and comprehending text. Readers who lack background knowledge about a text topic will find comprehension more difficult (Pearson, Hansen, & Gordon, 1979). Even if students do possess high prior knowledge about text topics, many do not spontaneously activate relevant knowledge (Paris & Lindauer, 1976). Therefore, it is important to investigate instructional processes that aid the activation and use of prior knowledge before and during reading. The instructional processes that facilitate prior knowledge activation include the use of modeling, prereading purpose questions, and small-group discussions.

Self-Questioning and Comprehension Monitoring

The metacognitive strategy of self-questioning leads to deeper comprehension of text by enabling readers to engage in goal-directed, organized thinking (Williamson, 1996). Students who self-question are able to read text actively for meaning, independent of teacher-supplied learning aids (Rosenshine, 1979). Comprehension monitoring refers to the ability to *evaluate* one's own understanding of text, as well as the ability to *regulate* misunderstandings by applying "fix-up" strategies such as rereading or changing reading speed (Baker, 1985). Such monitoring strategies are important because readers are better able to construct meaning from text when they are aware of their comprehension performance and use fix-up strategies to alleviate comprehension difficulties (Guthrie, 1983). The instructional processes that enhance monitoring skills are teacher modeling and explanation of the strategies' functional value—explanation about what, why, how, and when to use strategies and direct strategy instruction.

Summarizing

Summarizing is a valuable tool to help students understand and remember important ideas as they make decisions as to what information to delete and what to retain. Summarizing improves students' reading comprehension (Armbruster, Anderson, & Ostertag, 1987) as well as their writing ability (Taylor, 1983). Furthermore, by increasing early readers' summarization skills, teachers can help move young readers from an egocentric, "What is important to me" viewpoint of text to what is important according to others (Bereiter & Scardamalia, 1989).

Unfortunately, students are not naturally motivated to learn cognitive strategies. Learning strategies takes time, energy, and effort. Teachers rarely hear students say, "I really want to learn how to monitor my comprehension." Consequently, making strategy instruction motivating is a challenge for teachers.

Motivation for Engaged Reading

At least two aspects of motivation influence reading: intrinsic motivation and self-efficacy. Deci and Ryan (1985) defined intrinsic motivation to learn as "the innate, natural propensity to engage one's interests and exercise one's capacities, and in so doing, to seek and conquer optimal challenges" (p. 43). It is related in the literature to personal investment (Maehr, 1984), ownership of learning (Au & Asam, 1996), engaged learning (Guthrie & Wigfield, 1997), and the continuing impulse to learn (Thomas & Oldfather, 1997). A motivated student is an active learner who rises to challenges, solves problems, seeks to understand, takes pleasure in academic activities, and engages in learning with enthusiasm, effort, and intensity (Stipek, 1996).

As defined by Bandura (1986), self-efficacy is "people's judgments of their capabilities to organize and execute courses of action required to attain designated types of performances" (p. 391). Self-efficacy influences people's choices of activities; moreover, their persistence, effort expenditure, and task accomplishments are influenced by their self-efficacy. It also influences the learning of new skills and knowledge, as well as the activation and application of previously learned skills or knowledge. Self-efficacy for learning involves assessing what will be required in the learning context and how well one can use one's knowledge and skills to produce new learning (Schunk, 1984). When self-efficacy is low, the gap between prior knowledge and new knowledge is perceived to be relatively large. Thus, students with low self-efficacy come to view new learning as difficult, and hence learning is hindered. Therefore, promoting students' self-efficacy is central to increasing students' learning. Research has shown that intrinsic motivation to learn and self-efficacy are aspects of motivation that can be supported by instructional processes (Guthrie, Cox, et al., 1998).

Conceptual Knowledge in Engaged Reading

A cursory glance at the most recent research journals indicates the importance of conceptual knowledge growth as a primary goal of education (see Wigfield & Guthrie, 1997; Alexander, 1997). Researchers and laypersons alike agree that our teaching must involve conceptual understanding and higher-level thinking (McCombs, 1997). Conceptual knowledge goals are particularly essential for elementary school students in light of the current research that connects early reading ability and reading amount with growth in conceptual knowledge (Cunningham & Stanovich, 1997). Cunningham and Stanovich (1997) informed educators that "an early start in reading is important in predicting a *lifetime* of literacy experience" (p. 941). In their work, they found that early reading ability predicted general domain knowledge with a correlation of .59 in grade 11 even when accounting for background. Indeed, reading is one of the primary modes of gaining knowledge.

Engaged readers gain knowledge and experience as they read by continually activating and extending their understanding. As they read informational texts, engaged readers look for the big ideas that lie at the heart of the domain (Alexander, Jetton, & Kulikowich, 1996). In addition to gaining knowledge, engaged readers apply knowledge to answer a new question or to solve a problem. In narrative texts, these problems relate to comprehending plot, character, and theme (Graesser et al., 1991).

Defining Conceptual Knowledge

For decades, researchers have been discussing how people organize knowledge in their minds. This research highlights the notion that knowledge acquisition is seamlessly integrative, ever evolving, and dynamic (Alexander, 1997). "Concepts as mental structures are the building blocks of a person's cognitive structure. . . . [T]hey are the fundamental agents of all thinking processes" (Klausmeier, 1992, p. 268). Klausmeier explained that concept learning involves the interplay of knowledge at both the micro and the macro level. For example, at the micro level, students would be able to identify examples and nonexamples. At the macro level, students would create understandings involving principles, taxonomic relationships, and hierarchical processes. Hence, rather than viewing knowledge from a linear and static stance, we now realize that the highest levels of knowledge include basic facts, relational understandings, principles, and finally multiple viewpoints about the domain. Typically, at this last level of conceptual understanding, students are able to accurately use principled knowledge to reason in order to solve novel problems in the domain (Chi et al., 1994; Guthrie et al., 1996).

Most teachers want their students to gain knowledge and understanding of content. But teaching knowledge is not simple. Students are not empty vessels to be filled by "telling." Teachers help students to construct knowledge by assisting them in being active and staying active as learners. Two of the many methods of activating students' knowledge building are (1) to ask students to *explain* new information they encounter, and (2) to ask students to *map* the concepts of the information they are learning.

Self-Explanation

An instructional method that encourages students to actively manipulate and process information during reading is self-explanation (Chi, Bassok, Lewis, Reimann, & Glaser, 1989). Self-explanation supports meaningful learning by requiring students to become more reflective about their incoming knowledge (Menke & Pressley, 1994). Self-explaining can be facilitated through writing or through conversation with peers (Brown & Campione, 1998). Irrespective of the method, self-explaining enables students to forge new knowledge connections, which promotes deep understanding of a concept.

In their work on self-explanations, Chi and her colleagues (1994) found that students who were asked to explain the text improved in comprehension. They answered more complex questions, induced more correct inferences about the reading, made more elaborate mental models, and reached conceptually higher levels of knowledge than did other students. Moreover, although the good comprehenders generated many incorrect inferences and explanations, these students self-repaired along the way because the explaining process was ongoing. Unlike the poor comprehenders, the good comprehenders did not refer to the text to answer high-level questions because they knew the answers were not there. King, Staffieri, and Adelgais (1998) found similar benefits in an intervention that combined ongoing inquiry and self-explanation. These findings suggest that teachers should teach students to ask and answer "why" questions as they read.

Concept Mapping

Constructing concept maps facilitates meaningful learning by requiring students to integrate information from the text into existing knowledge in their minds (Lonka, Lindblom-Ylanne, & Maury, 1994). Concept maps are visual representations of a student's knowledge. They organize concepts and represent the relationships among concepts (Novak, 1995). Although concept maps can be used to represent a variety of domains for all age levels, much of the research has focused on high school or college students in science-related areas (Horton et al., 1993). However, studies with elementary school populations demonstrate that younger children are successful in constructing concept maps and displaying learning outcomes similar to those of older populations (Stice & Alvarez, 1987).

Using concept maps in classroom instruction results in improved knowledge retention (Heinze-Fry & Novak, 1990) and high performance on achievement tests (Okebukola, 1990). Concept mapping also affects the structure and organization of students' knowledge by increasing students' awareness of the relations among concepts (Novak, 1995). Student misconceptions are easily diagnosed through concept maps as well. Thus, concept maps play a significant role in students' construction of meaningful knowledge.

Concept mapping has also been linked to positive affective outcomes. Students who used concept maps tended to have more positive attitudes toward meaningful learning (Horton et al., 1993) and decreased levels of anxiety (Jegede, Alaiymelo, & Okebukola, 1990) compared to students who did not use concept maps in their classrooms.

The strategies of self-explanation and concept mapping help students gain knowledge from text. Because the strategies are intricately tied to the content, they are best taught in an extended topic of study. Strategy instruction requires depth and breadth. Depth of learning within a topic enables students to gain mastery. Breadth of application across topics enables students to transfer strategies to new domains. Strategies are best taught when they are coordinated with learning goals for content. Since both strategy learning and conceptual knowledge acquisition are difficult, motivational support is needed on a sustained basis. When reading strategies, aspects of motivation, and knowledge are active simultaneously, students are engaged. When reading engagement is sustained over an extended unit, instruction has probably been coherent.

Social Interaction

Reading is a social act. Beginning with the reader–author relationship, reading is a transaction between persons. When children are highly social, sharing their reading and writing frequently, they are likely to be active, interested readers (Guthrie, Schafer, Wang, & Afflerbach, 1995). The interchange among students can further increase interpretation competence (Almasi, 1995) and conceptual understanding of science or social studies topics (Brown & Campione, 1998). This process of engagement is not discussed further here, as it is emphasized elsewhere in this volume by Gambrell, Mazzoni, and Almasi (Chapter 6) and Wigfield (Chapter 7).

ASPECTS OF COHERENT INSTRUCTION

Coherent instruction makes engagement possible. Several aspects of the classroom impact engagement processes and learning outcomes (see Guthrie & Alao, 1997; Guthrie, Cox, et al., 1998). These are depicted in the outside ellipses of Figure 10.1. When these instructional processes work together, we say instruction is coherent.

Learning and Knowledge Goals

The goals of learning and knowledge refer to core learning goals that are codeveloped by the teacher and the students in conjunction with external requirements in the school. Roeser, Midgley, and Urdan (1996) showed that teachers' learning-goal orientation in the classroom contributed to their students' self-efficacy. When students believed that teachers thought that understanding the work was more important than just getting right answers, students were likely to believe in their capacity to do the hardest work. Students who were learning-goal oriented (e.g., dedicated to understanding content, using strategies effectively, and linking their new knowledge to previous experiences) were likely to be more highly engaged than other students. In contrast, when students' goals are dominated by the performance orientation of seeking to outperform others or demonstrate their competence, they will be less engaged in learning (Meece, Blumenfeld, & Hoyle, 1988). Teachers can create learning goals in the classroom by using long-term conceptual themes to organize instruction. The theme of colonial life, for example, is a learning goal. Reading comprehension skills can be set up as learning goals, too. If comprehension is valued for its own sake, it becomes a learning goal. However, if reading comprehension is valued because it improves points, competitive advantages, or grades, then reading will not be a learning goal.

Real-World Interactions

Real-world interactions are enjoyable, immediately interesting activities that can provide motivation for reading and learning from text (Brophy, 1998). If students are learning from text as they role-play in a historical drama, they are demonstrating that this merger of reading and real-world interaction can occur. Many teachers believe that reading motivation can be increased when texts and books are connected to stimulating activities (Nolen & Nichols, 1994), related to learning events (Guthrie, Alao, & Rinehart, 1997), or connected to personally significant projects (McCombs & Whistler, 1997). Further, teachers often report using variety, diversity, and high-interest tasks to motivate learning activities (Pressley, Rankin, & Yokoi, 1996).

Real-world experiences are powerful because they are intrinsically motivating. They are designed to, and usually do, evoke keen attention and a sense of wonder. For example, when elementary students see a Native American in original dress in a social studies unit or observe a monarch butterfly hatch in a life science activity, they are excited and brimming with questions. Ross (1988) confirmed these effects in an extensive literature review. He found that "hands-on" science activities aroused attention, questions, and active learning. Guthrie, Van Meter, et al. (1998) studied the benefits of Concept-Oriented Reading Instruction (CORI) which embedded reading instruction within an intrinsically motivating, "hands-on" science curriculum. It increased reading comprehension, strategy use, and problem solving in grade 3 and 5 students. Romance and Vitale (1992) reported similar results of an integrated curriculum that combined reading and hands-on activities in science. Students in the integrated curriculum scored higher on measures of reading achievement and science knowledge than students in a traditional form of instruction.

To explain the benefits of real-world interactions, Anderson (1998) reasoned that hands-on science activities would motivate students to read deeply and thus increase their conceptual learning from text. She found that students who read texts in association with hands-on activities (i.e., dealing with live crabs and turtles in the classroom) had better comprehension and conceptual knowledge gain than students who read the same texts without the intrinsically motivating context. Further, a year-long intervention study showed that reading engagement initiated with a life science unit transferred flexibly to reading in earth science (Guthrie, Anderson, Alao, & Rinehart, 1999).

Autonomy Support

It has been argued that in many schools the educative process has divorced children from an authentic need to learn and a vital context in which to do so (Ryan & Powelson, 1991). However, giving students opportunities to "self-rule" or "self-determine" can make learning more personally meaningful and intrinsically motivating (Deci & Ryan, 1985; Ryan & Powelson, 1991). Student choice in the classroom can manifest itself variously as the selection of topics, resources, tasks, media, learning goals, and more (Guthrie & McCann, 1997). Student choice can help students develop autonomy as well as increase their sense of ownership and responsibility for the learning process (Morrow, 1992). High achievers are most often accorded a wide array of opportunities for choice and self-direction within classrooms, whereas lower achievers are often micromanaged by their teachers. Research supports the use of choice for *all* students as a way to increase their motivation to learn (Brophy, 1998).

Autonomy support is the teacher's guidance in making choices among meaningful alternatives relevant to the knowledge and learning goals. Providing choices is a prominent practice among reading teachers (Baumann, Hoffman, Moon, & Duffy-Hester, 1998). Researchers studying elementary school teachers' beliefs about motivation in general (Nolen & Nichols, 1994) and reading motivation specifically (Sweet, Guthrie, & Ng, 1998) have found that teachers believe that children need choice to develop independence. Turner (1995) found that teachers who develop reputations as highly motivating often provide a myriad of choices during a lesson. Teachers often promote choice by giving students input into which books will be read, whether students will participate in reading aloud or silently, and what sequence of activities will be undertaken (Pressley et al., 1996). Choice is motivating because it affords students control over their activities. Children seek to be in command of their environment, rather than being manipulated by powerful others. This need for self-direction can be met in reading instruction through well-designed choices. Specific to reading, Grolnick and Ryan (1987) showed that an autonomy-supportive context increased motivation and comprehension in reading. Students who read social studies texts to answer their own personally formulated questions showed better comprehension than groups of students who were instructed to memorize the content or to read without direction. Legitimating the students' questions as purposes for reading increased student control and autonomy in the text reading situation.

Teacher style and orientation greatly affect the level to which student autonomy and self-direction is supported in classrooms. Deci, Schwartz, Scheinman, and Ryan (1981) studied 610 elementary classroom teachers in an attempt to analyze the teachers' attitudes regarding student autonomy versus control and the effects these attitudes had on their students. Teachers who possessed an orientation toward autonomy of their students (vs. a controlling orientation) were found to produce students with "more curiosity for learning, more desire for challenge, and more independent mastery attempts. In addition, these children experienced greater perceived competence in school and reported greater general self-worth" (Ryan & Powelson, 1991, p. 55). Grolnick and Ryan (1987) found that students who were pressured with the external reward/punishment of grades had less text comprehension and less recall a week later than students who were told that they would not be graded. Of course, grades are necessary, but overemphasizing grades often decreases motivation. Giving students opportunities to be agents in their own learning appears to increase their motivation to learn.

Choice, whether in the form of texts, tasks, goals, learning centers, or even simply the order of work completed, gives students a sense of ownership and inner control of the educative process. Providing support for autonomy and self-direction positively influences intrinsic motivation to learn. However, motivation in isolation does not increase reading comprehension and achievement. Motivation must be harnessed to interesting texts.

Interesting Texts for Instruction

Many teachers believe that students are motivated by interesting texts. The logic is that students will devote effort, attention, and persistence to reading about topics that they find enjoyable or intriguing. Here the phrase "interesting texts" refers to single-authored works in which the text matches the topic interest and cognitive competency of the reader. If a book is personally significant and easy to comprehend, it is likely to be rated as interesting (Schraw, Brüning, & Svoboda, 1995). One benefit is that students spend more time reading personally interesting texts than uninteresting ones (McLoyd, 1979). Another benefit is that students learn relatively more content from interesting texts even after accounting for their relatively high prior knowledge for the content of these texts (Schiefele, 1996). Providing an abundance of high-interest texts in the classroom enables teachers to adapt their reading instruction to the preexisting motivations of students. Such adaptation may explain the relatively high association between the size of a classroom library and student reading achievement, which has been documented across multiple nations (see Chambliss & McKillop, Chapter 5, this volume; Elley, 1992).

An interesting text has personal significance to the student, which increases learning (Brophy, 1998). Studies have shown that students who attach personal meaning to the material being read process the information at deeper levels (Alexander, Kulikowich, & Jetton, 1994). For example, learning of science was shown to increase when instruction was adapted to students' personal interests (Meece, 1991). Even in cases where the material was challenging, if the text and task were interesting to the students, the students sustained attention and involvement longer (Renninger, 1992). Heightened interest in texts has been related to a number of outcomes such as achievement (Deci, 1992), higher-level thinking (Corno & Kanfer, 1993), deep processing of content (Alexander et al., 1994), and reading comprehension (Schiefele, 1991). "Teachers can cultivate personal significance in text by verbalizing why students should value it, connecting it with previously known ideas, pointing out everyday applications, and mentioning the new and challenging aspects" (Brophy, 1998, p. 192).

Strategy Instruction

Strategy instruction consists of teachers' direct instruction, scaffolding, and guided practice in comprehending text. If students are able to complete the classroom reading tasks and are aware of their abilities and limitations, they will be more motivated than if they are less capable or less aware (Harter, 1981). Consequently, strategy instruction in reading is likely to be empowering and motivating. Strategies for reading and writing are difficult to learn and use. Many investigators report that strategies require long-term teaching and, once learned, strategies may not be frequently used (Gaskins & Elliot, 1991). Consequently, students learning must be intentional (Bereiter & Scardamalia, 1989). Students want to understand and learn the content for which the strategies will be useful. In reading, intrinsic motivation is vital to strategy learning. Guthrie, Van Meter, et al. (1996) found that all students who increased in intrinsic motivation during a year increased in reading strategy use. However, only 50% of the students who were stable or declined in intrinsic motivation increased in reading strategy use. Possession of strategies and the motivation for using them are likely to be mutually enhancing.

Teachers can provide direct instruction in using prior knowledge to improve comprehension. In a study comparing the effects of prior knowledge and main idea/supporting detail instruction on reading comprehension, Spires (1990) used a direct instruction model with two experimental groups. Direct instruction consisted of providing a rationale for why the strategy was useful, how the strategy benefited reading comprehension, teacher modeling of relating known information to text-based ideas, and guided practice with teacher and peer feedback during small-group practice. This occurred over eight 45-minute instructional sessions. In this study, ninth graders in the prior knowledge group outperformed the main idea/supporting detail group on a measure that assessed responses to follow-up application questions.

Another instructional process that facilitates children's comprehension is the use of prereading purpose questions. In a study by Rowe and Rayford (1987), students in grades 1, 6, and 10 read purpose questions, guessed about passage content, and made predictions about the passage. The children were also informed that the function of prereading purpose questions was to help the reader begin thinking about the passage before reading. Regardless of grade level, the children who used purpose questions activated their prior knowledge effectively.

The instructional processes that enhance self-questioning include (1) instructing students to pose "think-type" questions, (2) direct explicit instruction, (3) verbal explanation about why self-questioning is important, and (4) use of question prompt cards. Some researchers integrate comprehension monitoring strategies within a package of comprehension strategies and employ many of the instructional processes we have described. For example, Payne and Manning (1992) examined teacher modeling of several comprehension strategies, along with guided practice using the different strategies while reading basal texts, and independent practice using the strategies over the school year. This instruction resulted in gains in fourth graders' comprehension strategy use and reading comprehension scores, as well as superior reading attitude over students who participated in a regular basal reading program. Direct instruction in self-questioning is clearly an effective approach for teachers to use.

Collaboration Support

Collaboration refers to the interaction among students in a learning community. Many teachers use collaboration to activate and maintain intrinsic motivation. Teachers believe that social collaboration in the classroom will increase interest in the content to be learned (Hootstein, 1995; Zoharik, 1996) and maintain active learning over an extended period of time (Nolen & Nichols, 1994). Teachers also believe that collaboration increases motivation to read independently in the future (Morrow, 1996). When students have a caring teacher and a sense of belonging in the classroom (Wentzel, 1997), they are likely to be motivated for reading. Oldfather and Dahl (1994) suggested that students who felt that they were recognized, accepted, and affirmed as individuals in the classroom social structure were motivated to read, write, and express themselves forthrightly.

Small-group discussion can facilitate prior knowledge activation and result in improved reading comprehension. Hansen and Pearson (1983) employed a discussion approach with fourth graders in small groups of 10. The instructional processes for the experimental condition included a discussion of the importance of relating one's life to text, prereading questions that required the group to recall prior knowledge, requests for prediction about the upcoming text selection, independent reading, and postreading discussion of responses to inference questions. Poor readers demonstrated significant gains in their ability to answer inference questions; good readers did not. Teachers should support collaboration for all students—high achievers and low achievers alike.

Rewards and Praise

Abundant evidence supports the proposition that giving rewards and positive incentives for book-reading increases the time and effort in book reading activities. Further, reading incentive programs are quite common in elementary schools (Gambrell & Marinak, 1997). Giving rewards such as praise, points in a contest, gold stars, or self-selected books is relatively simple. Should not this solve the problem of increasing engaged reading? Unfortunately not, because rewards and incentives have a paradoxical effect. Rewards can increase short-term attention on specific activities, but students who experience an environment in which extrinsic rewards are dominant will become increasingly extrinsically motivated and focused on performance goals (Anderman, Maehr, & Midglan, 1999; Flink, Boggianno, Main, Barrett, & Katz, 1992). Such students become more committed to high grades, correct answers, and task completion (Anderman & Young, 1994), and less dedicated to comprehending content, gaining valuable reading skills, or enjoying reading and learning content (Maehr & Midgley, 1996).

A strong extrinsic orientation has several effects on students. Students with performance goals (who work for rewards) rely on memorizing, guessing, and other surface-learning strategies for reading. They attempt to avoid challenging tasks and give up easily when frustrated. These students are not cognitively engaged in reading and frequently adopt work-avoidant goals, attempting to meet their performance goals with minimal effort (Meece & Holt, 1993). Ultimately, extrinsic incentives can undermine the engagement of a literate, learning community.

Rewards and praise do have a place. Effective teachers can be seen to provide informative compliments that make learners feel a sense of accomplishment and pride in their work. Brophy (1981) reviewed the literature on the effects of praise. Effective praise is given contingently on effort and achievement, specifies the particulars of the accomplishment, shows spontaneity, orients students toward better appreciation of their work, attributes success to effort, and fosters appreciation of task-relevant strategies. Wlodkowski (1985) suggested that praise should be "3S–3P," which stands for praise that is sincere, specific, sufficient, and properly given for praiseworthy success in the manner preferred by the learner. However, teachers' attempts at effective praise are not always successful. If students interpret praise to be manipulative, their motivation may decline because they feel they are being treated as objects (Flink et al., 1992). Rewards and praise are valuable if they are not dominant in the classroom. If rewards are dominant, students become extrinsically motivated, which reduces their achievement. Unfortunately, beginning teachers are especially inclined to emphasize praise and punishment as their primary motivational strategies. Newby (1991) found that first-year teachers used praise and punishment more than 75% of the time as their motivational strategies. With experience, teachers gain command of an optimal contribution of autonomy-support, real-world interaction, and other processes, along with rewards and praise (see Brophy, 1998).

Evaluation for Engagement

Evaluation can emphasize either an absolute standard or student progress. Using an absolute standard, teachers grade everyone on the same scale of how proficient they are. This sets up a competition where there are few winners and many losers. Because being a loser is demoralizing, this grading approach reduces motivation for all but a few high achievers. Evaluating students on their progress, teachers can make everyone a winner. All can progress and thus succeed. Of course, evaluation for progress requires goals for improvement. Goals provide a clear standard against which students can gauge their progress. Feedback from the teacher conveys the progress that students have made and useful strategies to attain the goal. Feedback may contain some persuasive information, such as telling students that the goal is attainable and is valuable (Locke & Latham, 1990). Such information helps students become more committed to the goal. Several studies indicate that combining goal setting and progress feedback creates the most effective results in promoting students' performance, including strategy transfer and self-efficacy (Schunk & Rice, 1991).

Children's goals can take two different forms that affect their achievement patterns (Elliott & Dweck, 1988). Children with *learning goals* seek to develop skills and increase their ability or mastery; in contrast, children with *performance goals* seek to get positive or favorable judgments and avoid negative judgments about their ability. Learning-oriented students judge their competence in terms of efforts and whether they have achieved mastery, whereas performance-oriented students judge competence by comparing their performance with others and by people's opinions of their performance. Learning goals but not performance goals tend to foster achievement.

Students' motivation can be promoted when they participate in the process of goal setting. But before letting students set goals by themselves, some guidance and feedback are needed. This ensures that students select or establish their goals within a range that the teacher provides for them. For example, Schunk (1985) helped students set upper and lower page limits for their work each day. Gaa (1973) allowed students to check items, list the goals they wanted to accomplish, and gave them progress feedback at a weekly conference. In both cases, students became more realistic about their abilities and goal setting.

Teachers' methods of evaluation affect students' perceptions of their abilities (Blumenfeld, Pintrich, Meece, & Wessels, 1982). Although social comparison is harmful to children's growth of self-efficacy, traditional forms of schooling facilitate social comparison via grades and competition. In order to reduce social comparison during evaluation, researchers provided the following suggestions for teachers (Rosenholtz & Simpson, 1984): (1) give a variety of tasks and let students express their knowledge in different ways; (2) minimize student comparisons; (3) evaluate students in terms of their effort and improvement as well as their performance; and (4) provide written comments on students' work.

Teacher Involvement

Teacher involvement represents teachers' knowledge of individual learners, caring about their students' progress, and pedagogical understanding of how to foster students' active participation. Skinner, Wellborn, and Connell (1990) showed that teacher involvement increases student engagement. The involved teacher knows about the students' personal interests, cares about each student's learning, and holds realistic but positive goals for their effort and learning. When students perceived teachers to be involved (i.e., interested in their progress) and autonomy supportive (i.e., providing students some control of learning), the students tended to be engaged in the classroom (e.g., participating in class discussions, actively learning, and appearing happy) (Skinner & Belmont; 1993). Highly engaged students were relatively high achievers, as indicated by school grades and achievement test scores across all school subjects, including reading, mathematics, and science.

COHERENCE OF INSTRUCTIONAL PROCESSES

Coherence refers to important interconnections among all the instructional elements. For example, when real-world interactions are closely aligned with interesting texts, coherence is increased. When strategy instruction is linked to central knowledge goals, coherence is forged. When teacher involvement is evident in evaluation, coherence among the instructional processes is present (see Guthrie & Cox, 1998, for teaching guidelines). In addition to fusing the pedagogical approaches, coherent instruction links reading, writing, and rich knowledge domains. In coherent instruction, student engagement is increased (Guthrie, Van Meter, et al., 1998), conceptual learning from text is facilitated (Anderson, 1998), reading achievement is fostered (Romance & Vitale, 1992), and reading within content areas can be sustained (Gaskins et al., 1994; Santa, 1997).

The opposite of coherence is compartmentalization. If there are different times, texts, and activities for reading, spelling, writing, science, social studies, fine arts, mathematics, health, and literature, then instruction is extremely compartmentalized. One clear disadvantage of compartmentalization is that students cannot connect: they cannot easily use their reading strategies to do social studies, and so on. Such fragmentation is disengaging. Interest wanes, and effort is not sustained. With compartmentalization, students' interest in stories, authors, or information gets lost. Students' learning goals become fragmented and diminish. Consequently, it is vital to create coherence.

Instructional processes can be linked in multiple ways. Strategy instruction can be linked to authentic books, for example. Summarization can be taught with a text students find interesting in their social studies unit. The link does not imply that direct, separate teaching should not occur. For instance, strategy instruction in summarizing could occur daily for 20 minutes in a focused series of lessons. If the lessons are grounded in texts of interest for which students possess some background knowledge, coherence increases. Further, if the lessons include real-world interactions that aid students' text comprehension, then the instructional coherence increases again. In Figure 10.1, each instructional process can be linked with every other instructional process. These links constitute the coherence of instruction. A high linkage across processes is like a finely woven fabric in the classroom, maintaining the engagement of all learners.

A Classroom Example of Coherence

One type of instruction that constructs a thematic, motivating context for reading strategy learning is Concept-Oriented Reading Instruction (CORI) (Guthrie, Van Meter, et al., 1998). Examples from CORI will be used to illustrate the connections among several aspects of instruction. CORI provides a conceptual theme—in this case the theme of adaptation, with a hands-on science unit to motivate reading strategy instruction. In the following, grade 5 students conducted a cricket hunt in the early fall as a basis for learning principles of feeding, shelter, defense, and reproduction in the life cycle of insects. Then, they progressed to mammals and beyond. Examples will show how reading strategy learning is connected to motivation.

In CORI, strategy instruction is situated in intrinsically motivating contexts within a conceptual domain. In our example, a fifth-grade classroom study of animals, habitats, and adaptation, the teacher piqued children's interest by first asking them to work together to find crickets in the school's backyard. The children hunted for the crickets and expressed delight upon finding them. In the hunt, one child yelled to his team members, "I found one!"—calling the other children to see his successful find. Another child shared his personal concern for the cricket's life as well as his prior knowledge when he told another student, "Don't put the cricket with the spider!" As children closely observed and studied the crickets in the classroom, their curiosity was aroused and they gained observational information. The students' cricket search in the school's backyard habitat, their in-class observations of them, as well as their prior knowledge provided a source of personalized information that they could use to generate meaningful questions about crickets and their habitats. By initiating the study of animals and their habitats in a real-world, hands-on, relevant way, the teacher provided an intrinsically motivating activity. This activity served to lay the foundation for stimulating children to learn how to generate questions and search for information about crickets.

The teacher supported the children's intrinsic motivation by asking them to think about what they were *curious* about or what more they would like to *know* about crickets. She encouraged them to form their own questions as a basis for extended learning. The teacher modeled how to write one's curiosities or questions about crickets on a sentence strip that was then posted on a chart displaying the question, "What do we want to know about crickets?" This placed motivation in the context of conceptual knowledge development. The teacher made the link to personal interest explicit. She gave students the opportunity to express their own specific interests and set an agenda for their own line of inquiry. As the teacher modeled how to write a question, she drew an example from the class saying, "Sarah might write something like this," and then she verified it with Sarah. In the way that she directed the class's attention to Sarah's example, she validated Sarah's developing expertise and affirmed to the class that students are valuable sources of knowledge. This step also supported the development of autonomy and self-efficacy.

Before children generated their questions, the teacher modeled the strategy of self-questioning. This modeling was an important instructional process for teaching self-questioning. In addition, the teacher facilitated children's self-efficacy for generating questions *while* modeling by picking up one particular child's question. The teacher used this question as a model and wrote it word for word on a sentence strip in front of the class. As children came to the front of the classroom to tape their questions to the chart paper labeled "Chart of Curiosities/Interest," the teacher also showed a natural curiosity and an interest in the children's questions. For example, as she posted one child's question, she said to the class with a curious look, "Yes, I wonder where the crickets do go in the wintertime? Where *do* the cricket sounds go?" The teacher allowed discussion among the children as they posted their questions. Encouraging children to discuss their questions, as well as posting individual questions for the whole class to read, served to situate strategy instruction within a conceptual theme and intrinsically motivating activities.

All reading strategies were taught in this context, revolving around a relevant, authentic, self-directed goal—to acquire conceptual knowledge of adaptation and life cycles. Students possessed intrinsic motivation to learn summarizing and comprehension-monitoring strategies because they desired to gain knowledge about self-generated questions. To provide a meaningful, effective context for strategy instruction, summarizing strategies were taught using the actual texts that students eventually utilized to find answers to their questions. In other words, the teacher's strategy instruction did not occur in isolation but with *relevant* curricular materials and tasks. Children were motivated to learn and to use strategies because they were grounded in self-directed conceptual goals.

It is clear that this inaugural activity to a unit on habitats addressed the need to support the students' development of intrinsic motivation. As they were catching crickets, the students had an authentic opportunity to make the act of learning personal and meaningful. Their engagement was intellectual as well as physical and affective. Three activities that opened the unit of study—the collection of crickets, the subsequent observations, and the sketches to generate interest, deep involvement, and curiosity—shared the characteristics of being challenging yet doable, personally significant, and highly engrossing on an intellectual as well as physical level. They very much supported a developing sense of student ownership of learning. The students found their own crickets, observed them in the new habitats they created, and did their own sketches of them.

The teacher used concept maps to structure students' knowledge gained from reading about the concept of adaptation. The concept map was organized hierarchically: "adaptation" was written in the center of the board with terms such as "climate" and "shelter" radiating from it. The map began with an abstract concept, but grew across time with more concrete concepts, which were more tangible and easy to understand. The map was a collection of student answers gained from using their strategies for reading. After learning how to search for information, comprehend main ideas, and integrate across multiple texts to answer their own questions, students possessed ownership of the knowledge. Their engagement in the form of unified motivation, strategies, and knowledge gain was evident to them.

Among the many ways to implement the instructional processes of Figure 10.1 coherently, CORI is one. There are other programs, some aimed more toward primary learners, that also will foster and ensure long-term engaged reading. It is our belief that these principles of coherence will apply to many types of classrooms.

Teacher Guide for Planning Coherent Instruction

We have discussed the principles for connecting strategies, aspects of motivation, and knowledge with examples from one classroom. We now recommend a framework for designing instruction. The planning guide shown in Figure 10.2 is one way to build coherence. It has succeeded for teachers in grades 3 and 5 who integrated their science and reading/language arts curricula successfully (Guthrie et al., 1996; Guthrie, Van Meter, et al., 1998).

The first step in implementing the guide is to identify a conceptual theme for an extended unit of instruction. The time for the unit should be not less than 3 weeks and may extend to 16 weeks or longer. Conceptual themes may be drawn from the science and/or social studies curriculum, and should invite interdisciplinary connections. For example, adaptation, the solar system, weather, North American colonial life, Native Americans, endangered species, or the conflict between the states are all possible themes. The grade level for implementation, as well as the teachers and other personnel (e.g., a media specialist) involved, should be identified. The theme should allow real-world interactions, extended reading and writing, and should be familiar and interesting to the teachers. Needless to say, the topic should address district-level expectations. An in-depth unit is needed. This may require reducing the time given to other topics in the curriculum. However, the reading and writing strategies learned in the in-depth curriculum will transfer to other areas. The short-term loss of "content coverage" will be compensated by the long-term benefit in content learning via use of effective learning strategies.

Conceptual Theme:_____ Grade:_____

	Goals	Student Activities	Teacher Strategies	Resources
Observe & Personalize				
Search & Retrieve				
Comprehend & Integrate				
Communicate to Others				

FIGURE 10.2. CORI unit planning guide.

In the planning guide there are four phases to instruction, consisting of (1) observe and personalize, (2) search and retrieve, (3) comprehend and integrate, and (4) communicate to others. In the planning guide, column headings show the parts of each phase. Goals should be written for each of the four phases. Goals should reflect the district, school, and teacher's priorities. In the observe-and-personalize phase, goals might state what types of science hands-on experiences will occur or with what historical artifacts students will interact. In the search and retrieve phase, the texts and other resources help to form learning. The trade books, narratives, and multimedia programs available should be identified. The methods for student recording, note taking, collecting, or organizing should be stipulated. Goals from the district curriculum are related to this phase. In the comprehend-and-integrate phase, goals from the reading and writing curriculum should be stated. What types of comprehending strategies will be taught explicitly, with what types of texts?

The planning column of "student activities" is an opportunity to state what students will be doing. How will students interact with the texts in the comprehend-and-integrate phase? Will they read aloud, read to answer questions, take notes, summarize, or locate contrasts or conflicts in different accounts? For the communicating-to-others phase , the "student activities" section may contain statements of the writing process such as planning, outlining, drafting, revising, or conferencing. It may contain script writing for voice-over narrative on video taken by students.

The teacher strategies column is a section to contain statements of what teachers will do to help students in their activities. For example, in the comprehend-and-integrate phase, the teacher strategies needed to help students comprehend text may include teacher modeling and peer modeling. These strategies can be listed. The last planning phase of "resources" lists the materials, books, manipulables, or classroom tools such as journals that will be needed to accomplish the goals.

This planning guide may be expanded. Each phase of instruction (e.g., the comprehend-and-integrate phase) may be written on one page or more. This allows for a fuller statement of what specific techniques or lessons will look like. Some teachers begin by filling out the overall guide. Next, they write lessons for each day. Other teachers do not want that much detail, and they proceed from the one-page overview guide (as in Figure 10.2), followed up by four single-page statements for each of the four phases. This planning guide is a tool to fashion coherence in teaching (see Guthrie & Cox, 1998, for steps for teachers).

CONCLUSION

Coherence in instruction is extremely valuable for engaged reading. Coherence refers to the connections among the separate parts of teaching, such as reading strategy instruction, knowledge goals, real-world interactions, autonomy support, and rewards for learning. When the separate parts are integrated and coherent, students become engaged. Engagement includes long-term motivation, uses of multiple strategies, and conceptual learning through reading and writing. To support all these aspects of engagement, coherent instruction coordinates eight dimensions of the teaching environment. When they are synchronized, these eight instructional processes sustain students' reading engagement. Coherent instruction enables students to become independent readers, and it fosters reading achievement. With these growing capacities of independence and competence, students gain world knowledge, self-knowledge, and the disposition to expand both through reading widely and frequently.

RECOMMENDED READINGS

Guthrie, J. T., & Cox, K. E. (1998). Portrait of an engaging classroom: Principles of Concept-Oriented Reading Instruction for diverse students. In K. Harris (Ed.), *Teaching every child every day: Learning in diverse schools and classrooms* (pp. 70–130). Cambridge, MA: Brookline Books.

As a practical guide for teachers, this chapter presents all the steps for creating engaging instruction. Examples from classroom practices are provided.

Guthrie, J. T., Van Meter, P., Hancock, G. R., Alao, S., Anderson, E., & McCann, A. (1998). Does Concept-Oriented Reading Instruction increase strategy use and conceptual learning from text? *Journal of Educational Psychology, 90,* 261–278.

This study describes research on the effects of CORI. Students' reading, comprehension, strategy use, and problem solving increased more in CORI classrooms than in classrooms using traditional instruction.

Jones, B. F., Rasmussen, C. M., & Moffitt, M. C. (1997). *Real-life problem solving: A collaborative approach to interdisciplinary learning.* Washington, DC: American Psychological Association.

This book is a resource for integrating reading with content. Teachers' classroom ideas with directions for application are provided.

Miller, S. D., & Meece, J. L. (1997). Enhancing elementary students' motivation to read and write: A classroom intervention study. *Journal of Educational Research, 90,* 286–301.

A highly challenging language arts program is compared to a less challenging, more skill-based program. Motivation for reading improved in the well-implemented, high-challenge classroom.

REFERENCES

Alexander, P. A. (1997). Mapping the multidimensional nature of domain learning: The interplay of cognitive, motivational, and strategic forces. In P. R. Pintrich & M. L. Maehr (Eds.), *Advances in motivation and achievement* (Vol. 10, pp. 213–250). Greenwich, CT: JAI Press.

Alexander, P. A., Jetton, T. L., & Kulikowich, J. M. (1996). Interrelationship of knowledge, interest, and recall: Assessing a model of domain learning. *Journal of Educational Psychology, 87,* 559–575.

Alexander, P. A., Kulikowich, J. M., & Jetton, T. L. (1994). The role of subject-matter knowledge and interest in the processing of linear and nonlinear texts. *Review of Educational Research, 64,* 201–252.

Almasi, J. F. (1995). The nature of fourth graders' sociocognitive conflicts in peer-led and teacher-led discussions of literature. *Reading Research Quarterly, 30,* 314–351.

Anderman, E. M., Maehr, M. L., & Midgley, C. (1999). *Declining motivation after the transition to middle school: Schools can make a difference.* Manuscript in preparation.

Anderman, E. M., & Young, A. J. (1994). Motivation and strategy use in science: Individual differences and classroom effects. *Journal of Research in Science Teaching, 31,* 811–831.

Anderson, E. (1998). *Motivational and cognitive influences on conceptual knowledge acquisition: The combination of science observation and interesting texts.* Unpublished doctoral dissertation, University of Maryland, College Park.

Armbruster, B. B., Anderson, T. H., & Ostertag, J. (1987). Does text structure/summarization facilitate learning from expository text? *Reading Research Quarterly, 22,* 331–345.

Au, K. H., & Asam, C. L. (1996). Improving the literacy achievement of low-income students of diverse backgrounds. In M. F. Graves, P. van den Broek, & B. M. Taylor (Eds.), *The first R: Every child's right to read* (pp. 199–223). New York: Teachers College Press.

Baker, L. (1985). How do we know when we don't understand? Standards for evaluating comprehension. In D. L. Forrest, G. E. MacKinnon, & T. G. Waller (Eds.), *Metacognition, cognition, and human performance* (pp. 155–205). New York: Academic Press.

Bandura, A. (1986). *Social foundations of thought and action: A social cognitive theory*. Englewood Cliffs, NJ: Prentice Hall.

Baumann, J., Hoffman, J., Moon, J., & Duffy-Hester, A. M. (1998). Where are teachers' voices in the phonics/whole language debate? Results from a survey of U.S. elementary teachers. *The Reading Teacher, 51*, 636–652.

Bereiter, C., & Scardamalia, M. (1989). Intentional learning as a goal of instruction. In L. B. Resnick (Ed.), *Knowing, learning, and instruction: Essays in honor of Robert Glaser* (pp. 361–392). Hillsdale, NJ: Erlbaum.

Blumenfeld, P., Pintrich, P., Meece, J., & Wessels, K. (1982). The formation and role of self perceptions of ability in elementary classroom. *Elementary School Journal, 82*, 401–420.

Brophy, J. (1981). Teacher praise: A functional analysis. *Review of Educational Research, 51*, 5–32.

Brophy, J. (1998). *Motivating students to learn*. Boston: McGraw-Hill.

Brown, A. L., & Campione, J. C. (1998). Designing a community of young learners: Theoretical and practical lessons. In N. M. Lambert & B. McCombs (Eds.), *How students learn: Reforming schools through learner-centered education* (pp. 33–52). Washington, DC: American Psychological Association.

Chi, M., Bassok, M., Lewis, M., Reimann, P., & Glaser, R. (1989). Self-explanations: How students study and use examples to solve problems. *Cognitive Science, 13*, 145–182.

Chi, M. T. H., DeLeeun, N., Chiu, M., & Lavancher, C. (1994). Eliciting self-explanations improves understanding. *Cognitive Science, 18*, 439–477.

Corno, L., & Kanfer, R. (1993). The role of volition in learning and performance. In L. Darling-Hammond (Ed.), *Review of research in education* (pp. 301–341). Washington, DC: American Educational Research Association.

Cunningham, A., & Stanovich, K. (1997). Early reading acquisition and its relation to reading experience and ability 10 years later. *Developmental Psychology, 33*, 934–945.

Deci, E. L. (1992). The relation of interest to the motivation of behavior. In K. A. Renninger, S. Hidi, & A. Krapp (Eds.), *The role of interest in learning and development* (pp. 43–70). Hillsdale, NJ: Erlbaum.

Deci, E. L., & Ryan, R. M. (1985). *Intrinsic motivation and self-determination in human behavior*. New York: Plenum Press.

Deci, E. L., Schwartz, A. J., Scheinman, L., & Ryan, R. M. (1981). An instrument to assess adults' orientations toward control versus autonomy with children: Reflections on intrinsic motivation and perceived competence. *Journal of Educational Psychology, 73*, 642–650.

Dole, J. A., Duffy, G. G., Roehler, L. R., & Pearson, P. D. (1991). Moving from the old to the new: Research on reading comprehension instruction. *Review of Educational Research, 61*, 239–264.

Elley, W. B. (1992). *How in the world do students read?* Hamburg, Germany: International Reading Association.

Elliott, E. S., & Dweck, C. S. (1988). Goals: An approach to motivation and achievement. *Journal of Personality and Social Psychology, 54*, 5–12.

Flink, C., Boggiano, A. K., Main, D. S., Barrett, M., & Katz, P. A. (1992). Children's achievement-related behaviors: The role of extrinsic and intrinsic motivational orientations. In A. K. Boggiano & T. S. Pittman (Eds.), *Achievement and motivation: A social-developmental perspective* (pp. 189–214). New York: Cambridge University Press.

Flower, L., Stein, V., Ackerman, J., Kantz, M. J., McCormick, K., & Peck, W. C. (Eds.). (1990). *Reading to write: Exploring a cognitive and social process*. New York: Oxford University Press.

Gaa, J. P. (1973). Effects of individual goal-setting conferences on achievement, attitudes, and goal-setting behavior. *Journal of Experimental Education, 42,* 22–28.

Gambrell, L., & Marinak, B. (1997). Incentives and intrinsic motivation to read. In J. T. Guthrie & A. Wigfield (Eds.), *Reading engagement: Motivating readers through integrated instruction* (pp. 205–217). Newark, DE: International Reading Association.

Gaskins, I., & Elliot, T. (Eds.). (1991). *Implementing cognitive strategy training across the school: The benchmark manual for teachers.* Cambridge, MA: Brookline Books.

Gaskins, I., Guthrie, J. T., Satlow, E., Ostertag, F., Six, L., Byrne, J., & Conner, B. (1994). Integrating instruction of science, reading, and writing: Goals, teacher development, and assessment. *Journal of Research in Science Teaching, 31,* 1039–1056.

Graesser, A., Golding, J. M., & Long, D. L. (1991). Narrative representation and comprehension. In R. Barr, M. L. Kamil, P. Mosenthal, & P. D. Pearson (Eds.), *Handbook of reading research* (Vol. 2, pp. 171–205). New York: Longman.

Grolnick, W., & Ryan, R. (1987). Autonomy support in education: Creating the facilitating environment. In N. Hastings & J. Schwieso (Eds.), *New directions in educational psychology: Behaviour and motivation in the classroom* (pp. 213–231). London: Falmer.

Guthrie, J. T. (1983). Teaching comprehension monitoring. *Journal of Reading, 27*(2), 190–191.

Guthrie, J. T., & Alao, S. (1997). Designing contexts to increase motivations for reading. *Educational Psychologist, 32,* 95–107.

Guthrie, J. T., Alao, S., & Rinehart, J. M. (1997). Engagement in reading for young adolescents. *Journal of Adolescent and Adult Literacy, 40,* 438–446.

Guthrie, J. T., Anderson, E., Alao, S., & Rinehart, J. (1999). Influences of Concept-Oriented Reading Instruction on strategy use and conceptual learning from text. *Elementary School Journal, 99*(4), 343–366.

Guthrie, J. T., & Cox, K. (1998). Portrait of an engaging classroom: Principles of Concept-Oriented Reading Instruction for diverse students. In K. Harris (Ed.), *Teaching every child every day: Learning in diverse schools and classrooms* (pp. 77–131). Cambridge, MA: Brookline Books.

Guthrie, J. T., Cox, K., Anderson, E., Harris, K., Mazzonni, S., & Rach, L. (1998). Principles of integrated instruction for engagement in reading. *Educational Psychology Review, 10,* 177–199.

Guthrie, J. T., & McCann, A. D. (1997). Characteristics of classrooms that promote motivations and strategies for learning. In J. T. Guthrie & A. Wigfield (Eds.), *Reading engagement: Motivating readers through integrated instruction* (pp. 128–148). Newark, DE: International Reading Association.

Guthrie, J. T., Schafer, W. D., Wang, Y. Y., & Afflerbach, P. (1995). Relationships of instruction of reading: An exploration of social, cognitive, and instructional connections. *Reading Research Quarterly, 30,* 8–25.

Guthrie, J. T., Van Meter, P., Hancock, G. R., McCann, A., Anderson, E., & Alao, S. (1998). Does Concept-Oriented Reading Instruction increase strategy-use and conceptual learning from text? *Journal of Educational Psychology, 90,* 261–278.

Guthrie, J. T., Van Meter, P., McCann, A. D., Wigfield, A., Bennett, L., Poundstone, C. C., Rice, M. E., Faibisch, F. M., Hunt, B., & Mitchell, A. M. (1996). Growth of literacy engagement: Changes in motivations and strategies during Concept-Oriented Reading Instruction. *Reading Research Quarterly, 31,* 306–332.

Guthrie, J. T., Weber, S., & Kimmerly, N. (1993). Searching documents: Cognitive processes and deficits in understanding graphs, tables, and illustrations. *Contemporary Educational Psychology, 18,* 186–221.

Guthrie, J. T., & Wigfield, A. (Eds.). (1997). *Reading engagement: Motivating readers through integrated instruction.* Newark, DE: International Reading Association.

Hansen, J., & Pearson, P. D. (1983). An instructional study: Improving the inferential comprehension of good and poor fourth-grade readers. *Journal of Educational Psychology, 75*(6), 821–829.

Harter, S. (1981). A new self-report scale of intrinsic versus extrinsic orientation in the classroom: Motivational and informational components. *Development Psychology, 17,* 300–312.

Heinze-Fry, J. A., & Novak, J. D. (1990). Concept mapping brings long-term movement towards meaningful learning. *Science Educational, 74,* 973–988.

Hootstein, H. (1995). Motivational strategies of middle school social studies teachers. *Social Education, 59,* 23–26.

Horton, P. B., McConney, A. A., Gallo, M., Woods, A. L., Senn, G. J., & Hamelin, D. (1993). An investigation of the effectiveness of concept mapping as an instructional tool. *Science Education, 77,* 95–111.

Jegede, O. J., Alaiymelo, F. F., & Okebukola, P. A. O. (1990). The effect of concept mapping on students' anxiety and achievement in biology. *Journal of Research in Science Teaching, 27,* 951–960.

King, A., Staffieri, A., & Adelgais, A. (1998). Mutual peer tutoring: Effects of structuring tutorial interaction to scaffold peer learning. *Journal of Educational Psychology, 90,* 134–152.

Klausmeier, H. J. (1992). Concept learning and concept teaching. *Educational Psychologist, 27,* 267–286.

Locke, E. A., & Latham, G. P. (1990). *A theory of goal setting and task performing.* Englewood Cliffs, NY: Prentice Hall.

Lonka, K., Lindblom-Ylanne, S., & Maury, S. (1994). The effect of study strategies on learning from text. *Learning and Instruction, 4,* 253–271.

Maehr, M. (1984). Meaning and motivation. In R. Ames & C. Ames (Eds.), *Research on motivation in education: Student motivation* (Vol. 1, pp. 115–144). New York: Academic Press.

Maehr, M., & Midgley, C. (1996). *Transforming school cultures.* Boulder, CO: Westview Press.

McCombs, B. (1997). Commentary: Reflections on motivations for reading—Through the looking glass of theory, practice, and reader experiences. *Educational Psychologist, 32,* 125–134.

McCombs, B. L., & Whistler, J. S. (1997). The learner-centered classroom and school: Strategies for increasing student motivation and achievement. In B. L. McCombs & J. S. Whistler (Eds.), *The learner-centered classroom* (pp. 63–101). San Francisco: Jossey-Bass.

McLoyd, V. (1979). The effects of extrinsic rewards of differential value on high and low intrinsic interest. *Child Development, 50,* 1010–1019.

Meece, J. L. (1991). The classroom context and students' motivational goals. In M. K. Maehr & P. R. Pintrich (Eds.), *Advances in motivation and achievement* (Vol. 7, pp. 261–285). Greenwich, CT: JAI Press.

Meece, J. L., Blumenfeld, P. C., & Hoyle, R. H. (1988). Students' goal orientations and cognitive engagement in classroom activities. *Journal of Educational Psychology, 80*(4), 514–523.

Meece, J. L., & Holt, K. (1993). A pattern analysis of students' achievement goals. *Journal of Educational Psychology, 85,* 582–590.

Menke, D. J., & Pressley, M. (1994). Elaborative interrogation: Using "why" questions to enhance the learning from text. *Journal of Reading, 37,* 642–646.

Morrow, L. M. (1992). The impact of a literature-based program on literacy achievement, use of literature, and attitudes of children from minority backgrounds. *Reading Research Quarterly, 27,* 250–275.

Morrow, L. M. (1996). *Motivating reading and writing in diverse classrooms* (NCTE Research Rep. No. 28). Urbana, IL: National Council of Teachers of English.

Newby, T. J. (1991). Classroom motivation: Strategies of first-year teachers. *Journal of Educational Psychology, 83,* 187–194.

Nolen, S. B., & Nichols, J. G. (1994). A place to begin (again) in research on student motivation: Teachers' beliefs. *Teaching and Teacher Education, 10,* 57–69.

Novak, J. D. (1995). Concept mapping: A strategy for organizing knowledge. In S. Glynn & R. Duit (Eds.), *Learning science in the schools: Research reforming practice* (pp. 229–245). Mahwah, NJ: Erlbaum.

Okebukola, P. A. (1990). Attaining meaningful learning concepts in genetics and ecology: An examination of the potency of the concept mapping technique. *Journal of Research in Science Teaching, 27*(5), 493–504.

Oldfather, P., & Dahl, K. (1994). Toward a social constructivist reconceptualization of intrinsic motivation for literacy learning. *Journal of Reading Behavior, 26,* 139–158.

Paris, S. G., & Lindauer, B. K. (1976). The role of inference in children's comprehension and memory. *Cognitive Psychology, 8,* 217–227.

Payne, B. D., & Manning, B. H. (1992). Basal reader instruction: Effects of comprehension monitoring training on reading comprehension, strategy use and attitude. *Reading Research and Instruction, 32*(1), 29–38.

Pearson, P. D., Hansen, J., & Gordon, C. (1979). The effect of background knowledge on young children's comprehension of explicit and implicit information. *Journal of Reading Behavior, 11,* 201–209.

Pressley, M., Rankin, J., & Yokoi, L. (1996). A survey of instructional practices of primary teachers nominated as effective in promoting literacy. *Elementary School Journal, 96*(4), 363–383.

Renninger, K. A. (1992). Individual interest and development: Implications for theory and practice. In K. A. Renninger, S. Hidi, & A. Krapp (Eds.), *The role of interest in learning and development* (pp. 361–396). Hillsdale, NJ: Erlbaum.

Roeser, R. W., Midgley, C., & Urdan, T. C. (1996). Perceptions of the school psychological environment and early adolescents' psychological and behavioral functioning in school: The mediating role of goals and belonging. *Journal of Educational Psychology, 88*(3), 408–422.

Romance, N. R., & Vitale, M. R. (1992). A curriculum strategy that expands time for in-depth elementary science instruction by using science-based reading strategies: Effects of a year-long study in grade four. *Journal of Research in Science Teaching, 29,* 545–554.

Rosenholtz, S. J., & Simpson, C. (1984). Classroom organization and student stratification. *Elementary School Journal, 85,* 21–38.

Rosenshine, B. (1979). Staff development for teaching basic skills. *Theory into Practice, 17,* 267–271.

Ross, J. A. (1988). Controlling variables: A meta-analysis of training studies. *Review of Educational Research, 58,* 405–437.

Rowe, D. W., & Rayford, L. (1987). Activating background knowledge in reading comprehension assessment. *Reading Research Quarterly, 22*(2), 160–176.

Ryan, R., & Powelson, C. (1991). Autonomy and relatedness as fundamental to motivation and education. *Journal of Experimental Education, 60*(1), 49–66.

Santa, C. (1997). School change and literacy engagement. In J. T. Guthrie & A. Wigfield (Eds.), *Reading engagement: Motivating readers through integrated instruction* (pp. 218–235) Newark, DE: International Reading Association.

Schiefele, U. (1991). Interest, learning, and motivation. *Educational Psychologist, 26,* 299–323.

Schiefele, U. (1996). Topic interest, text representation, and quality of experience. *Contemporary Educational Psychology, 21,* 3–18.

Schraw, G., Bruning, R., & Svoboda, C. (1995). Source of situational interest. *Journal of Reading Behavior, 27,* 1–17.

Schunk, D. H. (1984). Enhancing self-efficacy and achievement through rewards and goals: Motivational and informational effects. *Journal of Educational Research, 78*(1), 29–34.

Schunk, D. H. (1985). Participation in goal setting: Effects on self-efficacy and skills of learning-disabled children. *Journal of Special Education, 19,* 307–317.

Schunk, D. H., & Rice, J. M. (1991). Learning goals and progress feedback during reading comprehension instruction. *Journal of Reading Behavior, 3,* 351–365.

Skinner, E. A., & Belmont, M. J. (1993). Motivation in the classroom: Reciprocal effects of teacher behavior and student engagement across the school year. *Journal of Educational Psychology, 85,* 571–581.

Skinner, E. A., Wellborn, J. G., & Connell, J. P. (1990). What it takes to do well in school and whether I've got it: A process model of perceived control and children's engagement and achievement in school. *Journal of Educational Psychology, 82*(1), 22–32.

Spires, H. A. (1990). *Prior knowledge activation: Inducing text engagement in reading to learn.* Paper presented at the annual meeting of the American Educational Research Association, Boston, MA.

Stice, C. F., & Alvarez, M. C. (1987). Hierarchical concept mapping in the early grades. *Childhood Education, 64,* 86–96.

Stipek, D. (1996). Motivation and instruction. In D. C. Berliner & R. C. Calfee (Eds.), *Handbook of educational psychology* (pp. 85–113). New York: Simon & Schuster/Macmillan.

Sweet, A., Guthrie, J. T., & Ng, M. (1998). Teachers' perceptions and students reading motivations. *Journal of Educational Psychology, 90,* 210–223.

Taylor, K. K. (1983). Can college students summarize? *Journal of Reading, 26,* 524–528.

Thomas, S., & Oldfather, P. (1997). Intrinsic motivations, literacy, and assessment practices: "That's my grade. That's me?" *Educational Psychologist, 32*(2), 107–123.

Turner, J. C. (1995). The influence of classroom contexts on young children's motivation for literacy. *Reading Research Quarterly, 30,* 410–441.

Wentzel, K. R. (1997). Student motivation in middle school: The role of perceived pedagogical caring. *Journal of Educational Psychology, 89*(3), 411–419.

Wigfield, A., & Guthrie, J. T. (1996). *Educational Psychologist,* special issue.

Wigfield, A., & Guthrie, J. T. (1997). Motivation for reading: Individual, home, textual, and classroom perspective. *Educational Psychologist, 32*(2), 57–135.

Williamson, R. A. (1996). Self-questioning: An aid to metacognition. *Reading Horizons, 37,* 31–47.

Wlodkowski, R. (1985). *Enhancing adult motivation to learn.* San Francisco: Jossey-Bass.

Zahorik, J. (1996). Elementary and secondary teachers' reports of how they make learning interesting. *Elementary School Journal, 96,* 551–564.

CHAPTER ELEVEN

Facilitating Reading
Instruction through
School-Wide Coordination

LINDA VALLI

Like all social systems, schools can be dysfunctional. They can develop norms and modes of operating that impede rather than enhance their overall goals and mission. In complex organizations like schools, which operate within larger systems, highly coordinated efforts are needed to accomplish multiple and challenging goals. This chapter focuses on what the school as a social system, through the collective work of teachers and administrators, can do to facilitate early reading comprehension and engagement. Three aspects of school-wide coordination of reading are emphasized: (1) its positive impact on classroom instruction, (2) implications for ongoing professional development of teachers, and (3) the importance of close alignment with school district and state-level policies and procedures.

Some of the questions this chapter addresses are the following: Why is a coordinated program necessary? What aspects of a literacy program need to be coordinated, and how can that be accomplished? What kinds of planning are necessary to create such consistency? What professional development opportunities do teachers need? And what is the role of principals, reading specialists, and support staff in promoting school-wide coordination? Examples illustrate what schools can do at the level of the individual classroom, across grade levels, and in relation to local and state education agencies. This is not to suggest that change is easy. Significant school reform requires the aligned support of state boards of education, local school districts, and teacher associations. It is particularly difficult to accomplish in poor schools surrounded by urban blight and hopelessness (Anyon, 1997). In these situations, the revitalization of urban economies is a vital pre- or corequisite. Nonetheless, as the following research examples indicate, school reform can occur, even in schools in high-poverty communities.

WHY IS SCHOOL COORDINATION NECESSARY?

The answer to that question is deceptively simple: the principles of literacy instruction presented in this book are impossible to apply and sustain without school coordination. Educators and educational researchers are becoming increasingly convinced that a successful reading program needs more than the knowledge, skills, and motivation of individual teachers. It depends on the coordinated, collective work of teachers supported by institutional norms and structures. The characteristics of exemplary reading programs most often cited in research studies are those that need to be coordinated at the school level: "systematic procedures, comprehensive intervention strategies, frequent diagnosis, facilitator leadership, monitoring components, and extensive and ongoing staff development" (L. Smith, Ross, & Casey, 1996, p. 351).

Elmwood Elementary School: A Fictionalized Case

Consider what it is like for a principal, teacher, and student to function in a school that lacks a coordinated approach to reading. As the principal of this imaginary elementary school, which will be called Elmwood, you trust that your teachers have the knowledge, skills, and dedication to engage students in meaningful, age-appropriate learning. You give them a lot of autonomy in making decisions about instructional strategies and resources. At the beginning of each year, you provide them with information about students' scores on standardized achievement tests and goals set by the School Improvement Team (SIT). You also carefully construct the school schedule so that grade-level teams have weekly planning time. With some additional funds from a state grant, you order several sets of leveled reading books that teachers can use as either primary or supplementary materials. You encourage teacher participation in in-service workshops provided by your school district and augment the school's limited resources with numerous enrichment activities for both teachers and students. You see your responsibility as making teachers aware of the latest curricular materials and programs available to them—especially new computer software. Your main frustrations come from two sources: continuing to have large numbers of students, most of them in English as a Second Language (ESL) and Chapter I programs, reading below grade level; and being overwhelmed by the number of school-district and state-level offices with which you must interact and to which you must report about curriculum guidelines, resources, special services, and standardized assessments.

Imagine, next, what it is like to be a teacher at Elmwood. You spend most of the day teaching, planning, and correcting students' work on your own, often hurrying to cover the curriculum, locate resources, attend meetings, and respond to the learning and literacy needs of low-achieving students. Like many other teachers in your school, you experience having too much content to cover in too short a period of time with too few readily available resources. Your school day is *broken up* into small units so that all core subjects can be included every day and still give students time for lunch, recess, assemblies, field trips, extracurricular activities, and "specials" such as art, music, and physical education. As a consequence, you teach subject matter in discrete blocks of time. Your class schedule is also frequently *broken into* by announcements, disruptions, unanticipated events, and pull-out programs for special needs students (e.g., those in Special Education, gifted and talented, ESL, and Chapter I programs).

Each year you have a new room full of students who may have come from classrooms or other schools with highly divergent teaching approaches and materials and potentially conflicting philosophies of reading. The annual turnover rate in your school is 25–30%, and you do not know which students will be permanently assigned to your classroom until the end of September. Considerable work is involved in determining if what you plan to do builds on past teachers' efforts, is redundant, or makes unwarranted assumptions about students' prior knowledge. You, in turn, have little control over what kind of reading instruction your students receive in supplementary programs or in subsequent years.

The local teacher's union has successfully bargained for a certain number of staff development days each year. You are free to select from a variety of workshops. Like most teachers, you choose one-day sessions on technology, cooperative learning, and classroom discipline. You frequently bring back extra materials to put in teachers' mailboxes or the faculty lounge, but there are no formal expectations about what you will learn or share.

Now imagine yourself a student. In Elmwood's half-day kindergarten program you attended, you had a teacher who loved "Big Books." Because of the increased emphasis on exit skills and teacher accountability, your teacher made sure everyone knew the alphabet, kept journals, could recognize some words, and had science and social studies lessons. But what you remember most is the time she spent each day reading aloud to the whole class and letting you draw pictures, create your own costumes, and act out a variety of stories. Your first-grade teacher, in contrast, had a more discrete-skills approach to reading. She relied primarily on a basal series accompanied by worksheets to facilitate word recognition. You spent much of your time that year in a reading group with the same students and then worked alone at your desk to complete the assigned seatwork. You knew an adequate number of words for a 6-year-old, but they were words you had mostly memorized. When given free time or a choice of activities, you gravitated to drawing. The classroom had few books that interested you. The ones you tried to read had too many words you could not figure out.

In second grade, you were placed in a classroom with a whole-language orientation. Your teacher emphasized reading comprehension through fiction and narrative text. There were more books in this room, and you were supposed to add regularly to a word wall, a class dictionary, and a writing portfolio, which you were allowed to take home at the end of the year. You were struggling with science and social studies but did not receive much guidance in reading information texts. You were assigned a reading buddy from your classroom who listened to you read aloud and helped you sound out words. When you were in third grade, your school decided to create an individualized tutoring program using instructional assistants and community volunteers. Because you were reading below grade level, you were given a tutor for 30 minutes a day. The only time she was available was during your language arts block, and she did not have common planning time with your teacher. As a result of the tutoring, the number of words you recognized and could spell increased significantly. You developed some additional word recognition skills but continued to rely primarily on memorization and sounding out parts of words that looked familiar. Your tutoring ended after 8 weeks so that other students who were reading below grade level could receive individual assistance.

Elmwood: An Analysis

What the school experiences of this principal, teacher, and student indicate is that although the principal has developed a leadership style consistent with prevailing norms of teacher autonomy and professionalism, the inadvertent results are a less-than-optimal working/learning environment for both the teacher and the student. From a review of research on site-based management and school restructuring, Fullan (1995) concluded that high ideals and professional commitment are simply not sufficient to sustain teacher motivation and quality instruction over time. Institutional reliance on teacher dedication is almost guaranteed to fail because the problem is not that teachers lack dedication but that the task of helping all children learn to read and read to learn is so complex that it requires highly coordinated, comprehensive effort (Snow, Burns, & Griffin, 1998).

Most educators and policy makers now realize that to make a difference in students' opportunities to learn, efforts to provide quality teaching must be embedded within focused professional development and school improvement activities that are supported by a coherent and streamlined policy environment. In essence, they believe that schools must be restructured and recultured as learning organizations "in which people at all levels are collectively, continually enhancing their capacity to create things they really want to create" (P. Senge, quoted in O'Neil, 1995, p. 21). As Santa (1997) argued from her experience as a district reading coordinator, "we cannot teach students to be continuous learners, engaged readers, and effective collaborators if we do not work in school communities that have these same characteristics. Children's reading engagement and learning as inquiry cannot happen unless schools become places where teachers consume, critique and produce new knowledge" (pp. 220–221). But exactly what does that mean for those who are attempting the school-wide coordination of reading?

WHAT NEEDS TO BE COORDINATED?

This section discusses how the components of a strong reading program, as well as teachers' professional development opportunities, need to be coordinated through school-wide efforts. They are too important to be left to chance or the choice of individual teachers. The section then addresses the elements of a reading program that need to be coordinated with school-district and state-level agencies.

Coordination of the Reading Program

Unless attention is paid to coordinating various elements of the reading program, numerous problems are likely to occur. Findings from a 2-year study of 140 classrooms in high-poverty areas indicate that "the school day [can] become quite fragmented in logistical or programmatic terms" unless preventive measures are taken (Knapp, Shields, & Padilla, 1995, p. 164). This fragmentation severely hampers sound reading instruction. As can be seen in the Elmwood scenario, without coordinated effort, the reading program fails to establish coherent goals and focus, causing students to lose out on critical literacy connections and opportunities across time and learning contexts. To avoid such problems, school leaders must make programmatic and logistical coordination a priority.

Programmatic Coordination

The programmatic coordination of reading includes the alignment of curriculum goals, activities, and assessments that promote literacy; the integration of reading instruction with writing and other content areas; and connections made by the school with students' homes and community. Long blocks of uninterrupted learning time are generally required for students to engage in meaningful learning (see Byrnes, Chapter 9, this volume). But that provision often lies beyond the resources and decision-making power of the individual classroom teacher. It is, at least in part, a function of the school schedule (Knapp et al., 1995).

Looking at reading instruction in 66 classrooms in high-poverty communities, Adelman (1995) found that although some teachers created environments that offered students multiple opportunities to read in all subject matter areas, others severely restricted student opportunities, sometimes for reasons beyond their control. One primary factor was a school schedule that fragmented instructional time. Some of these classrooms devoted less than half an hour a day to reading. Apart from routinized seatwork assignments, students often spent less than 5 minutes a day engaged with text. In contrast, students in classrooms that provided extended opportunities to read and discuss text were able to focus on text comprehension and to combine reading with writing assignments.

These findings suggest that the kind of instructional coherence described by Guthrie, Cox, et al. (Chapter 10, this volume) is difficult to achieve without organizational coherence. The school schedule needs to be carefully constructed, with the primary aim of maximizing instructional time and coherence. Otherwise, the school schedule itself can militate against teachers contextualizing word study within meaningful reading, providing opportunities for social interactions around literacy, and integrating reading and language arts within content area thematic units. "Short-term worksheets and other skills-oriented instructional devices fit ... easily into small slices of time available for instruction" (Knapp et al., 1995, pp. 164–165), but they are unlikely to promote engaging, integrated, and interactive forms of instruction.

In addition to this "within-school" programmatic coordination, school investment in preschool and parental literacy programs is strongly recommended but again, is beyond the reach or role responsibility of the individual teacher. Literacy difficulties may start well before a child attends school and are related to what happens outside the school walls. Preschool children who engage in family and community-based literacy experiences are less likely to have long-term literacy problems (see Sonnenschein & Schmidt, Chapter 12, this volume). Both teachers and students are well served when schools commit resources to ensure that children "are exposed to appropriate literacy experiences before they come to school" (Allington & Walmsley, 1995, p. 255). Schools need to establish preschool programs, prepare parents and guardians to support literacy goals, and develop partnerships with community groups to emphasize the benefits of being a reader. Cross-sectional and longitudinal studies of James Comer's School Development Program have indicated that the creation of a caring and supportive school climate, attention to the psychosocial as well as the academic needs of students, and strong connections between school and home have a positive impact on reading achievement (Haynes, Emmons, & Woodruff, 1998).

Logistical Coordination

Reading programs also require logistical support, namely, the efficient organization and distribution of human and material resources. In addition to the school schedule, there are at least three other logistical areas that can support or undermine a coherent reading program. These are the ways in which (1) curriculum materials are ordered and distributed, (2) teacher meetings are scheduled and used, and (3) student progress within and across grade levels is monitored.

First, teachers need timely access to materials in order to create print-rich environments that sustain children's motivation. This means close coordination with the library media specialist to develop classroom libraries and with textbook committees to ensure sequencing and cohesion in reading materials across grade levels (see Chambliss & McKillop, Chapter 5, this volume). These collaborative efforts are especially important for young children who find reading challenging. Regular and special educators need to meet regularly with support staff and committees to match reading materials to these students' levels of proficiency.

Planning instruction around thematic units also requires support for materials acquisition. Without assistance in knowing what materials are available or possible to acquire, teachers understandably resist planning integrated units that include a variety of genres (biographies, histories, poetry anthologies, science texts, folk tales, and so forth). And yet these thematically related materials produce the type of classroom environments in which students read to learn as well as learn to read (see Dreher, Chapter 4, this volume). Educators must be wary, however, of what Guthrie (1996) called the "mirage of materials": the belief that a set of curriculum materials can substitute for a set of engaging instructional processes. The coordination of materials acquisition, described later in this chapter, is an essential component of a comprehensive, coherent reading program. But it is only the beginning.

Second, schools and school systems must coordinate personnel schedules so that classroom teachers and support staff can have regular planning times within and across grade levels. Although these meeting times are necessary for normal instructional planning, they are most needed to monitor the literacy progress of at-risk readers. Without such coordination and monitoring, students with the greatest literacy problems become "curriculum casualties." As Allington and Walmsley (1995) cautioned from their analysis of elementary school literacy programs:

> Because most schools are organized around one-year-at-a-time instructional programs, children take a series of "field trips" with different teachers who, if they are accountable at all, are accountable only for coverage of material in a given year. They have no responsibility for children other than during the year they have them, and so no one has responsibility for the literacy experiences or the literacy accomplishments of a child across the entire elementary or secondary years. Under these circumstances, at risk children routinely fall through the cracks. (p. 256)

A third and related point is that schools need to coordinate pull-out and regular classroom instructional programs. Knapp and Associates (1995) discovered in their study of classrooms in high-poverty communities that "programmatic connections between pullout services and regular classroom instruction were often weak or nonexistent" (p. 164). Not even the most highly skilled and dedicated classroom teachers can make a difference when special programs constantly pull students out of the room, making coherent classroom instruction impossible to achieve. Because "pull-out" students still spend 90% of their time in regular classrooms, supplementary programs cannot substitute or compensate for classroom reading instruction (Snow et al., 1998). A more sensible solution is to help regular teachers develop skills in working with at-risk readers by investing in their professional development. Otherwise, we will continue to have a situation "in which students who are in most need of instructional support may actually receive less of it . . . because classroom teachers . . . may not actually know how to provide this support, even if they wanted to" (Walmsley & Allington, 1995, p. 25).

Coordination of Professional Development

As indicated above, classroom teachers are often ill prepared to meet the needs of children at risk for reading difficulties. In its recent committee report on preventing reading difficulties in young children, the National Research Council (Snow et al., 1998) stated that "it is nothing short of foolhardy to make enormous investments in remedial instruction and then return children to classroom instruction that will not serve to maintain the gains that they have made in the remedial program" (p. 258). But contributing to a comprehensive and coherent reading program, motivating and enabling *all* children to read, and maintaining reading gains is intellectually challenging work. It is not something that teachers, especially beginning teachers, can do on their own (see Alexander & Fives, Chapter 13, this volume). Doing it well requires ongoing opportunities to learn in collaborative, supportive settings. Based on their meta-analysis of instructional change research, Joyce and Showers (1995) concluded that "without companionship, help in reflecting on practice, and instruction on fresh teaching strategies, most people can make very few changes in their behavior, however well-intentioned they are" (p. 6).

In order to expand their repertoire of teaching strategies, gain new knowledge about the reading process, and examine their beliefs about at-risk readers, teachers must be provided with carefully designed professional development on a long-term basis (Borko & Putnam, 1995; Hodges, 1996; Richardson, 1998). The National Research Council frames the problem well: We need to abandon the unreal expectation that everything that must be learned about teaching reading can be learned in formal preservice teacher education. Opportunities for professional development must be provided throughout the career continuum so that teachers are able to sustain "a deep and principled understanding of the reading process and its implications for instruction" (Snow et al., 1998, p. 258).

These opportunities are likely to have a more powerful impact on student learning if they are coordinated at the school level and explicitly linked to the school's reading goals (Richardson, 1998). Ongoing opportunities for teacher learning must literally be embedded in the daily activities of schooling. In fact, research on teacher development and school improvement suggests that the two processes are so closely connected that they are virtually impossible to analyze separately (Hawley & Valli, 1999). As one review of the research concluded, school improvement efforts will fail until schools become not only places for teachers to work but places for them to learn (Smylie, 1995).

Classroom teachers are in particular need of professional development to learn how to reinforce the skills and knowledge that pull-out students receive from expert tutors and reading specialists (see Graham & Harris, Chapter 3, this volume). Summarizing the research on Reading Recovery programs, L. Smith et al. (1996) reported that schools that use a one-on-one Reading Recovery tutoring model are beginning to attend more to the professional development needs of the classroom teacher. Realizing the need to reach a larger percentage of low-achieving students, these schools help classroom teachers learn how to reinforce tutoring strategies and align instruction across the two settings. Virtually all exemplary reading programs use systemic approaches that include ongoing staff development so that teachers are well prepared to understand and implement the various components (L. Smith et al., 1996). One-shot workshops, no matter how informative or engaging, are simply not sufficient (Ball & Cohen, 1996; Hawley & Valli, 1999).

Similarly, reading tutors themselves need to be trained, supported, and supervised. "Best-evidence research has indicated that one-to-one tutoring is the most effective intervention strategy for students with reading problems" (L. Smith et al., 1996, p. 333). However, this finding only holds when tutors receive adequate training and close supervision from reading specialists. In a study of nonprofessional community volunteers, Invernizzi, Rosemary, Juel, and Richards (1997) found that "two sessions of one-on-one tutoring per week, by a trained, supported, and supervised community volunteer for a minimum of 20 weeks, can be an effective and affordable alternative intervention for children at risk for reading failure" (p. 277). That effectiveness was dependent, however, on the on-site involvement of a reading specialist who provided the volunteers with continual support and assistance.

District- and State-Level Coordination

With the exception of private schools and charter schools, most schools operate within larger systems that impact their day-to-day operation. Therefore, those who assess the potential of school-wide projects to make a difference in reading achievement emphasize the necessity of adequate support and coordination at the district and state level (Santa, 1997; Winfield, 1995). But this is not a simple administrative task. Education in the United States has historically functioned as a loosely coupled system with little coordination or accountability among levels (Rowan, 1990). Personnel at each level of the organization—classroom, school, district, and state—have, and expect to have, considerable autonomy. This creates various types of relations among these levels, some of which are more productive and functional than others.

In their intensive case studies of three elementary schools, Elmore, Peterson, and McCarthey (1996) found three distinctly different types of relations between the schools and their local districts: indifferent and sometimes openly hostile; actively supportive and directive; and supportive, but laissez-faire. There is now general consensus (Cohen & Spillane, 1992; M. Smith & O'Day, 1990) that schools benefit most from organizational relations that are neither too directive (top–down) nor too laissez-faire (bottom–up). Although teachers are eager to develop new approaches if they are convinced of their value and receive the necessary support, loosely coupled systems make resistance to change easy. "One of the reasons why mandates rarely work is that teachers' work goes on in the relative privacy of a classroom, where it is impossible to monitor the day-to-day activities" (Allington & Walmsley, 1995, p. 261).

As Santa (1997) described from her perspective as a district-level coordinator:

> Integrating curriculum, promoting extensive reading, applying learning strategies, and involving children in their own assessments are key factors for creating environments for literacy engagement. Incorporating such sweeping changes into the core of teaching demands healthy learning environments for teachers. The changes are too complex to be mandated from the top and too difficult for teachers to manage on their own. Both sides must work together to put personal visions about making life better for children into practice. Change occurs within centers of inquiry where teachers seek answers to questions that truly matter. Teaching engagement and literacy engagement follow the same path. (p. 231)

Others concur. In her study of a school-wide project in a major urban school district, Winfield (1995) found that "connectedness" between the school and the school district/state agencies is what makes the difference between a typical school and a successfully reforming school. Classroom teachers need encouragement and support from school leaders, school districts, and state agencies; they seldom change on their own (Knapp et al., 1995). But because teachers work hard to achieve what they know how to do, they need support and opportunities for further learning, not threats and sanctions (Allington & Walmsley, 1995, p. 261).

What the school district can do best to help schools deliver coherent, comprehensive reading programs is to set high standards, ensure the delivery of instructional materials and resources that are aligned with those standards, and support professional development opportunities that encourage the formation of school-based professional communities. In a recent evaluation of her own research on professional development for reading instruction, Richardson (1998) reaffirmed her belief in the importance of teacher autonomy, choice, and voluntary change. These norms, however, can undermine school and school-district efforts to establish coherence within and across instructional programs. To reconcile this tension, Richardson recommended that districts support professional development programs that preserve teacher autonomy *within* a school-based community of practice. This would require ongoing opportunities for critical discussions about the nature of reading and the implications for reading instruction.

Other research supports this recommendation. Knapp and Associates (1995), for example, found distinct differences in the ways districts encouraged, discouraged, or ignored high-quality instruction, particularly in the

248 ENGAGING YOUNG READERS

areas of curriculum policies, textbook adoption, assessment, and professional development. In districts that set high standards and curriculum expectations but encouraged flexibility in using and adapting curriculum guidelines, teachers were more receptive and invested in the success of the program. This again suggests that the type of support needed is quite different from bureaucratic mandate.

School-wide coordination should be supported by a well-integrated, "connected" school-district and state bureaucracy: "District-level initiatives that work to provide needed resources to schools and seek to simplify the potential maze of red tape that school personnel encounter can have a major impact on how schools deliver instruction to students and are critically important in fostering and perpetuating school improvement" (Winfield, 1995, p. 217). To upgrade reading programs on a school-wide basis, especially in schools with high concentrations of low-income students, Winfield (1995) recommended that control and governance at the district and state levels become less fragmented with regard to budgets, constituencies, and expertise. Bureaucratic divisions can be obstacles to coordinated programs because school administrators often must make requests to several different offices. Separately funded support programs create instructional fragmentation and resentment among teachers who also have need for resources but are denied access.

School districts can also assist with the alignment of textbooks, student assessments, and professional development opportunities with curriculum goals. Curriculum materials that are up to date and high quality are too often in short supply in schools, especially schools in high-poverty communities. Sometimes textbooks have been purchased but languish in warehouses because delivery systems are inadequate. Assessments are too often mismatched with curriculum frameworks, and professional development opportunities are inadequate—too weak, short term, and infrequent.

One district, for example, introduced a new language arts curriculum with integrated reading and writing. Teachers were expected to reconceptualize their notions of literacy, redesign instruction in reading and writing, and use these materials well after only a one-day workshop provided by the textbook publishing company (Knapp et al., 1995). In contrast, districts with strong professional development provided ongoing, school-based learning opportunities for teachers. Reading specialists were called upon for workshops, demonstrations, and ongoing informal support. In their study of successful school restructuring, Newmann and Wehlage (1995) reached a similar conclusion: staff development that immerses entire faculties in continuous, coordinated programs has a far more powerful school-wide impact than does staff development that encourages individual choice of multiple and discrete topics.

Textbook decisions, generally made in the central office, go hand in glove with curriculum assessment and professional development opportunities. Instructional difficulties at the classroom level and coordination problems at the school level are often exacerbated by the failure of textbook and resource materials to be aligned with curriculum frameworks, assessments, and professional development opportunities (Ball & Cohen, 1996). When the costs of important innovations (e.g., for staff development and new curriculum materials) are prohibitive at the school level, a comprehensive initiative at the district or state level is the only way that schools can afford to participate in such reforms (Biggam, Teitelbaum, & Willey, 1995).

HOW DOES SCHOOL-WIDE COORDINATION HAPPEN?

For most schools, the coordination of reading requires significant change in customary ways of operating. School change theorists talk about the necessity of both "reculturing" and "restructuring" the school (Fullan, 1993; Hargreaves, 1995). A return visit to Elmwood Elementary School, now under the leadership of a new principal, will help us envision how that can happen. This scenario is presented as one possible way to create greater school cohesion, not as the only feasible model. Its value is in enabling us to "see" what reculturing and restructuring mean in action.

Elmwood Revisited*

This is Ms. Williams's first year as Elmwood's new principal. She has been charged by her local superintendent to improve literacy achievement, especially in the primary unit, where student test scores are among the lowest in the district. During the first week of school, as Ms. Williams toured the building, she found orderly classrooms with teachers and students on task but noticeably unenthused. She also observed a wide range of approaches and materials used in reading instruction, with few teachers, even those at the same grade level, knowing what each other was doing. What teachers did at one grade level seemed to have little relation to what they did at another, or to the literacy expectations reflected in the county's instructional framework and the state's standardized assessments. Ms. Williams and the School Improvement Team (SIT) concluded that a major problem in the school was a lack of common literacy goals. Teachers had

---

*To create this scenario, I have drawn liberally from a videotape by Goldenberg (1977). I have also drawn from a case study of an elementary school written by Donna Muncey.

never agreed upon, never even seriously discussed, what reading and writing achievements they expected at each grade level. They had no standards to guide them.

This basic insight prompted the SIT to think about strategies to address this issue. With the assistance of a consultant from a nearby university, the SIT realized that what it was doing was developing a school change model. The SIT's ultimate goal was improved literacy scores. Because it had identified lack of common goals and standards as the core problem, the main task for the school that year was to create them. But goals, in and of themselves, would do little to change teaching and learning. Team members could all point to countless documents filled with goals and objectives that had little impact on student achievement. What the school needed was an infrastructure to assist teachers in making instructional change. That infrastructure needed to include leadership that both supported teachers and held them accountable, opportunities to learn new strategies, assessment to let them know whether or not they were successful, and time to collaboratively work on all these things.

To begin this instructional change process, Elmwood established several new committees. The first was the *literacy goals committee* (LGC), which included a representative from each grade level as well as the principal, the reading specialist, a TESOL teacher, the library-media specialist, and the Title I coordinator. The LGC established a meeting schedule at the beginning of the year with a target date for completion of its work. Between each meeting, grade-level teams reviewed the goals and gave feedback to the committee. The LGC used the school district's instructional framework to guide its effort.

In addition, a *literacy assessment committee* (LAC) was established to create classroom assessments such as running records, scoring rubrics, and portfolios that teachers and tutors could use to obtain concrete and immediate feedback on student progress. The LAC met often with an assessment consultant from the school district to help it develop classroom assessments and evaluate their "fit" with district tests. Given Elmwood's low literacy scores, the committee was particularly interested in knowing whether its literacy expectations were realistic. Some committee members initially recommended lowering expectations as a realistic accommodation to the school's high percentage of TESOL and Title I students. After much debate, they agreed that that decision was premature. They first needed to target low-achieving students and see if the appropriate instructional support and accommodations were in place for *each* of these students.

Teachers were invited to form *inquiry groups* on literacy topics such as word study, prevention strategies, use of time, classroom libraries, motivation, and integrated curriculum. In these groups, which met three or four times a month during the school day, teachers shared readings and experiences. They invited teachers with outstanding reputations from other schools to meet with them and visited these teachers' classrooms. Grade-level meetings and faculty meetings were also used to explore these topics in more depth.

One final structure that was eventually put into place was the *scoring sessions*, concentrated blocks of time during the summer where teachers collectively examined student work. The purpose of these sessions was to help teachers learn how to use student work so they could continuously improve their instruction. Although the literacy goals and assessments gave them a common frame of reference, teachers were still having difficulty knowing how to evaluate their progress. With the help of assessment consultants, scoring sessions taught them how to examine student products closely to determine what instructional changes they might make. Was the class as a whole having difficulty in a particular area? Were certain types of students having difficulties? Which individual students? What kind of group adjustments or individual assistance might be warranted? These were the questions the scoring sessions taught them how to answer and that helped them improve reading instruction, particularly for TESOL students.

Reculturing and Restructuring for School-Wide Coordination

The transformation at Elmwood is quite dramatic. It did not take place easily or quickly, but it did take place. For that to happen, serious attention had to be given to school cultures and school structures. Hargreaves (1995) and Fullan (1993) claimed that both reculturing and restructuring are essential in school change efforts. In their view, role expectations and relationships form the heart of school culture. "To develop or alter these relationships is to *reculture* the school" (Hargreaves, 1995, p. 16; his emphasis). Both argued for collaborative school cultures over individualistic or balkanized cultures in which teachers work alone or in isolated subgroups. Restructuring a school means attending to the time and space structures, such as classroom and committee arrangements, schedules, and student group and movement patterns that shape school cultures and relationships. Based on findings of school change efforts, Fullan (1993) believed that "reculturing leads to restructuring more effectively than the reverse" (p. 68). He encouraged educators to think about the types of behaviors and cultures they want to promote and then decide what and how existing structures need to be altered. As others have said, *form* should follow *function*. School-wide coordination will do little to improve reading achievement and independence unless it enhances teaching capacities and promotes coherent, comprehensive reading instruction.

In the case of Elmwood, the coordination of the reading program became what Sarason (1971) has called part of the "regularities" of school life. It was embedded into teachers' role relationships and the ways in which time and resources were used. Most schools are not yet restructured and recultured to facilitate collective work around shared goals and understandings. They must be redesigned so teachers can work together on a consistent, ongoing basis (Darling-Hammond, 1994; Sergiovanni, 1990). To establish more collegial norms and processes, teachers need time to engage in collaborative planning and in building professional communities that facilitate student learning (Little & McLaughlin, 1993). School cultures that promote a genuine sense of collective purpose and support systems motivate teacher engagement in coordinated efforts (Grimmett & Crehan, 1992; Hargreaves & Dawe, 1990; Joyce & Showers, 1995).

The following three subsections look more closely at ways in which role relationships and the use of planning time and resources can be recultured and restructured to facilitate the school-wide coordination of reading. The checklist in Table 11.1 summarizes these key components. School teams can use it as a way of determining where to put their coordination efforts. They might start with those components that received a weak rating.

Role Relationships

Patterns of relationships are an essential part of the school context. They create communication systems with both vertical and horizontal links. Vertical links attend to communication needs among individuals with shared responsibilities at one point in time. Horizontal links facilitate the sharing of information across time (Fullan, 1995). Both are needed for curriculum planning and student assessment. Classroom teachers need to communicate within and across grade levels about curriculum integration, goals, materials, and student progress. They need to discuss students' progress and provide continued support over time (see Leipzig & Afflerbach, Chapter 8, this volume). Clear and efficient communication systems must also be established among teachers, specialists, school leadership, the school district, and funding sources. Allington and Walmsley (1995) argued that "the working relationships among the various teachers, administrators, and specialists in the elementary school . . . need to move from a model in which each teacher works largely autonomously to an approach where far greater collaboration is expected" (p. 260).

What role relationships are most critical to reculturing for school-wide collaboration? There are at least three types: (1) among teachers and support staff, within and across grade levels; (2) with the principal and school leaders; and (3) with school-district and state personnel, and outside consultants. Although collaborative models of instruction generally do not

TABLE 11.1. School-Wide Coordination Checklist

Weak		Strong	
1	2	3	1. Teachers plan collaboratively for students' learning by discussing goals, curriculum, students' special needs, and literacy successes with colleagues.
1	2	3	2. Communication within and across grade levels emphasizes consistency in the program and allows for clear instructional goal setting.
1	2	3	3. Teachers' professional development is planned for as carefully as students' literacy development.
1	2	3	4. The school schedule is carefully constructed to maximize instructional time and coherence as well as collaborative planning time.
1	2	3	5. Pull-out programs are minimized and well coordinated with regular classroom instruction.
1	2	3	6. Individuals are identified who are responsible and supported for coordinating school-wide aspects of the reading program.
1	2	3	7. Everyone who works with special needs students receives coordinated preparation.
1	2	3	8. Curriculum materials are carefully coordinated with the school program.
1	2	3	9. The literacy progress of individual students is carefully tracked across grade-level so they receive timely, appropriate support.
1	2	3	10. The school invests in preschool and parental literacy programs that are coordinated with the school's reading program.
1	2	3	11. Teachers and support staff have ongoing, collaborative opportunities tostrengthen their knowledge and skills in reading instruction that are explicitly linked to the school's reading goals.
1	2	3	12. Textbook decisions are aligned with the curriculum, assessments, and professional development opportunities.
1	2	3	13. The principal, reading specialists, and instructional support staff provide leadership in coordinating all aspects of the reading program at the school level.
1	2	3	14. Support from the school district and state are adequate and aligned with the school's reading goals, curriculum, and assessments.
1	2	3	15. There is a healthy reciprocal relationship with the local and state educational agencies that encourages school-level educators to be fully engaged partners in school renewal.

function well when they are simply imposed on teachers (Allington & Walmsley, 1995), research affirms the value of team teaching and close working relationships among tutors and classroom teachers to strengthen vertical communication. One powerful model involves Special Education teachers working with the regular classroom teacher on instructional improvement and demonstrating lessons for the whole class (Knapp et al.,

1995). Another has volunteer tutors working with classroom teachers so students receive more individualized and motivating practice following instruction (Snow et al., 1998). What is not recommended is using volunteer tutors as students' primary or remedial reading teachers.

Allington and Walmsley (1995) further recommended special attention to horizontal communication, which is the most often neglected:

> Improving communication between teachers and specialists both within and across grade levels should be a major goal in every school. . . . [T]his could be accomplished by having teams of teachers and specialists who routinely follow children through the grades, ensuring that their core and remedial programs are cumulative and that current approaches build on what has taken place before. It also assumes that someone (or a group) actually takes responsibility for this monitoring as opposed to leaving responsibility to individual teachers or to the "system" as a whole. (pp. 256–257)

School leaders, especially the principal and the reading specialist, can also use their roles to impact school coordination efforts. The National Research Council (Snow et al., 1998) strongly recommended that all schools have access to a reading consultant. Education change theorists caution, however, against traditional role definitions that are consistent with bureaucratic and individualistic, but not with collaborative, school cultures (Christensen, 1992; Fullan, 1993; Senge, 1990). They warn that the image of school leaders as charismatic crusading heroes who effect change single-handedly reinforces notions of teacher powerlessness and isolation. It creates the impression that teachers are basically deficient, lacking the commitment, vision, and ability to learn and change. In place of this traditional role, both Senge (1990) and Fullan (1993) recommended that school leaders be thought of as designers, stewards, and teachers—coordinators of a complex change process who "keep students as the central focus, share power, foster a risk-taking and inquiry climate and procedures, and take time to interact with students, teachers, community and help keep the larger vision in the forefront of debate, action, and continuous reassessment" (Fullan, 1993, p. 72).

School leaders can be especially helpful in garnering outside resources and expertise. Although policy makers, universities, businesses, and educational reform networks have become increasingly viewed as important parts of a system to promote school improvement efforts, these agencies often merely add to the proliferation of conflicting messages received by the school. School leadership must harness and focus the support of these outside agencies around a clear and persistent vision of student learning and school improvement (Fullan, 1995). School leadership means "managing external pressures" that have direct consequences for the cohesion and comprehensiveness of instructional programs (Knapp et al., 1995).

Like school-level leaders, district leaders can support instructional coordination and professional development efforts and can make resources available that are closely aligned with the reading program (Darling-Hammond & McLaughlin, 1995). They can also network resources and expertise across schools. The National Research Council (Snow et al., 1998) strongly encouraged local districts to set standards for materials and professional development, to provide teachers with sufficient support and assistance to ensure effective reading instruction, and to monitor reading instruction and achievement. Otherwise, the prevention of reading difficulties among young children, on a large scale, is unlikely to occur.

Winfield's (1995) case study of changes made by a district to support Chapter I projects is illustrative. The district reorganized at the central office level to become more connected to the instructional process and deliver more coordinated direct services. It created an Office of School-Wide Projects to provide an advocate and point person for principals. This administrator's primary responsibility was instructional improvement in schools serving large numbers of poor students. New school-based positions were defined as teacher agents of change and facilitators rather than supervisors. This reorganization successfully broke down the old structure of compensatory education monitors operating in isolation from curriculum supervisors.

Although school districts are often criticized for standing in the way of school improvement, districts such as New York City School District No. 2 have developed comprehensive strategies to bring about system-wide changes in teaching and learning based on organizing principles and a set of activities (Elmore, 1997). The district has established expectations of high standards for students and teachers. In addition, it has supported teacher development by providing incentives, opportunities, and resources to learn; a consistent focus on literacy improvement in the early grades; and a highly visible accountability system for teachers, principals and schools. Teachers know the district is committed to a long-term process and that the next educational "fad" will not distract from this sustained focus. Others have written similar descriptions of ways in which school districts can capitalize on the expertise of central office staff to provide collaborative leadership across schools (Knapp et. al, 1995; Morrow & O'Connor, 1995; Santa, 1997).

In each of these three types of role relationships (among teachers, with school leaders, and with outside personnel), the goal is to change isolated work roles to collaborative working relationships. As Darling-Hammond and McLaughlin (1995) stated:

Teachers individually cannot reconceive their practice and the culture of their workplace. Yet almost everything about school is oriented toward going it alone professionally. . . . Organizational structures must be redesigned so that they actively foster learning and collaboration about serious problems of practice. This requires rethinking schedules, staffing patterns, and grouping arrangements to create blocks of time for teachers to work and learn together. (p. 601)

When teachers have regular meeting times to share ideas and solve problems, when there is an inclusive school culture, and when teachers analyze, evaluate, and experiment collectively, there is greater implementation of research-based instructional strategies and teaching improvement (Fullan, 1993; Rosenholtz, 1991). But for most teachers, collaborative planning is a new skill for which they need ongoing support and assistance.

Planning Time

Successful restructuring for collaborative rather than fragmented school cultures and programs demands a reconsideration of the use of time. In traditional school cultures, planning time tends to be highly restricted; it is used to complete multiple unrelated tasks and is driven by administrative rather than instructional agendas. In schools with collaborative cultures, time is built into the school calendar for multiple types of meetings, with work that is highly coordinated across settings and focused on a limited set of core instructional goals. As L. Smith et al. (1996) found in their comparative research review, "an important difference between Success for All [SFA] and traditional Title I pull-out programs is that tutoring in SFA is directly integrated with the reading curriculum" (p. 334). This cannot happen if tutors, remedial teachers, reading specialists, and classroom teachers do not have regularly scheduled meeting times.

Setting aside planning time for these groups and establishing a school schedule that enables classroom teachers to meet regularly with support staff also creates a sound infrastructure of professional development. Adelman and Walking-Eagle (1997) found in their on-site study of 14 schools that a critical step in successful reform efforts is building in time for teachers to study new instructional materials, practice new teaching strategies, and consider new organizational structures. Unfortunately, this key step is often overlooked or truncated.

Organizational theorists have found that change generally begins with small pockets of new thinking and behaviors supported by flexible structures and a risk-taking environment where there is open questioning and testing new ideas (Fullan, 1993). As evident in the restructured Elmwood scenario, this can happen in a variety of collaborative work settings. Keys to success are ensuring linkages among groups that operate within a set of shared understandings and protecting teachers from undue administrative burdens. As Allington and Walmsley (1995) cautioned, "Despite public opinion to the contrary, elementary teachers already have a teaching day that is too crowded, and to expect that they take on administrative duties with no relief from teaching is simply unrealistic" (p. 261).

A variety of strategies are being used to free "prisoners of time" (as teachers have justifiably been called) for planning, professional development, and school improvement work (National Education Commission on Time and Learning, 1994). They include *blocking, banking, extending,* and *repurposing* current uses of time (Purnell & Hill, 1992; Raywid, 1993; Watts & Castle, 1993). One relatively simple mechanism to accomplish this goal is to block time in the school schedule by combining out-of-class time such as individual planning time, grade-level meeting time, and lunchtime. Fullan (1993) reported one school that created a common planning time of over an hour every day for teams of classroom teachers and resource teachers by carefully scheduling classes such as physical education, music, and art that are taught by specialists.

Another mechanism is to use existing time more efficiently by repurposing the agendas of faculty and team meetings and by exploiting the communication potential of technology: "Department meetings, for example, can be an administrative bore, or they can operate as 'mini-seminars,' engaging faculty members in examination of materials, student work, and curriculum plans" (Darling-Hammond & McLaughlin, 1995, p. 600). The case of Elmwood illustrates how current structures and meeting times can be used for school-wide coordination and teachers' ongoing learning.

A third thing schools can do is to create additional meeting time during the school day when teachers do not have classroom responsibilities. They can do this by using substitutes to cover classes or varying the length of the school day. Although regular substitutes can be expensive, some schools are finding creative and meaningful ways to use interns, instructional assistants, and community volunteers. And finally, schools can "bank" time for professional development by saving for it during the school day. Lunch periods can be shortened to save time. Schools can also add time at the beginning or end of 4 days a week. Students can then be released early or come late one day a week so teachers have that time for professional development. This strategy can be controversial, however, because of its impact on families, so it must be carefully negotiated with parents and the local community. Its success is dependent on community support.

And last, schools can increase the amount of time available to them by permanently lengthening the school day, extending the school week into weekends, or expanding the school year into the summer months. Allington and Walmsley (1995) recommended keeping schools open all day, on weekends, and throughout the year, "so that teachers can spend part of their time teaching, part engaged in professional development, part in administration, and part on vacation" (p. 262).

Resources

Curriculum resources can promote or impede instructional coherence. In the hypothetical example of the untransformed Elmwood Elementary School presented at the start of this chapter, curriculum materials were plentiful but randomly purchased, with little besides the criteria of "adequate quantity" and "variety" in mind. They were unaligned across classrooms or with a comprehensive set of literacy goals. Whether decisions are made at the classroom, school, district, or state level, basals readers, tradebooks, "Big Books," and other literacy materials must be carefully chosen to support students' literacy needs within a coherent literacy curriculum.

All forms of curriculum materials (frameworks, objectives, assessments, manuals, and textbooks) should reinforce one another (Snow et al., 1998). This requires careful planning and decision-making by diverse members of the school community, including the library media specialist and the reading specialist. Without carefully selected materials that are integrated with professional development opportunities, teachers are frustrated in their attempts to create engaging literacy environments and flounder in attempts to fully exploit the materials' potential. Without adequate professional development, teachers also find ways to adapt materials, sometimes inappropriately, to their own beliefs about literacy instruction, which might be inconsistent with principles of sound literacy instruction. One reason why curriculum materials have not had a more significant impact on classroom practice is because curriculum designers have failed to appreciate the new learning required to use them. Learning to use new materials is seldom viewed as an essential component of professional development (Ball & Cohen, 1996).

Classroom libraries and literacy manuals can also promote instructional coherence. Regular meetings between classroom teachers and the library-media specialist are important communication vehicles to create well-designed classroom libraries. School literacy manuals are also a way of developing shared goals and understandings around intended outcomes and the use of curriculum materials. One recommended version states the school's philosophy and literacy goals, describes how the school is organized to teach reading and writing, outlines literacy objectives and activities at the classroom level, and indicates the leadership, organizational structures, and resources that support the program (Erickson, 1995). Were such a manual created, updated, and collectively used by the school staff for both planning and monitoring purposes, it would foster instructional and organizational coherence.

CONCLUSION

Various historical and organizational factors have acted as constraints on school-wide coordination efforts. First, even though current rhetoric defines the principal as the school's instructional leader, that has only recently been the case. Nor have teachers been encouraged to be curriculum developers, reflective practitioners, or collaborative problem solvers. Because teachers have not been involved, they have not developed a collaborative culture around the improvement of teaching and learning. Second, when budget cuts are in effect, class sizes and expectations for teaching load increase and resources, including time, materials, and support staff decrease. Teachers feel pressured to simply manage "the daily grind" (Jackson, 1968) and resist school change and coordination efforts. Third, teaching in the United States has historically been individually, not socially, organized work. Lortie's (1975) metaphor of egg-crate schools is, unfortunately, still an apt description of the working conditions in most schools. Teachers continue to work in rows of separated classrooms, much like eggs in an egg carton. And, fourth, federal programs inadvertently aggravate the problem with separate funding sources for different types of at-risk students. This loose coupling at the federal level ripples through the educational system. The fundamental reculturing and restructuring of deeply entrenched policies, norms, and practices that school-wide coordination requires is made difficult by the very educational policy context in which schools operate.

And yet there are increasingly robust examples of highly coherent and comprehensive literacy programs to guide reform efforts. Evidence from disparate sources indicates that school-wide coordination is possible and makes a difference for student learning, teacher learning, and the overall creation of schools as learning communities. Without school-wide support and coordination, teachers have scant means of enacting a coherent program of reading. This results in reading instruction that is fragmented, haphazard, and nonreinforcing. With school-wide coordination, many of these problems can be overcome. Shared goals can be established with high expectations for reading achievement, a coherent reading program with supporting resources can be developed across grade levels, reading instruction can be better integrated with other subject areas, special-needs students can be better served, and an ongoing assessment system can be established to monitor student growth. School-wide coordination is an essential—but too frequently overlooked—basis for successful reading instruction.

ACKNOWLEDGMENTS

I would like to thank the editors of this book as well as Mary Lou Watkins and Maureen Cooney for their helpful suggestions.

RECOMMENDED READINGS

Allington, R., & Walmsley, S. (Eds.). (1995). *No quick fix: Rethinking literacy programs in America's elementary schools.* New York: Teachers College Press.

The chapters in this edited volume deal with the many issues involved in promoting literacy for at-risk readers that must be dealt with at the school and school-district level. The many research-based examples and ideas presented in the book should be helpful to principals, policy makers, staff developers, and teachers who want to work as agents of school change.

Elmore, R., Peterson, P., & McCarthey, S. (1996). *Restructuring in the classroom: Teaching, learning, and school organization.* San Francisco: Jossey-Bass.

This book provides detailed portraits of the ways that policy and school organization affect classroom practice in three elementary schools in three different school districts. It gives compelling evidence that changing teaching practice is primarily dependent on teacher knowledge and skills, not just organizational structures, and suggests ways in which schools can systematically address that issue.

Erickson, L. (1995). *Supervision of literacy programs: Teachers as grass-roots change agents.* Boston: Allyn & Bacon.

The author writes directly to classroom teachers and offers practical suggestions about being change agents for literacy improvement. Some of the key topics are how to initiate change, how to form collaborative teams, how to develop school-wide manuals, and how to fund learning communities.

Fullan, M. (1993). *Change forces: Probing the depths of educational reform.* New York: Falmer Press.

The book tackles the "chaotic" process of educational change. It provides clear insights and vivid examples of successful reform strategies.

Goldenberg, C. (1997). *Settings for change* [Videotape]. Long Beach, CA: Small Island Multimedia.

This videotape is the basis for the "transformed" Elmwood scenario. It provides an overview of Goldenberg's work with Felton Elementary School personnel in creating both a model and settings for school change that had a dramatic, positive effect on primary-level reading scores. A copy of the videotape can be obtained by e-mailing the author [cgolden@ucla.edu].

Knapp, M., & Associates. (Eds.). (1995). *Teaching for meaning in high poverty classrooms.* New York: Teachers College Press.

Based on a study of 140 classrooms that serve large numbers of students from low-income families, this book describes factors that encourage "teaching for meaning" in the areas of reading, writing, and mathematics. Two chapters of particular interest are "Aiming Reading Instruction at Deeper Understanding" and "The School and District Environment for Meaning-Oriented Instruction."

Santa, C. M. (1997). School change and literacy engagement: Preparing teaching and learning environments. In J. T. Guthrie & A. Wigfield (Eds.), *Reading engagement: Motivating readers through integrated instruction* (pp. 218–233). Newark, DE: International Reading Association.

The author is a school-district reading supervisor who uses her experience to describe how principles of school change and research in reading engagement can play a critical role in transforming teaching and curriculum.

REFERENCES

Adelman, N. (1995). Aiming reading instruction at deeper understanding. In M. Knapp & Associates (Eds.), *Teaching for meaning in high poverty classrooms* (pp. 64–83). New York: Teachers College Press.

Adelman, N., & Walking-Eagle, K. P. (1997). Teachers, time, and school reform. In A. Hargreaves (Ed.), *Rethinking educational change with heart and mind: ASCD yearbook* (pp. 92–110). Alexandria, VA: Association for Supervision & Curriculum Development.

Allington, R., & Walmsley, S. (Eds.). (1995). *No quick fix: Rethinking literacy programs in America's elementary schools*. New York: Teachers College Press.

Anyon, J. (1997). *Ghetto schooling: A political economy of urban educational reform*. New York: Teachers College Press.

Ball, D. L., & Cohen, D. (1996). Reform by the book: What is—or might be— the role of curriculum materials in teacher learning and instructional reform? *Educational Researcher, 25*(9), 6–8, 14.

Biggam, S. C., Teitelbaum, N., & Willey, J. (1995). Improving early literacy: Vermont stories of educational change from the bottom up and the top down. In R. Allington & S. Walmsley (Eds.), *No quick fix: Rethinking literacy programs in America's elementary schools* (pp. 197–213). New York: Teachers College Press.

Borko, H., & Putnam, R. T. (1995). Expanding a teacher's knowledge base: A cognitive psychological perspective on professional development. In T. R. Guskey & M. Huberman (Eds.), *Professional development in education: New paradigms and practices* (pp. 35–66). New York: Teachers College Press.

Christensen, G. (1992). *The changing role of the administrator in an accelerated school*. Paper presented at the annual meeting of the American Educational Research Association, San Francisco, CA.

Cohen, D., & Spillane, J. (1992). Policy and practice: The relations between governance and instruction. In G. Grant (Ed.), *Review of research in education* (Vol. 18, pp. 3–49). Washington, DC: American Educational Research Association.

Darling-Hammond, L. (Ed.). (1994). *Professional development schools: Schools for developing a profession*. New York: Teachers College Press.

Darling-Hammond, L., & McLaughlin, M. (1995, April). Policies that support professional development in an era of reform. *Phi Delta Kappan*, 597–604.

Elmore, R. (1997). *Investing in teacher learning: Staff development and instructional improvement in Community School District #2, New York City*. New York: National Commission on

Teaching & America's Future (NCTAF) & Consortium for Policy Research in Education (CPRE).

Elmore, R., Peterson, P., & McCarthey, S. (1996). *Restructuring in the classroom: Teaching, learning, and school organization.* San Francisco: Jossey-Bass.

Erickson, L. (1995). *Supervision of literacy programs: Teachers as grass-roots change agents.* Boston: Allyn & Bacon.

Fullan, M. (1993). *Change forces: Probing the depths of educational reform.* New York: Falmer Press.

Fullan, M. (1995). The school as a learning organization: Distant dreams. *Theory into Practice,* 34(4), 230–245.

Goldenberg, C. (1997). *Settings for change* [Videotape]. Long Beach, CA: Small Island Multimedia.

Grimmett, P., & Crehan, E. P. (1992). The nature of collegiality in teacher development: The case of clinical supervision. In M. Fullan & A. Hargreaves (Eds.), *Teacher development and educational change* (pp. 56–85). London: Falmer Press.

Guthrie, J. T. (1996). Educational contexts for engagement in literacy. *The Reading Teacher, 49,* 432–445.

Hargreaves, A. (1995). Renewal in the age of paradox. *Educational Leadership, 52*(7), 14–19.

Hargreaves, A., & Dawe, R. (1990). Paths of professional development: Contrived collegiality, collaborative culture, and the case of peer coaching. *Teaching and Teacher Education, 6,* 227–241.

Hawley, W., & Valli, L. (1999). The essentials of effective professional development: A new consensus. In L. Darling-Hammond & G. Sykes (Eds.), *Teaching as a learning profession: Handbook of policy and practice* (pp. 127–150). San Francisco: Jossey-Bass.

Haynes, N., Emmons, C., & Woodruff, D. (1998). School development program effects: Linking implementation to outcomes. *Journal of Education for Students Placed at Risk, 3,* 71–85.

Hodges, H. L. B. (1996). Using research to inform practice in urban schools: 10 key strategies for success. *Educational Policy, 10,* 223–252.

Invernizzi, M., Rosemary, C., Juel, C., & Richards, H. (1997). At-risk readers and community volunteers: A three-year perspective. *Scientific Studies of Reading, 1,* 277–300.

Jackson, P. (1968). *Life in classrooms.* New York: Holt, Rinehart & Winston.

Joyce, B., & Showers, B. (1995). *Student achievement through staff development: Fundamentals of school renewal* (2nd ed.). White Plains, NY: Longman.

Knapp, M., & Associates. (Eds.). (1995). *Teaching for meaning in high poverty classrooms.* New York: Teachers College Press.

Knapp, M., Shields, P., & Padilla, C. (1995). The school and district environment for meaning-oriented instruction. In M. Knapp & Associates (Eds.), *Teaching for meaning in high poverty classrooms* (pp. 160–182). New York: Teachers College Press.

Little, J. W., & McLaughlin, M. W. (Eds.). (1993). *Teachers' work: Individuals, colleagues, and contexts.* New York: Teachers College Press.

Lortie, D. (1975). *Schoolteacher: A sociological study.* Chicago: University of Chicago Press.

Morrow, L. M., & O'Connor, E. (1995). Literacy partnerships for change with "at-risk" kindergartners. In R. Allington & S. Walmsley (Eds.), *No quick fix: Rethinking literacy programs in America's elementary schools* (pp. 97–115). New York: Teachers College Press.

National Education Commission on Time and Learning. (1994). *Prisoners of time: Schools and programs making time work for students and teachers.* Washington, DC: U.S. Government Printing Office.

Newmann, F. M., & Wehlage, G. G. (1995). *Successful school restructuring* (A report to the public and educators by the Center on Organization and Restructuring of Schools). Madison: University of Wisconsin–Madison.

O'Neil, J. (1995). On schools as learning organizations: A conversation with Peter Senge. *Educational Leadership, 52*(7), 20–23.

Purnell, S., & Hill, P. (1992). *Time for reform.* Santa Monica, CA: RAND.

Raywid, M. (1993). Finding time for collaboration. *Educational Leadership, 51*(1), 30–34.

Richardson, V. (1998). Professional development in the instruction of reading. In J. Osborn & F. Lehr (Eds.), *Literacy for all: Issues in teaching and learning* (pp. 303–318). New York: Guilford Press.

Rosenholtz, S. (1991). *Teachers' workplace: The social organization of schools.* New York: Teachers College Press.

Rowan, B. (1990). Commitment and control: Alternative strategies for the organizational design of schools. In C. Cazden (Ed.), *Review of research in education* (Vol. 16, pp. 353–389). Washington, DC: American Educational Research Association.

Santa, C. M. (1997). School change and literacy engagement: Preparing teaching and learning environments. In J. Guthrie & A. Wigfield (Eds.), *Reading engagement: Motivating readers through integrated instruction* (pp. 218–233). Newark, DE: International Reading Association.

Sarason, S. (1971). *The culture of the school and the problem of change.* Boston: Allyn & Bacon.

Senge, P. (1990). *The fifth discipline.* New York: Doubleday.

Sergiovanni, T. J. (1990). *Value-added leadership: How to get extraordinary performance in schools.* New York: Harcourt Brace Jovanovich.

Smith, L., Ross, S., & Casey, J. (1996). Multi-site comparison of the effects of Success for All on reading achievement. *Journal of Literacy Research, 28*, 329–353.

Smith, M., & O'Day, J. (1990). Systemic school reform. In S. Fuhrman & B. Malen (Eds.), *The politics of curriculum and testing* (pp. 233–267). Philadelphia: Falmer Press.

Smylie, M. A. (1995). Teacher learning in the workplace: Implications for school reform. In T. R. Guskey & M. Huberman (Eds.), *Professional development in education: New paradigms and practices* (pp. 92–113). New York: Teachers College Press.

Snow, C. E., Burns, M. S., & Griffin, P. (Eds.). (1998). *Preventing reading difficulties in young children.* Washington, DC: National Academy Press.

Walmsley, S., & Allington, R. (1995). Redefining and reforming instructional support programs for at-risk students. In R. Allington & S. Walmsley (Eds.), *No quick fix: Rethinking literacy programs in America's elementary schools* (pp. 19–44). New York: Teachers College Press.

Watts, G. D., & Castle, S. (1993). The time dilemma in school restructuring. *Phi Delta Kappan, 75*, 306–310.

Winfield, L. (1995). Change in urban schools with high concentrations of low-income children: Chapter I schoolwide projects. In R. Allington & S. Walmsley (Eds.), *No quick fix: Rethinking literacy programs in America's elementary schools* (pp. 214–235). New York: Teachers College Press.

CHAPTER TWELVE

Fostering Home and Community Connections to Support Children's Reading

SUSAN SONNENSCHEIN
DIANE SCHMIDT

There is now a large body of evidence showing that parental involvement in children's schooling has an important influence on children's attitudes and achievement (e.g., Cairney, 1997; Dauber & Epstein, 1993). Parental involvement during the preschool years helps the child develop a foundation for the teacher to build upon when the child enters school and continues to be important even afterward (Adams, 1990; Baker, 1999). Parental involvement can be beneficial for at least three reasons:

1. Parental involvement may increase the frequency of children's literacy and literacy-related experiences.
2. Parental involvement may convey a message to the *child* about the importance of school.
3. Parental involvement may convey a message to the *teacher* that this parent cares about his/her child's schooling.

Unfortunately, too often what teachers want and expect of parents may be inconsistent either with what parents think is expected of them *or* with what they have to offer. The mismatch in expectations is most likely to occur when teachers and families come from different backgrounds. It is the child who typically bears the brunt of a mismatch between the home and the school by not doing well in school.

The goal of this chapter is to suggest some ways that teachers can facilitate effective parental involvement in children's education and can utilize community resources to benefit children. The chapter is organized into sections corresponding to five guiding principles, each of which serves as the heading of the relevant section. The first section discusses the importance of establishing a partnership between parents and teachers. The second section provides a brief review of parental practices that contribute to children's reading development. Although most of the data in this section focus on the role of the home, some data about the importance of congruence between home and school are presented as well. The third section focuses on the importance of understanding parental beliefs about children's learning and development in order to understand differences in parents' practices. In the fourth section, we discuss factors that can lead to parents' involvement in their children's schooling, including specific suggestions that teachers can implement to facilitate such involvement. The fifth section presents community resources that a teacher can draw upon to augment opportunities available at home.

THE FOUNDATION FOR EFFECTIVE HOME–SCHOOL CONNECTIONS SHOULD BE A PARTNERSHIP BASED ON RESPECT AND UNDERSTANDING

Many theorists and practitioners believe that a child's success in school is facilitated when there is a partnership between the child's home and school (e.g., Bronfenbrenner, 1979; Comer & Haynes, 1991; Connors & Epstein, 1995; Swap, 1993). In fact, establishing partnerships between schools, homes and communities is mandated by current federal policy and legislation such as Goals 2000 and Title I (Epstein, Coates, Salinas, Sanders, & Simon, 1997) and is the keystone for several nationally recognized intervention programs. For example, Epstein et al. (1997) discussed six types of involvement to increase communication and to improve working relationships between home, school, and community: (1) *parenting*—helping all families establish home environments supportive of students' learning; (2) *communicating*—designing effective means of school-to-home and home-to-school communication; (3) *volunteering*—recruiting and organizing parental help and support; (4) *learning at home*—providing information and ideas to families to increase knowledge about ways to help with homework and to increase knowledge of the curriculum; (5) *decision making*—including parents in school decisions; and (6) *collaborating with the community*—identifying and integrating community resources into the school curriculum. Similar approaches attempting to foster alliances between home, school, and community have been developed by Slavin in his Success for All program (see Madden, Slavin, Karweit, Dolan, & Wasik, 1993) and by James Comer in his School Development Program (see Comer & Haynes, 1991).

The cornerstone of any successful relationship between home and school needs to be a shared understanding and agreement about the respective roles of each. Without such an understanding, the home–school relationship will be less than optimal. MacLeod (1996) discussed two reasons why teachers' attempts to get parents more involved in their children's education may not work. First, teachers often assume a background or ability that parents do not have. Second, teachers assume that parents need to accommodate to the school without the school similarly accommodating to the parents' interests and needs. We consider ways that teachers can address these issues in some of the subsequent sections.

THE HOME PLAYS AN IMPORTANT ROLE IN FOSTERING CHILDREN'S LITERACY ENGAGEMENT AND DEVELOPMENT

Children growing up in industrialized societies have many opportunities before starting school to interact with print and engage in activities relevant to literacy development (Baker, 1999; Snow, Burns, & Griffin, 1998; Sonnenschein, Brody, & Munsterman, 1996). Although storybook reading is the prototypical activity, other everyday experiences also can be relevant for learning to read. The many forms of printed materials that children see in their environment even before they enter school (e.g., shopping lists, television guides) can help foster an awareness of the purpose of print. The songs children sing can foster a sensitivity to the sounds of one's language, which is an aspect of phonological awareness. Listening to people tell stories about their lives can increase narrative skills. Going on outings and watching television stories can increase one's knowledge of the world. Print awareness, phonological awareness, narrative skills, and world knowledge are all considered relevant for reading development (Baker, Serpell, & Sonnenschein, 1995).

Growing up in a home rich in literacy-relevant opportunities not only influences literacy development but also has a long-lasting impact on a child's desire to learn (Gottfried, Fleming, & Gottfried, 1998). Gottfried et al. (1998) asked parents of 8-year-olds to complete a set of questionnaires focusing on the type and amount of cognitive stimulation available at home. Most of the families were European American, but they varied in socioeconomic status (SES). Children's intrinsic motivations for reading and mathematics were assessed when they were 9, 10, and 13 years old. Regardless of the family's SES, growing up in a cognitively stimulating environment positively influenced the children's motivation at each age.

Although all children in industrialized societies have exposure to literacy-relevant materials, there are differences in the nature and frequency of experiences as a function of SES. Before the average middle-income child starts elementary school, he/she has spent hundreds of hours at home reading with family members (Adams, 1990). Such reading interactions help children develop a foundation of relevant early literacy knowledge (e.g., knowledge about print, phonological awareness) upon which teachers can build. Equally important, these early home experiences help foster a positive attitude toward reading (Baker, Scher, & Mackler, 1997; Scarborough & Dobrich, 1994).

What appear to be normative experiences for most middle-income children are not necessarily so for low-income children. Heath (1983) has suggested that children from low-income backgrounds engage in different types of reading interactions and oral conversations with their families than do middle-income children. For example, in low-income families there often is less parent–child storybook reading and less discussion about books that are read. Even when parents discuss books with their children, such discussions are less likely to go beyond the immediate text and therefore these children are less likely to acquire skills thought to be relevant for later reading development (Snow, 1991).

In addition to differences in the amount and nature of book reading experiences, mother–child conversational patterns may vary across low-income and middle-income families. For example, Snow (1983) suggested that middle-income mothers are more likely than low-income mothers to require their children to make remarks contingent upon prior ones. Such discourse prepares children for the type of explicit language commonly used in text.

Until recently many schools seem to have operated under the assumption that all children arrive at school with middle-income experiences and knowledge (Tharp & Gallimore, 1988). Due to the nature of their home experiences prior to entering school, children from low-income families often do not display the knowledge expected by their teachers and have difficulty succeeding in school. The differences evident when children start school increase as they proceed through school (Alexander & Entwisle, 1988).

Once middle-income children enter elementary school, their parents continue to be involved in their education (Dauber & Epstein, 1993; Eccles & Harold, 1996). These parents, especially mothers, are particularly involved when their children are in elementary school; they monitor homework, read with their children, and are generally supportive of the schools. When middle-income parents have concerns about how their children are doing, they initiate contact with teachers. Teachers expect this form of support and inter-action. When it does not occur, teachers may erroneously assume that parents do not care or are not involved in their children's education.

Lareau (1996) described differences between middle- and low-income families in parents' involvement in their children's schooling. Middle-income parents were more likely to initiate interactions with their children's teachers than were low-income parents. Low-income parents, in contrast, even when they had concerns about their child's success in school, did not initiate interactions with the teachers. Teachers' assumptions about parental involvement may influence teachers' expectations for children's success in school, which in turn influences how teachers interact with the students (Snow, Barnes, Chandler, Goodman, & Hemphill, 1991).

Although what goes on at home and what goes on at school both contribute to children's reading development, there has been little research explicitly relating the two. Snow et al. (1991) considered how the relation between the home and the school can affect growth in children's reading comprehension. They interviewed and observed parents and teachers of around 30 low-income elementary school children. Children's classrooms were rated over a 2-year period for instructional quality, emotional climate, and literacy environment. Homes were rated for parental literacy, availability of literacy experiences for the child, organization, and emotional stability. Ratings in each category were summed for a home and a school composite. Each child's home and class were categorized, based on the composite ratings, as high or low. If a child's class were rated as high one year but low the next, the final rating for school was mixed. Children were classified based on whether they showed 2 years of growth in reading comprehension. The sample size was low, so the findings should be viewed as only suggestive. Nevertheless, they illustrate the importance of considering the relation between home and school factors. A home with a high rating could compensate for 1 year but not 2 years of low-rated school experiences. Two years of high-rated schooling could compensate for a low-rated home, but 1 year of high and 1 year of low school experiences could not.

TEACHERS NEED TO LEARN ABOUT THE STRENGTHS, NEEDS, BELIEFS, AND PRACTICES OF EACH STUDENT'S FAMILY IN ORDER TO DESIGN MORE EFFECTIVE PROGRAMS AND MAXIMIZE PARENTS' INVOLVEMENT

Although it is reasonable to assume that all parents want their children to learn and do well in school, it is not reasonable to assume that there is a shared understanding of how to accomplish the goal of success in school.

A teacher needs to understand the child's cultural and linguistic background and, more specifically, the beliefs and practices of each child's family. As McCarthey (1997) concluded after noting that establishing home–school connections was easier with students from middle-income backgrounds than with students from nonmainstream backgrounds, "An interest in making home–school connections is not enough—it is imperative for teachers to understand the complexity of students' lives, especially of those students whose backgrounds are different from their own" (p. 176).

Teachers should consider: the language or languages spoken at home, the educational background of the family, the family's beliefs about how children should be taught and their role in the child's education, and the parents' availability to assist with homework. Information about families can be obtained through questionnaires, interviews, or conversations. Although getting the information may add hours to what already is a long day for teachers, the extra time spent should prove beneficial for the students and thus for the teachers as well.

There are several examples in the literature of what happens when there is not consensus between teacher and parents on how children should be taught. Goldenberg, Reese, and Gallimore (1992) discovered that parents of low-income Hispanic kindergartners, when sent Spanish storybooks to read with their children, did not discuss the story, a frequently occurring practice in middle-income families that is thought to foster understanding of narrative text. Instead, the low-income families discussed aspects of the printed words (naming letters, sounding out words) in a manner comparable to what they did when children brought home workbooks.

Delpit (1986) described her experience as a new teacher in an inner-city school as an illustration of how a mismatch in what parents think their children need to learn and what the teacher comes prepared to teach can impact on children. She began by utilizing practices that emphasized the use of authentic literature as a tool for instruction. Her approach was consistent with recommendations from theorists and researchers. However, Delpit's African American students did not progress and their parents were critical of her approach. The parents wanted Delpit to use a more traditional approach that emphasized fundamental skills. When Delpit changed her approach to a more traditional one, the children progressed. Whether children improved due to greater congruence between Delpit's practices and parents' ideas or due to her providing instruction more tailored to the children's needs or both cannot be determined.

There is growing awareness that parents' practices may be influenced by their beliefs, which in turn may be influenced by their cultural background (Sonnenschein et al., 1996). Teachers need to understand parents' beliefs about their children's development in order to design effective instructional programs. As Goldenberg et al. (1992) suggested, "Parent involvement efforts in the area of early literacy might be more effective . . . when [teachers] build on parents' understandings and beliefs about how children learn to become literate" (p. 53).

The need for teachers to understand parental beliefs is particularly important when families do not share the same cultural background as the teacher. Valdes (1996), in an ethnographic study of school children growing up in a Mexican American community, showed that the many differences in beliefs about how children should behave in school or how parents should interact with teachers resulted in these children having a less than optimal educational experience. Consider the beginning-of-the-year "Open House," an annual tradition in most schools in this country. It is a time when parents can meet their children's teachers and learn something about the school program. Valdes (1996) noted that most of the families in her study did not introduce themselves to their children's teachers during their visit and did not view this as an opportunity to get an idea about the nature of the school program.

Three types of parental beliefs may be particularly important for children's reading: ideas about the importance of education, notions of how children learn, and expectations for parental involvement in schooling. Almost all parents stress the importance of education (Sonnenschein, Baker, Serpell, & Schmidt, in press). However, there appear to be differences in how parents from different social groups socialize their young children for school (Baker, 1999; Baker et al., 1995).

The results of a 5-year longitudinal investigation with children from Baltimore, Maryland, called the Early Childhood Project showed that differences in parental beliefs influenced children's literacy acquisition in late preschool and the first few years of elementary school. Low-income parents of children starting elementary school were more likely to view reading as fostered through an emphasis on skills, stressing the use of flashcards and workbooks. Middle-income families were more likely to attempt to engage the child by making interactions enjoyable and allowing the child to choose and initiate activities. The latter approach, one which emphasized engagement, facilitated the development of early literacy competencies, which in turn influenced later reading development.

Stipek, Milburn, Clements, and Daniels (1992) had similar findings. They interviewed parents of preschoolers about the appropriate way to teach basic academic skills to young children. Low-income parents in contrast to middle-income ones were more likely to stress a didactic approach.

After learning about the children's families, teachers should look for opportunities where parents or other family members can engage in relevant activities consistent with their own beliefs about what is important.

There are many areas that are relevant for reading development, including knowledge of the world, phonological analysis, and comprehension. It is also important to engage the child. Teachers should look for situations where there is an intersection between activities parents may value and those important for development. For example, Pelligrini, Perlmutter, Galda, and Brody (1990) found that low-income mothers of preschoolers were more likely to elicit their children's participation when reading expository rather than narrative text. Although we traditionally think of parents reading storybooks with their young children, teachers should encourage the reading of any type of text if there is the potential for engaging the child (see Dreher, Chapter 4, this volume). If parents attempt to elicit their child's participation, the child will probably become more interested in the reading interaction.

In addition to suggesting activities congruent with parents' beliefs, teachers can use their knowledge of a child's family to suggest activities not currently being implemented. Teachers can encourage parents to make children aware of the print in their environments. For example, parents can look with their children at advertisements in newspaper circulars. Children can be encouraged to cut out words from certain categories (food, etc.) and bring these to school to make a word tree that can serve as the basis for a conceptual learning unit (e.g., items sold at stores).

Learning about the backgrounds of one's students should enable teachers to make lessons congruent with the experiences of these students. McCarthey (1997) conducted an ethnographic study of nine children (aged 8–10 years) attending a public school in the Southwest. These children's teachers provided many opportunities for students to read novels, to reflect upon what they had read, and to attempt to draw connections between what they were reading in school and what they were doing at home. Nevertheless, despite the teachers' attempts to connect the world of the home and the school for their students, the program was more suited to students from mainstream backgrounds. Students from low-income *or* minority backgrounds had much more difficulty relating what they were doing at home (which in reality was very different from what was done at school) to what they were doing at school. Consequently the school lessons were less meaningful for them. McCarthey (1997) concluded:

> Selecting books that were not relevant to many students' lives and inadvertently excluding some students from classroom discussions seemed to be rooted in teachers having more information about middle-class students than students from working class or culturally diverse backgrounds. The teachers' practices were rooted in their (erroneous) assumptions that just providing literacy opportunities . . . would result in students' automatically making home–school connections. . . ." (p. 176)

Instead, teachers need to learn what is going on in their students' lives to better tailor instruction.

URGING PARENTS TO BECOME INVOLVED IN THEIR CHILDREN'S EDUCATION IS NOT ENOUGH; TEACHERS OFTEN MUST PROVIDE PARENTS WITH THE TOOLS ENABLING THEM TO DO SO

Although parental involvement may be beneficial for students, not all parents become involved, at least to the degree that some teachers would hope. Better-educated parents are more likely to be actively involved in their children's education than are less-educated parents (MacLeod, 1996). It is the children of this latter group who are more frequently counted among children having difficulty in school.

In the previous section, we reviewed research showing the importance of learning about parents' practices and, especially, their beliefs about how children learn. We included some discussion of how such knowledge could inform teachers' programs and interactions with children and their families. In this section we focus on increasing parents' involvement at home and at school. The section begins by considering factors that influence parents' involvement in their children's schooling and concludes by presenting suggestions for what teachers can do to involve families.

Hoover-Dempsey and Sandler (1997) reviewed research suggesting that a parent's decision to be involved in his/her child's education is based primarily on three factors: the parent's beliefs about the parental role, the parent's sense of efficacy for helping the child succeed in school, and the general push for involvement from the school. There appear to be differences due to sociocultural background in how parents view their role in their child's schooling. For example, although Asian American families push their children to excel in school, this is reflected in their home interactions rather than their presence in their children's schools (Dornbush & Glasgow, 1996). The lack of parental appearance in the classroom may be less of an issue when the child is doing well. It becomes more of an issue when the child is having difficulties. In such cases the parent is viewed as not caring, and the teacher may give the child less attention (Snow et al., 1991).

There is a positive relation between parents' beliefs that they can help their children succeed in school and parents' involvement in their children's schooling (Hoover-Dempsey & Sandler, 1997). Obviously parental self-efficacy is related to parental education. Even parents who have limited education, however, feel able to assist their young children during the first few years of school. Dauber and Epstein (1993) reported that around 75% of their sample of inner-city parents felt able to assist their elementary school children with reading. On the other hand, parents may have competing demands upon their time that limit their availability to assist their children. Dauber and Epstein (1993) found that inner-city parents who worked outside the home were less likely to assist in school, but working status did not deter many of these parents from assisting their children at home. However, working parents reported spending less time helping their children with homework than did nonworking parents.

We also need to consider parents' self-efficacy in conjunction with their ideas about what factors can cause a child to be successful in school and their notions of intelligence (Hoover-Dempsey & Sandler, 1997). For example, if a parent believes a child's school success is due solely to nonmalleable ability, the parent will be less likely to assist his/her child than would a parent who believes school success is due to effort.

A third influence on parental involvement is the parents' perception that their involvement is desired and welcome. Parents tend to be more involved when teachers actively encourage involvement; such pushes for parental involvement are also correlated with children's academic success (Dauber & Epstein, 1993; see Hoover-Dempsey & Sandler, 1997, for a review of research). Merely requesting or welcoming parents' involvement may not be sufficient, however. Teachers should offer suggestions for how parents can assist their children. In fact, one of the best predictors of parental involvement is parents' perceptions that teachers offered them guidelines (Dauber & Epstein, 1993). It is important to realize that parents who feel unsure of themselves may need more encouragement to become involved as well as instruction in how to do so. Unfortunately, in the Dauber and Epstein study (1993), only a third of the elementary school parents reported receiving guidance for checking their children's homework.

Parents' perception that they do not receive guidance about how to help children with homework is one shared by teachers. Eccles and Harold (1996) asked teachers of elementary students to note the frequency with which they made certain types of requests from parents or offered them certain types of guidance. Teachers viewed themselves as frequently (several times a month) encouraging parents to become involved in classroom activities or to monitor their children's work at home. However, only rarely did they offer suggestions for what parents could do to help their children with schoolwork.

Even when parents perceive that their assistance is welcome, requests from teachers may come at nonoptimal times. Dauber and Epstein (1993) examined parental involvement practices and what schools are requesting of them in eight inner-city schools in Baltimore. Parents reported that they had the most time to assist on weekends, a time when most young children are unlikely to be given homework. If teachers truly want parents to be involved with their children's homework, they should give assignments at times when parents are the most available to help.

Grolnick, Benjet, Kurowski, and Apostoleris (1997) also have considered the factors that predict parents' involvement in children's schooling. They discussed three types of involvement: *behavioral*—participating in school activities and/or helping with homework; *cognitive-intellectual*—exposing one's child to intellectually stimulating activities; *personal*—knowing what is going on with the child at school. Different factors or combinations of factors, including self-efficacy of the parent, social support, socioeconomic status of the family, attitude of the teacher, and parental beliefs, predicted each of the three types of involvement. For example, mothers who saw themselves as teachers and who felt able to assist their children were more receptive to teachers' attempts to involve them than were other mothers. Teachers' attempts to involve mothers who were experiencing stress or who had values or attitudes different from the teacher were less receptive to becoming involved.

The remainder of this section addresses what teachers can do to foster parents' participation at home and at school. As teachers attempt to get parents more involved in their children's education, it is important not to become discouraged. Several attempts may be necessary before a parent becomes involved. What works with one parent may not work with another.

Communicating with Families

A key element in getting parents involved in children's educational programs is for teachers to establish a means of communication by soliciting parents' input and being responsive to their concerns (Fredericks & Rasinski, 1990; Rasinski & Fredericks, 1989). Pryor and Church (1995) distinguished between giving parents information relevant to all the children in a class and giving parents information tailored to the specific needs of an individual child. Both types of information are necessary. At the start of the year, teachers should convey to parents, either orally or in writing, what they would like to see in terms of parental assistance with homework. Newsletters or other such communications should be sent frequently from teachers to parents indicating what is occurring in class and informing them of upcoming events.

Additional communication should be tailored to the profile of the individual family. For example, Betty Shockley and Barbara Michalove, teachers in a school in a low-income community in Georgia, used journals to dialogue with parents about what their children were doing in the classroom (see Shockley, Michalove, & Allen, 1995). Children brought the journals back and forth each day between home and school. Parents wrote their reactions to what children were reading at home or concerns they might have; the teacher responded and made additional comments. When later in the year parents reflected upon the year, most families noted how useful and rewarding they had found the journals.

A similar technique was used by Lazar and Weisberg (1996) with the parents of children attending a summer reading clinic. These authors reported that comments in parents' journals were particularly helpful as a source of topics to incorporate into the classroom instructional program.

Although requiring daily journal entries and daily responses by teachers might prove too taxing, teachers could ask parents to keep a weekly journal in which they expressed their concerns or satisfactions with what their child was doing. Teachers could use these journals as a means of offering individualized suggestions for how parents could assist their children. Teachers could also use the knowledge they gain about a child from these journals to structure classroom experiences. Parents whose literacy levels are too low to keep a written journal could be encouraged to tape their thoughts. As part of the ongoing dialogue between teachers and parents, teachers should indicate either how they are modifying the child's program in response to parent-noted concerns or why the concerns may not be consistent with the teacher's opinion.

Fostering Parents' Involvement at Home

Parents will be more likely to become involved if they have the time and believe they have the ability to help their child. Many teachers like parents to assist their children with homework. In planning children's homework assignments, teachers should think about the complexity of people's lives. Assignments, if possible, should be planned for times when parents are available to help. A fairly common and important assignment is having children read at home with a family member. The success of such an assignment depends upon the child having a book, having someone who can listen to the him/her read, and especially having someone whose literacy skills are sufficient to engage the child. All three can be problem areas for certain families.

Many researchers have implemented programs where books from a classroom library are sent home with children (e.g., Come & Fredericks, 1995; Morrow & Young, 1997). Some have even sent home audiocassettes and tape recorders (Koskinen et al., 1995). The results in terms of children's engagement and development were very positive. Interested teachers could create a class-based lending library and send books or stories home with their students. Sending home magazines or books that children have read in class is often useful when the children's parents' literacy levels are low because the children can assist with the reading.

Although having books available is a necessary first step when reading with a child, many parents need additional suggestions about ways to make the interactions engaging and beneficial for the child. In fact, Hannon (1987) found that just sending books home to parents did not increase children's subsequent scores on reading measures relative to a control group. In contrast, Morrow and Young (1997) found that a parent intervention program that provided parents with information about activities that parents could do with their children was more effective in boosting children's reading scores (both their achievement and motivation) than just a school-based intervention.

The discussion that occurs around text is important. By discussing the text, parents can ensure that their children have understood it and can model strategies for comprehension. Parents should ask children questions that encourage them to go beyond the literal meaning of the text. Thus, they should ask children to consider why certain actions took place, to predict events, and so on (see Whitehurst et al., 1994, for additional information).

A common reading experience for many young children is storybook reading. However, narrative is but one genre. Parents should be encouraged to read different genres as well with their children (see Dreher, Chapter 4, this volume). It is important to realize that reading a novel to a child and reading an expository text require the use of different strategies to facilitate comprehension on the part of the child. Warren and Fitzgerald (1997) developed an effective technique for showing parents from different socioeconomic backgrounds ways to read such expository text with their children that resulted in the children being able to understand unfamiliar text when they later independently read it. The critical element in the intervention was that parents taught their children steps for identifying main ideas and supporting details. When parents merely read to their children and asked them to recall as much as they could, understanding was not facilitated.

Teachers interested in providing parents with guidelines for reading with children might invite parents to a workshop where strategies for discussing both narrative and expository text are presented. They could offer parents copies of a videotape demonstrating these strategies to take home with them. Key points could be copied onto a chart distributed to parents as well.

Teachers also should encourage parents to have children read to younger siblings. Fox and Wright (1997) found that having children read age-appropriate stories to their younger siblings was an effective means of fostering fluency and comprehension. It also helped boost the children's self-esteem.

Although reading with children is important, it is not the only activity relevant to facilitating literacy development (Baker, 1999). Some parents have a limited awareness of the array of experiences that foster literacy development. For example, some might overemphasize the use of flashcards or workbooks (Baker, 1999; Sonnenschein et al., 1999). Although developing skills is important, skills may be better acquired in a setting that is more fun and fosters engagement (Sonnenschein et al., 1999).

Providing families with information about activities that foster literacy development is often useful. Thus, parents need to know that listening to and telling stories about events in their lives can foster narrative skills. Playing word games can increase children's phonological awareness. World knowledge is also important for reading development. Judicious selection of television programs by an adult can help increase a child's knowledge about the world as-well as facilitate narrative comprehension, especially if the adult watches with the child and discusses the programs with him/her. Although television shows that have a purposeful educational focus obviously are relevant, even shows that emphasize entertainment often contain useful information. When children are young, mundane activities such as trips to the supermarket can be learning tools. Teachers might also want to include in their newsletter to parents a calendar of upcoming local events of interest, especially free ones, that children and their families could attend.

Fostering Parents' Involvement at School

In addition to encouraging involvement at home, parents should be encouraged to be involved at school. Such involvement can increase their awareness of what is done at school and their support for school programs. Seeing parents involved at school may reinforce for children the notion that school is important and increase their motivation for learning.

Parents need to feel welcome at the school. As much as possible, special events should be scheduled at times convenient for most families. The availability of child care is a necessity for certain families.

Parents should be encouraged to serve as volunteers at the school. Volunteering might be based on a parent's area of expertise. The work of Moll and Greenberg (1990) in Mexican American communities in Arizona is one example of utilizing parents' expertise; the authors used families' "funds of knowledge" to serve as the basis for the curriculum. Teachers visited families of their students to learn about these families' activities and social networks. The goal was to develop instructional modules incorporating family resources and knowledge.

Using families's funds of knowledge can have positive consequences for both children and their families. It can increase children's knowledge of the world, which is important for comprehension. Seeing one's parents playing a role in what is taught at school also can affect children's motivation to learn. Incorporating family knowledge into classroom activities can increase the parents' motivation by helping the parents (who otherwise might feel marginalized due to differences in background, language, or education) realize that their experiences are relevant.

Publicizing contributions by family members is a nice way of thanking participants and encouraging others to participate. Thus, mention can be made in a newsletter or a section of a classroom bulletin board of who has recently volunteered in the class or assisted with an activity.

EFFECTIVE TEACHERS MAKE USE
OF COMMUNITY RESOURCES
TO AUGMENT WHAT IS AVAILABLE AT HOME

Teachers can draw upon a broad array of community resources. Although the specifics of what is available will vary depending upon both the community in which a school is located and the teacher's ingenuity, community resources can be grouped into three broad categories: programs designed to improve adults' literacy skills; mentors or volunteers; and sources of supplies, services, and programs.

Adult or Family Literacy Programs

Some parents do not become involved in their child's education because their own literacy levels are low. However, many communities have adult literacy programs designed to improve parents' reading abilities. Research has shown that adults completing such programs read more to their children, who in turn show improved language and literacy skills (Neuman, 1995; Neuman, Caperelli, & Kee, 1998). The programs vary: some are federally sponsored (e.g., Even Start) whereas others are locally sponsored. Teachers can get information about some family literacy programs from the Internet (e.g., www.ed.gov/Family/Brochures.html; also www.ed.gov/FPIE). Additional descriptions of several such programs are available in a book by Morrow (1995). These are some of the characteristics of successful programs: they provide literacy instruction to any and all members of the family, use a broad-based variety of recruitment plans, emphasize participant involvement in planning and development of the program, use creative scheduling, offer transportation and child care, use experienced teaching staff, have ongoing monitoring of program quality, and have staff who are knowledgeable about the community and resources (Neuman et al., 1998).

Mentors or Volunteers

Teachers can draw on the services of other community members to substitute for unavailable parents. For example, many schools use local senior citizens as volunteers in the classroom. Other schools have started partnerships with community groups (e.g., the Boy Scouts) or businesses (the local post office, newspapers). The nature of these partnerships can vary. In some cases, the partners commit time to helping in the classroom. In other cases, partners serve as role models or mentors to students.

Although volunteers can be effective supplements to a teacher's program, volunteers need training to be effective. Teachers should not assume that any literate adult can just step in and tutor a young child. Wasik (1998) reviewed the characteristics of 17 volunteer tutoring programs. Successful programs, that is, programs where children's reading improved, shared certain common characteristics. They provided sufficient training for the tutors prior to beginning tutoring and monitored progress once tutoring started. Successful tutoring programs included similar core components— reading new material, rereading familiar text, writing activities, activities focusing on word analysis. Successful programs also ensured that the child was an active participant in each session. Thus, if teachers want to make volunteer tutors part of their reading program, they need to provide sufficient training to their tutors prior to commencing the program and to monitor the progress of the children during the program, making changes in instruction as necessary. Training for tutors should include information about what learning to read entails as well as instruction in how to actively involve the child.

Sources of Supplies, Services, or Programs

Teachers also can use community agencies or organizations to give children experiences that they otherwise might not have. Such experiences provide information about the world, which in turn is related to academic achievement. Organizations can serve as the site of a field trip, an instructional module, or an afterschool or summer program. For example, many museums and zoos offer programs that might well be employed as learning tools by schools.

The public library is an important but often underutilized resource, especially by lower-income children (see Baker, 1999, for a discussion). Yet libraries can provide these children access to books and other activities. Ramos and Krashen (1998) described how taking a class of inner-city Hispanic students to a local library and allowing them to take home some books increased their self-reported frequency of reading. These children's self-reports were confirmed by independent reports given by their parents.

Teachers can ask businesses and groups in the community to donate needed supplies. For example, stores and businesses in the neighborhood might have a book drop where customers could bring in children's books they no longer wanted. These books could then form the basis of an in-class library or a class-based lending library (see Chambliss & McKillop, Chapter 5, this volume).

Churches or religious organizations often provide or support family literacy services. Teachers can contact leaders of such organizations to request support for their efforts. For example, ministers can discuss with parents the importance of participating in family literacy programs and becoming more involved in children's education. In addition, ministers might be able to encourage congregants to volunteer in the schools.

The Internet also can serve as a resource to teachers. A recent search indicated many sites pertinent for teachers. There were three that seemed particularly pertinent. The web page for the U.S. Department of Education (http://www.ed.gov/) has links to listings of government-published pamphlets for parents (www.ed.gov/pubs/parents.html) and links to a site listing ways to foster family and community involvement (Family Involvement Partnership for Learning, www.ed.gov/Family/Brochures. html). The Web page for the Partnership for Family Involvement (http:// www.ed.gov/PFIE) provides information about current developments in education with an emphasis on ways to foster involvement from families and other groups. The Web page for Read Write Now (http://www. udel.edu/ETL/RWN/) provides a listing of reading and writing activities for children from birth through sixth grade that parents can encourage at home.

CONCLUSIONS

Home and community connections are critical to children's reading development. Both the home and the school play important roles in fostering children's literacy engagement and development. A parent's influence on a child's literacy development starts before the child enters school and continues throughout the school years. Once a child enters school, effective teachers help facilitate the establishment of a partnership between home and school, one based on mutual respect and understanding.

Although all parents want their children to succeed in school, there are individual and sociocultural differences in parents' involvement in their children's schooling. It is often not sufficient just to urge parents to become involved in their child's education; teachers must provide parents with the tools to enable effective involvement. Such tools can only be developed after teachers learn about each student's family—their strengths, needs, beliefs, and practices. By understanding a child's family situation, teachers can improve communication with the family; they can devise instructional programs that capitalize upon the strengths of the family; they can offer suggestions to compensate for weaknesses within the family.

Effective teachers also make use of community resources. Community members and organizations can augment what is available at home, provide role models, and be a source of supplies and information.

RECOMMENDED READINGS

Baker, L. (1999). Opportunities at home and in the community that foster reading engagement. In J. T. Guthrie & D. E. Alvermann (Eds.), *Engaged reading: Processes, practices and policy implications* (pp. 105–133). New York: Teachers College Press.

This chapter provides general information about reading development and, more specifically, home influences on reading development.

Epstein, J. L., Coates, L., Salinas, K. C., Sanders, M. G., & Simon, B. S. (1997). *School, family, and community partnerships: Your handbook for action.* Thousand Oaks, CA: Corwin Press.

This book is particularly helpful in addressing ways to involve community members in school programs. It contains many handouts for teachers to use.

Fredericks, A. D., & Rasinski, T. V. (1990). Involving the uninvolved: How to. *The Reading Teacher, 43,* 424–425.

The article contains many helpful suggestions for ways to involve family members in their children's schooling.

Shockley, B., Michalove, B., & Allen, J. B. (1995). *Engaging families: Connecting home and school literacy communities.* Portsmouth, NH: Heinemann.

The authors include a detailed description of the journal exchange used as a means of communication between parents and teachers.

REFERENCES

Adams, M. J. (1990). *Beginning to read: Thinking and learning about print.* Cambridge, MA: MIT Press.

Alexander, K. L., & Entwisle, D. R. (1988). Achievement in the first 2 years of school: Patterns and processes. *Monographs of the Society for Research in Child Development, 53,* 1–157.

Baker, L. (1999). Opportunities at home and in the community that foster reading engagement. In J. T. Guthrie & D. E. Alvermann (Eds.), *Engaged reading: Processes, practices and policy implications* (pp. 105–133). New York: Teachers College Press.

Baker, L., Scher, D., & Mackler, K. (1997). Home and family influences on motivations for reading. *Educational Psychologist, 32,* 69–82.

Baker, L., Serpell, R., & Sonnenschein, S. (1995). Opportunities for literacy-related learning in the homes of urban preschoolers. In L. Morrow (Ed.), *Family literacy: Multiple perspectives to enhance literacy development* (pp. 236–252). Newark, DE: International Reading Association.

Bronfenbrenner, U. (1979). *The ecology of human development.* Cambridge, MA: Harvard University Press.

Cairney, T. H. (1997). Acknowledging diversity in home literacy practices: Moving towards partnership with parents. *Early Child Development and Care, 127/128,* 61–73.

Come, B., & Fredericks, A. D. (1995). Family literacy in urban schools: Meeting the needs of at-risk children. *The Reading Teacher, 48,* 566–570.

Comer, J., & Haynes, N. (1991). Parent involvement in the schools: An ecological approach. *Elementary School Journal, 91,* 271–277.

Connors, L. J., & Epstein, J. L. (1995). Parent and school partnerships. In M. H. Bornstein (Ed.), *Handbook of parenting* (Vol. 2, pp. 437–458). Hillsdale, NJ: Erlbaum.

Dauber, S. L., & Epstein, J. L. (1993). Parents' attitudes and practices of involvement in inner-city elementary and middle schools. In N. F. Chavkin (Ed.), *Families and schools in a pluralistic society* (pp. 2–71). Albany: State University of New York Press.

Delpit, L. D. (1986). Skills and other dilemmas of a progressive black educator. *Harvard Educational Review, 56,* 379–385.

Dornbush, S. M., & Glasgow, K. L. (1996). The structural context of family–school relations. In A. Booth & J. F. Dunn (Eds.), *Family–school links: How do they affect educational outcomes?* (pp. 35–44). Mahwah, NJ: Erlbaum.

Eccles, J. S., & Harold, R. D. (1996). Family involvement in children's and adolescents' schooling. In A. Booth & J. F. Dunn (Eds.), *Family–school links: How do they affect educational outcomes?* (pp. 3–34). Mahwah, NJ: Erlbaum.

Epstein, J. L., Coates, L., Salinas, K. C., Sanders, M. G., & Simon, B. S. (1997). *School, family, and community partnerships: Your handbook for action.* Thousand Oaks, CA: Corwin Press.

Fox, B. J., & Wright, M. (1997). Connecting school and home literacy experiences. *The Reading Teacher, 1997,* 396–403.

Fredericks, A. D., & Rasinski, T. V. (1990). Involving the uninvolved: How to. *The Reading Teacher, 43,* 424–425.

Goldenberg, C., Reese, L., & Gallimore, R. (1992). Effects of literacy materials from school on Latino children's home experiences and early reading achievement. *American Journal of Education, 100,* 497–537.

Gottfried, A. E., Fleming, J. S., & Gottfried, A. W. (1998). Role of cognitively stimulating home environment in children's academic intrinsic motivation: A longitudinal study. *Child Development, 69,* 1448–1460.

Grolnick, W. S., Benjet, C., Kurowski, C. O., & Apostoleris, N. H. (1997). Predictors of parent involvement in children's schooling. *Journal of Educational Psychology, 89,* 538–548.

Hannon, P. (1987). A study of the effects of parental involvement in the teaching of reading on children's reading test performance. *British Journal of Educational Psychology, 57,* 56–72.

Heath, S. B. (1983). *Way with words: Language, life, and work in communities and classrooms.* Cambridge, MA: Harvard University Press.

Hoover-Demsey, K. V., & Sandler, H. M. (1997). Why do parents become involved in their children's education? *Review of Educational Research, 67,* 3–42.

Koskinen, P. S., Blum, I. H., Tennant, N., Parker, E. M., Straub, M. W., & Curry, C. (1995). Have you heard any good books lately?: Encouraging shared reading at home with books and audiotapes. In L. Morrow (Ed.), *Family literacy: Multiple perspectives to enhance literacy development* (pp. 236–252). Newark, DE: International Reading Association.

Lareau, A. (1996). Assessing parent involvement in schooling: A critical analysis. In A. Booth & J. F. Dunn (Eds.), *Family–school links: How do they affect educational outcomes?* (pp. 54–64). Mahwah, NJ: Erlbaum.

Lazar, A. M., & Weisberg, R. (1996). Inviting parents' perspectives: Building home–school partnerships to support children who struggle with literacy. *The Reading Teacher, 50*, 228–237.

MacLeod, F. (1996). Integrating home and school resources to raise literacy levels of parents and children. *Early Child Development and Care, 117*, 123–132.

Madden, N. A., Slavin, R. E., Karweit, N. L., Dolan, L. J., & Wasik, B. A. (1993). Success for all: Longitudinal effects of a restructuring program for inner-city elementary schools. *American Educational Research Journal, 30*, 123–148.

McCarthey, S. J. (1997). Connecting home and school literacy practices in classrooms with diverse populations. *Journal of Literacy Research, 29*, 145–182.

Moll, L., & Greenberg, J. (1990). Creating zones of possibilities: Combining social contexts for instruction. In L. C. Moll (Ed.), *Vygotsky and education* (pp. 319–348). NY: Cambridge University Press.

Morrow, L. M. (Ed.). (1995). *Family literacy: Connections in schools and communities.* Newark, DE: International Reading Association.

Morrow, L. M., & Young, J. (1997). A family literacy program connecting school and home: Effects on attitude, motivation, and literacy achievement. *Journal of Educational Psychology, 89*, 736–742.

Neuman, S. B. (1995). Enhancing adolescent mothers' guided participation in literacy. In L. Morrow (Ed.), *Family literacy: Multiple perspectives to enhance literacy development* (pp. 104–114). Newark, DE: International Reading Association.

Neuman, S. B., Caperelli, B. J., & Kee, C. (1998). Literacy learning, a family matter. *The Reading Teacher, 52*, 244–252.

Pei, A., Pelligrini, A. D., Perlmutter, J. C., Galda, L., & Brody, G. H. (1990). Joint book reading between black Head Start children and their mothers. *Child Development, 61*, 443–453.

Pryor, E., & Church, B. (1995). Family–school partnerships for the 21st century. *Reading and Writing Quarterly: Overcoming Learning Difficulties, 11*, 297–303.

Ramos, F., & Krashen, S. (1998). The impact of one trip to the public library: Making books available may be the best incentive for reading. *The Reading Teacher, 57*, 614–615.

Rasinski, T. V., & Fredericks, A. D. (1989). Can parents make a difference? *The Reading Teacher, 43*, 84–85.

Scarborough, H. S., & Dobrich, W. (1994). On the efficacy of reading to preschoolers. *Developmental Review, 14*, 245–302.

Shockley, B., Michalove, B., & Allen, J. B. (1995). *Engaging families: Connecting home and school literacy communities.* Portsmouth, NH: Heinemann.

Snow, C. E. (1983). Literacy and language: Relationships during the preschool years. *Harvard Educational Review, 53*, 165–189.

Snow, C. E. (1991). The theoretical basis for relationships between language and literacy in development. *Journal of Research in Childhood Education, 6*, 5–10.

Snow, C. E., Barnes, W. S., Chandler, J., Goodman, I. F., & Hemphill, L. (1991). *Unfulfilled expectations: Home and school influences on literacy.* Cambridge, MA: Harvard University Press.

Snow, C. E., Burns, M. S., & Griffin, P. (Eds.). (1998). *Preventing reading difficulties in young children.* Washington, DC: National Academy Press.

Sonnenschein, S., Baker, L., Serpell, R., & Schmidt, D. (in press). Reading is a source of entertainment: The importance of the home perspective for children's literacy development. In K. Roskos & J. Christie (Eds.), *Literacy and play in the early years: Cognitive, ecological, and sociocultural perspectives.* Mahwah, NJ: Erlbaum.

Sonnenschein, S., Brody, G., & Munsterman, K. (1996). The influence of family beliefs and practices on children's early reading development. In L. Baker, P. Afflerbach, & D. Reinking (Eds.), *Developing engaged readers in school and home communities* (pp. 1–20). Mahwah, NJ: Erlbaum.

Stipek, D., Milburn, S., Clements, D., & Daniels, D. H. (1992). Parents' beliefs about appropriate education for young children. *Journal of Applied Developmental Psychology, 13,* 293–
300.

Swap, S. (1993). *Developing home–school partnerships.* New York: Teachers College Press.

Tharp, R. R., & Gallimore, R. (1988). *Rousing minds to life.* Cambridge, UK: Cambridge University Press.

Valdes, G. (1996). Con respeto: *Bridging the distances between culturally diverse families and
schools–An ethnographic portrait.* New York: Teachers College Press.

Warren, L., & Fitzgerald, J. (1997). Helping parents to read expository literature to their children: Promoting main-idea and detail understanding. *Reading Research and Instruction,
36,* 341–360.

Wasik, B. A. (1998). Volunteer tutoring programs in reading: A review. *Reading Research Quarterly, 33,* 266–292.

Whitehurst, G. J., Epstein, J. N., Angell, A. L., Payne, A. C., Crone, D. A., & Fischel, J. E. (1994).
Outcomes of an emergent literacy intervention in Head Start. *Journal of Educational Psychology, 86,* 542–555.

CHAPTER THIRTEEN

Achieving Expertise
in Teaching Reading

PATRICIA A. ALEXANDER
HELENROSE FIVES

As the second graders arrive for another day of school, Moira Redcliff greets each with a warm smile and a few words that convey her interest and concern for her students: "Hi, Emma. Is your grandmother still visiting?" "Boy, I like that sweater, Jackson." "Morris, did you bring that permission slip for the field trip?"

This same kind of interest and concern is evident in the way Moira has approached her first year of teaching at Milam Elementary School. Moira began this first year armed with the latest theories and techniques she learned in her elementary education program and with a real desire to make a difference in students' lives. But her desires and expectations have not been realized in the way she hoped. Moira spent many a long night designing her lessons and preparing instructional materials, proof of which can be seen in a quick glance around the room. There are several colorful bulletin boards or learning areas, for instance, and samples of the children's work hang everywhere. But there are visual clues that things are not operating to perfection in Room 240. Books that are apparently part of the reading corner are pretty scant in number and in poor condition. Some are strewn on the floor. There is also a behavior management chart prominently displayed on the front board, and it is filled with names and strings of check marks. What appear to be the remnants of an unfinished project on Native Americans sit on the window ledge, along with piles of unmarked papers and workbooks.

As we observe Moira during her language arts period, we witness what might best be described as controlled chaos. Two children move aimlessly around the room. Others work together on an assigned worksheet or gather in the reading corner for Sustained Silent Reading. Within these clusters, however, one or two students are bickering about what they are supposed to do, while several others are clearly engaged in off-task behaviors.

At the moment, Moira is sitting with a group of six children who are reading aloud from a storybook about a young Native American girl. Except when she occasionally stops to reprimand the class about their behavior or to answer some child's question about the worksheet assignment, Moira directs her attention to the group in front of her. We note that the book seems pretty difficult for several of the children who struggle along with Ms. Redcliff's periodic assistance: "The word is teepee, Aman. See the teepee in the picture. Do you remember the teepees we made during art on Tuesday? Good. Now you read, Nadeen."

When we have a chance to sit down with Moira and talk about the class, we sense her concern and frustration. The techniques she learned about in college, like discovery learning and reciprocal teaching, are not working the way they should. Even though she knows she is expected to be doing multiple groups, she finds it difficult to maintain control. Not only that—she is not sure what the children are getting from these different activities. Having had only one reading class just did not prepare her for the diversity and complexity she faces every day. Mrs. Robinson, Moira's mentor teacher, makes all this look so easy.

Concerns about grading and testing also loom large for Moira. She finds it difficult to judge her students' reading skills. There are the standardized test scores, of course, but relating those to what the children are doing in the classroom or explaining them to the parents are other things entirely. So, here she sits with this district curriculum that she is expected to cover—a laundry list of techniques and methods she feels she should be implementing—and 19 lively and diverse second graders who need her constant attention. No wonder she goes home each day with sore feet and a terrible headache. Moira had heard that the first year of teaching is the toughest, and she is certainly no quitter. However, there are days when she is simply not sure if she will make it. Is she ever going to learn how to help her students become good readers or writers, as she has dreamed? What does it take to become a master teacher like Mrs. Robinson anyway?

It is easy to understand Moira's admiration for Mrs. Robinson. Dorothy Robinson certainly deserves her reputation as a master teacher. After 12 years, her classroom literally hums with activity, and every corner of the classroom is alive with learning. Currently, five children sit in beanbag chairs or on carpet squares in the library corner engrossed in reading, while two others work at the computer composing a book critique for the class' Web page. Mrs. Robinson modified the concept of book clubs to create Web Book Buddies—an on-line book club. She is sharing this idea with colleagues next week at a literacy conference.

These second graders love having their own classroom Web page. Children from all over the world have read their book reviews and creative writings. Some of the books that their Web buddies have suggested are now in their classroom library. The parents are also excited about the Web page and other activities going on in Mrs. Robinson's room. They often volunteer to help on class projects, like the book quilt in which each child designs and sews a quilt square portraying his/her favorite book.

Mrs. Robinson is presently working with a small group of students on the skill of fact versus fiction. After she discussed and modeled strategies for telling fact from fiction, she asked the children to find three examples of each in the pile of magazines and newspapers spread on the table. The children are now engaged in sharing their choices. If the group agrees with the student's explanation, the example becomes part of a "Fact or Fiction Collage."

Suddenly Mrs. Robinson becomes aware that another group of students, working in pairs on their practice and reinforcement sheets, is skirting the edges of "on-task" behavior. Without saying a word or moving from her chair, Mrs. Robinson raises two fingers in the air. As students take notice, they mimic the gesture until the room is suddenly still. Then Mrs. Robinson simply lowers her hand and the children return to their activities in a more focused way. This is one technique that Dorothy Robinson plans to share with Moira Redcliff at their next coffee chat.

All who have entered the teaching profession can identify and sympathize with Moira Redcliff, our beginning teacher. Her story may not be unique, but it is an excellent reminder that achieving expertise in the teaching of reading takes more than desire and a college diploma. The challenges facing even proficient teachers like Mrs. Robinson, dedicated to guiding the development of young readers, are great. Certainly, the editors and authors of this volume understand those many challenges, which is why this rich and informative portrayal of effective reading practices has been offered. Yet, as our opening scenario suggests, success at teaching reading is not just a matter of understanding assessment or grouping practices, or of knowing how to infuse reading throughout the curriculum. It is all of these—and more. Effective teaching of reading demands that educators weave these bodies of knowledge together into coherent principles and practices for reading instruction that direct everyday interactions within classrooms. This, of course, is no simple matter.

Nor should it be assumed that any educator, no matter how well intentioned, well taught, or highly committed, can manifest expertise in these many areas within a few days, a few months, or a few years of professional practice. The road to expertise in any profession is long and, at times, arduous. The field of reading education is no exception. As a matter of fact, the inherent difficulty and complexity of teaching any content to a learner of any age is exacerbated when we weigh the demands of teaching as fundamental and controversial a subject matter as reading. Add to this formula the fact that young children, the focus of this instruction, are undergoing tremendous cognitive growth and development during this period. For these young minds, the whole social and cultural experience of formal schooling is, itself, new and confusing.

Although Mrs. Robinson, Moira's mentor teacher, conveys ease, naturalness, and confidence in her teaching, she was not born an expert reading teacher. She has undoubtedly honed her skills over the years. Indeed, it has been said that it often takes up to 10 years of dedicated study and practice to become a master in any field of endeavor (Gardner, 1993). This is true even for recognized geniuses in their fields like Wolfgang Amadeus Mozart or Stephen Hawking. However, time alone does not ensure that a person will master music or astrophysics, or the domain of reading education. To the contrary, the seeds of development must be present if a teacher like Ms. Redcliff ever hopes to become an expert at teaching reading like Mrs. Robinson. The seeds of development we discuss here are knowledge, motivation, and strategic processing. When these seeds exist and are suitably nurtured, time and opportunity allow them to mature and flower.

Further, one does not change overnight from a novice to an expert. The journey toward expertise takes time and entails the crucial intermediary period of competence. Moreover, not everyone who sets out to become an expert teacher of reading will realize this laudable goal. Some will even fail to become competent at this endeavor. That is because individuals on the path to expertise must progress through certain identifiable stages of development, each marked by particular challenges of mind and spirit (Alexander, 1997). Only if these challenges are met can an individual continue to grow and develop as a reading educator. An awareness of the challenges that lie ahead can serve as a road map for educators undertaking this important journey.

Thus, our purpose in this chapter is to identify the seeds of professional development and to describe the journey toward expertise in the form of stages that teachers of reading must reach. We also explore each of these developmental stages in terms of the defining attributes that become benchmarks of significant progress toward expertise. The goal is to furnish those interested in teaching reading with crucial landmarks against which they can judge their own performance or that of others. Finally, we draw on research in literacy, expertise, motivation, development, and teacher education to forward recommendations that can aid those interested in becoming expert teachers of reading in the elementary grades.

THE SEEDS OF DEVELOPMENT

If the contents of this volume were distilled to their essence, we would find at least three fundamental ingredients that define effective reading instruction: knowledge, motivation, and strategic processing. We refer to these as the seeds of development.

Knowledge

What some call the most rudimentary seed of development in any complex domain is knowledge (e.g., Chi, Glaser, & Farr, 1988; diSessa, 1982). In relation to becoming expert teachers of reading, there are at least two categories of knowledge that are mandatory and highly integrated. These are literacy knowledge and pedagogical knowledge. Literacy knowledge encompasses one's breadth of understanding about reading and its related language domains (i.e., writing, listening, and speech). Pedagogical knowledge, by definition, entails an individual's general knowledge about the art, science, or profession of teaching. In effect, it is a truism to say that better teachers of reading know more about reading and more about teaching (Alexander & Jetton, in press). Whether the authors of this volume are discussing word study or comprehension, they are conveying basic literacy content. When they move beyond the summarization of research on word study and detail ways that word study can be instructionally addressed, they are presenting pedagogical knowledge.

All knowledge, including literacy and pedagogical knowledge, can take three forms: declarative, procedural, and conditional. It is the ownership and use of these three forms of knowledge that make a teacher effective. Grasping the definitions of reading terms, such as "digraph" or "comprehension," is an example of declarative knowledge, or "knowing what" (Ryle, 1949), in the realm of literacy. Memorizing the components of particular instructional techniques like reciprocal teaching (Palincsar & Brown, 1984) would be indicative of declarative pedagogical knowledge. Success in the reading classroom demands that teachers not only comprehend the meaning of such ideas but that they can also incorporate such concepts fluidly into their everyday practice, as Mrs. Robinson has done. That means that teachers' procedural understanding, or "knowing how," must be equally well articulated (Anderson, 1987). In addition, fluid execution requires that teachers recognize the instructional conditions under which these aspects of the domain are suitably applied and adjust their instruction accordingly to conform to specific sociocontextual circumstances. This is what Paris, Lipson, and Wixson (1983) describe as conditional knowledge, or "knowing when or where."

For the fluid practice of reading instruction, however, literacy knowledge alone cannot suffice. Literacy knowledge must be continuously wedded to knowledge of teaching (i.e., pedagogical knowledge), as well as to a deep understanding of the developing child. One reason that particular reading techniques such as K-W-L (Ogle, 1986; Dreher, Chapter 4, this volume) or reciprocal teaching have gained favor in the classroom is because they bring strong literacy knowledge and effective pedagogical practice together. Important principles of pedagogical knowledge are also clearly outlined elsewhere in this volume in the chapters addressing strategies for learning from reading (Dreher, Chapter 4), motivation (Wigfield, Chapter 7), and intervention (Graham & Harris, Chapter 3). Further, the consideration of developmental appropriateness in the selection and use of reading and assessment materials (Chambliss & McKillop, Chapter 5, and Leipzig & Afflerbach, Chapter 8, respectively, this volume) amplifies the necessity of both literacy and pedagogical knowledge.

Even as a novice teacher, Ms. Redcliff is aware of the value of knowledge about reading and about pedagogy to effective education. Her words punctuate the fact that declarative knowledge about various reading components or methods must be accompanied by well-developed procedural knowledge. Without both forms of understanding, the "laundry list" of reading methods that she acquired during her education will not necessarily translate into improved reading performance for her 19 second graders. Moira Redcliff is also right to question whether sufficient literacy knowledge can be attained from one course in reading during her preservice preparation. Still, increasing the number of preservice courses, while probably enriching declarative knowledge, may not ensure internalization and effortless execution of such acquired knowledge.

Motivation

The second seed of development is motivation, a term that applies to a wide array of constructs, including teachers' interests, goals, and self-beliefs (Pintrich & Schunk, 1996). Just as it is critical to address children's motivation to read (Wigfield, Chapter 7, this volume), it is imperative to understand what drives teachers' actions and underlies their development as reading instructors. That is to say, teachers' interest in reading and in teaching, their personal goals, and perceptions of their abilities have much to do with their subsequent growth toward proficiency.

For all her concerns, frustrations, and observed limits, Ms. Redcliff conveys a sincere interest in her students and their academic future, as well as a deep commitment to improving her performance. These are positive motivational indicators. They are also hopeful signs that this novice teacher will overcome any initial shortcomings in her instruction and ultimately achieve expertise in teaching reading. Mrs. Robinson's passion for her chosen profession is also quite evident. Yet, even expert teachers face unbelievable complexities every day in the classroom. They also shoulder tremendous responsibility for fostering children's literacy development. Being personally invested in the teaching of reading and believing in their ability to succeed are just two aspects of motivation that can make these complexities and responsibilities bearable (Ashton & Webb, 1986). Later in this chapter, we examine how particular motivational characteristics help propel teachers toward expertise and how these characteristics undergo transformation as the journey toward expertise progresses.

Strategic Processing

The third seed of development that must take root is strategic processing. As defined here, strategic processing entails teachers' capacity to respond to an array of instructional problems, to reason critically and creatively about existing social and contextual circumstances. Graham and Harris's overview of exemplary instructional strategies in Chapter 3 of this volume focuses specifically on this component of professional development. Strategies can be understood as procedures that are purposefully and intentionally invoked when teachers confront certain dilemmas or unexpected events in the classroom (Alexander, Graham, & Harris, 1998). Defined this way, strategic processing differs from skilled performance, because skills are essentially routine practices. Whereas strategies require thought and effort, skills represent more instinctive, habitual forms of problem solving. Mrs. Robinson's use of a simple routine to calm a noisy classroom is an example of her skillful teaching. When this routine fails, undoubtedly she is strategic and utilizes alternative methods to bring about order.

In this chapter, we consider how teachers' patterns of strategic processing change as they progress toward expertise. These changes encompass transformations both in the quantity and the quality of strategies that teachers employ. What is important to remember, however, is that these strategic transformations are accompanied by shifts in teachers' knowledge and in their motivation. Every stage in a teacher's development is marked by this interplay between knowledge, motivation, and strategic processing. Therefore, even though we discussed each of these seeds separately, all three work in synchronicity and significantly impact the others. Thus, if a particular teacher's personal commitment to professional growth is weak, it is unlikely that he/she will exert strategic energy or pursue relevant literacy or pedagogical knowledge. Similarly, if another teacher has a limited strategic repertoire or does not respond well to unexpected events, it is likely that his/her self-beliefs and interest in the profession may be negatively affected over time. For instance, teachers' limited strategies thwart success in the classroom, which in turn influences their self-concept. If educators continue to experience limited success, their interest and dedication decrease, as does their willingness to attempt new innovations and strategies (Ashton & Webb, 1986; Fritz, Miller-Heyl, Kreutzer, & MacPhee, 1995; Tschannen-Moran, Woolfolk-Hoy, & Hoy, 1998). The failure of any one of these seeds of development to survive or to thrive has significant consequences not only for teachers' personal growth but also for the well-being of those they teach.

STAGES ON THE JOURNEY TOWARD EXPERTISE

When individuals set out on any long-term quest, they often envision their journey as occurring in stages. This is certainly true for those educators who seek to become expert teachers of reading. Specifically, in this particular professional quest, teachers endeavoring to become experts must move through three distinct stages of professional development: acclimation, competency, and proficiency (Alexander, 1997). Each is marked by different configurations of knowledge, motivation, and strategic processing.

Acclimation

Acclimation is the initial and a requisite stage of professional growth and development. Every individual who wishes to teach reading must experience acclimation, however frustrating or unpleasant that prospect may seem. In the simplest terms, acclimation is a period of orientation to a complex field. It is a valuable time when educators come to explore and to familiarize themselves with the professional terrain that lies before them. In many complex fields such as medicine or law, this period of acclimation is an expected and appreciated aspect of professional growth and is therefore an orchestrated and extended portion of career development. This is not necessarily the case in education, where beginning teachers are required to achieve full membership in the profession after only a semester or perhaps a year of supervised practice.

Of course, as Moira Redcliff noted, new and veteran teachers alike know how difficult the first year or so of teaching can be. Nevertheless, beyond such an acknowledgment, there is little in the way of an apprenticeship model that supports and guides emerging professionals. Perhaps, because of societal beliefs about teaching and learning, or because of the nature of teacher preparation programs, many novice teachers do not fully appreciate the need to orient themselves to their profession. They mistakenly assume that they leave teacher preparation or certification programs with an adequate base of knowledge about reading and about teaching, resulting in an overconfidence in their existing knowledge and abilities. They may likewise underestimate the complexity of teaching reading to diverse learners with a wide range of abilities and motivation. There is certainly evidence of such prejudgments in the research on teachers' beliefs (Pajares, 1992).

The lack of understanding about the nature and importance of the acclimation period can help to explain the decline in self-confidence, coupled with a growing disillusionment, among those who move from education student to full-time educator. In fact, Soodak and Podell (1997) determined that preservice teachers enter the field with a high, inflated level of "teacher efficacy"—the individual's belief in his/her ability to teach effectively (Pintrich & Schunk, 1996). Generally, teachers' professed self-efficacy drops significantly during the first year of teaching, contributing to a perception of failure. This significant drop dramatically affects novice teachers' attitudes and willingness to continue in the teaching profession (Soodak & Podell, 1997). An accepted period of orientation, beginning during the preservice years, would potentially counter simplistic notions about the ease of teaching reading to children and make the practice of an extended initiation into the community of reading educators accepted and welcomed. The more that beginning teachers like Moira Redcliff recognize that teaching, like any complex profession, requires an extended period of acclimation, the more likely they are to survive and to thrive on their journey toward expertise.

From the studies of expertise in various fields, from arts to physics, we can identify several indicators of acclimation (diSessa, 1982; Ericsson & Smith, 1991). These indicators include restricted and piecemeal knowledge, situation- or task-specific goals and interests, wavering beliefs in one's ability and self-determination, and inefficient strategy use (Alexander, Jetton, & Kulikowich, 1995; Alexander & Murphy, 1998). In light of the minimal attention paid to this important initiation period, we want to consider these characteristics in some detail.

As teachers in acclimation progress toward expertise, there must be significant quantitative and qualitative transformations in their base of relevant knowledge. This is because teachers in acclimation begin their journey with limited knowledge of reading and related literacy domains. In addition, they often possess less knowledge about teaching, in general, than do competent or proficient teachers. This restrictive frame of knowledge is no reflection on these teachers' intellectual abilities or commitment, however, but on the time and opportunity that novice educators have had in which to acquire relevant knowledge. Moreover, what literacy and pedagogical knowledge that novice teachers like Moira Redcliff do possess is often fragmented or disjointed, and it is predominately declarative in nature (Gelman & Greeno, 1989).

Consequently, acclimating teachers may be able to recognize certain text genres, or describe certain instructional techniques to use with narrative, expository, or mixed texts. However, these novice teachers may not grasp the impact that text forms have in children's literacy development (Dreher, Chapter 4, this volume; Goldman, 1997). They may also be unable to convey these subtleties clearly to children or incorporate the different genres well in their everyday instruction. This means that teachers in acclimation may be unable to draw on their relevant literacy or pedagogical knowledge easily when it is called for, or even recognize its pertinence to a given situation or context. These novice teachers are often unable to make connections across content or curriculum and are frequently unable to draw on either their own or their students' prior knowledge during reading instruction (Westerman, 1991). In effect, their "knowing what" (i.e., declarative knowledge) is much richer than either their "knowing how" or their "knowing when or where" (i.e., procedural knowledge and conditional knowledge, respectively).

Beyond knowledge, however, there are motivational and strategic characteristics of acclimation. For instance, based on motivation research, one can conjecture that teachers in acclimation like Ms. Redcliff are more performance than mastery oriented in their goals (Meece & Holt, 1993), and more situationally than individually interested (Schiefele, 1991; Wade, 1992; Wigfield, Chapter 7, this volume). This means that teachers in this stage are, understandably, concerned with performing particular tasks well and winning the approval of others (Ames, 1992). The concept of mastering the domain of reading often gets buried in the daily demands of teaching. This is also evidenced in novice teachers' educational objectives for their students. These teachers tend to have narrow objectives that focus on individual skill acquisition rather than an overall learning goal (Westerman, 1991). Thus the focus of the teacher in acclimation is not on an integrated approach to reading instruction for their students but on the successful completion of the assigned tasks. We catch a glimpse of this performance orientation in Ms. Redcliff's remarks about running multiple groups in her classroom. She obviously wants to perform this particular aspect of her teaching job in a much more competent fashion. The broader desire to master reading instruction often takes a backseat when one is still working hard to learn the fundamentals or gain full admittance into the professional community. Performing well at the specifics, like grouping or assessment, subsequently allows teachers to think beyond the immediate tasks and to aim for a higher objective of becoming a master teacher. This is clearly evident in Mrs. Robinson's classroom, where reading groups operate so efficiently as to permit her and her students to concentrate on deeper literacy goals. Yet, until novice teachers acquire a strong base of knowledge and can achieve greater control over the learning environment, they rightly focus on executing specific tasks or functions successfully.

Just as her goals manifest a performance or task orientation, Ms. Redcliff probably exhibits more situational than personal or individual interest in the teaching of reading. *Situational interest*, by definition, refers to a temporary or fluctuating attention to or fascination with conditions within the immediate environment (Hidi, 1990). *Individual or personal interest*, in contrast, is a long-term and abiding interest that endures from situation to situation or context to context (Dewey, 1913). Because teachers in acclimation are just becoming enculturated into the community of reading educators, they likely have only a rudimentary understanding of their chosen profession. As they better understand what it means to teach reading, such educators may find that their professional interests grow deeper and stronger. Until that time, however, they are more apt to find their interests to be somewhat fleeting or temporal, and more dependent on the circumstances that unfold on a particular day or during a specific aspect of the lesson.

Given all the novelty and complexity neophyte teachers face, it is also understandable that their beliefs in their ability to succeed (i.e., self-efficacy beliefs) are likely lower than those of competent or proficient teachers (Schunk, 1991; Zimmerman, 1995). Moreover, as noted, these beliefs are likely to drop as the school year progresses and expectations that ignored a need for acclimation are not met (Soodak & Podell, 1997). When Moira Redcliff expresses her fear that she does not have what it takes to make it as a reading teacher, she is voicing negative self-efficacy beliefs. It is also logical that novice teachers, who are still struggling to gain a foothold in the domain, sense less control in their choice of curriculum and pedagogy than do their peers who have progressed to higher stages of professional development (Tschannen-Moran et al., 1998). The research on self-determination and autonomy demonstrates how important such self-perceptions are to continued growth and development (Deci, Valleran, Pelletier, & Ryan, 1991; Ryan, 1992). If teachers are to progress in their professional development, it is essential for them to feel that they are increasingly the captains of their own fates. That is, their instructional decisions and choices reflect personal judgments of what is appropriate or best for their young students and are not typically responses to external mandates or others' expectations. To proceed beyond acclimation, it is important for teachers to begin branching out beyond the given curricular objectives to include goals and objectives that they see as needed for their students (Westerman, 1991). This means that Moira Redcliff should articulate personal goals for herself that are not mandated by the reading curriculum in her district. Having a mentor like Mrs. Robinson can be invaluable to her in this process.

Finally, the strategic processing of acclimated teachers manifests certain qualities. Specifically, these beginning teachers encounter a high frequency of unexpected and unfamiliar situations or problems. In addition, these teachers' lack of knowledge allows many problems to arise at one time, making it nearly impossible for all situations to be resolved. These encounters demand that teachers react in a strategic manner. They must assess the problem critically, choose a reasonable solution procedure, and then execute that procedure well. The dilemma, however, is that even though acclimated teachers must rely on their strategic abilities more often than competent or expert teachers, their strategies are not always effectively and efficiently executed (Alexander & Judy, 1988). Ineffectiveness or inefficiency in strategy use could result because the problem is not well diagnosed, an appropriate solution strategy is unknown or overlooked, or the strategy is simply not implemented fluently or accurately. As with knowledge, progress toward competence will require a quantitative and qualitative shift in the strategic processing of acclimated teachers (Alexander et al., 1998).

Competence

Most educators who survive their initial years of classroom instruction can look forward to reaching competence in their professional development. Because most studies of expertise jump directly from acclimation to proficiency, competence is often a neglected and unheralded period of professional development. It should be the goal of every school district to promote competence in all teachers. Teachers know that they have left the stage of acclimation behind and have entered the stage of competence when they manifest certain characteristics. These hallmarks of competence include the emergence of a rich and principled body of knowledge and a deepening investment in reading and in literacy development (Alexander, 1997). Competent teachers possess a rich knowledge about reading, teaching, and human development, and they have an extensive repertoire of instructional strategies they can apply in the teaching of reading. This principled knowledge results not only from repeated opportunities for meaningful practice but also from an active and ongoing pursuit of knowledge (Valli, Chapter 11, this volume). Competent educators recognize that teaching and learning are inextricably intertwined and that they must be lifelong learners who value domain-specific knowledge.

Further, competent teachers deeply prize literacy and convey a true passion for reading. It is conceivable that some teachers can facilitate basic literacy skills in young students with only a marginal personal interest in reading. However, the prospect of creating a literacy-rich learning environment that fosters continued and optimal literacy development in all children is greatly enhanced when teachers find real pleasure and importance in reading. This personal interest also serves to maintain a teacher's resolve during trying instructional episodes, and it fuels strategic teaching that requires thoughtful, effortful processing.

From a motivational standpoint, competent teachers typically convey a mastery orientation, positive ratings of self-efficacy, and feelings of self-determination and autonomy in their teaching (Alexander, 1997; Pajares, 1992; Soodak & Podell, 1997; Woolfolk & Hoy, 1990). Moreover, they have reached a point in their development where they routinely handle commonplace tasks or problems effectively and efficiently. That is to say, competent reading educators have come to the point when they are not merely reacting to conditions around them but are predicting and orchestrating those conditions to a large extent. In effect, their knowledge of the content and of their students, their instructional goals, and their self-assuredness, along with their strategic abilities, allows them to anticipate how specific instructional approaches or materials will pan out (Carter, Cushing, Sabers, Stein, & Berliner, 1988; Westerman, 1991).

Unlike Ms. Redcliff, for instance, competent teachers would be careful to assign developmentally appropriate reading materials to their students, especially those children who are expected to work independently. When difficulties do arise, competent teachers are quick to read the situation and to make adjustments in the instructional environment, as warranted. Such fluid and flexible instruction is clearly a benchmark of educational competence (Alexander & Jetton, in press). This means that there is a degree of consistency and coherence in the learning environments of these able teachers (Guthrie, Cox, et al., Chapter 10, this volume). Both the teacher and the students know what behaviors are acceptable and desirable in this environment, and they perform simple day-to-day functions with efficiency and ease, allowing their energies to be focused on more important, novel, or complex reading activities (Jetton & Alexander, 1997).

In essence, there is a comfortable balance between routinization and creativity in the classrooms of competent reading teachers. What makes this possible is that competent teachers are informed and are pedagogically skilled. This combination of literacy and pedagogical knowledge is critical for competency among teachers of reading. Alexander, Jetton, Kulikowich, and Woehler (1994; also Jetton & Alexander, 1997) have found that a weakness in either of these knowledge areas has serious consequences for what and how well children learn.

Proficiency

The ultimate stage of development, and the one that Ms. Redcliff seemingly aspires to, is proficiency or expertise. Although, like Ms. Redcliff, many who set out on the journey of professional development voice a desire for proficiency, not all will realize this end. The reason is that expert teachers of reading must attain exceptional levels of knowledge, motivation, and strategic processing, and they must labor to maintain those performance levels. Thus, there will be those teachers who have a strong foundation of reading and pedagogical knowledge but who lack the personal drive required to move beyond competence (Alexander, 1997). Similarly, there may be those who are highly gifted pedagogically, who maintain an exciting and comfortable learning environment for their young students (Garner, 1990), yet are not as informed about reading as they could be and are not passionate about pursuing this understanding.

In many ways, the distinction between a highly competent teacher and a proficient teacher may not be readily apparent. All the positive instructional characteristics attributed to competent teachers are also expected of proficient teachers. You may have even thought of Mrs. Robinson as you considered the earlier description of competence. The difference is that even more is expected of those relative few we hold as the experts in a given field such as reading education. For example, in the area of knowledge, one thing that separates proficient teachers from competent ones deals with the creation of new knowledge (Alexander, 1997). That is, proficient or expert teachers not only possess extensive bodies of domain and pedagogical knowledge, but they also contribute new knowledge to the field. The way that Mrs. Robinson has modified traditional book clubs and included technology is one example of her instructional innovations. Those reading teachers who devise and test new instructional techniques to promote literacy or establish programs that reinforce literacy between home, community, and school (Sonnenschein & Schmidt, Chapter 12, this volume) would likewise show evidence of proficiency.

Simply put, educators at this level have a true command of the field and can communicate that understanding to others. That is why these experts are often called on to provide workshops or inservices for fellow teachers or take on the role of adjuncts or clinical teachers in university training programs. They make databased decisions that are founded on solid information and current knowledge (Leipzig & Afflerbach, Chapter 8, this volume), and they operate from a theory or model of teaching and learning that frames their actions. Thus, proficient teachers like Mrs. Robinson can explain the reasoning that underlies their strategic decisions and can justify the specific response they make under varying contextual conditions. For this reason, proficient teachers serve as excellent models or guides for others seeking access to the professional community (Valli, Chapter 11, this volume; Vygotsky, 1986). In an ideal world, all teachers in acclimation would have an extended opportunity to apprentice under the watchful and caring eye of a master teacher who can help to set them on the path to competence just as Moira Redcliff is being helped by Mrs. Robinson. Also, this mentorship would not cease the moment preservice teachers graduate from college and assume responsibility for their own classrooms, but would continue as long as the collaboration proved beneficial.

Even though proficient or expert teachers espouse strong beliefs and have well-articulated views about reading, education, and learning, they must remain open to new ideas and innovative practices. As we noted, the pursuit of understanding on the journey toward expertise is a never-ending quest. Reaching the stage of expertise does not allow educators to rest permanently on their laurels. Because knowledge about reading and pedagogy are always in formation, expert teachers must remain vigilant and invested (Csikszentmihalyi, 1990). Otherwise, their ideas and approaches can become dated and ineffective. Changes in society and culture can also impact schools in dramatic ways (Alexander, Murphy, & Woods, 1996). Consider, for instance, how technology has altered what and how people read and communicate (Kamil & Lane, 1998; Reinking, McKenna, Labbo, & Kieffer, 1998). Many of the children who come to school are already familiar with computers and can navigate well in this environment, whereas others have had virtually no exposure to this nonlinear form of text. Thus, proficient teachers must be able to respond appropriately by providing instruction that meets the needs of such a changing world.

RECOMMENDATIONS FOR ACHIEVING EXPERTISE

In light of the stages that teachers of reading must achieve in their journey toward expertise, the following 10 recommendations are forwarded to aid further professional growth. These recommendations acknowledge the interplay of knowledge, motivation, and strategic processing that occurs in each of the developmental stages.

Engage in Self-Assessment

The first step that teachers must take, if they wish to move forward on the path toward expertise, is to assess their current situation. Where do they stand in terms of their present stage of professional development, and what are their particular strengths and needs as teachers of reading? How would they judge their present knowledge, motivation, and strategic abilities? What efforts for self-improvement have they undertaken in the past, and how did these efforts contribute to their continued growth as a reading professional? It is also imperative that teachers acknowledge and enjoy their successes, as well as recognize their professional needs.

Self-assessment should be an ongoing process and should weigh not only the individual teacher's personal abilities and needs but also the instructional system as a whole. For instance, how does a teacher's philosophy of reading education and learning match with the goals and perceptions of the school leadership or with those of collaborating teachers? How does the support or nature of the local community influence the values of and expectations for literacy that exist (Valli, Chapter 11, this volume)? Schools should utilize formal teacher assessments as a constructive dialogue that can coax appropriate self-assessment. As a way to aid teachers in their self-assessment efforts, a simple guide like that displayed in Figure 13.1 may prove useful in focusing reflection on the essential areas of knowledge, strategies, and motivation.

Establish Personal Goals and Objectives

New teachers are often expected to do everything well, even from the first day of their professional careers. Doing everything well is an impossible task even for the most experienced teacher. For this reason, it is important for teachers to make specific and reasoned choices relative to professional

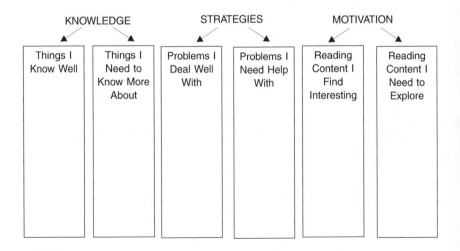

FIGURE 13.1. Teachers' self-assessment guide for the areas of knowledge, strategies, and motivation.

development, and to frame those choices as personal goals and objectives. These goals and objectives should address all the seeds of professional development (i.e., knowledge, motivation, and strategic processing), result from a careful self-assessment, and reflect personal values and aspirations.

Also, as seen in Figure 13.2, a professional development plan should identify the essential *target* area, explicitly state the desired *goal*, outline the *procedure* to be followed, and track the *outcomes* of the process. For example, a teacher in acclimation like Ms. Redcliff might decide that reading groups are a desired goal for the year, and she might set out to gain the knowledge and acquire strategies needed to make these groups function effectively. Our advice is to keep the list of goals and objectives reasonable, limited, and rather specific. Also, establish a means of monitoring progress. Know that each year, as teachers improve in specific areas or master particular strategies or methods, they move closer to the ultimate goal of achieving expertise.

Maintain Reasonable Self-Expectations

Recognize that the classroom environment is dynamic and multidimensional. This means that teachers of reading must acquire patience with themselves and with their abilities to implement their desired goals and

Target	Goal	Procedure	Outcomes
Example: KNOWLEDGE Reading Groups	To organize and work more effectively with multiple reading groups	• Read about grouping practices. • Discuss grouping alternatives with mentor. • Select most suitable technique for my purposes. • Monitor grouping effectiveness for 3 weeks.	• Met with mentor to identify some useful readings on homogeneous and heterogeneous grouping techniques. • Decided with mentor to use heterogeneous groups. • Created three groups; identified varied activities for independent groups. • Students adapted to new procedure; some difficulties persist such as off-task behavior and incomplete work.

FIGURE 13.2. Example of a segment of a professional agenda dealing with the formation of reading groups.

objectives. Implementing new procedures can be challenging and may ne-
cessitate repeated attempts and trials. Acknowledge that both instructor
and students are learning and developing, and a teaching method that did
not work the previous month may be the perfect solution this month. A
classic example of this principle would be teachers' attempts to implement
cooperative learning. Rarely has a teacher introduced this basic instructional procedure without some initial setbacks. Moreover, students need to
be taught how to function in cooperative groups—a process that clearly
demands time and patience from the reading teacher.

Seek a Mentor

Teachers, especially those in acclimation, should seek guidance and support from more knowledgeable and experienced peers. A professional relationship between apprentice and mentor serves as a conduit for essential
knowledge about reading and teaching, as well as an invaluable source of
motivational support. Moira Redcliff is already steps ahead in her professional journey by having someone like Mrs. Robinson to teach her the lay
of the land. If the school does not provide a mentor for new teachers, then
the responsibility for finding a mentor falls on the teachers themselves.
Observe how other teachers function, and openly pursue the advice of
those who appear well informed and effective. Few expert teachers will
turn down a request for help from an aspiring teacher. Look for a mentor
who demonstrates a highly integrated knowledge base and well-developed performance in instruction of reading and classroom management. If
one such person does not exist in the school, an alternative approach is to
choose multiple mentors from the professionals available: one for reading
instruction, another for management or other pedagogical needs. As with
self-assessment, the school structure should offer support and guidance
for the creation and maintenance of mentorships.

Actively Pursue New Knowledge

The amount of information available to teachers today may seem over-
whelming. However, recognize that you have a professional lifetime to acquire the information. As experiences in the classroom broaden, so will a
teacher's knowledge base. However, teachers should be active and asser-
tive in the pursuit of relevant knowledge. There are various sources of professional knowledge that can be tapped, including professional journals
and magazines, organized workshops or conferences, advanced courses,
on-line information exchanges, and of course fellow teachers. Reading, as
a field, is particularly rich in information sources. Yet, teachers must be
careful to select among these sources to ensure that the information they
receive is accurate and up to date. Teachers must also be mindful that al-

though a technique is new, it is not always better. Teachers need to be discerning in the incorporation of new theories into their repertoire, and need to rely on their own professional knowledge and instincts in making these decisions.

Establish a Professional Identity

Teaching is a profession that requires its members to establish an identity as functioning professionals. Gone are the days when teachers perceived of themselves as technicians or artists. Teaching is a demanding profession, and those who enter the profession must hold to that notion in their journey toward expertise. Although professionalism may be a state of mind, there are concrete steps that educators can take to promote this identity. Joining professional associations such as the International Reading Association is one way for teachers of reading to initiate themselves into communities of practice. Many of these reading associations have special interest groups expressly devoted to reading in the elementary grades. These associations give voice to the current research on reading instruction, and they can offer guidance on implementing effective practices. Professional associations can also be sources of mentors and can help make professional development a priority.

Become Self-Challenging

It is likely that every person reading this chapter is acquainted with a teacher who, as the old adage goes, taught 10 times rather than 10 years. In effect, these teachers fell into a professional rut from which they never emerged. Consequently, they went through the motions of teaching reading to their young students. As William James (1890) said, when we fail to challenge ourselves, we cease to live. This is certainly true for teaching. Teachers who lose their motivation to grow and improve are undeniably crippled in their quest for proficiency and fail to provide the best instruction possible for their students. Further, these challenges must come from within. Others cannot mandate them, regardless of how well intentioned these others may be. By becoming self-challenging, such as setting new goals, trying new techniques, or teaching new content, teachers can ignite their own motivational sparks and maintain their incentive to reach proficiency. Competent reading teachers may want to share their knowledge and interests with others, especially those still in acclimation.

Be a Model of Literacy

What is clear from the research on teacher effectiveness is that educators' passion for their subject matter is contagious. It is also apparent from the expert–novice research that no one can hope to achieve proficiency without an abiding interest in his/her chosen domain. One method of developing such an interest in reading instruction is by serving as a model of literacy. In becoming a model of literacy, an individual must experience reading and its importance on a personal level. Ideally, such exposure may deepen individual interest in reading. One way to demonstrate such deep-seated investment is to create a literacy-rich environment where print is everywhere and where the teacher is an active participant in the literacy community. In addition, it is important that there be a wide range of texts available in this environment. Such a wide range of reading materials ensures that developmentally appropriate and personally interesting materials can be found for readers of differing abilities and backgrounds. Also, implementing a variety of reading approaches, which encourage teachers and students to engage in joint "meaning-making," places reading in the foreground of instruction in an inviting way. In effect, teachers should share their love of reading by demonstrating its importance and beauty to children on a daily basis.

Be Prepared

As we have said repeatedly, teaching is a challenging profession. Even though highly competent and proficient teachers are better able to predict how certain events will unfold in the classroom than are teachers in acclimation, all must cope with the unexpected. That is why strategic processing is such a key to achieving and maintaining expertise. Still, being prepared goes a long way to promoting teachers' professional development, because it demands that they reflect on the nature of the reading instruction they provide. Preparedness also entails having backup plans or instructional alternatives ready for those times when the students do not respond to the reading instruction as predicted. Saying the same thing louder is not the solution to a child's confusion or inability to grasp a concept, for instance. Instead, teachers must be able to communicate that idea in an entirely different way. Reflecting on the lesson and the students and considering alternative approaches to instruction are just two ways to enhance one's preparedness. Both can augment teachers' knowledge of reading and of pedagogy and can contribute to positive feelings of self-efficacy and autonomy—critical ingredients in emerging proficiency.

Enjoy the Journey

Many who enter the teaching profession do so not because they seek money, power, or recognition but because they fervently desire to serve and share in the learning of children. Opening the world of reading to young people is truly a wondrous gift. It is a gift to the child who attains the ability to unlock the secrets of the written word and who can thus traverse time and space through text. It is a gift to the teacher who gets to re-visit that world of print through the eyes of a child. People rightly speak of the selflessness of teachers. Yet, teachers should also be encouraged to be selfish as they undertake this momentous journey of professional growth and development. Teachers are urged to enjoy every moment they spend with a child, learn from every experience, and recognize the critical role they play in these children's futures. If they can embrace this journey to-ward expertise with joy and abandon, then the difficulties and challenges they face will seem less daunting and much more worth the effort.

ACKNOWLEDGMENT

The authors wish to thank Joy Blackin for her helpful suggestions on an earlier ver-sion of this chapter.

RECOMMENDED READINGS

Alexander, P. A. (1997). Mapping the multidimensional nature of domain learning: The interplay of cognitive, motivational and strategic forces. In P. R. Pintrich & M. L. Maehr (Eds.), *Advances in motivation and achievement* (Vol. 10, pp. 213–250). Greenwich, CT: JAI Press.

Alexander outlines her Model of Domain Learning in this chapter. This theory is a developmental approach to understanding the acquisition of knowledge in a given domain. Outlined in the theory are the three stages of development (i.e., ac-climation, competency, expertise), as well as the forces that guide an individual through these stages.

Atwell, N. (1987). *In the middle: Writing, reading and learning with adolescents.* Portsmouth, NH: Boyton/Cook.

Atwell's book outlines her growth as a teacher, from competency to expertise. The book explains her Reading and Writing Workshops. Atwell worked with mid-dle school/junior high levels, but many of her techniques can be adapted to lower and higher grades. The book provides focused, detailed methods and strategies for reading instruction, as well as an opportunity to witness one teacher's growth as an educator.

Carter, K., Cushing, K., Sabers, D., Stein, P., & Berliner, D. (1988). Expert–novice dif-ferences in perceiving and processing visual classroom information. *Journal of Teacher Education, 39,* 25–31.

Carter and colleagues examined the type and depth of perceptions that nov-ice teachers, expert teachers, and nonteachers have when observing slides of class-room situations. Novice and nonteachers tended to be less able to perceive and in-terpret classroom information than experts. Experts were better able to determine importance, draw connections, and infer meaningful conclusions than the other two groups.

Kelly, P. R., & Farnan, N. (1990). Practicing what we teach in reading education programs. *Journal of Reading, 34,* 264–269.

Kelly and Farnan propose that teacher educators use specific reading strategies in their reading education programs. The article outlines key prereading, during-reading, and postreading strategies with specific examples that would be easy to apply in the classroom.

Soodak, L., & Podell, D. (1997). Efficacy and experience: Perceptions of efficacy among preservice and practicing teachers. *Journal of Research and Development in Education, 30,* 214–221.

Soodak and Podell examined the efficacy beliefs of preservice and practicing teachers in elementary and secondary schools. They concluded that preservice teachers have higher efficacy beliefs than do novices during the first two years of teaching. Novices' efficacy beliefs rose again with experience but never reached the same levels reported by preservice teachers. The article overviews the concept of teacher efficacy and gives an informative picture of how these beliefs change over time.

Westerman, D. A. (1991). Expert and novice teacher decision making. *Journal of Teacher Education, 42,* 292–305.

Westerman identified three levels of decision making: preactive, interactive, postactive. The author used these levels to study the decision-making trends of expert and novice teachers. Westerman found that experts were able to make more connections across the curriculum and content and were more able to adapt to the students' needs than were novices. Novices tended to focus on specific objectives and were less likely to divert from their lesson plans. This article identifies a series of techniques used by experts that could be applied by novices. Moreover, the procedure of this study offers an excellent means for self-assessment for teachers at all levels of professional development.

Woolfolk, A. E., & Hoy, W. K. (1990). Prospective teachers' sense of efficacy and beliefs about control. *Journal of Educational Psychology, 82,* 81–91.

Woolfolk and Hoy examined the interaction of teacher efficacy, personal efficacy, and management styles. The article suggests that the interaction of teacher efficacy (i.e., beliefs about one's teaching ability) and personal efficacy (i.e., beliefs about oneself generally) predict prospective teachers' views on pupil control, as well as their bureaucratic orientation to the school environment.

REFERENCES

Alexander, P. A. (1997). Mapping the multidimensional nature of domain learning: The interplay of cognitive, motivational, and strategic forces. In M. L. Maehr & P. R. Pintrich (Eds.), *Advances in motivation and achievement* (Vol. 10, pp. 213–250). Greenwich, CT: JAI Press.

Alexander, P. A., Graham, S., & Harris, K. (1998). A perspective on strategy research: Progress and prospects. *Educational Psychology Review, 10,* 129–154.

Alexander, P. A., & Jetton, T. L. (in press). Learning from text. In M. L. Kamil, P. B. Mosenthal, P. D. Pearson, & R. Barr (Eds.), *Handbook of reading research* (Vol. 3). Mahwah, NJ: Erlbaum.

Alexander, P. A., Jetton, T. L., & Kulikowich, J. M. (1995). Interrelationship of knowledge, interest, and recall: Assessing a model of domain learning. *Journal of Educational Psychology, 87*, 559–575.

Alexander, P. A., Jetton, T. L., Kulikowich, J. M., & Woehler, C. (1994). Contrasting instructional and structural importance: The seductive effect of teacher questions. *Journal of Reading Behavior, 26*, 19–45.

Alexander, P. A., & Judy, J. E. (1988). The interaction of domain-specific and strategic knowledge in academic performance. *Review of Educational Research, 58*, 375–404.

Alexander, P. A., & Murphy, P. K. (1998). Profiling the differences in students' knowledge, interest, and strategic processing. *Journal of Educational Psychology, 90*, 435–449.

Alexander, P. A., Murphy, P. K., & Woods, B. S. (1996). Of squalls and fathoms: Navigating the seas of educational innovation. *Educational Researcher, 25*(3), 31–36, 39.

Ames, C. (1992). Classrooms: Goals, structures, and student motivation. *Journal of Educational Psychology, 84*, 261–271.

Anderson, J. R. (1987). Skill acquisition: Compilation of weak-method problem solutions. *Psychological Review, 94*, 192–210.

Ashton, P. T., & Webb, R. B. (1986). *Making a difference: Teachers' sense of efficacy and student achievement.* New York: Longman.

Atwell, N. (1987). *In the middle: Writing, reading and learning with adolescents.* Portsmouth, NH: Boyton/Cook.

Carter, K., Cushing, K., Sabers, D., Stein, P., & Berliner, D. (1988). Expert–novice differences in perceiving and processing visual classroom information. *Journal of Teacher Education, 39*, 25–31.

Chi, M. T. H., Glaser, R., & Farr, M. J. (1988). *The nature of expertise.* Hillsdale, NJ: Erlbaum.

Csikszentmihalyi, M. (1990). *Flow: The psychology of optimal experience.* New York: Cambridge University Press.

Deci, E. L., Valleran, R. J., Pelletier, L. G., & Ryan, R. M. (1991). Motivation and education: The self-determination perspective. *Educational Psychologist, 26*, 325–346.

Dewey, J. (1913). *Interest and effort in education.* Boston: Riverside.

diSessa, A. A. (1982). Unlearning Aristotelian physics: A study of knowledge-based learning. *Cognitive Science, 6*, 37–75.

Ericsson, K. A., & Smith, J. (1991). *Toward a general theory of expertise: Prospects and limits.* Cambridge, UK: Cambridge University Press.

Fritz, J. J., Miller-Heyl, J., Kruetzer, J. C., & MacPhee, D. (1995). Fostering personal teaching efficacy through staff development and classroom activities. *Journal of Educational Research, 88*, 200–208.

Gardner, H. (1993). *Creating minds.* New York: Basic Books.

Garner, R. (1990). When children and adults do not use learning strategies: Toward a theory of settings. *Review of Educational Research, 60*, 517–529.

Gelman, R., & Greeno, J. G. (1989). On the nature of competence: Principles for understanding in a domain. In L. B. Resnick (Ed.), *Knowing, learning, and instruction: Essays in honor of Robert Glaser* (pp. 125–186). Hillsdale, NJ: Erlbaum.

Goldman, S. R. (1997). Learning from text: Reflections on the past and suggestions for the future. *Discourse Processes, 23*, 357–397.

Hidi, S. (1990). Interest and its contribution as a mental resource for learning. *Review of Educational Research, 60*, 549–571.

James, W. (1890). *Principles of psychology* (Vols. 1 & 2). New York: Holt.

Jetton, T. L., & Alexander, P. A. (1997). Instructional importance: What teachers value and what students learn. *Reading Research Quarterly, 32*, 290–308.

Kamil, M. L., & Lane, D. M. (1998). Researching the relationship between technology and literacy: An agenda for the 21st century. In D. Reinking, M. C. McKenna, L. D. Labbo, & R. D. Kieffer (Eds.), *Handbook of literacy and technology: Transformations in a post-typographic world* (pp. 323–341). Mahwah, NJ: Erlbaum.

Kelly, P. R., & Farnan, N. (1990). Practicing what we teach in reading education programs. *Journal of Reading, 34*, 264–269.

Meece, J. L., & Holt, K. (1993). A pattern analysis of students' achievement goals. *Journal of Educational Psychology, 85*, 582–590.

Ogle, D. (1986). A teaching model that develops active reading of expository text. *The Reading Teacher, 39*, 563–570.

Pajares, M. F. (1992). Teacher's beliefs and educational research: Cleaning up a messy construct. *Review of Educational Research, 62*, 307–332.

Palincsar, A. S., & Brown, A. L. (1984). Reciprocal teaching of comprehension-fostering and monitoring activities. *Cognition and Instruction, 1*, 117–175.

Paris, S. G., Lipson, M. Y., & Wixson, K. K. (1983). Becoming a strategic reader. *Contemporary Educational Psychology, 8*, 293–316.

Pintrich, P. R., & Schunk, D. H. (1996). *Motivation in education: Theory, research, and applications.* Englewood Cliffs, NJ: Prentice Hall.

Reinking, D., McKenna, M. C., Labbo, L. D., & Kieffer, R. O. (Eds.). (1998). *Handbook of literacy and technology: Transformations in a post-typographic world.* Mahwah, NJ: Erlbaum.

Ryan, R. M. (1992). Agency and organization: Intrinsic motivation, autonomy, and the self in psychological development. In J. Jacobs (Ed.), *Nebraska symposium on motivation* (Vol. 40, pp. 1–56). Lincoln: University of Nebraska Press.

Ryle, G. (1949). *The concept of mind.* London: Hutchinson.

Schiefele, U. (1991). Interest, learning, and motivation. *Educational Psychologist, 26*, 229–323.

Schunk, D. (1991). Self-efficacy and academic motivation. *Educational Psychologist, 26*, 207–231.

Soodak, L. C., & Podell, D. M. (1997). Efficacy and experience: Perceptions of efficacy among preservice and practicing teachers. *Journal of Research and Development in Education, 30*, 214–221.

Tschannen-Moran, M., Woolfolk-Hoy, A., & Hoy, W. K. (1998). Teacher efficacy: Its meaning and measure. *Review of Educational Research, 68*, 202–248.

Vygotsky, L. (1986). *Thought and language* (A. Kozulin, Trans.). Cambridge, MA: MIT Press. (Original work published 1934)

Wade, S. E. (1992). How interest affects learning from text. In K. A. Renninger, S. Hidi, & A. Krapp (Eds.), *The role of interest in learning and development* (pp. 255–277). Hillsdale, NJ: Erlbaum.

Westerman, D. A. (1991). Expert and novice teacher decision making. *Journal of Teacher Education, 42*, 292–305.

Woolfolk, A. E., & Hoy, W. K. (1990). Prospective teachers' sense of efficacy and beliefs about control. *Journal of Educational Psychology, 82*, 81–91.

Zimmerman, B. J. (1995). Self-regulation involves more than metacognition: A social cognitive perspective. *Educational Psychologist, 30*, 217–221.

CHAPTER FOURTEEN

Why Teacher Engagement Is Important to Student Achievement

JOHN T. GUTHRIE
MARIAM JEAN DREHER
LINDA BAKER

This book is intended to heighten the awareness of principles for improving engagement and achievement in reading. As teachers think more about their instruction and their students' reading, they will become more engaged in improving their teaching. In this final chapter, we discuss what it means to be engaged in teaching. We present some challenges facing teachers and administrators who are making renewed efforts to improve instruction, and we summarize the principles presented in this volume.

In the late 1990s, teacher quality has become the centerpiece for discussions of school improvement. Policy leaders, such as Darling-Hammond (1994) and Fuhrman and O'Day (1996), have focused attention on the needs of teachers for several reasons. Foremost among these is the current status of the systemic reform movement. Across many states, schools have embarked on systemic efforts to improve student achievement. Systemic reform has been led by efforts for accountability. As states seek to increase student achievement, they begin by forming learning goals for students. These desirable outcomes are stated in more or less detail, but they are generated with consensus and public involvement as fully as possible (Feuer, Holland, Green, Bertenthal, & Hemphill, 1999).

Accountability in the form of student assessment is prominent in the systemic reforms. Testing programs in the form of performance assessments, multiple-choice approaches, and occasionally portfolios are present in nearly every state as a source of leverage for school improvement.

Although high standards have been developed and accountability has been emphasized, student achievement has not increased markedly. Therefore, policy makers are increasing attention to teacher quality. This recognition of the teacher as a central force in helping students learn is long overdue. At present, national certification bodies, research and development centers, and institutions of higher education are asking, "How can we improve teacher quality to increase student achievement?" Answering this question puts the teacher's knowledge, dispositions, and incentives for good instruction at the center of the table.

In this book, we have suggested that students need instruction that is redesigned for a better balance between achievement and engagement. We believe that students need to be taught skills of word recognition and comprehension (Snow, Burns, & Griffin, 1998). However, students also need cultivation of motivation, interests, and the ability to share literacy with peers. These aspects of engaged reading have also been discussed in Guthrie and Alvermann (1999). This emphasis on student engagement places a challenge before teachers. To be capable of engaging students in productive reading, teachers must have an array of qualities. We call these qualities "teacher engagement." Engaged teachers are like engaged learners. They are motivated, strategic, knowledgeable, and social in their approach to teaching.

Engaged teachers are knowledgeable about students and pedagogy. They know how the reading process occurs, how children learn phonological awareness, word recognition, sentence comprehension, and story understanding. Yet, engaged teachers are also motivated. They desire to teach well and take pleasure in successfully reaching students. Motivated teachers are curious about what new techniques will work and are attentive to whether children are responding to the context for learning they create. Engagement in teaching includes a wide repertoire of effective strategies; they include knowing how to get children to respond to difficult tasks, knowing how to introduce appropriate texts for reading, and knowing how to ask questions that help students enter the world of the text. Engagement is not merely affect without practice. In other words, the motivations for teaching are not fluffy abstractions, but rather are tied tightly to effective practices.

The link between teacher and student engagement was expressed by Williams (1996) as follows:

Unless teachers engage in teaching and feel that they are effective, students are less likely to make rapid progress in learning. From the students' point of view, teacher engagement is a prerequisite for student engagement. This is particularly true for schools with a high concentration of low income and minority students. Because teachers' work and students' work are linked, alienated teachers pose a major stumbling block to students' engagement with their own education. (p. 125)

TEACHER EDUCATION THAT FACILITATES
TEACHER ENGAGEMENT

If reform efforts are to result in improved student achievement, we need to pay attention to teacher engagement. Alexander and Fives (Chapter 13, this volume) closed their chapter with recommended steps teachers can take to move themselves toward expertise (e.g., seek a mentor, actively pursue knowledge). Teachers taking such steps exhibit the qualities that characterize engaged teachers. They are likely to set up classroom and school contexts so that their students develop those same qualities.

Teachers who work to develop from novice to competent to proficient, as Alexander and Fives (Chapter 13, this volume) described, are clearly engaged teachers. However, as Valli (Chapter 11, this volume) has made clear, school-wide, coordinated efforts are much more powerful than individual efforts. Further, the coherent instruction that Guthrie, Cox, et al. (Chapter 10, this volume) described is more effective when a whole school or school system provides coherence. We believe that preservice preparation and in-service professional development can do more to produce engaged teachers who seek expertise, and who in turn help facilitate more school-wide and system-wide instructional coherence.

One route toward increasing the number of engaged teachers is to improve preservice preparation. Moira Redcliff, the teacher in Alexander and Fives's vignette (Chapter 13, this volume), took only one reading course in her teacher preparation program. That level of preparation is typical, with most states requiring one course and some two. As Goodlad (1997) has pointed out, that level may be enough to enable teachers to provide some help to children who encounter little trouble learning to read but does not provide enough background to make a difference for children having difficulty. Many would agree that more courses are needed. In 1998, for instance, the Maryland State Board of Education passed new certification regulations requiring that all early childhood and elementary teachers take 12 semester hours dealing with various aspects of reading.

The knowledge teachers need for effective reading instruction is wide ranging. It comes from fields such as linguistics, psycholinguistics, rhetoric, sociolinguistics, psychology of reading, as well as pedagogical methodology. Preservice programs can be more effective in providing prospective teachers with such knowledge. However, even if we improve preservice preparation, beginning teachers will still not have all the knowledge they need. Expertise involves not only considerable knowledge of literacy and pedagogy, but years of opportunity to refine pedagogical knowledge and skill (Alexander & Fives, Chapter 13, this volume; Sabers, Cushing, & Berliner, 1991).

Thus, to increase the number of engaged teachers, preservice education must be more thorough. But, in addition, teacher education needs to be viewed as a long-term process, extending well beyond receipt of a teaching credential. This long-term conception takes into account what we know about developing instructional expertise.

This reconceptualization extends to professional development opportunities. Relatively little money is spent on professional development, and what is spent is likely misspent on ineffective short-term efforts (Cuban, 1984; Darling-Hammond, 1996). Yet, evidence indicates that money spent on highly qualified teachers results in greater improvement in student achievement than any other type of increased spending (Ferguson, 1991). Hence, allocating resources to quality professional development involving long-term efforts, with modeling, coaching, and feedback (Joyce & Showers, 1988), may be more cost effective than it initially appears.

To help teachers become and stay engaged, we also need to rethink the training model in which experts tell teachers exactly what to do (Duffy, 1991). Teachers are frequently viewed as semiprofessionals whose role is to deliver a prescribed program (Darling-Hammond, 1988). This "de-skilling" of teachers is not only demoralizing but also leads to passivity (Duffy, 1991). Teachers see their role as one of following what the experts say (Dreher & Singer, 1989; Duffy, Roehler, & Putman, 1987), and authors of instructional programs try to devise teacher-proof methods. Balmuth (1998), in her testimony before the National Reading Panel, argued for "the transcendence of the teacher variable—good teachers do better with any method than do poor teachers. What may be needed instead of one grounded teacher-proof method is a universe of well-grounded method-proof teachers" (p. 2).

Outstanding teachers, such as those observed by Pressley, Wharton-McDonald, Allington, Block, and Morrow (1998), do not follow canned programs. They bring creativity and professional decision making to their roles. If we want to develop engaged teachers—teachers who are empowered and who have a vision for learning—then teacher education needs to equip teachers with the knowledge and attitudes to enable them to be professionals. Well-prepared teachers who are supported by effective professional development will more likely become engaged teachers.

CHALLENGES FACING TEACHERS ENGAGED
IN IMPROVING INSTRUCTION

Within any school, constraints and choices are present. When the constraints on teachers are excessive and teachers feel that they have little freedom of movement, teacher engagement will be suffocated. Under these conditions, student achievement is likely to decrease as a consequence. In the opposite situation, when teacher choices are too widely available and the structure is too loose, student achievement also languishes. These constraints and choices exist for several important dimensions of teaching, including (1) vision for learning, (2) accountability for outcomes, (3) empowerment of teachers, (4) curriculum clarity, (5) the tools and resources for instruction, (6) time use, and (7) sustainability of teaching improvement.

Vision for Learning

Teachers in an elementary school have a right to participate in the construction of a vision for learning in the school. If the state, district, or school provides high constraints on the knowledge and skills students should learn, teachers have little role in evolving a vision for learning. If every reading skill is listed and mandated to be taught, teachers are totally constrained. This results in disenchantment with the school program. At the opposite end, if the vision for learning is left open to every teacher, then a coherent framework cannot exist in a grade level or department. To balance the constraints and choices, teachers in a school should take time to identify, articulate, and write their vision for student learning in reading and language arts. The vision may include objectives from the district and school but will also include their own special topics, unique areas of interest, and priorities for children's learning. If the process of vision forming is unduly constrained and limited or excessively open and unguided, teachers are entitled to request a balance from the team leaders and school principal.

Accountability for Outcomes

Having participated in constructing a vision for learning, teachers desire both constraints and choices in coping with accountability. In most states and schools, tests are used to determine student achievement and may be used to reflect the school quality or teacher quality. Teachers often cannot choose the tests. However, they can create multiple indicators of student success to decide grades and reporting procedures. Further, teachers can participate in decisions of how much coaching to provide for the test. Although some coaching on formats is valuable, excessive coaching is disruptive to the curriculum. Teachers should participate in deciding how much of the student instruction should be disrupted by the necessity of test preparation. If the test used for accountability becomes the curriculum, student achievement will decrease and teacher engagement will be reduced.

Empowerment of Teachers

In the process of creating a school teaching program or an improvement plan, teachers should be empowered as decision makers over matters that are substantial enough to influence student achievement. Simply empowering teachers to decide when to perform trivial tasks is disengaging. The engaged teacher has a need for decision-making responsibility, opportunity for input into the school program, and recognition for professional expertise. If the teacher's role is too constrained, teachers will lose motivation to invest their best thinking and energy. In contrast, if teachers are expected to make too many decisions, their knowledge may be insufficient and the benefits of other experts may not be adequately tapped.

Curriculum Clarity

The reading and language arts curriculum at the primary and intermediate grades can vary from highly specific to extremely general. In the highly specific case, teaching objectives may be mandated, a basal reader may be required, regular assessments may be demanded, and a schedule of basal coverage across the weeks, months, and year may be expected. In such a case, student grouping is often predetermined by others and classroom activities may be highly prescribed by someone other than the teacher. Such constraints prevent the teachers as professionals from using their knowledge about word recognition or student collaboration for learning. However, with the underprescribed curriculum, differences across classrooms and grade levels in the school may lead to a chaotic scope and sequence of reading objectives, which is likely to be confusing to learners. Teachers should seek a middle ground between the overprescribed curriculum that does not tap their professional knowledge and the underprescribed curriculum in which inadequate guidance is provided.

Materials and Resources

Chapters in this volume have emphasized the role of a book-rich environment (e.g., Chambliss & McKillop, Chapter 5; Dreher, Chapter 4). Diversity of trade books, literature, poetry, and multimedia is a hallmark of good instruction. When well-informed teachers have the opportunity to grow a classroom collection of diverse genres, authors, and topics, student achievement is consistently improved. Whether teachers are relying exclusively on trade books or are supplementing an existing prescribed approach (such as a basal reader) with children's literature and specific activities for word recognition, spelling, or language arts, student learning needs should be primary. The focus must be on the students' needs, rather than on the materials used. Addressing these needs will require ingenuity and flexibility by the teacher. The balance of constraints and choices in supporting teacher decision making about materials and resources for learning should be weighed toward teacher choice.

Time Use

Time allocated for the reading/language arts program in the elementary grades often ranges from 120 to 140 minutes per day. Constraints and choices regarding this time allocation itself may be negotiable. For example, teachers who provide an integration of reading/language arts with social studies or science may effectively negotiate increased time for reading instruction (see Byrnes, Chapter 9, this volume). Within the 120 to 140 minutes, teachers are usually at liberty to structure time use according to their preferences. This is a choice that is important and valuable. If this choice is reduced or eliminated, such that teachers are required to spend specific allocated time for spelling, writing, and reading skills and literature, then teachers are too constrained. This limitation will be disengaging. It is valuable to identify the choices about time available within a reading and writing/language arts program. With a focus on available time choices, teachers can optimize their effectiveness.

Sustainability of Teaching Improvements

When teachers are engaged with improving their own instruction, creative things will happen in the classroom. Often student excitement and improvement will be evident to the teacher and others outside the classroom. But how can these improvements be retained? How can advances that engaged teachers make in their own effectiveness be maintained? Engagement involves high effort that merits recognition. Individual teachers and teacher teams who are engaged and who are improving merit public validation. More fundamentally, however, teachers who sustain their excellence and maintain their improvements in instruction should be given increased professional decision making and freedom. They should be afforded expanded opportunity for exchange with other teachers (see Valli, Chapter 11, this volume).

Development of long-term engagement is based on believing in one's competence, having the opportunity to enjoy more freedom to grow as a teacher, and having expanded social networking in the professional community. These positive qualities of the school environment are theoretically confirmed (Deci, Vallerand, Pelletier, & Ryan, 1991), and they are recommended for the improvement of teacher quality (Fuhrman & O'Day, 1996). Our message to teachers is that it is in your interest as well as the children's interest to find ways to sustain your own engagement in teaching. That is, identify how well you are doing and how your competence is growing. Seek to expand your personal freedom and choices as a teacher and form liaisons with other teachers who think and teach as you do. Our message to administrators is that successful schools place their highest priority on undergirding the engagement of teachers as growing professionals.

PRINCIPLES ON WHICH TEACHERS CAN RELY

To rise successfully to these challenges, teachers can use the principles presented in this volume. In forming a vision for learning or deciding how to allocate precious time, teachers can use our suggested guidelines. The chapters in this volume focus on different facets of reading and reading instruction that foster the development of reading engagement. Each chapter explicates a simply stated prescription for what children need to become engaged and achieving readers. We saw that children need the following supports:

1. A good foundation at the word level
2. Help if they are in trouble
3. Opportunity to read for learning
4. Ample materials for reading
5. Opportunities to share in a community of learners
6. Instructional contexts that are motivating
7. Teachers who are familiar with their strengths and weaknesses
8. Time to read
9. Coherent instruction that pulls all of the pieces together
10. Classrooms that are coordinated with the school as a whole
11. Continuities between home and school
12. Masterful teaching by teachers knowledgeable about engagement and achievement

We now go beyond these simple statements to synthesize the key points in each chapter in terms of instructional design principles. The principles are based on best practices culled from the research literature. The chapter titles themselves reflect the engaged role that the teacher plays in implementing each of the processes that lead to engagement and achievement.

"Building the Word-Level Foundation for Engaged Reading" (Baker, Chapter 2): Focused instruction at the word level is explicit and developmentally appropriate, connected to the extent possible with meaningful reading and writing. Components of instruction include phonemic awareness, phonics, oral reading fluency, spelling, word analysis, and vocabulary, tailored to the needs of the students. Emphasis is placed on providing students with the strategies and knowledge to identify words and their meanings independently. Contexts of instruction are motivating and socially interactive, supportive of reading engagement.

"Helping Children Who Experience Reading Difficulties" (Graham & Harris, Chapter 3): Exemplary reading instruction is provided to all children. Reading instruction is tailored to meet the individual needs of children who experience difficulty learning to read. Intervention occurs early, with a coherent and sustained effort to improve the literacy skills of children who experience reading difficulties. Teachers hold the expectation that each child will learn to read. Academic and nonacademic roadblocks to reading and school success are identified and addressed.

"Fostering Reading for Learning" (Dreher, Chapter 4): Children need to have the opportunity to read for learning in order to become engaged readers. Teachers give children exposure to, practice with, and instruction relevant to reading for acquiring new concepts. Children are immersed in inquiry tasks, and they experience instruction that integrates literacy and content area learning. By balancing learning to read and reading for learning, teachers increase the likelihood of producing readers who can interact capably with all genres of text and who are also motivated to read.

"Creating a Print- and Technology-Rich Classroom Library to Entice Children to Read" (Chambliss & McKillop, Chapter 5): Each classroom includes a substantial collection of reading materials in a classroom library. Print represents a variety of genres including information books, narratives, poetry, reference books, and multimedia. A variety of cultural backgrounds is represented in the collection. Books encompass a range of difficulty and interests so that they are accessible and appropriate to all students. Children use technology to increase their access to print.

"Promoting Collaboration, Social Interaction, and Engagement with Text" (Gambrell, Mazzoni, & Almasi, Chapter 6): Collaborative literacy experiences promote engaged reading. Literacy development is enhanced when children work together to discuss and reflect on their reading and writing. Teachers create different kinds of social structures to enable peer collaboration. These structures may include small groups, teams, and partnerships. Peer-led discussions help students take responsibility for their own literacy learning. Peers play important roles in promoting one another's competence and motivation for reading.

"Facilitating Children's Reading Motivation" (Wigfield, Chapter 7): Teachers are concerned with facilitating children's motivation to read along with their cognitive reading skills, in order that children become lifelong self-directed readers. Teachers facilitate children's reading motivation when they (1) provide children opportunities to choose books based on their interests and from topics they are learning about in school; (2) use interesting texts and provide challenging tasks and activities; (3) foster children's beliefs that they are competent readers, and teach them the skills to be competent readers; and (4) encourage children to collaborate with others on projects related to their reading.

"Determining the Suitability of Assessments" (Leipzig & Afflerbach, Chapter 8): Teachers develop and evaluate reading assessments with a clear sense of how they conceptualize reading for the students in their classrooms. Teachers keep in mind five separate but closely intertwined concepts related to assessment: consequences, usefulness, roles of teachers and students, reliability, and validity. Effective reading assessments are engaging to students and teachers, and they reflect the multiple aspects of engaged reading. Assessment in itself is a means to promote student achievement and engagement.

"Using Instructional Time Effectively" (Byrnes, Chapter 9): Time to read is an important ingredient in the overall process of reading development. Children who read more frequently have higher reading achievement. Teachers provide children with ample opportunity to read diverse and challenging books of their own choosing. Teachers also provide guidance and support children as they practice their reading skills; they recognize that Sustained Silent Reading is necessary but not sufficient for engagement.

"Building toward Coherent Instruction" (Guthrie, Cox, Knowles, Buehl, Mazzoni, & Fasulo, Chapter 10): Coherence in instruction is extremely valuable for engaged reading. Coherence refers to the connections among the separate parts of teaching, such as reading strategy instruction, knowledge goals, real-world interactions, autonomy support, and rewards for learning. When these eight dimensions are integrated and coherent, students become engaged. Coherent instruction enables students to become independent readers and fosters reading achievement.

"Facilitating Reading Instruction through School-Wide Coordination" (Valli, Chapter 11): Teachers plan collaboratively for student learning by discussing goals, curriculum, students' special needs, and literacy successes with colleagues. Communication within and across grade levels and with support staff emphasizes consistency in the program and allows for clear instructional goal setting. Teachers' professional development is aligned with students' literacy development.

"Fostering Home and Community Connections to Support Children's Reading" (Sonnenschein & Schmidt, Chapter 12): Connections with the home and the community are important in fostering children's engagement and achievement. Effective teachers facilitate the establishment of a partnership between home and school based on mutual respect and understanding. Teachers provide parents with the tools to enable effective involvement once they have learned about the strengths, needs, beliefs, and practices of each student's family. Effective teachers use community resources to augment what is available at home and school.

"Achieving Expertise in Teaching Reading" (Alexander & Fives, Chapter 13): Effective reading instruction depends on the teacher's knowledge, motivation, and strategic processing. Teachers progress through developmental stages as they move toward expertise in teaching reading, each with its own distinct set of challenges. Teachers who are on the road to expertise: engage in self-assessment; establish personal goals and objectives; maintain reasonable self-expectations; seek a mentor; actively pursue new knowledge; establish a professional identify; are self-challenging; serve as a model of literacy; are prepared; and enjoy the journey.

This volume contains our guidelines for effective reading instruction. We believe they will benefit teachers and students. However, there are several purposes this book does not attempt to accomplish. First, we are not making recommendations for how to provide professional development. The best means for communicating the principles of this book to preservice and in-service teachers is another matter. Second, we are not trying to suggest how to assess the knowledge and competencies recommended here. The controversial issues of testing teachers are not addressed. It was not our goal to set standards or construct benchmarks for teachers. National professional organizations and teacher development institutes are discussing those issues. Finally, we are not proposing research questions, although we believe there are many important ones. Despite these limitations, we do believe that teachers who understand these principles will be more effective. Classroom instruction that exemplifies the ideas presented here will yield positive dividends to teachers, administrators, and students.

REFERENCES

Balmuth, M. (1998, June 23). Comments about reading instruction presented to the National Reading Panel at the New York City regional meeting.

Cuban, L. (1984). *How teachers taught: Consistency and change in American classroom, 1890–1980*. New York: Longman.

Darling-Hammond, L. (1988). The futures of teaching. *Educational Leadership, 46,* 4–10.

Darling-Hammond, L. (1994). *Professional development schools: Schools for developing a profession.* New York: Teachers College Press.

Darling-Hammond, L. (1996). The quiet revolution: Rethinking teacher development. *Educational Leadership, 53*(6), 4–10.

Deci, E. L., Vallerand, R. J., Pelletier, L. G., & Ryan, R. M. (1991). Motivation and education: The self-determination perspective. *Educational Psychologist, 26,* 325–346.

Dreher, M. J., & Singer, H. A. (1989). The teacher's role in students' success. *The Reading Teacher, 42,* 612–617.

Duffy, G. G. (1991). What counts in teacher education? Dilemmas in educating empowered teachers. In J. Zutell & S. McCormick (Eds.), *Learner factors/teacher factors: Issues in literacy research and instruction* (Fortieth yearbook of the National Reading Conference, pp. 1–18). Chicago: National Reading Conference.

Duffy, G. G., Roehler, L., & Putman, J. (1987). Putting the teacher in control: Basal reading textbooks and instructional decision making. *Elementary School Journal, 87,* 357–366.

Ferguson, R. (1991). Paying for public education: New evidence on how and why money matters. *Harvard Journal on Legislation, 28,* 465–498.

Feuer, M. J., Holland, P. W., Green, B. F., Bertenthal, M. W., & Hemphill, F. C. (1999). *Uncommon measures: Equivalence and linkage among educational tests.* Washington, DC: National Academy Press.

Fuhrman, S. H., & O'Day, J. A. (1996). *Rewards and reform: Creating incentives that work.* San Francisco: Jossey-Bass.

Goodlad, J. (1997). Producing teachers who understand, believe, and care. *Education Week, 16*(48), 36–37.

Guthrie, J. T., & Alvermann, D. E. (Eds.). (1999). *Engaged reading: Processes, practices, and policy implications.* New York: Teachers College Press.

Joyce, B., & Showers, B. (1988). *Student achievement through staff development.* White Plains, NY: Longman.

Pressley, M., Wharton-McDonald, R., Allington, R., Block, C. C., & Morrow, L. (1998). *The nature of effective first-grade literacy instruction* (CELA Research Rep. No. 11007). Albany: State University of New York at Albany, The National Center on English Learning & Achievement. [http://cela.albany.edu/1stgradelit/index.html]

Sabers, D. S., Cushing, K., & Berliner, D. (1991). Differences among teachers in a task characterized by simultaneity, multidimensionality, and immediacy. *American Educational Research Journal, 28,* 63–88.

Snow, C., Burns, M., & Griffin, P. (Eds.). (1998). *Preventing reading difficulties in young children.* Washington, DC: National Academy Press.

Williams, B. (Ed.). (1996). *Closing the achievement gap: A vision for changing beliefs and practices.* Alexandria, VA: Association for Supervision & Curriculum Development.

Index